Data Structures and Algorithms Using Python

D1708312

Rance D. Necaise

Department of Computer Science
College of William and Mary

WILEY
JOHN WILEY & SONS, INC.

ACQUISITIONS EDITOR	Beth Golub
MARKETING MANAGER	Christopher Ruel
EDITORIAL ASSISTANT	Michael Berlin
SENIOR DESIGNER	Jeof Vita
MEDIA EDITOR	Thomas Kulesa
PRODUCTION MANAGER	Micheline Frederick
PRODUCTION EDITOR	Amy Weintraub

This book was printed and bound by Hamilton Printing Company. The cover was printed by Hamilton Printing Company

This book is printed on acid free paper. ∞

Library of Congress Cataloging-in-Publication Data

Necaise, Rance D.
Data structures and algorithms using Python / Rance D. Necaise.
    p. cm.
Includes bibliographical references and index.
ISBN 978-0-470-61829-5 (pbk.)
    1. Python (Computer program language) 2. Algorithms.
    3. Data structures (Computer science) I. Title.
QA76.73.P98N43 2011
005.13'3—dc22   2010039903

Printed in the United States of America

10 9 8 7 6 5 4 3 2 1

To my nieces and nephews
Allison, Janey, Kevin, RJ, and Maria

Contents

Preface

The standard second course in computer science has traditionally covered the fundamental data structures and algorithms, but more recently these topics have been included in the broader topic of abstract data types. This book is no exception, with the main focus on the design, use, and implementation of abstract data types. The importance of designing and using abstract data types for easier modular programming is emphasized throughout the text. The traditional data structures are also presented throughout the text in terms of implementing the various abstract data types. Multiple implementations using different data structures are used throughout the text to reinforce the abstraction concept. Common algorithms are also presented throughout the text as appropriate to provide complete coverage of the typical data structures course.

Overview

The typical data structures course, which introduces a collection of fundamental data structures and algorithms, can be taught using any of the different programming languages available today. In recent years, more colleges have begun to adopt the Python language for introducing students to programming and problem solving. Python provides several benefits over other languages such as C++ and Java, the most important of which is that Python has a simple syntax that is easier to learn. This book expands upon that use of Python by providing a Python-centric text for the data structures course. The clean syntax and powerful features of the language are used throughout, but the underlying mechanisms of these features are fully explored not only to expose the "magic" but also to study their overall efficiency.

For a number of years, many data structures textbooks have been written to serve a dual role of introducing data structures and providing an in-depth study of object-oriented programming (OOP). In some instances, this dual role may compromise the original purpose of the data structures course by placing more focus on OOP and less on the abstract data types and their underlying data structures. To stress the importance of abstract data types, data structures, and algorithms, we limit the discussion of OOP to the use of base classes for implementing the various abstract data types. We do not use class inheritance or polymorphism in the main part of the text but instead provide a basic introduction as an appendix. This choice was made for several reasons. First, our objective is to provide a "back to basics" approach to learning data structures and algorithms without overwhelming the reader with all of the OOP terminology and concepts, which is especially important when the instructor has no plans to cover such topics. Second, different instructors take different approaches with Python in their first course. Our aim is to provide an excellent text to the widest possible audience. We do this by placing the focus on the data structures and algorithms, while designing the examples to allow the introduction of object-oriented programming if so desired.

The text also introduces the concept of algorithm analysis and explores the efficiency of algorithms and data structures throughout the text. The major presentation of complexity analysis is contained in a single chapter, which allows it to be omitted by instructors who do not normally cover such material in their data structures course. Additional evaluations are provided throughout the text as new algorithms and data structures are introduced, with the major details contained in individual sections. When algorithm analysis is covered, examples of the various complexity functions are introduced, including amortized cost. The latter is important when using Python since many of the list operations have a very efficient amortized cost.

Prerequisites

This book assumes that the student has completed the standard introduction to programming and problem-solving course using the Python language. Since the contents of the first course can differ from college to college and instructor to instructor, we assume the students are familiar with or can do the following:

- Design and implement complete programs in Python, including the use of modules and namespaces

- Apply the basic data types and constructs, including loops, selection statements, and subprograms (functions)

- Create and use the built-in list and dictionary structures

- Design and implement basics classes, including the use of helper methods and private attributes

Contents and Organization

The text is organized into fourteen chapters and four appendices. The basic concepts related to abstract data types, data structures, and algorithms are presented in the first four chapters. Later chapters build on these earlier concepts to present more advanced topics and introduce the student to additional abstract data types and more advanced data structures. The book contains several topic threads that run throughout the text, in which the topics are revisited in various chapters as appropriate. The layout of the text does not force a rigid outline, but allows for the reordering of some topics. For example, the chapters on recursion and hashing can be presented at any time after the discussion of algorithm analysis in Chapter 4.

Chapter 1: Abstract Data Types.   Introduces the concept of abstract data types (ADTs) for both simple types, those containing individual data fields, and the more complex types, those containing data structures. ADTs are presented in terms of their definition, use, and implementation. After discussing the importance of abstraction, we define several ADTs and then show how a well-defined ADT can be used without knowing how its actually implemented. The focus then turns to the implementation of the ADTs with an emphasis placed on the importance of selecting an appropriate data structure. The chapter includes an introduction to the Python iterator mechanism and provides an example of a user-defined iterator for use with a container type ADT.

Chapter 2: Arrays.   Introduces the student to the array structure, which is important since Python only provides the list structure and students are unlikely to have seen the concept of the array as a fixed-sized structure in a first course using Python. We define an ADT for a one-dimensional array and implement it using a hardware array provided through a special mechanism of the C-implemented version of Python. The two-dimensional array is also introduced and implemented using a 1-D array of arrays. The array structures will be used throughout the text in place of the Python's list when it is the appropriate choice. The implementation of the list structure provided by Python is presented to show how the various operations are implemented using a 1-D array. The Matrix ADT is introduced and includes an implementation using a two-dimensional array that exposes the students to an example of an ADT that is best implemented using a structure other than the list or dictionary.

Chapter 3: Sets and Maps.   This chapter reintroduces the students to both the Set and Map (or dictionary) ADTs with which they are likely to be familiar from their first programming course using Python. Even though Python provides these ADTs, they both provide great examples of abstract data types that can be implemented in many different ways. The chapter also continues the discussion of arrays from the previous chapter by introducing multi-dimensional arrays (those of two or more dimensions) along with the concept of physically storing these using a one-dimensional array in either row-major or column-major order. The chapter concludes with an example application that can benefit from the use of a three-dimensional array.

Chapter 4: Algorithm Analysis.   Introduces the basic concept and importance of complexity analysis by evaluating the operations of Python's list structure and the Set ADT as implemented in the previous chapter. This information will be used to provide a more efficient implementation of the Set ADT in the following chapter. The chapter concludes by introducing the Sparse Matrix ADT and providing a more efficient implementation with the use of a list in place of a two-dimensional array.

Chapter 5: Searching and Sorting. Introduces the concepts of searching and sorting and illustrates how the efficiency of some ADTs can be improved when working with sorted sequences. Search operations for an unsorted sequence are discussed and the binary search algorithm is introduced as a way of improving this operation. Three of the basic sorting algorithms are also introduced to further illustrate the use of algorithm analysis. A new implementation of the Set ADT is provided to show how different data structures or data organizations can change the efficiency of an ADT.

Chapter 6: Linked Structures. Provides an introduction to dynamic structures by illustrating the construction and use of the singly linked list using dynamic storage allocation. The common operations — traversal, searching, insertion, and deletion — are presented as is the use of a tail reference when appropriate. Several of the ADTs presented in earlier chapters are reimplemented using the singly linked list, and the run times of their operations are compared to the earlier versions. A new implementation of the Sparse Matrix is especially eye-opening to many students as it uses an array of sorted linked lists instead of a single Python list as was done in an earlier chapter.

Chapter 7: Stacks. Introduces the Stack ADT and includes implementations using both a Python list and a linked list. Several common stack applications are then presented, including balanced delimiter verification and the evaluation of postfix expressions. The concept of backtracking is also introduced as part of the application for solving a maze. A detailed discussion is provided in designing a solution and a partial implementation.

Chapter 8: Queues. Introduces the Queue ADT and includes three different implementations: Python list, circular array, and linked list. The priority queue is introduced to provide an opportunity to discuss different structures and data organization for an efficient implementation. The application of the queue presents the concept of discrete event computer simulations using an airline ticket counter as the example.

Chapter 9: Advanced Linked Lists. Continues the discussion of dynamic structures by introducing a collection of more advanced linked lists. These include the doubly linked, circularly linked, and multi linked lists. The latter provides an example of a linked structure containing multiple chains and is applied by reimplementing the Sparse Matrix to use two arrays of linked lists, one for the rows and one for the columns. The doubly linked list is applied to the problem of designing and implementing an Edit Buffer ADT for use with a basic text editor.

Chapter 10: Recursion. Introduces the use of recursion to solve various programming problems. The properties of creating recursive functions are presented along with common examples, including factorial, greatest common divisor, and the Towers of Hanoi. The concept of backtracking is revisited to use recursion for solving the eight-queens problem.

Chapter 11: Hash Tables.   Introduces the concept of hashing and the use of hash tables for performing fast searches. Different addressing techniques are presented, including those for both closed and open addressing. Collision resolution techniques and hash function design are also discussed. The magic behind Python's dictionary structure, which uses a hash table, is exposed and its efficiency evaluated.

Chapter 12: Advanced Sorting.   Continues the discussion of the sorting problem by introducing the recursive sorting algorithms—merge sort and quick sort—along with the radix distribution sort algorithm, all of which can be used to sort sequences. Some of the common techniques for sorting linked lists are also presented.

Chapter 13: Binary Trees.   Presents the tree structure and the general binary tree specifically. The construction and use of the binary tree is presented along with various properties and the various traversal operations. The binary tree is used to build and evaluate arithmetic expressions and in decoding Morse Code sequences. The tree-based heap structure is also introduced along with its use in implementing a priority queue and the heapsort algorithm.

Chapter 14: Search Trees.   Continues the discussion from the previous chapter by using the tree structure to solve the search problem. The basic binary search tree and the balanced binary search tree (AVL) are both introduced along with new implementations of the Map ADT. Finally, a brief introduction to the 2-3 multi-way tree is also provided, which shows an alternative to both the binary search and AVL trees.

Appendix A: Python Review.   Provides a review of the Python language and concepts learned in the traditional first course. The review includes a presentation of the basic constructs and built-in data structures.

Appendix B: User-Defined Modules.   Describes the use of modules in creating well structured programs. The different approaches for importing modules is also discussed along with the use of namespaces.

Appendix C: Exceptions.   Provides a basic introduction to the use of exceptions for handling and raising errors during program execution.

Appendix D: Classes.   Introduces the basic concepts of object-oriented programming, including encapsulation, inheritance, and polymorphism. The presentation is divided into two main parts. The first part presents the basic design and use of classes for those instructors who use a "back to basics" approach in teaching data structures. The second part briefly explores the more advanced features of inheritance and polymorphism for those instructors who typically include these topics in their course.

Acknowledgments

There are a number of individuals I would like to thank for helping to make this book possible. First, I must acknowledge two individuals who served as mentors in the early part of my career. Mary Dayne Gregg (University of Southern Mississippi), who was the best computer science teacher I have ever known, shared her love of teaching and provided a great role model in academia. Richard Prosl (Professor Emeritus, College of William and Mary) served not only as my graduate advisor but also shared great insight into teaching and helped me to become a good teacher.

A special thanks to the many students I have taught over the years, especially those at Washington and Lee University, who during the past five years used draft versions of the manuscript and provided helpful suggestions. I would also like to thank some of my colleagues who provided great advice and the encouragement to complete the project: Sara Sprenkle (Washington and Lee University), Debbie Noonan (College of William and Mary), and Robert Noonan (College of William and Mary).

I am also grateful to the following individuals who served as outside reviewers and provided valuable feedback and helpful suggestions: Esmail Bonakdarian (Franklin University), David Dubin (University of Illinois at Urbana-Champaign) Mark E. Fenner (Norwich University), Robert Franks (Central College), Charles J. Leska (Randolph-Macon College), Fernando Martincic (Wayne State University), Joseph D. Sloan (Wofford College), David A. Sykes (Wofford College), and Stan Thomas (Wake Forest University).

Finally, I would like to thank everyone at John Wiley & Sons who helped make this book possible. I would especially like to thank Beth Golub, Mike Berlin, and Amy Weintraub, with whom I worked closely throughout the process and who helped to make this first book an enjoyable experience.

RANCE D. NECAISE

## CHAPTER 1

Abstract Data Types

The foundation of computer science is based on the study of algorithms. An *algorithm* is a sequence of clear and precise step-by-step instructions for solving a problem in a finite amount of time. Algorithms are implemented by translating the step-by-step instructions into a *computer program* that can be executed by a computer. This translation process is called *computer programming* or simply *programming*. Computer programs are constructed using a *programming language* appropriate to the problem. While programming is an important part of computer science, computer science is not the study of programming. Nor is it about learning a particular programming language. Instead, programming and programming languages are tools used by computer scientists to solve problems.

1.1 Introduction

Data items are represented within a computer as a sequence of binary digits. These sequences can appear very similar but have different meanings since computers can store and manipulate different types of data. For example, the binary sequence 01001100110010110101110011011100 could be a string of characters, an integer value, or a real value. To distinguish between the different types of data, the term *type* is often used to refer to a collection of values and the term *data type* to refer to a given type along with a collection of operations for manipulating values of the given type.

Programming languages commonly provide data types as part of the language itself. These data types, known as *primitives*, come in two categories: simple and complex. The *simple data types* consist of values that are in the most basic form and cannot be decomposed into smaller parts. Integer and real types, for example, consist of single numeric values. The *complex data types*, on the other hand, are constructed of multiple components consisting of simple types or other complex types. In Python, objects, strings, lists, and dictionaries, which can contain multiple values, are all examples of complex types. The primitive types provided by a language may not be sufficient for solving large complex problems. Thus, most languages allow for the construction of additional data types, known as *user-defined types* since they are defined by the programmer and not the language. Some of these data types can themselves be very complex.

1.1.1 Abstractions

To help manage complex problems and complex data types, computer scientists typically work with abstractions. An *abstraction* is a mechanism for separating the properties of an object and restricting the focus to those relevant in the current context. The user of the abstraction does not have to understand all of the details in order to utilize the object, but only those relevant to the current task or problem.

Two common types of abstractions encountered in computer science are procedural, or functional, abstraction and data abstraction. *Procedural abstraction* is the use of a function or method knowing what it does but ignoring how it's accomplished. Consider the mathematical square root function which you have probably used at some point. You know the function will compute the square root of a given number, but do you know how the square root is computed? Does it matter if you know how it is computed, or is simply knowing how to correctly use the function sufficient? *Data abstraction* is the separation of the properties of a data type (its values and operations) from the implementation of that data type. You have used strings in Python many times. But do you know how they are implemented? That is, do you know how the data is structured internally or how the various operations are implemented?

Typically, abstractions of complex problems occur in layers, with each higher layer adding more abstraction than the previous. Consider the problem of representing integer values on computers and performing arithmetic operations on those values. Figure 1.1 illustrates the common levels of abstractions used with integer arithmetic. At the lowest level is the hardware with little to no abstraction since it includes binary representations of the values and logic circuits for performing the arithmetic. Hardware designers would deal with integer arithmetic at this level and be concerned with its correct implementation. A higher level of abstraction for integer values and arithmetic is provided through assembly language, which involves working with binary values and individual instructions corresponding to the underlying hardware. Compiler writers and assembly language programmers would work with integer arithmetic at this level and must ensure the proper selection of assembly language instructions to compute a given mathematical expression. For example, suppose we wish to compute $x = a + b - 5$. At the assembly language level, this expression must be split into multiple instructions for loading the values from memory, storing them into registers, and then performing each arithmetic operation separately, as shown in the following psuedocode:

```
loadFromMem( R1, 'a' )
loadFromMem( R2, 'b' )
```

```
add R0, R1, R2
sub R0, R0, 5
storeToMem( R0, 'x' )
```

To avoid this level of complexity, high-level programming languages add another layer of abstraction above the assembly language level. This abstraction is provided through a primitive data type for storing integer values and a set of well-defined operations that can be performed on those values. By providing this level of abstraction, programmers can work with variables storing decimal values and specify mathematical expressions in a more familiar notation $(x = a + b - 5)$ than is possible with assembly language instructions. Thus, a programmer does not need to know the assembly language instructions required to evaluate a mathematical expression or understand the hardware implementation in order to use integer arithmetic in a computer program.

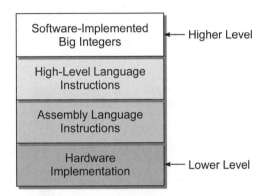

Figure 1.1: Levels of abstraction used with integer arithmetic.

One problem with the integer arithmetic provided by most high-level languages and in computer hardware is that it works with values of a limited size. On 32-bit architecture computers, for example, signed integer values are limited to the range $-2^{31} \ldots (2^{31} - 1)$. What if we need larger values? In this case, we can provide long or "big integers" implemented in software to allow values of unlimited size. This would involve storing the individual digits and implementing functions or methods for performing the various arithmetic operations. The implementation of the operations would use the primitive data types and instructions provided by the high-level language. Software libraries that provide big integer implementations are available for most common programming languages. Python, however, actually provides software-implemented big integers as part of the language itself.

1.1.2 Abstract Data Types

An *abstract data type* (or *ADT*) is a programmer-defined data type that specifies a set of data values and a collection of well-defined operations that can be performed on those values. Abstract data types are defined independent of their implementation, allowing us to focus on the use of the new data type instead of how it's implemented. This separation is typically enforced by requiring interaction with the abstract data type through an *interface* or defined set of operations. This is known as *information hiding*. By hiding the implementation details and requiring ADTs to be accessed through an interface, we can work with an abstraction and focus on what functionality the ADT provides instead of how that functionality is implemented.

Abstract data types can be viewed like black boxes as illustrated in Figure 1.2. User programs interact with instances of the ADT by invoking one of the several operations defined by its interface. The set of operations can be grouped into four categories:

- *Constructors*: Create and initialize new instances of the ADT.
- *Accessors*: Return data contained in an instance without modifying it.
- *Mutators*: Modify the contents of an ADT instance.
- *Iterators*: Process individual data components sequentially.

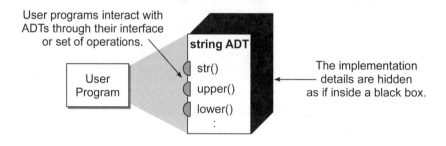

Figure 1.2: Separating the ADT definition from its implementation.

The implementation of the various operations are hidden inside the black box, the contents of which we do not have to know in order to utilize the ADT. There are several advantages of working with abstract data types and focusing on the "what" instead of the "how."

- *We can focus on solving the problem at hand instead of getting bogged down in the implementation details.* For example, suppose we need to extract a collection of values from a file on disk and store them for later use in our program. If we focus on the implementation details, then we have to worry about what type of storage structure to use, how it should be used, and whether it is the most efficient choice.

- *We can reduce logical errors that can occur from accidental misuse of storage structures and data types by preventing direct access to the implementation.* If we used a list to store the collection of values in the previous example, there is the opportunity to accidentally modify its contents in a part of our code where it was not intended. This type of logical error can be difficult to track down. By using ADTs and requiring access via the interface, we have fewer access points to debug.

- *The implementation of the abstract data type can be changed without having to modify the program code that uses the ADT.* There are many times when we discover the initial implementation of an ADT is not the most efficient or we need the data organized in a different way. Suppose our initial approach to the previous problem of storing a collection of values is to simply append new values to the end of the list. What happens if we later decide the items should be arranged in a different order than simply appending them to the end? If we are accessing the list directly, then we will have to modify our code at every point where values are added and make sure they are not rearranged in other places. By requiring access via the interface, we can easily "swap out" the black box with a new implementation with no impact on code segments that use the ADT.

- *It's easier to manage and divide larger programs into smaller modules, allowing different members of a team to work on the separate modules.* Large programming projects are commonly developed by teams of programmers in which the workload is divided among the members. By working with ADTs and agreeing on their definition, the team can better ensure the individual modules will work together when all the pieces are combined. Using our previous example, if each member of the team directly accessed the list storing the collection of values, they may inadvertently organize the data in different ways or modify the list in some unexpected way. When the various modules are combined, the results may be unpredictable.

1.1.3 Data Structures

Working with abstract data types, which separate the definition from the implementation, is advantageous in solving problems and writing programs. At some point, however, we must provide a concrete implementation in order for the program to execute. ADTs provided in language libraries, like Python, are implemented by the maintainers of the library. When you define and create your own abstract data types, you must eventually provide an implementation. The choices you make in implementing your ADT can affect its functionality and efficiency.

Abstract data types can be simple or complex. A *simple ADT* is composed of a single or several individually named data fields such as those used to represent a date or rational number. The *complex ADTs* are composed of a collection of data values such as the Python list or dictionary. Complex abstract data types are implemented using a particular *data structure*, which is the physical representation of how data is organized and manipulated. Data structures can be characterized by how they store and organize the individual data elements and what operations are available for accessing and manipulating the data.

There are many common data structures, including arrays, linked lists, stacks, queues, and trees, to name a few. All data structures store a collection of values, but differ in how they organize the individual data items and by what operations can be applied to manage the collection. The choice of a particular data structure depends on the ADT and the problem at hand. Some data structures are better suited to particular problems. For example, the queue structure is perfect for implementing a printer queue, while the B-Tree is the better choice for a database index. No matter which data structure we use to implement an ADT, by keeping the implementation separate from the definition, we can use an abstract data type within our program and later change to a different implementation, as needed, without having to modify our existing code.

1.1.4 General Definitions

There are many different terms used in computer science. Some of these can have different meanings among the various textbooks and programming languages. To aide the reader and to avoid confusion, we define some of the common terms we will be using throughout the text.

A *collection* is a group of values with no implied organization or relationship between the individual values. Sometimes we may restrict the elements to a specific data type such as a collection of integers or floating-point values.

A *container* is any data structure or abstract data type that stores and organizes a collection. The individual values of the collection are known as *elements* of the container and a container with no elements is said to be *empty*. The organization or arrangement of the elements can vary from one container to the next as can the operations available for accessing the elements. Python provides a number of built-in containers, which include strings, tuples, lists, dictionaries, and sets.

A *sequence* is a container in which the elements are arranged in linear order from front to back, with each element accessible by position. Throughout the text, we assume that access to the individual elements based on their position within the linear order is provided using the subscript operator. Python provides two immutable sequences, strings and tuples, and one mutable sequence, the list. In the next chapter, we introduce the array structure, which is also a commonly used mutable sequence.

A *sorted sequence* is one in which the position of the elements is based on a prescribed relationship between each element and its successor. For example, we can create a sorted sequence of integers in which the elements are arranged in ascending or increasing order from smallest to largest value.

In computer science, the term list is commonly used to refer to any collection with a linear ordering. The ordering is such that every element in the collection, except the first one, has a unique predecessor and every element, except the last one, has a unique successor. By this definition, a sequence is a list, but a list is not necessarily a sequence since there is no requirement that a list provide access to the elements by position. Python, unfortunately, uses the same name for its built-in mutable sequence type, which in other languages would be called an array list or vector abstract data type. To avoid confusion, we will use the term *list* to refer to the data type provided by Python and use the terms *general list* or *list structure* when referring to the more general list structure as defined earlier.

1.2   The Date Abstract Data Type

An abstract data type is defined by specifying the domain of the data elements that compose the ADT and the set of operations that can be performed on that domain. The definition should provide a clear description of the ADT including both its domain and each of its operations as only those operations specified can be performed on an instance of the ADT. Next, we provide the definition of a simple abstract data type for representing a date in the proleptic Gregorian calendar.

1.2.1   Defining the ADT

The Gregorian calendar was introduced in the year 1582 by Pope Gregory XIII to replace the Julian calendar. The new calendar corrected for the miscalculation of the lunar year and introduced the leap year. The official first date of the Gregorian calendar is Friday, October 15, 1582. The proleptic Gregorian calendar is an extension for accommodating earlier dates with the first date on November 24, 4713 BC. This extension simplifies the handling of dates across older calendars and its use can be found in many software applications.

Define   **Date ADT**

A *date* represents a single day in the proleptic Gregorian calendar in which the first day starts on November 24, 4713 BC.

- `Date( month, day, year )`: Creates a new `Date` instance initialized to the given Gregorian date which must be valid. Year 1 BC and earlier are indicated by negative year components.

- `day()`: Returns the Gregorian day number of this date.

- `month()`: Returns the Gregorian month number of this date.

- `year()`: Returns the Gregorian year of this date.

- `monthName()`: Returns the Gregorian month name of this date.

- `dayOfWeek()`: Returns the day of the week as a number between 0 and 6 with 0 representing Monday and 6 representing Sunday.

- `numDays( otherDate )`: Returns the number of days as a positive integer between this date and the `otherDate`.

- `isLeapYear()`: Determines if this date falls in a leap year and returns the appropriate boolean value.

- advanceBy(days): Advances the date by the given number of days. The date is incremented if days is positive and decremented if days is negative. The date is capped to November 24, 4714 BC, if necessary.

- *comparable* (otherDate): Compares this date to the otherDate to determine their logical ordering. This comparison can be done using any of the logical operators <, <=, >, >=, ==, !=.

- *toString* (): Returns a string representing the Gregorian date in the format mm/dd/yyyy. Implemented as the Python operator that is automatically called via the str() constructor.

The abstract data types defined in the text will be implemented as Python classes. When defining an ADT, we specify the ADT operations as method prototypes. The class constructor, which is used to create an instance of the ADT, is indicated by the name of the class used in the implementation.

Python allows classes to define or overload various operators that can be used more naturally in a program without having to call a method by name. We define all ADT operations as named methods, but implement some of them as operators when appropriate instead of using the named method. The ADT operations that will be implemented as Python operators are indicated in italicized text and a brief comment is provided in the ADT definition indicating the corresponding operator. This approach allows us to focus on the general ADT specification that can be easily translated to other languages if the need arises but also allows us to take advantage of Python's simple syntax in various sample programs.

1.2.2   Using the ADT

To illustrate the use of the Date ADT, consider the program in Listing 1.1, which processes a collection of birth dates. The dates are extracted from standard input and examined. Those dates that indicate the individual is at least 21 years of age based on a target date are printed to standard output. The user is continuously prompted to enter a birth date until zero is entered for the month.

This simple example illustrates an advantage of working with an abstraction by focusing on what functionality the ADT provides instead of how that functionality is implemented. By hiding the implementation details, we can use an ADT independent of its implementation. In fact, the choice of implementation for the Date ADT will have no effect on the instructions in our example program.

> **NOTE**
>
> ⚠ **Class Definitions.** Classes are the foundation of object-oriented programing languages and they provide a convenient mechanism for defining and implementing abstract data types. A review of Python classes is provided in Appendix D.

Listing 1.1   The `checkdates.py` program.

```python
 1  # Extracts a collection of birth dates from the user and determines
 2  # if each individual is at least 21 years of age.
 3  from date import Date
 4
 5  def main():
 6      # Date before which a person must have been born to be 21 or older.
 7      bornBefore = Date(6, 1, 1988)
 8
 9      # Extract birth dates from the user and determine if 21 or older.
10      date = promptAndExtractDate()
11      while date is not None :
12          if date <= bornBefore :
13              print( "Is at least 21 years of age: ", date )
14          date = promptAndExtractDate()
15
16  # Prompts for and extracts the Gregorian date components. Returns a
17  # Date object or None when the user has finished entering dates.
18  def promptAndExtractDate():
19      print( "Enter a birth date." )
20      month = int( input("month (0 to quit): ") )
21      if month == 0 :
22          return None
23      else :
24          day = int( input("day: ") )
25          year = int( input("year: ") )
26          return Date( month, day, year )
27
28  # Call the main routine.
29  main()
```

1.2.3 Preconditions and Postconditions

In defining the operations, we must include a specification of required inputs and the resulting output, if any. In addition, we must specify the preconditions and postconditions for each operation. A *precondition* indicates the condition or state of the ADT instance and inputs before the operation can be performed. A *postcondition* indicates the result or ending state of the ADT instance after the operation is performed. The precondition is assumed to be true while the postcondition is a guarantee as long as the preconditions are met. Attempting to perform an operation in which the precondition is not satisfied should be flagged as an error. Consider the use of the `pop(i)` method for removing a value from a list. When this method is called, the precondition states the supplied index must be within the legal range. Upon successful completion of the operation, the postcondition guarantees the item has been removed from the list. If an invalid index, one that is out of the legal range, is passed to the `pop()` method, an exception is raised.

All operations have at least one precondition, which is that the ADT instance has to have been previously initialized. In an object-oriented language, this precondition is automatically verified since an object must be created and initialized via the constructor before any operation can be used. Other than the initialization requirement, an operation may not have any other preconditions. It all depends on the type of ADT and the respective operation. Likewise, some operations may not have a postcondition, as is the case for simple access methods, which simply return a value without modifying the ADT instance itself. Throughout the text, we do not explicitly state the precondition and postcondition as such, but they are easily identified from the description of the ADT operations.

When implementing abstract data types, it's important that we ensure the proper execution of the various operations by verifying any stated preconditions. The appropriate mechanism when testing preconditions for abstract data types is to test the precondition and raise an exception when the precondition fails. You then allow the user of the ADT to decide how they wish to handle the error, either catch it or allow the program to abort.

Python, like many other object-oriented programming languages, raises an exception when an error occurs. An *exception* is an event that can be triggered and optionally handled during program execution. When an exception is raised indicating an error, the program can contain code to catch and gracefully handle the exception; otherwise, the program will abort. Python also provides the `assert` statement, which can be used to raise an `AssertionError` exception. The `assert` statement is used to state what we assume to be true at a given point in the program. If the assertion fails, Python automatically raises an `AssertionError` and aborts the program, unless the exception is caught.

Throughout the text, we use the `assert` statement to test the preconditions when implementing abstract data types. This allows us to focus on the implementation of the ADTs instead of having to spend time selecting the proper exception to raise or creating new exceptions for use with our ADTs. For more information on exceptions and assertions, refer to Appendix C.

1.2.4 Implementing the ADT

After defining the ADT, we need to provide an implementation in an appropriate language. In our case, we will always use Python and class definitions, but any programming language could be used. A partial implementation of the `Date` class is provided in Listing 1.2, with the implementation of some methods left as exercises.

Date Representations

There are two common approaches to storing a date in an object. One approach stores the three components—month, day, and year—as three separate fields. With this format, it is easy to access the individual components, but it's difficult to compare two dates or to compute the number of days between two dates since the number of days in a month varies from month to month. The second approach stores the date as an integer value representing the Julian day, which is the number of days elapsed since the initial date of November 24, 4713 BC (using the Gregorian calendar notation). Given a Julian day number, we can compute any of the three Gregorian components and simply subtract the two integer values to determine which occurs first or how many days separate the two dates. We are going to use the latter approach as it is very common for storing dates in computer applications and provides for an easy implementation.

Listing 1.2   Partial implementation of the `date.py` module.

```
1   # Implements a proleptic Gregorian calendar date as a Julian day number.
2
3   class Date :
4     # Creates an object instance for the specified Gregorian date.
5     def __init__( self, month, day, year ):
6       self._julianDay = 0
7       assert self._isValidGregorian( month, day, year ), \
8             "Invalid Gregorian date."
9
10      # The first line of the equation, T = (M - 14) / 12, has to be changed
11      # since Python's implementation of integer division is not the same
12      # as the mathematical definition.
13      tmp = 0
14      if month < 3 :
15        tmp = -1
16      self._julianDay = day - 32075 + \
17              (1461 * (year + 4800 + tmp) // 4) + \
18              (367 * (month - 2 - tmp * 12) // 12) - \
19              (3 * ((year + 4900 + tmp) // 100) // 4)
20
21    # Extracts the appropriate Gregorian date component.
22    def month( self ):
23      return (self._toGregorian())[0]  # returning M from (M, d, y)
24
25    def day( self ):
26      return (self._toGregorian())[1]  # returning D from (m, D, y)
27
28    def year( self ):
29      return (self._toGregorian())[2]  # returning Y from (m, d, Y)
30
31    # Returns day of the week as an int between 0 (Mon) and 6 (Sun).
32    def dayOfWeek( self ):
33      month, day, year = self._toGregorian()
34      if month < 3 :
35        month = month + 12
36        year = year - 1
37      return ((13 * month + 3) // 5 + day + \
38              year + year // 4 - year // 100 + year // 400) % 7
39
40    # Returns the date as a string in Gregorian format.
41    def __str__( self ):
42      month, day, year = self._toGregorian()
43      return "%02d/%02d/%04d" % (month, day, year)
44
45    # Logically compares the two dates.
46    def __eq__( self, otherDate ):
47      return self._julianDay == otherDate._julianDay
48
```

(Listing Continued)

Listing 1.2   Continued . . .

```
49    def __lt__( self, otherDate ):
50      return self._julianDay < otherDate._julianDay
51
52    def __le__( self, otherDate ):
53      return self._julianDay <= otherDate._julianDay
54
55    # The remaining methods are to be included at this point.
56    # ......
57
58    # Returns the Gregorian date as a tuple: (month, day, year).
59    def _toGregorian( self ):
60      A = self._julianDay + 68569
61      B = 4 * A // 146097
62      A = A - (146097 * B + 3) // 4
63      year = 4000 * (A + 1) // 1461001
64      A = A - (1461 * year // 4) + 31
65      month = 80 * A // 2447
66      day = A - (2447 * month // 80)
67      A = month // 11
68      month = month + 2 - (12 * A)
69      year = 100 * (B - 49) + year + A
70      return month, day, year
```

Constructing the Date

We begin our discussion of the implementation with the constructor, which is shown in lines 5–19 of Listing 1.2. The Date ADT will need only a single attribute to store the Julian day representing the given Gregorian date. To convert a Gregorian date to a Julian day number, we use the following formula[1] where day 0 corresponds to November 24, 4713 BC and all operations involve integer arithmetic.

```
T = (M - 14) / 12
jday = D - 32075 + (1461 * (Y + 4800 + T) / 4) +
                   (367 * (M - 2 - T * 12) / 12) -
                   (3 * ((Y + 4900 + T) / 100) / 4)
```

Before attempting to convert the Gregorian date to a Julian day, we need to verify it's a valid date. This is necessary since the precondition states the supplied Gregorian date must be valid. The _isValidGregorian() helper method is used to verify the validity of the given Gregorian date. This helper method, the implementation of which is left as an exercise, tests the supplied Gregorian date components and returns the appropriate boolean value. If a valid date is supplied to the constructor, it is converted to the equivalent Julian day using the equation provided earlier. Note the statements in lines 13–15. The equation for converting a Gregorian date to a Julian day number uses integer arithmetic, but

---

[1]Seidelmann, P. Kenneth (ed.) (1992). *Explanatory Supplement to the Astronomical Almanac*, Chapter 12, pp. 604—606, University Science Books.

> **NOTE**
>
> ⓘ **Comments.** Class definitions and methods should be properly commented to aide the user in knowing what the class and/or methods do. To conserve space, however, classes and methods presented in this book do not routinely include these comments since the surrounding text provides a full explanation.

the equation line T = (M - 14) / 12 produces an incorrect result in Python due to its implementation of integer division, which is not the same as the mathematical definition. By definition, the result of the integer division -11/12 is 0, but Python computes this as $\lfloor -11/12.0 \rfloor$ resulting in -1. Thus, we had to modify the first line of the equation to produce the correct Julian day when the month component is greater than 2.

> **CAUTION**
>
> ⚠ **Protected Attributes and Methods.** Python does not provide a technique to protect attributes and helper methods in order to prevent their use outside the class definition. In this text, we use identifier names, which begin with a single underscore to flag those attributes and methods that should be considered protected and rely on the user of the class to not attempt a direct access.

The Gregorian Date

To access the Gregorian date components the Julian day must be converted back to Gregorian. This conversion is needed in several of the ADT operations. Instead of duplicating the formula each time it's needed, we create a helper method to handle the conversion as illustrated in lines 59–70 of Listing 1.2.

The _toGregorian() method returns a tuple containing the day, month, and year components. As with the conversion from Gregorian to Julian, integer arithmetic operations are used throughout the conversion formula. By returning a tuple, we can call the helper method and use the appropriate component from the tuple for the given Gregorian component access method, as illustrated in lines 22–29.

The dayOfWeek() method, shown in lines 32–38, also uses the _toGregorian() conversion helper method. We determine the day of the week based on the Gregorian components using a simple formula that returns an integer value between 0 and 6, where 0 represents Monday, 1 represents Tuesday, and so on.

The *toString* operation defined by the ADT is implemented in lines 41–43 by overloading Python's __str__ method. It creates a string representation of a date in Gregorian format. This can be done using the string format operator and supplying the values returned from the conversion helper method. By using Python's __str__ method, Python automatically calls this method on the object when you attempt to print or convert an object to a string as in the following example:

```
firstDay = Date( 9, 1, 2006 )
print( firstDay )
```

Comparing Date Objects

We can logically compare two `Date` instances to determine their calendar order. When using a Julian day to represent the dates, the date comparison is as simple as comparing the two integer values and returning the appropriate boolean value based on the result of that comparison. The "comparable" ADT operation is implemented using Python's logical comparison operators as shown in lines 46–53 of Listing 1.2. By implementing the methods for the logical comparison operators, instances of the class become *comparable* objects. That is, the objects can be compared against each other to produce a logical ordering.

You will notice that we implemented only three of the logical comparison operators. The reason for this is that starting with Python version 3, Python will automatically swap the operands and call the appropriate reflective method when necessary. For example, if we use the expression `a > b` with `Date` objects in our program, Python will automatically swap the operands and call `b < a` instead since the `__lt__` method is defined but not `__gt__`. It will do the same for `a >= b` and `a <= b`. When testing for equality, Python will automatically invert the result when only one of the equality operators (`==` or `!=`) is defined. Thus, we need only define one operator from each of the following pairs to achieve the full range of logical comparisons: `<` or `>`, `<=` or `>=`, and `==` or `!=`. For more information on overloading operators, refer to Appendix D.

> **TIP**
>
> 🗩 **Overloading Operators.** User-defined classes can implement methods to define many of the standard Python operators such as +, *, %, and ==, as well as the standard named operators such as `in` and `not in`. This allows for a more natural use of the objects instead of having to call specific named methods. It can be tempting to define operators for every class you create, but you should limit the definition of operator methods for classes where the specific operator has a meaningful purpose.

1.3 Bags

The Date ADT provided an example of a simple abstract data type. To illustrate the design and implementation of a complex abstract data type, we define the Bag ADT. A *bag* is a simple container like a shopping bag that can be used to store a collection of items. The bag container restricts access to the individual items by only defining operations for adding and removing individual items, for determining if an item is in the bag, and for traversing over the collection of items.

1.3.1   The Bag Abstract Data Type

There are several variations of the Bag ADT with the one described here being a simple bag. A grab bag is similar to the simple bag but the items are removed from the bag at random. Another common variation is the counting bag, which includes an operation that returns the number of occurrences in the bag of a given item. Implementations of the grab bag and counting bag are left as exercises.

Define   **Bag ADT**

A *bag* is a container that stores a collection in which duplicate values are allowed. The items, each of which is individually stored, have no particular order but they must be comparable.

- Bag(): Creates a bag that is initially empty.

- *length* (): Returns the number of items stored in the bag. Accessed using the len() function.

- *contains* (item): Determines if the given target item is stored in the bag and returns the appropriate boolean value. Accessed using the in operator.

- add(item): Adds the given item to the bag.

- remove(item): Removes and returns an occurrence of item from the bag. An exception is raised if the element is not in the bag.

- *iterator* (): Creates and returns an iterator that can be used to iterate over the collection of items.

You may have noticed our definition of the Bag ADT does not include an operation to convert the container to a string. We could include such an operation, but creating a string for a large collection is time consuming and requires a large amount of memory. Such an operation can be beneficial when debugging a program that uses an instance of the Bag ADT. Thus, it's not uncommon to include the __str__ operator method for debugging purposes, but it would not typically be used in production software. We will usually omit the inclusion of a __str__ operator method in the definition of our abstract data types, except in those cases where it's meaningful, but you may want to include one temporarily for debugging purposes.

Examples

Given the abstract definition of the Bag ADT, we can create and use a bag without knowing how it is actually implemented. Consider the following simple example, which creates a bag and asks the user to guess one of the values it contains.

```
myBag = Bag()
myBag.add( 19 )
myBag.add( 74 )
myBag.add( 23 )
myBag.add( 19 )
myBag.add( 12 )

value = int( input("Guess a value contained in the bag.") )
if value in myBag:
  print( "The bag contains the value", value )
else :
  print( "The bag does not contain the value", value )
```

Next, consider the `checkdates.py` sample program from the previous section where we extracted birth dates from the user and determined which ones were for individuals who were at least 21 years of age. Suppose we want to keep the collection of birth dates for later use. It wouldn't make sense to require the user to re-enter the dates multiple times. Instead, we can store the birth dates in a bag as they are entered and access them later, as many times as needed. The Bag ADT is a perfect container for storing objects when the position or order of a specific item does not matter. The following is a new version of the main routine for our birth date checking program from Listing 1.1:

```
#pgm: checkdates2.py (modified main() from checkdates.py)
from linearbag import Bag
from date import Date

def main():
  bornBefore = Date( 6, 1, 1988 )
  bag = Bag()

  # Extract dates from the user and place them in the bag.
  date = promptAndExtractDate()
  while date is not None :
    bag.add( date )
    date = promptAndExtractDate()

  # Iterate over the bag and check the age.
  for date in bag :
    if date <= bornBefore :
      print( "Is at least 21 years of age: ", date )
```

Why a Bag ADT?

You may be wondering, why do we need the Bag ADT when we could simply use the list to store the items? For a small program and a small collection of data, using a list would be appropriate. When working with large programs and multiple team members, however, abstract data types provide several advantages as described earlier in Section 1.1.2. By working with the abstraction of a bag, we can: a) focus on solving the problem at hand instead of worrying about the implementation of the container, b) reduce the chance of introducing errors from misuse of the list since it provides additional operations that are not appropriate for a bag, c) provide better coordination between different modules and designers, and d) easily swap out our current implementation of the Bag ADT for a different, possibly more efficient, version later.

1.3.2 Selecting a Data Structure

The implementation of a complex abstract data type typically requires the use of a data structure for organizing and managing the collection of data items. There are many different structures from which to choose. So how do we know which to use? We have to evaluate the suitability of a data structure for implementing a given abstract data type, which we base on the following criteria:

1. *Does the data structure provide for the storage requirements as specified by the domain of the ADT?* Abstract data types are defined to work with a specific domain of data values. The data structure we choose must be capable of storing all possible values in that domain, taking into consideration any restrictions or limitations placed on the individual items.

2. *Does the data structure provide the necessary data access and manipulation functionality to fully implement the ADT?* The functionality of an abstract data type is provided through its defined set of operations. The data structure must allow for a full and correct implementation of the ADT without having to violate the abstraction principle by exposing the implementation details to the user.

3. *Does the data structure lend itself to an efficient implementation of the operations?* An important goal in the implementation of an abstract data type is to provide an efficient solution. Some data structures allow for a more efficient implementation than others, but not every data structure is suitable for implementing every ADT. Efficiency considerations can help to select the best structure from among multiple candidates.

There may be multiple data structures suitable for implementing a given abstract data type, but we attempt to select the best possible based on the context in which the ADT will be used. To accommodate different contexts, language libraries will commonly provide several implementations of some ADTs, allowing the programmer to choose the most appropriate. Following this approach, we introduce a number of abstract data types throughout the text and present multiple implementations as new data structures are introduced.

The efficiency of an implementation is based on complexity analysis, which is not introduced until later in Chapter 3. Thus, we postpone consideration of the efficiency of an implementation in selecting a data structure until that time. In the meantime, we only consider the suitability of a data structure based on the storage and functional requirements of the abstract data type.

We now turn our attention to selecting a data structure for implementing the Bag ADT. The possible candidates at this point include the list and dictionary structures. The list can store any type of comparable object, including duplicates. Each item is stored individually, including duplicates, which means the reference to each individual object is stored and later accessible when needed. This satisfies the storage requirements of the Bag ADT, making the list a candidate structure for its implementation.

The dictionary stores key/value pairs in which the key component must be comparable and unique. To use the dictionary in implementing the Bag ADT, we must have a way to store duplicate items as required by the definition of the abstract data type. To accomplish this, each unique item can be stored in the key part of the key/value pair and a counter can be stored in the value part. The counter would be used to indicate the number of occurrences of the corresponding item in the bag. When a duplicate item is added, the counter is incremented; when a duplicate is removed, the counter is decremented.

Both the list and dictionary structures could be used to implement the Bag ADT. For the simple version of the bag, however, the list is a better choice since the dictionary would require twice as much space to store the contents of the bag in the case where most of the items are unique. The dictionary is an excellent choice for the implementation of the counting bag variation of the ADT.

Having chosen the list, we must ensure it provides the means to implement the complete set of bag operations. When implementing an ADT, we must use the functionality provided by the underlying data structure. Sometimes, an ADT operation is identical to one already provided by the data structure. In this case, the implementation can be quite simple and may consist of a single call to the corresponding operation of the structure, while in other cases, we have to use multiple operations provided by the structure. To help verify a correct implementation of the Bag ADT using the list, we can outline how each bag operation will be implemented:

- An empty bag can be represented by an empty list.
- The size of the bag can be determined by the size of the list.
- Determining if the bag contains a specific item can be done using the equivalent list operation.
- When a new item is added to the bag, it can be appended to the end of the list since there is no specific ordering of the items in a bag.
- Removing an item from the bag can also be handled by the equivalent list operation.
- The items in a list can be traversed using a `for` loop and Python provides for user-defined iterators that be used with a bag.

From this itemized list, we see that each Bag ADT operation can be implemented using the available functionality of the list. Thus, the list is suitable for implementing the bag.

1.3.3 List-Based Implementation

The implementation of the Bag ADT using a list is shown in Listing 1.3. The constructor defines a single data field, which is initialized to an empty list. This corresponds to the definition of the constructor for the Bag ADT in which the container is initially created empty. A sample instance of the `Bag` class created from the example `checkdates2.py` program provided earlier is illustrated in Figure 1.3.

Listing 1.3   The `linearbag.py` module.

```python
1  # Implements the Bag ADT container using a Python list.
2  class Bag :
3    # Constructs an empty bag.
4    def __init__( self ):
5      self._theItems = list()
6
7    # Returns the number of items in the bag.
8    def __len__( self ):
9      return len( self._theItems )
10
11   # Determines if an item is contained in the bag.
12   def __contains__( self, item ):
13     return item in self._theItems
14
15   # Adds a new item to the bag.
16   def add( self, item ):
17     self._theItems.append( item )
18
19   # Removes and returns an instance of the item from the bag.
20   def remove( self, item ):
21     assert item in self._theItems, "The item must be in the bag."
22     ndx = self._theItems.index( item )
23     return self._theItems.pop( ndx )
24
25   # Returns an iterator for traversing the list of items.
26   def __iter__( self, item ):
27     ......
```

Most of the implementation details follow the specifics discussed in the previous section. There are some additional details, however. First, the ADT definition of the `remove()` operation specifies the precondition that the item must exist in the bag in order to be removed. Thus, we must first assert that condition and verify the existence of the item. Second, we need to provide an iteration mechanism that allows us to iterate over the individual items in the bag. We delay

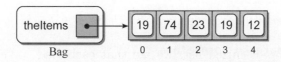

Figure 1.3: Sample instance of the `Bag` class implemented using a list.

the implementation of this operation until the next section where we discuss the creation and use of iterators in Python.

A list stores references to objects and technically would be illustrated as shown in the figure to the right. To conserve space and reduce the clutter that can result in some figures, however, we illustrate objects in the text as boxes with rounded edges and show them stored directly within the list structure. Variables will be illustrated as square boxes with a bullet in the middle and the name of the variable printed nearby.

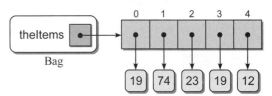

1.4 Iterators

Traversals are very common operations, especially on containers. A traversal iterates over the entire collection, providing access to each individual element. Traversals can be used for a number of operations, including searching for a specific item or printing an entire collection.

Python's container types—strings, tuples, lists, and dictionaries—can be traversed using the **for** loop construct. For our user-defined abstract data types, we can add methods that perform specific traversal operations when necessary. For example, if we wanted to save every item contained in a bag to a text file, we could add a **saveElements()** method that traverses over the vector and writes each value to a file. But this would limit the format of the resulting text file to that specified in the new method. In addition to saving the items, perhaps we would like to simply print the items to the screen in a specific way. To perform the latter, we would have to add yet another operation to our ADT.

Not all abstract data types should provide a traversal operation, but it is appropriate for most container types. Thus, we need a way to allow generic traversals to be performed. One way would be to provide the user with access to the underlying data structure used to implement the ADT. But this would violate the abstraction principle and defeat the purpose of defining new abstract data types.

Python, like many of today's object-oriented languages, provides a built-in iterator construct that can be used to perform traversals on user-defined ADTs. An *iterator* is an object that provides a mechanism for performing generic traversals through a container without having to expose the underlying implementation. Iterators are used with Python's **for** loop construct to provide a traversal mechanism for both built-in and user-defined containers. Consider the code segment from the **checkdates2.py** program in Section 1.3 that uses the **for** loop to traverse the collection of dates:

```
 # Iterate over the bag and check the ages.
for date in bag :
  if date <= bornBefore :
    print( "Is at least 21 years of age: ", date )
```

1.4.1   Designing an Iterator

To use Python's traversal mechanism with our own abstract data types, we must define an iterator class, which is a class in Python containing two special methods, `__iter__` and `__next__`. Iterator classes are commonly defined in the same module as the corresponding container class.

The implementation of the `_BagIterator` class is shown in Listing 1.4. The constructor defines two data fields. One is an alias to the list used to store the items in the bag, and the other is a loop index variable that will be used to iterate over that list. The loop variable is initialized to zero in order to start from the beginning of the list. The `__iter__` method simply returns a reference to the object itself and is always implemented to do so.

Listing 1.4   The _BagIterator class, which is part of the `linearbag.py` module.

```python
1  # An iterator for the Bag ADT implemented as a Python list.
2  class _BagIterator :
3    def __init__( self, theList ):
4      self._bagItems = theList
5      self._curItem = 0
6
7    def __iter__( self ):
8      return self
9
10   def __next__( self ):
11     if self._curItem < len( self._bagItems ) :
12       item = self._bagItems[ self._curItem ]
13       self._curItem += 1
14       return item
15     else :
16       raise StopIteration
```

The `__next__` method is called to return the next item in the container. The method first saves a reference to the current item indicated by the loop variable. The loop variable is then incremented by one to prepare it for the next invocation of the `__next__` method. If there are no additional items, the method must raise a `StopIteration` exception that flags the `for` loop to terminate. Finally, we must add an `__iter__` method to our `Bag` class, as shown here:

```python
def __iter__( self ):
  return _BagIterator( self._theItems )
```

This method, which is responsible for creating and returning an instance of the `_BagIterator` class, is automatically called at the beginning of the `for` loop to create an iterator object for use with the loop construct.

1.4.2 Using Iterators

With the definition of the _BagIterator class and the modifications to the Bag class, we can now use Python's for loop with a Bag instance. When the for loop

```
for item in bag :
    print( item )
```

is executed, Python automatically calls the __iter__ method on the bag object to create an iterator object. Figure 1.4 illustrates the state of the _BagIterator object immediately after being created. Notice the _bagItems field of the iterator object references _theItems field of the bag object. This reference was assigned by the constructor when the _BagIterator object was created.

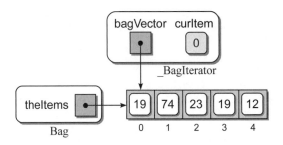

Figure 1.4: The Bag and _BagIterator objects before the first loop iteration.

The for loop then automatically calls the __next__ method on the iterator object to access the next item in the container. The state of the iterator object changes with the _curItem field having been incremented by one. This process continues until a StopIteration exception is raised by the __next__ method when the items have been exhausted as indicated by the _curItem. After all of the items have been processed, the iteration is terminated and execution continues with the next statement following the loop. The following code segment illustrates how Python actually performs the iteration when a for loop is used with an instance of the Bag class:

```
# Create a BagIterator object for myBag.
iterator = myBag.__iter__()

# Repeat the while loop until break is called.
while True :
  try:
      # Get the next item from the bag. If there are no
      # more items, the StopIteration exception is raised.
      item = iterator.__next__()
      # Perform the body of the for loop.
      print( item )

  # Catch the exception and break from the loop when we are done.
  except StopIteration:
      break
```

1.5 Application: Student Records

Most computer applications are written to process and manipulate data that is stored external to the program. Data is commonly extracted from files stored on disk, from databases, and even from remote sites through web services. For example, suppose we have a collection of records stored on disk that contain information related to students at Smalltown College. We have been assigned the task to extract this information and produce a report similar to the following in which the records are sorted by identification number.

```
                       LIST OF STUDENTS

     ID    NAME                      CLASS       GPA
     -----  ------------------------  ----------  ----
     10015  Smith, John               Sophomore   3.01
     10167  Jones, Wendy              Junior      2.85
     10175  Smith, Jane               Senior      3.92
     10188  Wales, Sam                Senior      3.25
     10200  Roberts, Sally            Freshman    4.00
     10208  Green, Patrick            Freshman    3.95
     10226  Nelson, Amy               Sophomore   2.95
     10334  Roberts, Jane             Senior      3.81
     10387  Taylor, Susan             Sophomore   2.15
     10400  Logan, Mark               Junior      3.33
     10485  Brown, Jessica            Sophomore   2.91
     -------------------------------------------------

     Number of students: 11
```

Our contact in the Registrar's office, who assigned the task, has provided some information about the data. We know each record contains five pieces of information for an individual student: (1) the student's id number represented as an integer; (2) their first and last names, which are strings; (3) an integer classification code in the range $[1 \ldots 4]$ that indicates if the student is a freshman, sophomore, junior, or senior; and (4) their current grade point average represented as a floating-point value. What we have not been told, however, is how the data is stored on disk. It could be stored in a plain text file, in a binary file, or even in a database. In addition, if the data is stored in a text or binary file, we will need to know how the data is formatted in the file, and if it's in a relational database, we will need to know the type and the structure of the database.

1.5.1 Designing a Solution

Even though we have not yet been told the type of file or the format used to store the data, we can begin designing and implementing a solution by working with an abstraction of the input source. No matter the source or format of the data, the extraction of data records from external storage requires similar steps: open a connection, extract the individual records, then close the connection. To aide in our effort, we define a Student File Reader ADT to represent the extraction of data from an external file or database. In computer programming, an object used to input data into a program is sometimes referred to as a *reader* while an object used to output data is referred to as a *writer*.

Define   **Student File Reader ADT**

A *student file reader* is used to extract student records from external storage. The five data components of the individual records are extracted and stored in a storage object specific for this collection of student records.

- `StudentFileReader( filename )`: Creates a student reader instance for extracting student records from the given file. The type and format of the file is dependent on the specific implementation.

- `open()`: Opens a connection to the input source and prepares it for extracting student records. If a connection cannot be opened, an exception is raised.

- `close()`: Closes the connection to the input source. If the connection is not currently open, an exception is raised.

- `fetchRecord()`: Extracts the next student record from the input source and returns a reference to a storage object containing the data. `None` is returned when there are no additional records to be extracted. An exception is raised if the connection to the input source was previously closed.

- `fetchAll()`: The same as `fetchRecord()`, but extracts all student records (or those remaining) from the input source and returns them in a Python list.

Creating the Report

The program in Listing 1.5 uses the Student File Reader ADT to produce the sample report illustrated earlier. The program extracts the student records from the input source, sorts the records by student identification number, and produces the report. This program illustrates some of the advantages of applying abstraction to problem solving by focusing on the "what" instead of the "how."

By using the Student File Reader ADT, we are able to design a solution and construct a program for the problem at hand without knowing exactly how the data is stored in the external source. We import the `StudentFileReader` class from the `studentfile.py` module, which we assume will be an implementation of the ADT that handles the actual data extraction. Further, if we want to use this same program with a data file having a different format, the only modifications required will be to indicate a different module in the `import` statement and possibly a change to the filename specified by the constant variable `FILE_NAME`.

The `studentreport.py` program consists of two functions: `printReport()` and `main()`. The main routine uses an instance of the ADT to connect to the external source in order to extract the student records into a list. The list of records is then

Listing 1.5	The `studentreport.py` program.

```python
1   # Produces a student report from data extracted from an external source.
2   from studentfile import StudentFileReader
3
4   # Name of the file to open.
5   FILE_NAME = "students.txt"
6
7   def main():
8       # Extract the student records from the given text file.
9       reader = StudentFileReader( FILE_NAME )
10      reader.open()
11      studentList = reader.fetchAll()
12      reader.close()
13
14      # Sort the list by id number. Each object is passed to the lambda
15      # expression which returns the idNum field of the object.
16      studentList.sort( key = lambda rec: rec.idNum )
17
18      # Print the student report.
19      printReport( studentList )
20
21  # Prints the student report.
22  def printReport( theList ):
23      # The class names associated with the class codes.
24      classNames = ( None, "Freshman", "Sophomore", "Junior", "Senior" )
25
26      # Print the header.
27      print( "LIST OF STUDENTS".center(50) )
28      print( "" )
29      print( "%-5s  %-25s  %-10s  %-4s" % ('ID', 'NAME', 'CLASS', 'GPA' ) )
30      print( "%5s  %25s  %10s  %4s" % ('-' * 5, '-' * 25, '-' * 10, '-' * 4))
31      # Print the body.
32      for record in theList :
33          print( "%5d  %-25s  %-10s  %4.2f" % \
34                      (record.idNum, \
35                       record.lastName + ', ' + record.firstName,
36                       classNames[record.classCode], record.gpa) )
37      # Add a footer.
38      print( "-" * 50 )
39      print( "Number of students:", len(theList) )
40
41  # Executes the main routine.
42  main()
```

sorted in ascending order based on the student identification number. The actual report is produced by passing the sorted list to the `printReport()` function.

Storage Class

When the data for an individual student is extracted from the input file, it will need to be saved in a storage object that can be added to a list in order to first sort and then print the records. We could use tuples to store the records, but we avoid the use of tuples when storing structured data since it's better practice to use classes with named fields. Thus, we define the `StudentRecord` class

```
class StudentRecord :
  def __init__( self ):
    self.idNum = 0
    self.firstName = None
    self.lastName = None
    self.classCode = 0
    self.gpa = 0.0
```

to store the data related to an individual student. You may notice there is only a constructor with no additional methods. This is a complete class as defined and represents a ***storage class***. The constructor is all that's needed to define the two data fields for storing the two component values.

Storage classes should be defined within the same module as the class with which they will be used. For this application, the `StudentRecord` class is defined at the end of the `studentfile.py` module. Some storage classes may be intended for internal use by a specific class and not meant to be accessed from outside the module. In those cases, the name of the storage class will begin with a single underscore, which flags it as being private to the module in which it's defined. The `StudentRecord` class, however, has not been defined as being private to the module since instances of the storage class are not confined to the ADT but instead are returned to the client code by methods of the `StudentFileReader` class. The storage class can be imported along with the `StudentFileReader` class when needed.

You will note the data fields in the storage class are public (by our notation) since their names do not begin with an underscore as they have been in other classes presented earlier. The reason we do not include a restrictive interface for accessing the data fields is that storage objects are meant to be used exclusively for storing data and not as an instance of some abstract data type. Given their limited use, we access the data fields directly as needed.

1.5.2 Implementation

The implementation of the Student File Reader ADT does not require a data structure since it does not store data but instead extracts data from an external source. The ADT has to be implemented to extract data based on the format in which the data is stored. For this example, we are going to extract the data from

> **CAUTION**
>
> ⚠ **Python Tuples.** The tuple can be used to store structured data, with each element corresponding to an individual data field. This is not good practice, however, since the elements are not named and you would have to remember what piece of data is stored in each element. A better practice is to use objects with named data fields. In this book, we limit the use of tuples for returning multiple values from methods and functions.

a text file in which the records are listed one after the other. The five fields of the record are each stored on a separate line. The first line contains the id number, the second and third contain the first and last names, the fourth line contains the classification code, and the grade point average follows on the fifth line. The following text block illustrates the format for a file containing two records:

```
10015
John
Smith
2
3.01
10334
Jane
Roberts
4
3.81
```

Listing 1.6 provides the implementation of the ADT for extracting the records from the text file in the given format. The constructor simply initializes an instance of the class by creating two attributes, one to store the name the text file and the other to store a reference to the file object after it's opened. The open() method is responsible for opening the input file using the name saved in the constructor. The resulting file object is saved in the inputFile attribute so it can be used in the other methods. After the records are extracted, the file is closed by calling the close() method.

Listing 1.6   The studentfile.py module.

```
 1  # Implementation of the StudentFileReader ADT using a text file as the
 2  # input source in which each field is stored on a separate line.
 3
 4  class StudentFileReader :
 5    # Create a new student reader instance.
 6    def __init__( self, inputSrc ):
 7      self._inputSrc = inputSrc
 8      self._inputFile = None
 9
10    # Open a connection to the input file.
11    def open( self ):
12      self._inputFile = open( self._inputSrc, "r" )
13
14    # Close the connection to the input file.
15    def close( self ):
16      self._inputFile.close()
17      self._inputFile = None
18
19    # Extract all student records and store them in a list.
20    def fetchAll( self ):
21      theRecords = list()
22      student = self.fetchRecord()
```

(Listing Continued)

Listing 1.6   Continued ...

```
23        while student != None :
24          theRecords.append( student )
25          student = self.fetchRecord()
26        return theRecords
27
28      # Extract the next student record from the file.
29      def fetchRecord( self ):
30        # Read the first line of the record.
31        line = self._inputFile.readline()
32        if line == "" :
33          return None
34
35        # If there is another record, create a storage object and fill it.
36        student = StudentRecord()
37        student.idNum = int( line )
38        student.firstName = self._inputFile.readline().rstrip()
39        student.lastName = self._inputFile.readline().rstrip()
40        student.classCode = int( self._inputFile.readline() )
41        student.gpa = float( self._inputFile.readline() )
42        return student
43
44  # Storage class used for an individual student record.
45  class StudentRecord :
46    def __init__( self ):
47      self.idNum = 0
48      self.firstName = None
49      self.lastName = None
50      self.classCode = 0
51      self.gpa = 0.0
```

The `fetchAll()` method, at lines 20–26, is a simple event-controlled loop that builds and returns a list of `StudentRecord` objects. This is done by repeatedly calling the `fetchRecord()` method. Thus, the actual extraction of a record from the text file is handled by the `fetchRecord()` method, as shown in lines 29–42. To extract the student records from a file in which the data is stored in a different format, we need only modify this method to accommodate the new format.

The Student File Reader ADT provides a framework that can be used to extract any type of records from a text file. The only change required would be in the `fetchRecord()` method to create the appropriate storage object and to extract the data from the file in the given format.

Exercises

1.1 Complete the partial implementation of the `Date` class by implementing the remaining methods: `monthName()`, `isLeapYear()`, `numDays()`, `advanceBy()`, and _isValidGregorian(). The _isValidGregorian() method should determine if the three components of the given Gregorian date are valid.

1.2 Add additional operations to the Date class:

(a) dayOfWeekName(): returns a string containing the name of the day.

(b) dayOfYear(): returns an integer indicating the day of the year. For example, the first day of February is day 32 of the year.

(c) isWeekday(): determines if the date is a weekday.

(d) isEquinox(): determines if the date is the spring or autumn equinox.

(e) isSolstice(): determines if the date is the summer or winter solstice.

(f) asGregorian(divchar = '/'): similar to the _str() method but uses the optional argument divchar as the dividing character between the three components of the Gregorian date.

1.3 Implement a function named printCalendar() that accepts a Date object and prints a calendar for the month of the given date. For example, if the Date object passed to the function contained the date 11/5/2007, the function should print

```
           November 2007
    Su  Mo  Tu  We  Th  Fr  Sa
                     1   2   3
     4   5   6   7   8   9  10
    11  12  13  14  15  16  17
    18  19  20  21  22  23  24
    25  26  27  28  29  30
```

1.4 Modify the Date() constructor to make each of the three arguments optional, with an initial value of zero. When no argument is supplied to the constructor, the object should be initialized to the current date. Hint: You will need to use Python's date() function from the time.py module.

Programming Projects

1.1 A click counter is a small hand-held device that contains a push button and a count display. To increment the counter, the button is pushed and the new count shows in the display. Clicker counters also contain a button that can be pressed to reset the counter to zero. Design and implement the Counter ADT that functions as a hand-held clicker.

1.2 A Grab Bag ADT is similar to the Bag ADT with one difference. A grab bag does not have a remove() operation, but in place of it has a grabItem() operation, which allows for the random removal of an item from the bag. Implement the Grab Bag ADT.

1.3 A Counting Bag ADT is just like the Bag ADT but includes the `numOf(item)` operation, which returns the number of occurrences of the given item in the bag. Implement the Counting Bag ADT and defend your selection of data structure.

1.4 The use of the Student File Reader ADT makes it easy to extract student records from a text file no matter the format used to store the data. Implement a new version of the ADT to extract the data from a text file in which each record is stored on a separate line and the individual fields are separated by commas. For example, the following illustrates the format of a sample file containing three student records:

```
10015, John, Smith, 2, 3.01
10334, Jane, Roberts, 4, 3.81
10208, Patrick, Green, 1, 3.95
```

1.5 In the chapter, we defined and implemented the Student File Reader ADT for extracting student records from an external source. We can define and use a similar ADT for output.

(a) Design a Student File Writer ADT that can be used to display, or store to an output device, student records contained in a **StudentRecord** object.

(b) Provide an implementation of your ADT to output the records by displaying them to the terminal in a neatly formatted fashion.

(c) Provide an implementation of your ADT to output the records to a text file using the same format described in the text.

(d) Design and implement a complete program that extracts student records from a text file, sorts them by either student id or student name, and displays them to the terminal using your ADT. The choice of sort keys should be extracted from the user.

1.6 We can use a Time ADT to represent the time of day, for any 24-hour period, as the number of seconds that have elapsed since midnight. Given the following list of operations, implement the Time ADT.

- `Time(hours, minutes, seconds)`: Creates a new `Time` instance and initializes it with the given time.
- `hour()`: Returns the hour part of the time.
- `minutes()`: Returns the minutes part of the time.
- `seconds()`: Returns the seconds part of the time.
- `numSeconds(otherTime)`: Returns the number of seconds as a positive integer between this time and the `otherTime`.
- `isAM()`: Determines if this time is ante meridiem or before midday (at or before 12 o'clock noon).

- isPM(): Determines if this time is post meridiem or after midday (after 12 o'clock noon).

- *comparable* (otherTime): Compares this time to the otherTime to determine their logical ordering. This comparison can be done using any of the Python logical operators.

- *toString* (): Returns a string representing the time in the 12-hour format hh:mm:ss. Invoked by calling Python's str() constructor.

1.7 Design and implement a TimeDate ADT that can be used to represent both a date and time as a single entity.

1.8 A line segment is a straight line bounded by two endpoints. The Line Segment ADT, whose operations are described below, represents a line segment defined by points in the two-dimensional Cartesian coordinate system. Use the Point class from Appendix D and implement the Line Segment ADT.

- LineSegment(ptA, ptB): Creates a new Line Segment instance defined by the two Point objects.

- endPointA(): Returns the first endpoint of the line.

- endPointB(): Returns the second endpoint of the line.

- *length* (): Returns the length of the line segment given as the Euclidean distance between the two endpoints.

- *toString* (): Returns a string representation of the line segment in the format (Ax, Ay)#(Bx, By).

- isVertical(): Is the line segment parallel to the y-axis?

- isHorizontal(): Is the line segment parallel to the x-axis?

- isParallel(otherLine): Is this line segment parallel to the otherLine?

- isPerpendicular(otherLine): Is this line segment perpendicular to the otherLine?

- intersects(otherLine): Does this line segment intersect the otherLine?

- bisects(otherLine): Does this line segment bisect the otherLine?

- slope(): Returns the slope of the line segment given as the rise over the run. If the line segment is vertical, None is returned.

- shift(xInc, yInc): Shifts the line segment by xInc amount along the x-axis and yInc amount along the y-axis.

- midpoint(): Returns the midpoint of the line segment as a Point object.

1.9 A polygon is a closed geometric shape consisting of three or more line segments that are connected end to end. The endpoints of the line segments are known as vertices, which can be defined by points in the two-dimensional Cartesian coordinate system.

(a) Define a Polygon ADT to represent a geometric polygon and provide a set of appropriate operations.

(b) Provide a Python implementation of your Polygon ADT.

1.10 Anyone who is involved in many activities typically uses a calendar to keep track of the various activities. Colleges commonly maintain several calendars such as an academic calendar, a school events calendar, and a sporting events calendar. We have defined an Activities Calendar ADT below that can keep track of one activity per day over a given range of dates. Select a data structure and implement the ADT.

- `ActivitiesCalendar( dateFrom, dateTo )`: Creates a new empty activities calendar initialized to the given range of dates. The date range can be specified for any non-overlapping period. The only requirements are that `dateFrom` must precede `dateTo` and `dateTo` cannot overlap the day and month of `dateFrom` for the next year.
- `length ()`: Returns the number of activities on the calendar.
- `getActivity( date )`: Returns the string that describes the activity for the given date if an activity exists for the given date; otherwise, `None` is returned.
- `addActivity( date, activity )`: Adds the given activity description to the calendar for the given date. The date must be within the valid date range for the calendar.
- `displayMonth( month )`: Displays to standard output all activities for the given month. The display includes the year and name of the month and the list of activities for the month. The display of each activity includes the day of the month on which the activity occurs and the description of the activity.

1.11 Python provides a numeric class for working with floating-point values. But not all real numbers can be represented precisely on a computer since they are stored as binary values. In applications where the precision of real numbers is important, we can use rational numbers or fractions to store exact values. A fraction, such as $\frac{7}{8}$, consists of two parts, both of which are integers. The top value, which can be any integer value, is known as the numerator. The bottom value, which must be greater than zero, is known as the denominator.

(a) Define a Fraction ADT to represent and store rational numbers. The ADT should include all of the common mathematical and logical operations. In addition, your ADT should provide for the conversion between floating-point values and fractions and the ability to produce a string version of the fraction.

(b) Provide a Python implementation of your Fraction ADT.

## CHAPTER 2

Arrays

The most basic structure for storing and accessing a collection of data is the array. Arrays can be used to solve a wide range of problems in computer science. Most programming languages provide this structured data type as a primitive and allow for the creation of arrays with multiple dimensions. In this chapter, we implement an array structure for a one-dimensional array and then use it to implement a two-dimensional array and the related matrix structure.

2.1 The Array Structure

At the hardware level, most computer architectures provide a mechanism for creating and using one-dimensional arrays. A *one-dimensional array*, as illustrated in Figure 2.1, is composed of multiple sequential elements stored in contiguous bytes of memory and allows for random access to the individual elements.

The entire contents of an array are identified by a single name. Individual elements within the array can be accessed directly by specifying an integer subscript or index value, which indicates an offset from the start of the array. This is similar to the mathematics notation (x_i), which allows for multiple variables of the same name. The difference is that programming languages typically use square brackets following the array name to specify the subscript, x[i].

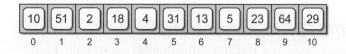

Figure 2.1: A sample 1-D array consisting of 11 elements.

2.1.1 Why Study Arrays?

You will notice the array structure looks very similar to Python's list structure. That's because the two structures are both sequences that are composed of multiple sequential elements that can be accessed by position. But there are two major differences between the array and the list. First, an array has a limited number of operations, which commonly include those for array creation, reading a value from a specific element, and writing a value to a specific element. The list, on the other hand, provides a large number of operations for working with the contents of the list. Second, the list can grow and shrink during execution as elements are added or removed while the size of an array cannot be changed after it has been created.

You may be wondering, if Python provides the list structure as its mutable sequence type, why are we bothering to discuss the array structure, much less plan to implement an abstract data type for working with arrays in Python? The short answer is that both structures have their uses. There are many problems that only require the use of a basic array in which the number of elements is known beforehand and the flexible set of operations available with the list is not needed.

The array is best suited for problems requiring a sequence in which the maximum number of elements are known up front, whereas the list is the better choice when the size of the sequence needs to change after it has been created. As you will learn later in the chapter, a list contains more storage space than is needed to store the items currently in the list. This extra space, the size of which can be up to twice the necessary capacity, allows for quick and easy expansion as new items are added to the list. But the extra space is wasteful when using a list to store a fixed number of elements. For example, suppose we need a sequence structure with 100,000 elements. We could create a list with the given number of elements using the replication operator:

```
values = [ None ] * 100000
```

But underneath, this results in the allocation of space for up to 200,000 elements, half of which will go to waste. In this case, an array would be a better choice.

The decision as to whether an array or list should be used is not limited to the size of the sequence structure. It also depends on how it will be used. The list provides a large set of operations for managing the items contained in the list. Some of these include inserting an item at a specific location, searching for an item, removing an item by value or location, easily extracting a subset of items, and sorting the items. The array structure, on the other hand, only provides a limited set of operations for accessing the individual elements comprising the array. Thus, if the problem at hand requires these types of operations, the list is the better choice.

2.1.2 The Array Abstract Data Type

The array structure is commonly found in most programming languages as a primitive type, but Python only provides the list structure for creating mutable sequences. We can define the Array ADT to represent a one-dimensional array for use in Python that works similarly to arrays found in other languages. It will be used throughout the text when an array structure is required.

Define	Array ADT

A *one-dimensional array* is a collection of contiguous elements in which individual elements are identified by a unique integer subscript starting with zero. Once an array is created, its size cannot be changed.

- Array(size): Creates a one-dimensional array consisting of size elements with each element initially set to None. size must be greater than zero.

- *length* (): Returns the length or number of elements in the array.

- *getitem* (index): Returns the value stored in the array at element position index. The index argument must be within the valid range. Accessed using the subscript operator.

- *setitem* (index, value): Modifies the contents of the array element at position index to contain value. The index must be within the valid range. Accessed using the subscript operator.

- clearing(value): Clears the array by setting every element to value.

- *iterator* (): Creates and returns an iterator that can be used to traverse the elements of the array.

Some computer scientists consider the array a physical structure and not an abstraction since arrays are implemented at the hardware level. But remember, there are only three basic operations available with the hardware-implemented array. As part of our Array ADT, we have provided for these operations but have also included an iterator and operations for obtaining the size of the array and for setting every element to a given value. In this case, we have provided a higher level of abstraction than that provided by the underlying hardware-implemented array.

The following simple program illustrates the creation and use of an array object based on the Array ADT. Comments are provided to highlight the use of the operator methods.

```
# Fill a 1-D array with random values, then print them, one per line.

from array import Array
import random

# The constructor is called to create the array.
valueList = Array( 100 )
```

```
# Fill the array with random floating-point values.
for i in range( len( valueList ) ) :
  valueList[ i ] = random.random()

# Print the values, one per line.
for value in valueList :
  print( value )
```

As a second example, suppose you need to read the contents of a text file and count the number of letters occurring in the file with the results printed to the terminal. We know that characters are represented by the ASCII code, which consists of integer values. The letters of the alphabet, both upper- and lowercase, are part of what's known as the printable range of the ASCII code. This includes the ASCII values in the range $[32 \ldots 126]$ along with some of the codes with smaller values. The latter are known control characters and can include the tab, newline, and form-feed codes. Since all of the letters will have ASCII values less than 127, we can create an array of this size and let each element represent a counter for the corresponding ASCII value. After processing the file, we can traverse over the elements used as counters for the letters of the alphabet and ignore the others. The following program provides a solution to this problem using the Array ADT:

```
#Count the number of occurrences of each letter in a text file.

from array import Array

# Create an array for the counters and initialize each element to 0.
theCounters = Array( 127 )
theCounters.clear( 0 )

# Open the text file for reading and extract each line from the file
# and iterate over each character in the line.
theFile = open( 'atextfile.txt', 'r' )
for line in theFile :
  for letter in line :
    code = ord( letter )
    theCounters[code] += 1
# Close the file
theFile.close()

# Print the results. The uppercase letters have ASCII values in the
# range 65..90 and the lowercase letters are in the range 97..122.
for i in range( 26 ) :
  print( "%c - %4d          %c - %4d" % \
    (chr(65+i), theCounters[65+i], chr(97+i), theCounters[97+i]) )
```

2.1.3 Implementing the Array

Python is a scripting language built using the C language, a high-level language that requires a program's source code be compiled into executable code before it can be used. The C language is a very powerful programming language that provides syntax for working with the complete functionality available by the underlying hardware. That syntax, however, can be somewhat cryptic compared to Python, especially for a Python programmer who may not be familiar with C.

The ctypes **Module**

Many of the data types and classes available in Python are actually implemented using appropriate types from the C language. While Python does not provide the array structure as part of the language itself, it now includes the **ctypes** module as part of the Python Standard Library. This module provides access to the diverse set of data types available in the C language and the complete functionality provided by a wide range of C libraries.

The **ctypes** module provides the capability to create hardware-supported arrays just like the ones used to implement Python's string, list, tuple, and dictionary collection types. But the **ctypes** module is not meant for everyday use in Python programs as it was designed for use by module developers to aide in creating more portable Python modules by bridging the gap between Python and the C language. Much of the functionality provided by the **ctypes** module requires some knowledge of the C language. Thus, the technique provided by the module for creating an array should not typically be used directly within a Python program. But we can use it within our **Array** class to provide the functionality defined by the Array ADT since the details will be hidden within the class.

Creating a Hardware Array

The **ctypes** module provides a technique for creating arrays that can store references to Python objects. The following code segment

```
import ctypes

ArrayType = ctypes.py_object * 5
slots = ArrayType()
```

creates an array named **slots** that contains five elements

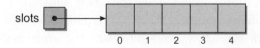

each of which can store a reference to an object. After the array has been created, the elements can be accessed using the same integer subscript notation as used with Python's own sequence types. For the **slots** array, the legal range is $[0 \ldots 4]$.

The elements of the array have to be initialized before they can be used. If we attempt to read the contents of an element in the **slots** array before it has been initialized

```
print( slots[0] )
```

an exception would be raised in the same way as if we tried to print the value of a variable `sum`, that had not previously been assigned a value. Thus, the array should be initialized immediately after it has been created by assigning a value to each element using the subscript notation. Any value can be used, but a logical choice is to assign `None` to each element:

```
for i in range( 5 ) :
    slots[i] = None
```

The elements of the array can now be treated like any other variable in Python that contains a null reference:

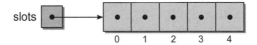

You may have noticed that we used the literal 5 with the `range()` function to indicate the number of elements to be initialized. This was necessary because a hardware-supported array does not keep track of the array size; it's up to the programmer to remember or maintain this value. Likewise, the programmer must also ensure they do not access an element outside the legal range.

References to any type of Python object can be stored in any element of the array. For example, the following code segment stores three integers in various elements of the array:

```
slots[1] = 12
slots[3] = 54
slots[4] = 37
```

the result of which is illustrated here:

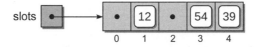

The operations provided by the array only allow for setting a given element to a given reference or accessing a reference stored in a given element. To remove an item from the array, we simply set the corresponding element to `None`. For example, suppose we want to remove value 54 from the array

```
slots[3] = None
```

which results in the following change to the `slots` array:

The size of the array can never change, so removing an item from an array has no effect on the size of the array or on the items stored in other elements. The array does not provide any of the list type operations such as appending or popping items, searching for a specific item, or sorting the items. To use such an operation with an array, you would have to provide the necessary code yourself.

The Class Definition

The implementation of the Array ADT using a hardware-supported array created with the use of the `ctypes` module is provided in Listing 2.1.

Listing 2.1   The `array.py` module with the `Array` class.

```
1  # Implements the Array ADT using array capabilities of the ctypes module.
2  import ctypes
3
4  class Array :
5    # Creates an array with size elements.
6    def __init__( self, size ):
7      assert size > 0, "Array size must be > 0"
8      self._size = size
9       # Create the array structure using the ctypes module.
10     PyArrayType = ctypes.py_object * size
11     self._elements = PyArrayType()
12      # Initialize each element.
13     self.clear( None )
14
15    # Returns the size of the array.
16    def __len__( self ):
17      return self._size
18
19    # Gets the contents of the index element.
20    def __getitem__( self, index ):
21      assert index >= 0 and index < len(self), "Array subscript out of range"
22      return self._elements[ index ]
23
24    # Puts the value in the array element at index position.
25    def __setitem__( self, index, value ):
26      assert index >= 0 and index < len(self), "Array subscript out of range"
27      self._elements[ index ] = value
28
29    # Clears the array by setting each element to the given value.
30    def clear( self, value ):
31      for i in range( len(self) ) :
32        self._elements[i] = value
33
34    # Returns the array's iterator for traversing the elements.
35    def __iter__( self ):
36      return _ArrayIterator( self._elements )
37
38  # An iterator for the Array ADT.
39  class _ArrayIterator :
```

(Listing Continued)

Listing 2.1	Continued ...

```
40    def __init__( self, theArray ):
41      self._arrayRef = theArray
42      self._curNdx = 0
43
44    def __iter__( self ):
45      return self
46
47    def __next__( self ):
48      if self._curNdx < len( self._arrayRef ) :
49        entry = self._arrayRef[ self._curNdx ]
50        self._curNdx += 1
51        return entry
52      else :
53        raise StopIteration
```

The constructor, as shown in lines 6–13, handles the creation and initialization of the array using the technique described earlier. It also defines two data fields needed for the implementation of the Array ADT: one to store a reference to the array structure and another to store the number of elements allocated for the array. The latter is needed since hardware-supported arrays do not keep track of this value. The initialization of the array is done by calling the clear() method.

The clear() method is used to set each element of the array to a given value, which it does by iterating over the elements using an index variable. The __len__ method, which returns the number of elements in the array, simply returns the value of _size that was saved in the constructor. The __iter__ method creates and returns an instance of the _ArrayIterator private iterator class, which is provided in lines 39–53 of Listing 2.1.

The definition of the Array ADT calls for the implementation of the subscript operator, which allows for the use of array objects in a manner similar to other Python collection types. In Python, as in most languages, the subscript notation can be used to read the contents of an array element or to modify an element. Thus, there are two different methods that must be defined, as shown in lines 20–27. First, the __getitem__ operator method takes the array index as an argument and returns the value of the corresponding element. The precondition must first be verified to ensure the subscript is within the valid range.

When the subscript notation is used in a program, y = x[i], Python will call the __getitem__ method, passing the value of i to the index parameter. Since Python expects the __getitem__ method to return a value, it is your responsibility to make sure this occurs.

The __setitem__ operator method is used to set or change the contents of a specific element of the array. It takes two arguments: the array index of the element being modified and the new value that will be stored in that element. Before the element is modified, the precondition must be tested to verify the subscript is within the valid range. Python automatically calls the __setitem__ method when the subscript notation is used to assign a value to a specific element, x[i] = y. The index, i, specified in the subscript is passed as the first argument and the value to be assigned is passed as the second argument, __setitem__(i,y).

2.2 The Python List

Python, as indicated earlier, is built using the C language with many of the data types and classes available in Python actually implemented using appropriate types available in C. Python's list structure is a mutable sequence container that can change size as items are added or removed. It is an abstract data type that is implemented using an array structure to store the items contained in the list.

In this section, we examine the implementation of Python's list, which can be very beneficial not only for learning more about abstract data types and their implementations but also to illustrate the major differences between an array and Python's list structure. We explore some of the more common list operations and describe how they are implemented using an array structure.

2.2.1 Creating a Python List

Suppose we create a list containing several values:

```
pyList = [ 4, 12, 2, 34, 17 ]
```

which results in the `list()` constructor being called to create a list object and fill it with the given values. When the `list()` constructor is called, an array structure is created to store the items contained in the list. The array is initially created bigger than needed, leaving capacity for future expansion. The values stored in the list comprise a **subarray** in which only a contiguous subset of the array elements are actually used.

Figure 2.2 illustrates the abstract and physical views of our sample list. In the physical view, the elements of the array structure used to store the actual contents of the list are enclosed inside the dashed gray box. The elements with null references shown outside the dashed gray box are the remaining elements of the underlying array structure that are still available for use. This notation will be used throughout the section to illustrate the contents of the list and the underlying array used to implement it.

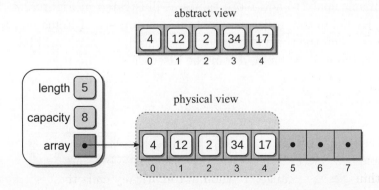

Figure 2.2: The abstract and physical views of a list implemented using an array.

The length of the list, obtained using `len()`, is the number of items currently in the subarray and not the size of the underlying array. The size or capacity of the array used to implement the list must be maintained in order to know when the array is full. Python does not provide a method to access the capacity value since that information is not part of the list definition.

2.2.2 Appending Items

What happens when a new item is appended to the end of a list as in the following statement?

```
pyList.append( 50 )
```

If there is room in the array, the item is stored in the next available slot of the array and the length field is incremented by one. The result of appending 50 to `pyList` is illustrated in Figure 2.3.

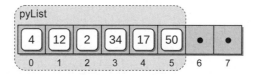

Figure 2.3: Result of appending value 50 to the list.

What happens when the array becomes full and there are no free elements in which to add a new list item? For example, consider the following list operations:

```
pyList.append( 18 )
pyList.append( 64 )
pyList.append( 6 )
```

After the second statement is executed, the array becomes full and there is no available space to add more values as illustrated in Figure 2.4.

By definition, a list can contain any number of items and never becomes full. Thus, when the third statement is executed, the array will have to be expanded to make room for value 6. From the discussion in the previous section, we know an array cannot change size once it has been created. To allow for the expansion of

Figure 2.4: A full array resulting after appending three values.

the list, the following steps have to be performed: (1) a new array is created with additional capacity, (2) the items from the original array are copied to the new array, (3) the new larger array is set as the data structure for the list, and (4) the original smaller array is destroyed. After the array has been expanded, the value can be appended to the end of the list. In Python, the amount by which the size of the array is increased is proportional to the current array size. For illustration purposes, we assume an expansion creates a new array that is double the size of the original. The result of expanding the array and appending value 6 to the list is shown in Figure 2.5.

(1) A new array, double the size of the original, is created.

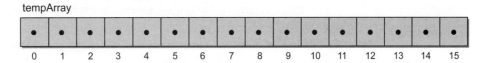

(2) The values from the original array are copied to the new larger array.

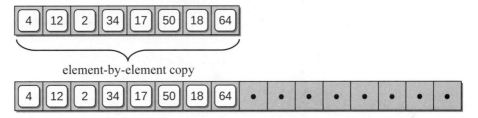

(3) The new array replaces the original in the list.

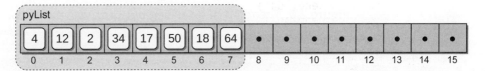

(4) Value 6 is appended to the end of the list.

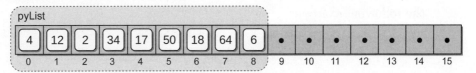

Figure 2.5: The steps required to expand the array to provide space for value 6.

2.2.3   Extending A List

A list can be appended to a second list using the **extend()** method as shown in the following example:

```
pyListA = [ 34, 12 ]
pyListB = [ 4, 6, 31, 9 ]
pyListA.extend( pyListB )
```

If the list being extended has the capacity to store all of the elements from the second list, the elements are simply copied, element by element. If there is not enough capacity for all of the elements, the underlying array has to be expanded as was done with the **append()** method. Since Python knows how big the array needs to be in order to store all of the elements from both lists, it only requires a single expansion of the destination list, **pyListA**. The new array will be created larger than needed to allow more items to be added to the list without first requiring an immediate expansion of the array. After the new array is created, elements from the destination list are copied to the new array followed by the elements from the source list, **pyListB**, as illustrated in Figure 2.6.

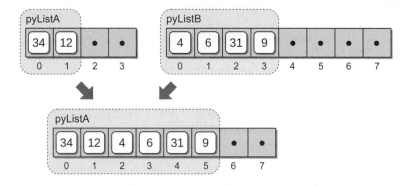

Figure 2.6: The result of extending `pyListA` with `pyListB`.

2.2.4   Inserting Items

An item can be inserted anywhere within the list using the **insert()** method. In the following example

```
pyList.insert( 3, 79 )
```

we insert the value 79 at index position 3. Since there is already an item at that position, we must make room for the new item by shifting all of the items down one position starting with the item at index position 3. After shifting the items, the value 79 is then inserted at position 3 as illustrated in Figure 2.7. If there are no free slots for the new item, the list will be expanded in the same fashion as described earlier.

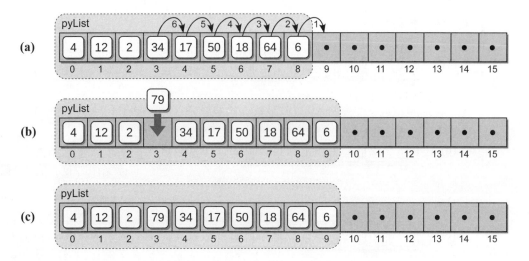

Figure 2.7: Inserting an item into a list: (a) the array elements are shifted to the right one at a time, traversing from right to left; (b) the new value is then inserted into the array at the given position; (c) the result after inserting the item.

Removing Items

An item can be removed from any position within the list using the `pop()` method. Consider the following code segment, which removes both the first and last items from the sample list:

```
pyList.pop( 0 )    # remove the first item
pyList.pop()       # remove the last item
```

The first statement removes the first item from the list. After the item is removed, typically by setting the reference variable to `None`, the items following it within the array are shifted down, from left to right, to close the gap. Finally, the length of the list is decremented to reflect the smaller size. Figure 2.8 on the next page illustrates the process of removing the first item from the sample list. The second `pop()` operation in the example code removes the last item from the list. Since there are no items following the last one, the only operations required are to remove the item and decrement the size of the list.

After removing an item from the list, the size of the array may be reduced using a technique similar to that for expansion. This reduction occurs when the number of available slots in the internal array falls below a certain threshold. For example, when more than half of the array elements are empty, the size of the array may be cut in half.

2.2.5 List Slice

Slicing is an operation that creates a new list consisting of a contiguous subset of elements from the original list. The original list is not modified by this operation. Instead, references to the corresponding elements are copied and stored in the

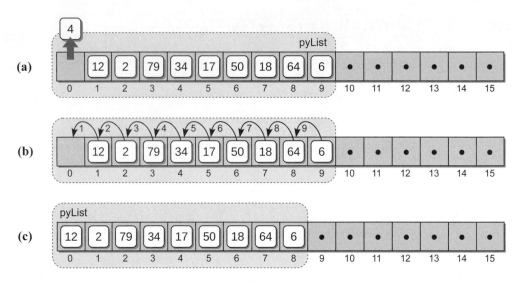

Figure 2.8: Removing an item from a list: (a) a copy of the item is saved; (b) the array elements are shifted to the left one at a time, traversing left to right; and (c) the size of the list is decremented by one.

new list. In Python, slicing is performed on a list using the colon operator and specifying the beginning element index and the number of elements included in the subset. Consider the following example code segment, which creates a slice from our sample list:

```
aSlice = theVector[2:3]
```

To slice a list, a new list is created with a capacity large enough to store the entire subset of elements plus additional space for future insertions. The elements within the specified range are then copied, element by element, to the new list. The result of creating the sample slice is illustrated in Figure 2.9.

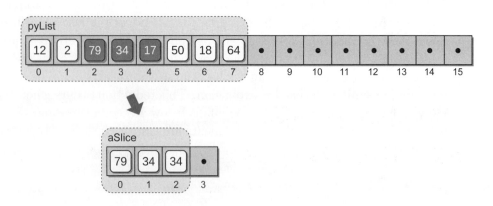

Figure 2.9: The result of creating a list slice.

2.3 Two-Dimensional Arrays

Arrays are not limited to a single dimension. Some problems require the use of a ***two-dimensional array***, which organizes data into rows and columns similar to a table or grid. The individual elements are accessed by specifying two indices, one for the row and one for the column, [i,j]. Figure 2.10 shows an abstract view of both a one- and a two-dimensional array.

While computer architectures provide a mechanism at the hardware level for creating and using one-dimensional arrays, they do not typically support arrays of higher dimensions. Instead, programming languages typically provide their own mechanism for creating and managing arrays that consist of multiple dimensions. In this section, we explore two-dimensional arrays while arrays of higher dimensions are discussed later in the chapter.

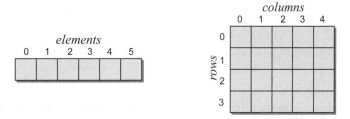

Figure 2.10: Sample arrays: (left) a 1-D array viewed as a sequential list and (right) a 2-D array viewed as a rectangular table or grid.

2.3.1 The Array2D Abstract Data Type

As we saw earlier, Python does not directly support built-in arrays of any dimension. But, in the previous section, we were able to use the `ctypes` module to create a one-dimensional hardware-supported array that we used to implement the Array ADT. Two-dimensional arrays are also very common in computer programming, where they are used to solve problems that require data to be organized into rows and columns. Since 2-D arrays are not provided by Python, we define the Array2D abstract data type for creating 2-D arrays. It consists of a limited set of operations similar to those provided by the one-dimensional Array ADT.

Define	Array2D ADT

A ***two-dimensional array*** consists of a collection of elements organized into rows and columns. Individual elements are referenced by specifying the specific row and column indices (r, c), both of which start at 0.

- **Array2D(nrows, ncols):** Creates a two-dimensional array organized into rows and columns. The **nrows** and **ncols** arguments indicate the size of the table. The individual elements of the table are initialized to **None**.

- **numRows():** Returns the number of rows in the 2-D array.

- numCols(): Returns the number of columns in the 2-D array.

- clear(value): Clears the array by setting each element to the given value.

- getitem(i_1, i_2): Returns the value stored in the 2-D array element at the position indicated by the 2-tuple (i_1, i_2), both of which must be within the valid range. Accessed using the subscript operator: y = x[1,2].

- setitem(i_1, i_2, value): Modifies the contents of the 2-D array element indicated by the 2-tuple (i_1, i_2) with the new value. Both indices must be within the valid range. Accessed using the subscript operator: x[0,3] = y.

To illustrate the use of a 2-D array, suppose we have a collection of exam grades stored in a text file for a group of students that we need to process. For example, we may want to compute the average exam grade for each student or the average grade for each exam, or both. A sample text file is illustrated on the left in Figure 2.11. The file contains the grades for multiple students, each of whom have grades for multiple exams. The first line indicates the number of students for whom we have grades, and the second line indicates the number of exams for which each student has a grade. The remaining lines contain the actual exam grades. Each line contains the grade for an individual student, with the grades listed in exam order.

Since we have multiple grades for multiple students, we can store the grades in a 2-D array in which each row contains the grades for an individual student and each column contains the grades for a given exam. A 2-D array used to store the exam grades from the sample file is illustrated on the right in Figure 2.11.

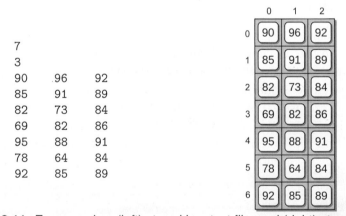

```
7
3
90    .96    92
85    91    89
82    73    84
69    82    86
95    88    91
78    64    84
92    85    89
```

Figure 2.11: Exam grades: (left) stored in a text file; and (right) stored in a 2-D array.

The following code segment shows the implementation needed to extract the exam grades from the text file and store them into a 2-D array. Notice that we create the array after extracting the first two values from the file. These values indicate the number of students and the number of exams that correspond to the number of rows and columns needed in the array.

```
from array import Array2D

# Open the text file for reading.
gradeFile = open( filename, "r" )

# Extract the first two values which indicate the size of the array.
numExams = int( gradeFile.readline() )
numStudents = int( gradeFile.readline() )

# Create the 2-D array to store the grades.
examGrades = Array2D( numStudents, numExams )

# Extract the grades from the remaining lines.
i = 0
for student in gradeFile :
  grades = student.split()
  for j in range( numExams ):
    examGrades[i,j] = int( grades[j] )
  i += 1
# Close the text file.
gradeFile.close()
```

With the grades extracted from the file and stored in the 2-D array, we can now process the grades as needed. Suppose we want to compute and display each student's exam grade, which we can do with the following code:

```
# Compute each student's average exam grade.
for i in range( numStudents ) :
  # Tally the exam grades for the ith student.
  total = 0
  for j in range( numExams ) :
    total += examGrades[i,j]

  # Compute average for the ith student.
  examAvg = total / numExams
  print( "%2d:  %6.2f" % (i+1, examAvg) )
```

2.3.2 Implementing the 2-D Array

We now turn our attention to the implementation of the 2-D array. There are several approaches that we can use to store and organize the data for a 2-D array. Two of the more common approaches include the use of a single 1-D array to physically store the elements of the 2-D array by arranging them in order based on either row or column, whereas the other uses an array of arrays. We are going to use the latter approach to implement the Array2D abstract data type and delay discussion of the former approach until later in the chapter.

When using an array of arrays to store the elements of a 2-D array, we store each row of the 2-D array within its own 1-D array. Then, another 1-D array is used to store references to each of the arrays used to store the row elements. Figure 2.12 shows the abstract view of a 2-D array and the physical storage of that 2-D array using an array of arrays.

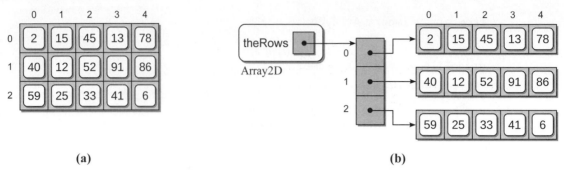

Figure 2.12: A sample 2-D array: (a) the abstract view organized into rows and columns and (b) the physical storage of the 2-D array using an array of arrays.

Some languages that use the array of arrays approach for implementing a 2-D array provide access to the individual arrays used to store the row elements. Having access to the given 1-D array, these languages use the subscript notation x[r][c] for referencing an individual element. To be consistent in our approach of hiding the implementation details, we do not provide access to any of the 1-D arrays used to store the elements of the 2-D array. Thus, our implementation requires the use of the subscript notation x[r,c].

The implementation of the Array2D abstract data type using an array of arrays is provided in Listing 2.2. The constructor creates a data field named _theRows to which an **Array** object is assigned. This is the main array used to store the references to the other arrays that are created for each row in the 2-D array.

Listing 2.2	The array.py module with the Array2D class.

```python
1   # Implementation of the Array2D ADT using an array of arrays.
2
3   class Array2D :
4     # Creates a 2-D array of size numRows x numCols.
5     def __init__( self, numRows, numCols ):
6       # Create a 1-D array to store an array reference for each row.
7       self._theRows = Array( numRows )
8
9       # Create the 1-D arrays for each row of the 2-D array.
10      for i in range( numRows ) :
11        self._theRows[i] = Array( numCols )
12
13    # Returns the number of rows in the 2-D array.
14    def numRows( self ):
15      return len( self._theRows )
16
17    # Returns the number of columns in the 2-D array.
18    def numCols( self ):
19      return len( self._theRows[0] )
20
21    # Clears the array by setting every element to the given value.
22    def clear( self, value ):
23      for row in range( self.numRows() ):
24        row.clear( value )
```

```
25
26      # Gets the contents of the element at position [i, j]
27    def __getitem__( self, ndxTuple ):
28      assert len(ndxTuple) == 2, "Invalid number of array subscripts."
29      row = ndxTuple[0]
30      col = ndxTuple[1]
31      assert row >= 0 and row < self.numRows() \
32          and col >= 0 and col < self.numCols(), \
33              "Array subscript out of range."
34      the1dArray = self._theRows[row]
35      return the1dArray[col]
36
37      # Sets the contents of the element at position [i,j] to value.
38    def __setitem__( self, ndxTuple, value ):
39      assert len(ndxTuple) == 2, "Invalid number of array subscripts."
40      row = ndxTuple[0]
41      col = ndxTuple[1]
42      assert row >= 0 and row < self.numRows() \
43          and col >= 0 and col < self.numCols(), \
44              "Array subscript out of range."
45      the1dArray = self._theRows[row]
46      the1dArray[col] = value
```

Basic Operations

Note that the size of the array that is passed as arguments to the constructor is not saved in data fields. The numRows() method can obtain the number of rows by checking the length of the main array, which contains an element for each row in the 2-D array. To determine the number of columns in the 2-D array, the numCols() method can simply check the length of any of the 1-D arrays used to store the individual rows.

The clear() method can set every element to the given value by calling the clear() method on each of the 1-D arrays used to store the individual rows. This is easily done by iterating over the array stored in _theRows.

Element Access

Access to individual elements within an 2-D array requires a 2-tuple or two-component subscript, one for each dimension. In mathematics, the 2-tuple subscript is generally notated as $x_{r,c}$. In modern programming languages, a 2-tuple subscript is given either as x[r][c] or x[r,c]. In Python, we can use the latter notation in conjunction with the __getitem__ and __setitem__ subscript operators. This will allow for a more natural use of the two-dimensional array instead of having to invoke a named method.

The Python subscript operator method __getitem__, which is shown in lines 27–35, takes a single index argument as specified in the method definition. This does not restrict the subscript to a single index value, however. When a multi-component subscript is specified (i.e., y = x[i,j]), Python automatically stores the components in a tuple in the order listed within the brackets and passes the tuple to the `ndxTuple` argument of the `__getitem__` method.

The contents of the `ndxTuple` are used to extract the contents of the given element. After verifying both subscripts are within the valid range, we extract, from the data field `_theRows`, the reference to the array used to store the given row. With this reference stored in the local variable `the1dArray`, we can then apply the subscript operator to the 1-D array using the column value.

You may notice a second `assert` statement within the `__getitem__` method at line 28. This is needed because Python does not examine the number of components specified in the subscript before passing the tuple to the subscript operator method. For example, there is nothing to prevent us from incorrectly supplying three components such as `box[i,j,k]` instead of two. In fact, Python would have no way of knowing that we only need two components for the 2-D array subscript. Thus, we must first check to make sure the subscript tuple passed to the method contains only two elements.

When making the assertion about the size of the `ndxTuple`, we assume a tuple is passed to the subscript operator and use the `len()` function to verify its length. When a single-component subscript `x[0]` is supplied to a subscript operator method, as is done with the `Array` class, the argument is a single integer value. The `len()` method can only be used with the collection types and not individual values. It does generate its own error, however, when used improperly. Thus, Python's `len()` function is used to ensure two components are supplied for all `Array2D` objects.

The `__setitem__` operator method can be implemented in a similar fashion to `__getitem__`. The major differences are that this method requires a second argument to receive the value to which an element is set and it modifies the indicated element with the new value instead of returning a value.

2.4 The Matrix Abstract Data Type

In mathematics, a matrix is an $m \times n$ rectangular grid or table of numerical values divided into m rows and n columns. Matrices, which are an important tool in areas such as linear algebra and computer graphics, are used in a number of applications, including representing and solving systems of linear equations. The Matrix ADT is defined next.

Define | **Matrix ADT**

A *matrix* is a collection of scalar values arranged in rows and columns as a rectangular grid of a fixed size. The elements of the matrix can be accessed by specifying a given row and column index with indices starting at 0.

- `Matrix( rows, ncols )`: Creates a new matrix containing `nrows` and `ncols` with each element initialized to 0.

- `numRows()`: Returns the number of rows in the matrix.

- numCols(): Returns the number of columns in the matrix.

- *getitem*(row, col): Returns the value stored in the given matrix element. Both row and col must be within the valid range.

- *setitem*(row, col, scalar): Sets the matrix element at the given row and col to scalar. The element indices must be within the valid range.

- scaleBy(scalar): Multiplies each element of the matrix by the given scalar value. The matrix is modified by this operation.

- transpose(): Returns a new matrix that is the transpose of this matrix.

- *add*(rhsMatrix): Creates and returns a new matrix that is the result of adding this matrix to the given rhsMatrix. The size of the two matrices must be the same.

- *subtract*(rhsMatrix): The same as the add() operation but subtracts the two matrices.

- *multiply*(rhsMatrix): Creates and returns a new matrix that is the result of multiplying this matrix to the given rhsMatrix. The two matrices must be of appropriate sizes as defined for matrix multiplication.

2.4.1 Matrix Operations

A number of operations can be performed on matrices. We first describe some of the more common ones and provide examples as a review of matrix arithmetic.

Addition and Subtraction.   Two $m \times n$ matrices can be added or subtracted to create a third $m \times n$ matrix. When adding two $m \times n$ matrices, corresponding elements are summed as illustrated here. Subtraction is performed in a similar fashion but the corresponding elements are subtracted instead of summed.

$$\begin{bmatrix} 0 & 1 \\ 2 & 3 \\ 4 & 5 \end{bmatrix} + \begin{bmatrix} 6 & 7 \\ 8 & 9 \\ 1 & 0 \end{bmatrix} = \begin{bmatrix} 0+6 & 1+7 \\ 2+8 & 3+9 \\ 4+1 & 5+0 \end{bmatrix} = \begin{bmatrix} 6 & 8 \\ 10 & 12 \\ 5 & 5 \end{bmatrix}$$

Scaling.   A matrix can be uniformly scaled, which modifies each element of the matrix by the same scale factor. A scale factor of less than 1 has the effect of reducing the value of each element whereas a scale factor greater than 1 increases the value of each element. Scaling a matrix by a scale factor of 3 is illustrated here:

$$3 \begin{bmatrix} 6 & 7 \\ 8 & 9 \\ 1 & 0 \end{bmatrix} = \begin{bmatrix} 3*6 & 3*7 \\ 3*8 & 3*9 \\ 3*1 & 3*0 \end{bmatrix} = \begin{bmatrix} 18 & 21 \\ 24 & 27 \\ 3 & 0 \end{bmatrix}$$

Multiplication.   Matrix multiplication is only defined for matrices where the number of columns in the matrix on the lefthand side is equal to the number of rows in the matrix on the righthand side. The result is a new matrix that contains the same number of rows as the matrix on the lefthand side and the same number of columns as the matrix on the righthand side. In other words, given a matrix of size $m \times n$ multiplied by a matrix of size $n \times p$, the resulting matrix is of size $m \times p$. In multiplying two matrices, each element of the new matrix is the result of summing the product of a row in the lefthand side matrix by a column in the righthand side matrix. In the example matrix multiplication illustrated here, the row and column used to compute entry $(0,0)$ of the new matrix is shaded in gray.

$$
\begin{bmatrix} 0 & 1 \\ 2 & 3 \\ 4 & 5 \end{bmatrix} * \begin{bmatrix} 6 & 7 & 8 \\ 9 & 1 & 0 \end{bmatrix}
$$

$$
= \begin{bmatrix} (0*6+1*9) & (0*7+1*1) & (0*8+1*0) \\ (2*6+3*9) & (2*7+3*1) & (2*8+3*0) \\ (4*6+5*9) & (4*7+5*1) & (4*8+5*0) \end{bmatrix}
$$

$$
= \begin{bmatrix} 9 & 1 & 0 \\ 39 & 17 & 16 \\ 69 & 33 & 32 \end{bmatrix}
$$

Viewing matrix multiplication based on the element subscripts can help you to better understand the operation. Consider the two matrices from above and assume they are labeled A and B, respectively.

$$
A = \begin{bmatrix} A_{0,0} & A_{0,1} \\ A_{1,0} & A_{1,1} \\ A_{2,0} & A_{2,1} \end{bmatrix} \qquad B = \begin{bmatrix} B_{0,0} & B_{0,1} & B_{0,2} \\ B_{1,0} & B_{1,1} & B_{1,2} \end{bmatrix}
$$

The computation of the individual elements resulting from multiplying A and B (C = A * B) is performed as follows:

$$
\begin{aligned}
C_{0,0} &= A_{0,0} * B_{0,0} + A_{0,1} * B_{1,0} \\
C_{0,1} &= A_{0,0} * B_{0,1} + A_{0,1} * B_{1,1} \\
C_{0,2} &= A_{0,0} * B_{0,2} + A_{0,1} * B_{1,2} \\
C_{1,0} &= A_{1,0} * B_{0,0} + A_{1,1} * B_{1,0} \\
C_{1,1} &= A_{1,0} * B_{0,1} + A_{1,1} * B_{1,1} \\
C_{1,2} &= A_{1,0} * B_{0,2} + A_{1,1} * B_{1,2} \\
C_{2,0} &= A_{2,0} * B_{0,0} + A_{2,1} * B_{1,0} \\
C_{2,1} &= A_{2,0} * B_{0,1} + A_{2,1} * B_{1,1} \\
C_{2,2} &= A_{2,0} * B_{0,2} + A_{2,1} * B_{1,2}
\end{aligned}
$$

resulting in

$$C = \begin{bmatrix} \boxed{(A_{0,0} * B_{0,0} + A_{0,1} * B_{1,0})} & (A_{0,0} * B_{0,1} + A_{0,1} * B_{1,1}) & (A_{0,0} * B_{0,2} + A_{0,1} * B_{1,2}) \\ (A_{1,0} * B_{0,0} + A_{1,1} * B_{1,0}) & (A_{1,0} * B_{0,1} + A_{1,1} * B_{1,1}) & (A_{1,0} * B_{0,2} + A_{1,1} * B_{1,2}) \\ (A_{2,0} * B_{0,0} + A_{2,1} * B_{1,0}) & (A_{2,0} * B_{0,1} + A_{2,1} * B_{1,1}) & (A_{2,0} * B_{0,2} + A_{2,1} * B_{1,2}) \end{bmatrix}$$

Transpose. Another useful operation that can be applied to a matrix is the matrix transpose. Given a $m \times n$ matrix, a transpose swaps the rows and columns to create a new matrix of size $n \times m$ as illustrated here:

$$\begin{bmatrix} 0 & 1 \\ 2 & 3 \\ 4 & 5 \end{bmatrix}^T = \begin{bmatrix} 0 & 2 & 4 \\ 1 & 3 & 5 \end{bmatrix}$$

2.4.2 Implementing the Matrix

There are a number of ways to organize the data for the Matrix ADT, but the most obvious is with the use of a two-dimensional array or rectangular grid. Having defined and implemented the Array2D ADT, we can utilize it to implement the Matrix ADT as shown in Listing 2.3.

Listing 2.3   The `matrix.py` module.

```
1   # Implementation of the Matrix ADT using a 2-D array.
2   from array import Array2D
3
4   class Matrix :
5     # Creates a matrix of size numRows x numCols initialized to 0.
6     def __init__( self, numRows, numCols ):
7       self._theGrid = Array2D( numRows, numCols )
8       self._theGrid.clear( 0 )
9
10    # Returns the number of rows in the matrix.
11    def numRows( self ):
12      return self._theGrid.numRows()
13
14    # Returns the number of columns in the matrix.
15    def numCols( self ):
16      return self._theGrid.numCols()
17
18    # Returns the value of element (i, j): x[i,j]
19    def __getitem__( self, ndxTuple ):
20      return self._theGrid[ ndxTuple[0], ndxTuple[1] )
21
22    # Sets the value of element (i,j) to the value s: x[i,j] = s
23    def __setitem__( self, ndxTuple, scalar ):
24      self._theGrid[ ndxTuple[0], ndxTuple[1] ] = scalar
```

(Listing Continued)

Listing 2.3   Continued ...

```
25
26      # Scales the matrix by the given scalar.
27    def scaleBy( self, scalar ):
28      for r in range( self.numRows() ) :
29        for c in range( self.numCols() ) :
30          self[ r, c ] *= scalar
31
32      # Creates and returns a new matrix that is the transpose of this matrix.
33    def tranpose( self ):
34      ......
35
36      # Creates and returns a new matrix that results from matrix addition.
37    def __add__( self, rhsMatrix ):
38      assert rhsMatrix.numRows() == self.numRows() and \
39             rhsMatrix.numCols() == self.numCols(), \
40        "Matrix sizes not compatible for the add operation."
41      # Create the new matrix.
42      newMatrix = Matrix( self.numRows(), self.numCols() )
43      # Add the corresponding elements in the two matrices.
44      for r in range( self.numRows() ) :
45        for c in range( self.numCols() ) :
46          newMatrix[ r, c ] = self[ r, c ] + rhsMatrix[ r, c ]
47      return newMatrix
48
49      # Creates and returns a new matrix that results from matrix subtraction.
50    def __sub__( self, rhsMatrix ):
51      ......
52
53      # Creates and returns a new matrix resulting from matrix multiplication.
54    def __mul__( self, rhsMatrix ):
55      ......
```

A `Matrix` object only requires one data field for storing the 2-D array. After creating the array, its elements must be set to zero as specified by the definition of the Matrix ADT. The constructor is provided in lines 6–8.

The `numRows()` and `numCols()` methods are straightforward. They need only return the length of the corresponding dimension of the 2-D array. The element access methods are also rather simple as they need only call the corresponding method from the `Array2D` class. Note that we do not check for valid indices in these methods even though it is a precondition as defined by the Matrix ADT. The validation of the precondition is omitted here since we know the corresponding methods of the `Array2D` class have the same preconditions and they are verified by that class. If this were not the case, we would have to validate the indices and raise an exception directly within the methods of the `Matrix` class.

The scaling matrix operation, shown in lines 27–30, involves multiplying each element in the matrix by the given scalar value. The Matrix ADT calls for this operation to modify the matrix on which it is applied instead of creating a new matrix resulting from the multiplication. The matrix add operation, on the other hand, creates and returns a new `Matrix` object that is the result of adding the two given matrices. The first step is to ensure the two matrices are the same size as required by the rules of matrix addition. After verifying the sizes, a new `Matrix` object is created and its elements set by iterating over and summing the corresponding elements from the two sources. The new matrix resulting from this operation is then returned. The implementation of the remaining methods, which is left as an exercise, can be done in a similar fashion.

2.5 Application: The Game of Life

The *game of Life*, devised by British mathematician John H. Conway, is a Solitaire-type game that is analogous with "the rise, fall and alternations of a society of living organisms." The game, which is actually a zero-player game, was first introduced by Martin Gardner in his Mathematical Games column in the October 1970 issue of *Scientific American*. Since its introduction, Life has attracted much attention and has been widely studied as it can be used to observe how complex systems or patterns can evolve from a simple set of rules. The game of Life was an early example of a problem in the modern field of mathematics called cellular automata.

2.5.1 Rules of the Game

The game uses an infinite-sized rectangular grid of cells in which each cell is either empty or occupied by an organism. The occupied cells are said to be alive, whereas the empty ones are dead. The game is played over a specific period of time with each turn creating a new *"generation"* based on the arrangement of live organisms in the current *configuration*. The status of a cell in the next generation is determined by applying the following four basic rules to each cell in the current configuration:

1. If a cell is alive and has either two or three live neighbors, the cell remains alive in the next generation. The neighbors are the eight cells immediately surrounding a cell: vertically, horizontally, and diagonally.

2. A living cell that has no live neighbors or a single live neighbor dies from isolation in the next generation.

3. A living cell that has four or more live neighbors dies from overpopulation in the next generation.

4. A dead cell with exactly three live neighbors results in a birth and becomes alive in the next generation. All other dead cells remain dead in the next generation.

The game starts with an initial configuration supplied by the user. Successive generations are created by applying the set of rules simultaneously to each cell in the grid. Interesting patterns can develop as the population of organisms undergoes changes by expanding or eventually dying out. To illustrate the game of Life, consider the following simple configuration of live organisms:

Applying the rules to this configuration creates the next generation. This results in two organisms dying (shown below as the light gray boxes) based on rule 2, one remaining alive based on rule 1, and the generation of a new organism based on rule 4 (the black box marked with an x).

If we evolve the next generation, the system dies out since both live cells in the first generation have a single live neighbor.

While some systems may eventually die out, others can evolve into a "stable" state. Consider the following initial configuration and its first generation. The result is a stable state since the four live cells each have three neighbors and no dead cell has exactly three neighbors in order to produce a new live cell.

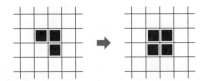

Another interesting patterns is the "two-phase oscillator," which alternates between successive generations:

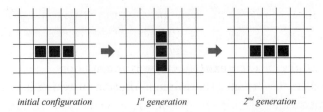

initial configuration   *1ˢᵗ generation*   *2ⁿᵈ generation*

2.5.2 Designing a Solution

The game of Life requires the use of a grid for storing the organisms. A Life Grid ADT can be defined to add a layer of abstraction between the algorithm for "playing" the game and the underlying structure used to store and manipulate the data.

Define   **Life Grid ADT**

A *life grid* is used to represent and store the area in the game of Life that contains organisms. The grid contains a rectangular grouping of cells of a finite size divided into rows and columns. The individual cells, which can be alive or dead, are referenced by row and column indices, both of which start at zero.

- **LifeGrid(nrows, ncols)**: Creates a new game grid consisting of **nrows** and **ncols**. All cells in the grid are set to dead.

- **numRows()**: Returns the number rows in the grid.

- **numCols()**: Returns the number of columns in the grid.

- **configure(coordList)**: Configures the grid for evolving the next generation. The **coordList** argument is a sequence of 2-tuples with each tuple representing the coordinates (r, c) of the cells to be set as alive. All remaining cells are cleared or set to dead.

- **clearCell(row, col)**: Clears the individual cell (**row**, **col**) and sets it to dead. The cell indices must be within the valid range of the grid.

- **setCell(row, col)**: Sets the indicated cell (**row**, **col**) to be alive. The cell indices must be within the valid range of the grid.

- **isLiveCell(row,col)**: Returns a boolean value indicating if the given cell (**row**, **col**) contains a live organism. The cell indices must be within the valid range of the grid.

- **numLiveNeighbors(row, col)**: Returns the number of live neighbors for the given cell (**row**, **col**). The neighbors of a cell include all of the cells immediately surrounding it in all directions. For the cells along the border of the grid, the neighbors that fall outside the grid are assumed to be dead. The cell indices must be within the valid range of the grid.

We now develop a program for the game of Life using the Life Grid ADT. The implementation of the program provided in Listing 2.4 on the next page was developed using a top-down design consisting of several functions. The main routine creates the game grid and evolves new generations of organisms. It relies on two additional functions: **draw()** and **evolve()**.

The **draw()** routine, the implementation of which is left as an exercise, prints a text-based representation of the game grid. The **evolve()** function generates

Listing 2.4   The gameoflife.py program.

```python
1  # Program for playing the game of Life.
2  from life import LifeGrid
3
4  # Define the initial configuration of live cells.
5  INIT_CONFIG = [ (1,1), (1,2), (2,2), (3,2) ]
6
7  # Set the size of the grid.
8  GRID_WIDTH = 5
9  GRID_HEIGHT = 5
10
11 # Indicate the number of generations.
12 NUM_GENS = 8
13
14 def main():
15    # Construct the game grid and configure it.
16    grid = LifeGrid( GRID_WIDTH, GRID_HEIGHT )
17    grid.configure( INIT_CONFIG )
18
19    # Play the game.
20    draw( grid )
21    for i in range( NUM_GENS ):
22      evolve( grid )
23      draw( grid )
24
25 # Generates the next generation of organisms.
26 def evolve( grid ):
27    # List for storing the live cells of the next generation.
28    liveCells = list()
29
30    # Iterate over the elements of the grid.
31    for i in range( grid.numRows() ) :
32      for j in range( grid.numCols() ) :
33
34         # Determine the number of live neighbors for this cell.
35         neighbors = grid.numLiveNeighbors( i, j )
36
37         # Add the (i,j) tuple to liveCells if this cell contains
38         # a live organism in the next generation.
39         if (neighbors == 2 and grid.isLiveCell( i, j )) or \
40            (neighbors == 3 ) :
41           liveCells.append( (i, j) )
42
43    # Reconfigure the grid using the liveCells coord list.
44    grid.configure( liveCells )
45
46 # Prints a text-based representation of the game grid.
47 def draw( grid ):
48    ......
49
50 # Executes the main routine.
51 main()
```

a new configuration of organisms based on the rules of the game. A list is used within `evolve()` to store the coordinates of live cells in the next generation. After iterating over all the cells, the grid is reconfigured using this list of coordinates. This is necessary since the current configuration stored in the game grid cannot be modified with the next generation until the neighbor count has been computed for each cell in the current generation.

The program also defines several constant variables. These are used to specify the grid size, the number of generations to be created, and the set of initial live cells. Using constant variables allows for easy modifications to any of these parameters as needed without having to modify other parts of the program. Of course, this information could be extracted from the user or a text file instead. The results of executing the `gameoflife.py` program are illustrated graphically in Figure 2.13.

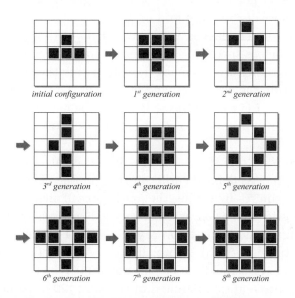

Figure 2.13: The results of using the `gameoflife.py` program on a sample grid configuration. Configurations after the eighth generation produce a two-phase oscillator, alternating between the configuration of the seventh and eighth generations.

2.5.3 Implementation

The actual game of Life specifies a rectangular grid of infinite size. When developing a computer solution for such a problem, we are limited to grids of a fixed size. The game of Life can still be implemented, however, by using a finite size for the grid. If the system grows too large where it does not fit into the space, it can be "played" again, with a larger grid.

Before implementing the `LifeGrid` class, we must decide how the data should be organized and select an appropriate structure. The most obvious is the use of a two-dimensional array to represent the grid. Next, we must decide what values to store in the grid to represent the organisms, both dead and alive. Any pair of values can be used. We are going to use the value 0 to represent the dead cells and the

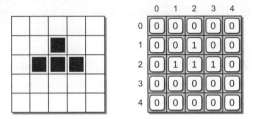

Figure 2.14: The game grid representation with live and dead cells: (left) the abstract view and (right) the physical view using a 2-D array of 0's and 1's.

value 1 for the live cells. This choice is based on the ease it creates when counting the number of neighbors for a given cell. Figure 2.14 illustrates the abstract and physical views of the game grid.

The `LifeGrid` class is implemented in Listing 2.5. At the top of the class definition, before specifying the constructor, two constant variables are initialized to store the values used to mark the cells within the game grid. These constants are defined within the class itself and outside of the methods since they are not actual data fields of a `LifeGrid` object. By using the named constants, the code is easier to read and the values used to represent the cell status could easily be changed if we were so inclined.

The constructor, shown in lines 10–14, creates a 2-D array for the grid using the `Array2D` class defined earlier in the chapter. The cells are cleared as the ADT definition requires by calling the `configure()` method with an empty coordinate list. The grid dimension accessor methods are easily implemented using the corresponding methods of the `Array2D` class. The three cell modification routines are also straightforward. Note that the ADT definition requires the cell indices specified for the `clearCell()` and `setCell()` methods must be valid. Since this is also the precondition required of the `Array2D` element access methods, we omit the direct specification of assertions in these methods. The `configure()` method, shown in lines 25–29, clears the grid cells by setting each to a dead organism. It then iterates through the coordinate list and uses the `setCell()` method to set the live cells.

The `numLiveNeighbors()` method is left as an exercise. Note, however, since we used the integer values 0 and 1 to represent the state of a cell, counting the number of live neighbors is as simple as summing the contents of the neighboring cells. Working with a fixed-size grid introduces the problem of how to deal with the cells around the border. A border cell will not have all eight neighbors since some of them lie outside the grid. Different approaches can be taken when a border cell

> **NOTE**
>
> ⟨i⟩ **Constant Variables.** Constant variables defined within a class are actually class variables that are unique to the class and not to individual objects. To reference a class constant variable, use the name of the class in place of the `self` keyword (i.e., `print( GameGrid.DEAD_CELL)`).

is examined. The most common is to assume any neighboring cell lying outside the grid contains a dead organism.

Listing 2.5   The `life.py` module.

```
1    # Implements the LifeGrid ADT for use with the game of Life.
2    from array import Array2D
3
4    class LifeGrid :
5      # Defines constants to represent the cell states.
6      DEAD_CELL = 0
7      LIVE_CELL = 1
8
9      # Creates the game grid and initializes the cells to dead.
10     def __init__( self, numRows, numCols ):
11       # Allocate the 2-D array for the grid.
12       self._grid = Array2D( numRows, numCols )
13       # Clear the grid and set all cells to dead.
14       self.configure( list() )
15
16     # Returns the number of rows in the grid.
17     def numRows( self ):
18       return self._grid.numRows()
19
20     # Returns the number of columns in the grid.
21     def numCols( self ):
22       return self._grid.numCols()
23
24     # Configures the grid to contain the given live cells.
25     def configure( self, coordList ):
26       # Clear the game grid.
27       for i in range( numRows ):
28         for j in range( numCols ):
29           self.clearCell( i, j )
30
31       # Set the indicated cells to be alive.
32       for coord in coordList :
33         self.setCell( coord[0], coord[1] )
34
35     # Does the indicated cell contain a live organism?
36     def isLiveCell( self, row, col ):
37       return self._grid[row, col] == GameGrid.LIVE_CELL
38
39     # Clears the indicated cell by setting it to dead.
40     def clearCell( self, row, col ):
41       self._grid[row, col] = GameGrid.DEAD_CELL
42
43     # Sets the indicated cell to be alive.
44     def setCell( self, row, col ):
45       self._grid[row, col] = GameGrid.LIVE_CELL
46
47     # Returns the number of live neighbors for the given cell.
48     def numLiveNeighbors( self, row, col ):
49       ......
```

Exercises

2.1 Complete the `Matrix` class by implementing the remaining methods: `__sub__`, `__mult__`, and `transpose()`.

2.2 Implement the `numLiveNeighbors()` method of the `LifeGrid` class.

2.3 Complete the implementation of the `gameoflife.py` program by implementing the `draw()` function. The output should look similar to the following, where dead cells are indicated using a period and live cells are indicated using the @ symbol.

```
. . @ . .
. @ . @ .
@ . . . @
. @ . @ .
. . @ . .
```

2.4 Modify the `gameoflife.py` program to prompt the user for the grid size and the number of generations to evolve.

2.5 Use your program from Exercise 2.4 to experiment with the initial configurations shown in Figure 2.15. Answer the following questions for each configuration using a variety of grid sizes and assuming no more than 10 generations.

   (a) Does the configuration die out?

   (b) Does the configuration become stable?

   (c) Does the configuration become an oscillator?

   (d) How many generations were required before each configuration resulted in one of the states indicated in parts (a) – (c)?

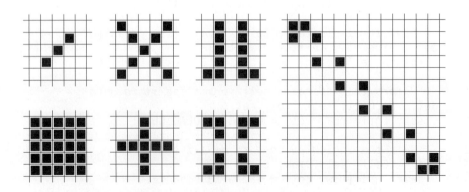

Figure 2.15: Sample game of Life configurations.

2.6 As indicated in the chapter, when a list is created using the replication operator `values = [ None ] * 10000` the size of the underlying array used to implement the list can be up to twice the size actually needed. This extra space is beneficial to the list itself, but it can be quite wasteful when a list is used to implement some abstract data types. Consider the implementation of the Array2D abstract data type as described in the chapter. If we had used a list of lists to implement the ADT, instead of the array of arrays, a large amount of extra storage space would be allocated that would never be used. Calculate the number of elements that will be allocated when using an array of arrays implementation and a list of lists implementation of the Array2D abstract data type for each of the following 2-D array sizes:

(a) 75×100 　　　　(b) $10,000 \times 25$ 　　　　(c) $10,000 \times 10,000$

Programming Projects

2.1 While Python provides the built-in list type for constructing and managing mutable sequences, many languages do not provide such a structure, at least not as part of the language itself. To help in further understanding how Python's built-in list works, implement the Vector ADT using the `Array` class implemented in the chapter. Your implementation should produce a mutable sequence type that works like Python's list structure. When the underlying array needs to be expanded, the new array should double the size of the original. The operations that can be performed on the ADT are described below. Assume the size of the underlying array never decreases.

- `Vector()`: Creates a new empty vector with an initial capacity of two elements.
- *length* (): Returns the number of items contained in the vector.
- *contains* (item): Determines if the given item is contained in the vector.
- *getitem* (ndx): Returns the item stored in the `ndx` element of the list. The value of `ndx` must be within the valid range.
- *setitem* (ndx, item): Sets the element at position `ndx` to contain the given `item`. The value of `ndx` must be within the valid range, which includes the first position past the last item.
- `append( item )`: Adds the given `item` to the end of the list.
- `insert( ndx, item )`: Inserts the given `item` in the element at position `ndx`. The items in the elements at and following the given position are shifted down to make room for the new item. `ndx` must be within the valid range.
- `remove( ndx )`: Removes and returns the item from the element from the given `ndx` position. The items in the elements at and following the given position are shifted up to close the gap created by the removed item. `ndx` must be within the valid range.

- `indexOf( item )`: Returns the index of the vector element containing the given `item`. The `item` must be in the list.

- `extend( otherVector )`: Extends this vector by appending the entire contents of the `otherVector` to this vector.

- `subVector( from, to )`: Creates and returns a new vector that contains a subsequence of the items in the vector between and including those indicated by the given `from` and `to` positions. Both the `from` and `to` positions must be within the valid range.

- *iterator* (): Creates and returns an iterator that can be used to traverse the elements of the vector.

2.2 In a typical Vector ADT, the size of the underlying array decreases after a sufficient number of items have been removed. Devise a strategy for decreasing the size of the array as items are removed. Modify your implementation of the Vector ADT from the previous question to include your reduction strategy.

2.3 A grayscale digital image is a two-dimensional raster image in which the picture elements, or pixels, store a single value representing a shade of gray that varies from black to white. In a discrete grayscale image, the shades of gray are represented by integer values in the range $[0 \ldots 255]$, where 0 is black and 255 is white. We can define the Grayscale Image ADT for storing and manipulating discrete grayscale digital images. Given the description of the operations, provide a complete implementation of the ADT using a 2-D array.

- `GrayscaleImage( nrows, ncols )`: Creates a new instance that consists of `nrows` and `ncols` of pixels each set to an initial value of 0.

- `width()`: Returns the width of the image.

- `height()`: Returns the height of the image.

- `clear( value )`: Clears the entire image by setting each pixel to the given intensity value. The intensity value will be clamped to 0 or 255 if it is less than 0 or greater than 255, respectively.

- *getitem* (row, col): Returns the intensity level of the given pixel. The pixel coordinates must be within the valid range.

- *setitem* (row, col, value): Sets the intensity level of the given pixel to the given `value`. The pixel coordinates must be within the valid range. The intensity value is clamped to 0 or 255 if it is outside the valid range.

2.4 Playing board games on a computer is very common. We can use abstraction to aide in the design of a board game by separating the game logic from the actual user interaction required to play the game. No matter the type of user interface provided to play the game (i.e., text based, desktop windowing environment, or web browser), the underlying logic remains the same. Consider the game of Reversi, which was invented in 1893 but has a more modern set of rules dating back to the 1970s. Reversi is played by two players on a game board divided into 64 squares arranged in 8 rows and 8 columns and a set of 64 chips. Each chip is painted a dark color on one side and a light color on the other, with each color belonging to one of the two players. The players place their chips on the board and flip the chips of their opponent with the goal of having the most chips of their color on the board at the end of the game. The game starts with a configuration as shown in part (a) of Figure 2.16.

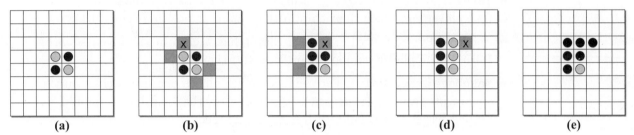

Figure 2.16: Moves in the game of Reversi.

The players take turns placing chips on the board with their color facing up. A chip can only be played in a square that is adjacent to a chip of the other player and that forms a straight line of attack (vertical, horizontal, or diagonal). A line of attack is formed between two squares containing the player's own chips in which there is one or more of the opponent's chips in between the two. For example, if player 1 (black) goes first, he has four options as shown in part (b). Suppose player 1 places a chip in the square marked with an x. After placing his chip, player 1 flips all of the chips of player 2 (white) that are in the line of attack. In this case, he flips the chip immediately below the new chip as shown in part (c). Player 2 then places one of her chips. She has three options from which to choose as shown by the dark squares in part (c). If player 2 places her chip in the square marked x, she flips the black chip below the new chip as shown in part (d). If there are multiple lines of attack that result from the placement of a chip, then all of the opponent's chips that are in all of the lines of attack are flipped. For example, suppose player 1 places a chip in the square marked with an x as shown in part (d). Then he flips both white chips, the one to the left and the one diagonally down to the left as shown in part (e). Play alternates between the players until all of the squares are filled or neither player can move. If one player cannot move but the other can, play proceeds with the other player. The winner is the player with the most chips at the end of the game. Given the following description of the operations, provide a complete implementation for the Reversi Game Logic ADT.

- `ReversiGameLogic()`: Creates a new instance of the Reversi game logic with the initial configuration.

- `whoseTurn()`: Returns the player number (1 or 2) for the current player or 0 if no player can move.

- `numChips( player )`: Returns the number of chips on the board belonging to the indicated player. The value of `player` must be 1 or 2.

- `numOpenSquares()`: Returns the number of squares still open and available for play.

- `getWinner()`: Returns the player number (1 or 2) for the player who has won the game or 0 if the game is not finished.

- `isLegalMove( row, col )`: Returns `True` or `False` to indicate if the current player can place their chip in the square at position (`row`, `col`).

- `occupiedBy( row, col )`: Which player has a chip in the given square? Returns the player number (1 or 2) or 0 if the square is empty.

- `makeMove( row, col )`: The current player places one of his chips in the square at position (`row`, `col`). All chips on the board that should be flipped based on the rules of Reversi are flipped.

2.5 Implement a text-based version of the Reversi game using your game logic ADT from the previous question.

2.6 Define a game logic ADT, similar to that of the Reversi Game Logic ADT, for the game of checkers.

## CHAPTER 3

Sets and Maps

In the previous chapters, we studied several complex abstract data types that required the use of a data structure for their implementation. In this chapter, we continue exploring abstract data types with a focus on several common containers. Two of these are provided by Python as part of the language itself: sets and dictionaries. Nevertheless, it's still important to understand how they work and some of the common ways in which they are implemented.

Your experience in programming will likely not be limited to the Python language. At some point in the future, you may use one if not several other common programming languages. While some of these do provide a wide range of abstract data types as part of the language itself or included in their standard library, others, like C, do not. Thus, it's important that you know how to implement a set or dictionary ADT if necessary, when one is not available as part of the language.

Further, both the set and dictionary types provide excellent examples of abstract data types that can be implemented using different data structures. As you learned in Chapter 1, there may be multiple data structures and ways to organize the data in those structures that are suitable for implementing an abstract data type. Thus, it's not uncommon for language libraries to provide multiple implementations of an abstract data type, which allows the programmer to choose the best option for a given problem. Your ability to choose from among these various implementations will depend not only on your knowledge of the abstract data type itself, but also on understanding the pros and cons of the various implementations.

3.1 Sets

The Set ADT is a common container used in computer science. But unlike the Bag ADT introduced in Chapter 1, a set stores unique values and represents the same structure found in mathematics. It is commonly used when you need to store a collection of unique values without regard to how they are stored or when you need to perform various mathematical set operations on collections.

3.1.1   The Set Abstract Data Type

The definition of the set abstract data type is provided here, followed by an implementation using a list. In later chapters, we will provide and evaluate alternate implementations for the Set ADT.

Define   **Set ADT**

A *set* is a container that stores a collection of unique values over a given comparable domain in which the stored values have no particular ordering.

- `Set()`: Creates a new set initialized to the empty set.

- *length*`()`: Returns the number of elements in the set, also known as the cardinality. Accessed using the `len()` function.

- *contains*`(element)`: Determines if the given value is an element of the set and returns the appropriate boolean value. Accessed using the `in` operator.

- `add(element)`: Modifies the set by adding the given value or element to the set if the element is not already a member. If the element is not unique, no action is taken and the operation is skipped.

- `remove(element)`: Removes the given value from the set if the value is contained in the set and raises an exception otherwise.

- *equals*`(setB)`: Determines if the set is equal to another set and returns a boolean value. For two sets, A and B, to be equal, both A and B must contain the same number of elements and all elements in A must also be elements in B. If both sets are empty, the sets are equal. Access with `==` or `!=`.

- `isSubsetOf(setB)`: Determines if the set is a subset of another set and returns a boolean value. For set A to be a subset of B, all elements in A must also be elements in B.

- `union(setB)`: Creates and returns a new set that is the union of this set and `setB`. The new set created from the union of two sets, A and B, contains all elements in A plus those elements in B that are not in A. Neither set A nor set B is modified by this operation.

- `intersect(setB)`: Creates and returns a new set that is the intersection of this set and `setB`. The intersection of sets A and B contains only those elements that are in both A and B. Neither set A nor set B is modified by this operation.

- `difference(setB)`: Creates and returns a new set that is the difference of this set and `setB`. The set difference, $A - B$, contains only those elements that are in A but not in B. Neither set A nor set B is modified by this operation.

■ *iterator*(): Creates and returns an iterator that can be used to iterate over the collection of items.

Example Use

To illustrate the use of the Set ADT, we create and use sets containing the courses currently being taken by two students. In the following code segment, we create two sets and add elements to each. The results are illustrated in Figure 3.1.

```
smith = Set()
smith.add( "CSCI-112" )
smith.add( "MATH-121" )
smith.add( "HIST-340" )
smith.add( "ECON-101" )

roberts = Set()
roberts.add( "POL-101" )
roberts.add( "ANTH-230" )
roberts.add( "CSCI-112" )
roberts.add( "ECON-101" )
```

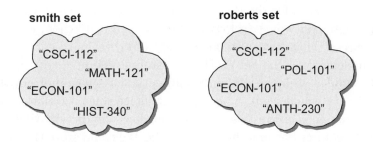

Figure 3.1: Abstract view of the two sample sets.

Next, we determine if the two students are taking the exact same courses. If not, then we want to know if they are taking any of the same courses. We can do this by computing the intersection between the two sets.

```
if smith == roberts :
    print( "Smith and Roberts are taking the same courses." )
else :
    sameCourses = smith.intersection( roberts )
    if sameCourses.isEmpty() :
        print( "Smith and Roberts are not taking any of "\
            + "the same courses." )
    else :
        print( "Smith and Roberts are taking some of the "\
            + "same courses:" )
        for course in sameCourses :
            print( course )
```

In this case, the two students are both taking CSCI-112 and ECON-101. Thus, the results of executing the previous code segment will be

```
Smith and Roberts are taking some of the same courses:
CSCI-112  ECON-101
```

Suppose we want to know which courses Smith is taking that Roberts is not taking. We can determine this using the set difference operation:

```
uniqueCourses = smith.difference( roberts )
for course in sameCourses :
  print( course )
```

This example reinforces one of the advantages of working with an abstraction by focusing on what functionality the ADT provides instead of how that functionality is implemented. By hiding the implementation details, we can use an ADT independent of its implementation. In fact, the choice of implementation for the Set ADT will have no effect on the instructions in our example program.

3.1.2   Selecting a Data Structure

To implement the Set ADT, we must select a data structure based on the same criteria we used for the Bag ADT from Chapter 1. Since we are trying to replicate the functionality of the set structure provided by Python, we don't want to use that structure. That leaves the array, list, and dictionary containers for consideration in implementing the Set ADT. The storage requirements for the bag and set are very similar with the difference being that a set cannot contain duplicates. The dictionary would seem to be the ideal choice since it can store unique items, but it would waste space in this case. Remember, the dictionary stores key/value pairs, which requires two data fields per entry. We could store the individual items of the set in the key fields and leave the value fields empty, but that would use twice the amount of storage than necessary. This waste does not occur with an array or list. An array could be used to implement the set, but a set can contain any number of elements and by definition an array has a fixed size. To use the array structure, we would have to manage the expansion of the array when necessary in the same fashion as it's done for the list. Since the list can grow as needed, it seems ideal for storing the elements of a set just as it was for the bag and it does provide for the complete functionality of the ADT. Since the list allows for duplicate values, however, we must make sure as part of the implementation that no duplicates are added to our set.

3.1.3   List-Based Implementation

Having selected the list structure, we can now implement the Set ADT as shown in Listing 3.1. Some of the operations of the set are very similar to those of the Bag ADT and are implemented in a similar fashion. Sample instances for the two sets from Figure 3.1 are illustrated in Figure 3.2.

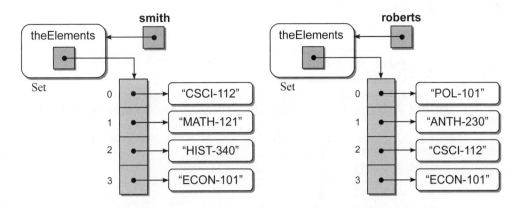

Figure 3.2: Two instances of the Set class implemented as a list.

Listing 3.1   The `linearset.py` module.

```python
1   # Implementation of the Set ADT container using a Python list.
2   class Set :
3     # Creates an empty set instance.
4     def __init__( self ):
5       self._theElements = list()
6
7     # Returns the number of items in the set.
8     def __len__( self ):
9       return len( self._theElements )
10
11    # Determines if an element is in the set.
12    def __contains__( self, element ):
13      return element in self._theElements
14
15    # Adds a new unique element to the set.
16    def add( self, element ):
17      if element not in self :
18        self._theElements.append( element )
19
20    # Removes an element from the set.
21    def remove( self, element ):
22      assert element in self, "The element must be in the set."
23      self._theElements.remove( item )
24
25    # Determines if two sets are equal.
26    def __eq__( self, setB ):
27      if len( self ) != len( setB ) :
28        return False
29      else :
30        return self.isSubsetOf( setB )
31
```

(Listing Continued)

```
32      # Determines if this set is a subset of setB.
33      def isSubsetOf( self, setB ):
34        for element in self :
35          if element not in setB :
36            return False
37        return True
38
39      # Creates a new set from the union of this set and setB.
40      def union( self, setB ):
41        newSet = Set()
42        newSet._theElements.extend( self._theElements )
43        for element in setB :
44          if element not in self :
45            newSet._theElements.append( element )
46        return newSet
47
48      # Creates a new set from the intersection: self set and setB.
49      def interset( self, setB ):
50        ......
51
52      # Creates a new set from the difference: self set and setB.
53      def difference( self, setB ):
54        ......
55
56      # Returns an iterator for traversing the list of items.
57      def __iter__( self ):
58        return _SetIterator( self._theElements )
```

Adding Elements

As indicated earlier, we must ensure that duplicate values are not added to the set since the list structure does not handle this for us. When implementing the add method, shown in lines 16–18, we must first determine if the supplied element is already in the list or not. If the element is not a duplicate, we can simply append the value to the end of the list; if the element is a duplicate, we do nothing. The reason for this is that the definition of the add() operation indicates no action is taken when an attempt is made to add a duplicate value. This is known as a *noop*, which is short for no operation and indicates no action is taken. Noops are appropriate in some cases, which will be stated implicitly in the definition of an abstract data type by indicating no action is to be taken when the precondition fails as we did with the add() operation.

Comparing Two Sets

For the operations that require a second set as an argument, we can use the operations of the Set ADT itself to access and manipulate the data of the second set. Consider the "equals" operation, implemented in lines 26–30 of Listing 3.1, which determines if both sets contain the exact same elements. We first check to make

> **TIP**
>
> **Avoid Reinventing the Wheel.** Using operations provided by an ADT to implement other methods of that same ADT allows you to take advantage of the abstraction and avoid "reinventing the wheel" by duplicating code in several places.

sure the two sets contain the same number of elements; otherwise, they cannot be equal. It would be inefficient to compare the individual elements since we already know the two sets cannot be equal. After verifying the size of the lists, we can test to see if the `self` set is a subset of `setB` by calling `self.isSubsetOf(setB)`. This is a valid test since two equal sets are subsets of each other and we already know they are of the same size.

To determine if one set is the subset of another, we can iterate over the list of elements in the `self` set and make sure each is contained in `setB`. If just one element in the `self` set is not in `setB`, then it is not a subset. The implementation of the `isSubsetOf()` method is shown in lines 33–37.

The Set Union

Some of the operations create and return a new set based on the original, but the original is not modified. This is accomplished by creating a new set and populating it with the appropriate data from the other sets. Consider the `union()` method, shown in lines 40–46, which creates a new set from the `self` set and `setB` passed as an argument to the method.

Creating a new set, populated with the unique elements of the other two sets, requires three steps: (1) create a new set; (2) fill the `newSet` with the elements from `setB`; and (3) iterate through the elements of the `self` set, during which each element is added to the `newSet` if that element is not in `setB`. For the first step, we simply create a new instance of the `Set` class. The second step is accomplished with the use of the list `extend()` method. It directly copies the entire contents of the list used to store the elements of the `self` set to the list used to store the elements of the `newSet`. For the final step, we iterate through the elements of `setB` and add those elements to the the `newSet` that are not in the `self` set. The unique elements are added to the `newSet` by appending them to the list used to store the elements of the `newSet`. The remaining operations of the Set ADT can be implemented in a similar fashion and are left as exercises.

3.2   Maps

Searching for data items based on unique key values is a very common application in computer science. An abstract data type that provides this type of search capability is often referred to as a *map* or *dictionary* since it maps a key to a corresponding value. Consider the problem of a university registrar having to manage and process large volumes of data related to students. To keep track of the information or records of data, the registrar assigns a unique student identification number to each individual student as illustrated in Figure 3.3. Later, when the registrar needs to search for a student's information, the identification number is used. Using this *keyed* approach allows access to a specific student record. If the names were used to identify the records instead, then what happens when multiple students have the same name? Or, what happens if the name was entered incorrectly when the record was initially created?

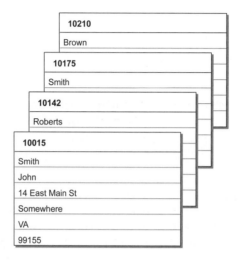

Figure 3.3: Unique key/data pairs.

In this section, we define our own Map ADT and then provide an implementation using a list. In later chapters, we will implement and evaluate the map using a variety of data structures. We use the term map to distinguish our ADT from the dictionary provided by Python. The Python dictionary is implemented using a hash table, which requires the key objects to contain the __hash__ method for generating a hash code. This can limit the type of problems with which a dictionary can be used. We define our Map ADT with the minimum requirement that the keys are comparable, which will allow it to be used in a wider range of problems. It's not uncommon to provide multiple implementations of an ADT as is done with many language libraries. We will explore the implementation details of Python's dictionary later in Chapter 11 when we discuss hash tables and the design of hash functions.

3.2.1 The Map Abstract Data Type

The Map ADT provides a great example of an ADT that can be implemented using one of many different data structures. Our definition of the Map ADT, which is provided next, includes the minimum set of operations necessary for using and managing a map.

Define	Map ADT

A *map* is a container for storing a collection of data records in which each record is associated with a unique key. The key components must be comparable.

- `Map()`: Creates a new empty map.

- *`length`* `()`: Returns the number of key/value pairs in the map.

- *`contains`* `(key)`: Determines if the given key is in the map and returns `True` if the key is found and `False` otherwise.

- `add(key, value)`: Adds a new key/value pair to the map if the key is not already in the map or replaces the data associated with the key if the key is in the map. Returns `True` if this is a new key and `False` if the data associated with the existing key is replaced.

- `remove(key)`: Removes the key/value pair for the given key if it is in the map and raises an exception otherwise.

- `valueOf(key)`: Returns the data record associated with the given key. The key must exist in the map or an exception is raised.

- *`iterator`* `()`: Creates and returns an iterator that can be used to iterate over the keys in the map.

3.2.2 List-Based Implementation

We indicated earlier that many different data structures can be used to implement a map. Since we are trying to replicate the functionality of the dictionary provided by Python, we don't want to use that structure. That leaves the use of an array or list. As with the Set ADT, both the array and list structures can be used, but the list is a better choice since it does not have a fixed size like an array and it can expand automatically as needed.

In the implementation of the Bag and Set ADTs, we used a single list to store the individual elements. For the Map ADT, however, we must store both a key component and the corresponding value component for each entry in the map. We cannot simply add the component pairs to the list without some means of maintaining their association.

One approach is to use two lists, one for the keys and one for the corresponding values. Accessing and manipulating the components is very similar to that used with the Bag and Set ADTs. The difference, however, is that the association between the component pairs must always be maintained as new entries are added and existing ones removed. To accomplish this, each key/value must be stored in corresponding elements of the parallel lists and that association must be maintained.

Instead of using two lists to store the key/value entries in the map, we can use a single list. The individual keys and corresponding values can both be saved in a single object, with that object then stored in the list. A sample instance illustrating the data organization required for this approach is shown in Figure 3.4.

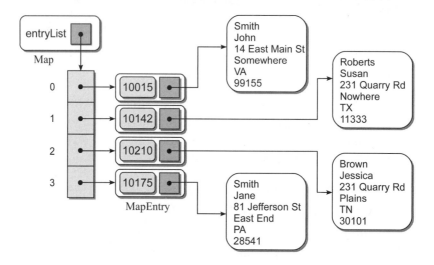

Figure 3.4: The Map ADT implemented using a single list.

The implementation of the Map ADT using a single list is provided in Listing 3.2. As we indicated earlier in Chapter 1, we want to avoid the use of tuples when storing structured data since it's better practice to use classes with named fields. The _MapEntry storage class, defined in lines 56–59, will be used to store the individual key/value pairs. Note this storage class is defined to be private since it's only intended for use by the Map class that provides the single list implementation of the Map ADT.

Listing 3.2	The `linearmap.py` module.

```
1   # Implementation of Map ADT using a single list.
2   class Map :
3     # Creates an empty map instance.
4     def __init__( self ):
5       self._entryList = list()
6
7     # Returns the number of entries in the map.
8     def __len__( self ):
9       return len( self._entryList )
10
11    # Determines if the map contains the given key.
12    def __contains__( self, key ):
13      ndx = self._findPosition( key )
14      return ndx is not None
15
16    # Adds a new entry to the map if the key does exist. Otherwise, the
```

```
17      # new value replaces the current value associated with the key.
18    def add( self, key, value ):
19      ndx = self._findPosition( key )
20      if ndx is not None :   # if the key was found
21        self._entryList[ndx].value = value
22        return False
23      else :  # otherwise add a new entry
24        entry = _MapEntry( key, value )
25        self._entryList.append( entry )
26        return True
27
28      # Returns the value associated with the key.
29    def valueOf( self, key ):
30      ndx = self._findPosition( key )
31      assert ndx is not None, "Invalid map key."
32      return self._entryList[ndx].value
33
34      # Removes the entry associated with the key.
35    def remove( self, key ):
36      ndx = self._findPosition( key )
37      assert ndx is not None, "Invalid map key."
38      self._entryList.pop( ndx )
39
40      # Returns an iterator for traversing the keys in the map.
41    def __iter__( self ):
42      return _MapIterator( self._entryList )
43
44      # Helper method used to find the index position of a category. If the
45      # key is not found, None is returned.
46    def _findPosition( self, key ):
47        # Iterate through each entry in the list.
48      for i in range( len(self) ) :
49          # Is the key stored in the ith entry?
50        if self._entryList[i].key == key :
51          return i
52      # When not found, return None.
53      return None
54
55  # Storage class for holding the key/value pairs.
56  class _MapEntry :
57    def __init__( self, key, value ):
58      self.key = key
59      self.value = value
```

Many of the methods require a search to determine if the map contains a given key. In this implementation, the standard **in** operator cannot be used since the list contains _MapEntry objects and not simply key entries. Instead, we have to search the list ourselves and examine the key field of each _MapEntry object. Likewise, we routinely have to locate within the list the position containing a specific key/value entry. Since these operations will be needed in several methods, we can create a helper method that combines the two searches and use it where needed.

The _findPosition() helper method searches the list for the given key. If the key is found, the index of its location is returned; otherwise, the function returns None to indicate the key is not contained in the map. When used by the other methods, the value returned can be evaluated to determine both the existence of the key and the location of the corresponding entry if the key is in the map. By combining the two searches into a single operation, we eliminate the need to first determine if the map contains the key and then searching again for its location. Given the helper method, the implementation of the various methods is straightforward. Implementation of the iterator method is left as an exercise.

3.3   Multi-Dimensional Arrays

In Chapter 2, we worked with one- and two-dimensional arrays, but arrays can be larger than two dimensions. In fact, arrays can contain any number of dimensions that may be needed for a given problem. A ***multi-dimensional array*** stores a collection of data in which the individual elements are accessed with multi-component subscripts: $x_{i,j}$ or $y_{i,j,k}$. Figure 3.5 illustrates the abstract view of a two- and three-dimensional array. As we saw earlier, a ***two-dimensional array*** is typically viewed as a table or grid consisting of rows and columns. An individual element is accessed by specifying two indices, one for the row and one for the column. The ***three-dimensional array*** can be visualized as a box of tables where each table is divided into rows and columns. Individual elements are accessed by specifying the index of the table followed by the row and column indices. Larger dimensions are used in the solutions for some problems, but they are more difficult to visualize.

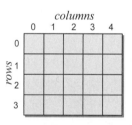 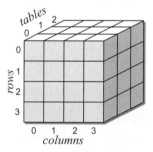

Figure 3.5: Sample multi-dimensional arrays: (left) a 2-D array viewed as a rectangular table and (right) a 3-D array viewed as a box of tables.

Most high-level programming languages provide a convenient way to create and manage multi-dimensional arrays while others require a more hands-on approach. C++ and Java are two examples of languages that provide multi-dimensional arrays as part of the language. Python, of course, does not directly support arrays of any dimension. But that did not prevent us from defining and implementing abstract data types in the previous chapter for one- and two-dimensional arrays. Likewise, we can define an abstract data type for creating and using arrays of any dimension.

3.3.1   The MultiArray Abstract Data Type

To accommodate multi-dimensional arrays of two or more dimensions, we define the MultiArray ADT and as with the earlier array abstract data types, we limit the operations to those commonly provided by arrays in most programming languages that provide the array structure.

Define   **MultiArray ADT**

A *multi-dimensional array* consists of a collection of elements organized into multiple dimensions. Individual elements are referenced by specifying an n-tuple or a subscript of multiple components, $(i_1, i_2, \ldots i_n)$, one for each dimension of the array. All indices of the n-tuple start at zero.

- MultiArray($d_1, d_2, \ldots d_n$): Creates a multi-dimensional array of elements organized into n-dimensions with each element initially set to None. The number of dimensions, which is specified by the number of arguments, must be greater than 1. The individual arguments, all of which must be greater than zero, indicate the lengths of the corresponding array dimensions. The dimensions are specified from highest to lowest, where d_1 is the highest possible dimension and d_n is the lowest.

- dims(): Returns the number of dimensions in the multi-dimensional array.

- length(dim): Returns the length of the given array dimension. The individual dimensions are numbered starting from 1, where 1 represents the first, or highest, dimension possible in the array. Thus, in an array with three dimensions, 1 indicates the number of tables in the box, 2 is the number of rows, and 3 is the number of columns.

- clear(value): Clears the array by setting each element to the given value.

- *getitem*($i_1, i_2, \ldots i_n$): Returns the value stored in the array at the element position indicated by the n-tuple $(i_1, i_2, \ldots i_n)$. All of the specified indices must be given and they must be within the valid range of the corresponding array dimensions. Accessed using the element operator: y = x[1, 2].

- *setitem*($i_1, i_2, \ldots i_n$, value): Modifies the contents of the specified array element to contain the given value. The element is specified by the n-tuple $(i_1, i_2, \ldots i_n)$. All of the subscript components must be given and they must be within the valid range of the corresponding array dimensions. Accessed using the element operator: x[1, 2] = y.

3.3.2   Data Organization

Most computer architectures provide a mechanism at the hardware level for creating and using one-dimensional arrays. Programming languages need only provide appropriate syntax to make use of a 1-D array. Multi-dimensional arrays are not handled at the hardware level. Instead, the programming language typically provides its own mechanism for creating and managing multi-dimensional arrays.

As we saw earlier, a one-dimensional array is composed of a group of sequential elements stored in successive memory locations. The index used to reference a particular element is simply the offset from the first element in the array. In most programming languages, a multi-dimensional array is actually created and stored in memory as a one-dimensional array. With this organization, a multi-dimensional array is simply an abstract view of a physical one-dimensional data structure.

Array Storage

A one-dimensional array is commonly used to physically store arrays of higher dimensions. Consider a two-dimensional array divided into a table of rows and columns as illustrated in Figure 3.6. How can the individual elements of the table be stored in the one-dimensional structure while maintaining direct access to the individual table elements? There are two common approaches. The elements can be stored in *row-major order* or *column-major order*. Most high-level programming languages use row-major order, with FORTRAN being one of the few languages that uses column-major ordering to store and manage 2-D arrays.

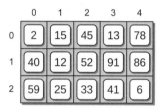

Figure 3.6: The abstract view of a sample 3×5 two-dimensional array.

In row-major order, the individual rows are stored sequentially, one at a time, as illustrated in Figure 3.7. The first row of 5 elements are stored in the first 5 sequential elements of the 1-D array, the second row of 5 elements are stored in the next five sequential elements, and so forth.

In column-major order, the 2-D array is stored sequentially, one entire column at a time, as illustrated in Figure 3.8. The first column of 3 elements are stored in the first 3 sequential elements of the 1-D array, followed by the 3 elements of the second column, and so on.

For larger dimensions, a similar approach can be used. With a three-dimensional array, the individual tables can be stored contiguously using either row-major or column-major ordering. As the number of dimensions grow, all elements within a single instance of each dimension are stored contiguously before the next instance. For example, given a four-dimensional array, which can be thought of as an array of boxes, all elements of an individual box (3-D array) are stored before the next box.

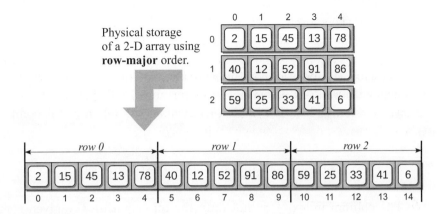

Figure 3.7: Physical storage of a sample 2-D array (top) in a 1-D array using row-major order (bottom).

Index Computation

Since multi-dimensional arrays are created and managed by instructions in the programming language, accessing an individual element must also be handled by the language. When an individual element of a 2-D array is accessed, the compiler must include additional instructions to calculate the offset of the specific element within the 1-D array. Given a 2-D array of size $m \times n$ and using row-major ordering, an equation can be derived to compute this offset.

To derive the formula, consider the 2-D array illustrated in Figure 3.7 and observe the physical storage location within the 1-D array for the first element in several of the rows. Element $(0, 0)$ maps to position 0 since it is the first element in both the abstract 2-D and physical 1-D arrays. The first entry of the second row $(1, 0)$ maps to position n since it follows the first n elements of the first row. Likewise, element $(2, 0)$ maps to position $2n$ since it follows the first $2n$ elements in the first two rows. We could continue in the same fashion through all of the rows, but you would soon notice the position for the first element of the ith row is

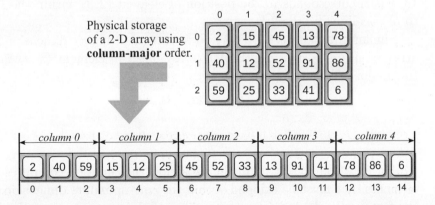

Figure 3.8: Physical storage of a sample 2-D array (top) in a 1-D array using column-major order (bottom).

$n * i$. Since the subscripts start from zero, the ith subscript not only represents a specific row but also indicates the number of complete rows skipped to reach the ith row.

Knowing the position of the first element of each row, the position for any element within a 2-D array can be determined. Given an element (i, j) of a 2-D array, the storage location of that element in the 1-D array is computed as

$$\text{index}_2(i, j) = i * n + j \tag{3.1}$$

The column index, j, is not only the offset within the given row but also the number of elements that must be skipped in the ith row to reach the jth column. To see this formula in action, again consider the 2-D array from Figure 3.7 and assume we want to access element $(2, 3)$. Finding the target element within the 1-D array requires skipping over the first 2 complete rows of elements:

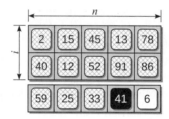

and the first 3 elements within row 2:

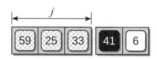

Plugging the indices into the equation from above results in an index position of 13, which corresponds to the position of element $(2, 3)$ within the 1-D array used to physically store the 2-D array.

Similar equations can be derived for arrays of higher dimensions. Given a 3-D array of size $d_1 \times d_2 \times d_3$, the 1-D array offset of element (i_1, i_2, i_3) stored using row-major order will be

$$\text{index}_3(i_1, i_2, i_3) = i_1 * (d_2 * d_3) + i_2 * d_3 + i_3 \tag{3.2}$$

For each component (i) in the subscript, the equation computes the number of elements that must be skipped within the corresponding dimension. For example, the factor $(d_2 * d_3)$ indicates the number of elements in a single table of the cube. When it's multiplied by i_1 we get the number of complete tables to skip and in turn the number of elements to skip in order to arrive at the first element of table i_1.

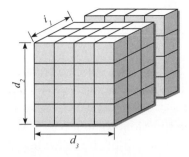

The remaining part of the equation $(i_2 * d_3 + i_3)$ is equivalent to $\text{index}_2(i_2, i_3)$, which indicates the number of elements to skip within the i_1 table. As the number of dimensions increase, additional products are added to the equation, one for each new dimension. For example, the equation to compute the offset for a 4-D array is

$$\text{index}_4(i_1, i_2, i_3, i_4) = i_1 * (d_2 * d_3 * d_4) + i_2 * (d_3 * d_4) + i_3 * d_4 + i_4 \qquad (3.3)$$

You may notice a pattern developing as the number of dimensions increase. This pattern leads to a general equation for computing the 1-D array offset for element $(i_1, i_2, \ldots, i_n)$ within an n-dimensional array:

$$\text{index}(i_1, i_2, \ldots, i_n) = i_1 * f_1 + i_2 * f_2 + \cdots + i_{n-1} * f_{n-1} + i_n * 1 \qquad (3.4)$$

where the f_j values are the factors representing the number of elements to be skipped within the corresponding dimension and are computed using

$$f_n = 1 \quad \text{and} \quad f_j = \prod_{k=j+1}^{n} d_k \ \ \forall_{0<j<n} \qquad (3.5)$$

The size of a multi-dimensional array is fixed at the time it's created and cannot change during execution. Likewise, the several f_j products used in the equation above will not change once the size of the array is set. This can be used to our advantage to reduce the number of multiplications required to compute the element offsets. Instead of computing the products every time an element is accessed, we can compute and store the factor values and simply plug them into the equation when needed.

3.3.3 Variable-Length Arguments

The definition of the MultiArray ADT requires a variable-length argument for the constructor and the two element access methods. The number of arguments passed to each method is supposed to equal the number of dimensions in the array. Python functions and methods can be defined to accept a variable number of arguments, which is exactly what we need to implement the MultiArray ADT. Consider the following function, which accepts any number of arguments (assumed to be numerical in this example) and then prints how many arguments were passed and the sum of those arguments:

```
def func( *args ):
  print "Number of arguments: ", len( args )
  sum = 0
  for value in args :
    sum += value
  print( "Sum of the arguments: ", sum )
```

When using the function, we can pass a variable number of arguments for each invocation. For example, all of the following are valid function calls:

```
func( 12 )
func( 5, 8, 2 )
func( 18, -2, 50, 21, 6 )
```

which results in the following output:

```
Number of arguments: 1
Sum of the arguments: 12
Number of arguments: 3
Sum of the arguments: 15
Number of arguments: 5
Sum of the arguments: 93
```

The asterisk next to the argument name (*args) tells Python to accept any number of arguments and to combine them into a tuple. The tuple is then passed to the function and assigned to the formal argument marked with the asterisk. Note the asterisk is only used in the argument list to indicate that the function or method can accept any number of arguments. It is not part of the argument name. The len() operation can be applied to the tuple to determine the number of actual arguments passed to the function. The individual arguments, which are elements in the tuple, can be accessed by using the subscript notation or by iterating the collection.

3.3.4   Implementing the MultiArray

To implement the MultiArray ADT, the elements of the multi-dimensional array can be stored in a single 1-D array in row-major order. Not only does this create a fast and compact array structure, but it's also the actual technique used by most programming languages. A partial implementation of the MultiArray class is provided in Listing 3.3.

Listing 3.3   The array.py module with the MultiArray class.

```
1  # Implementation of the MultiArray ADT using a 1-D array.
2  class MultiArray :
3    # Creates a multi-dimensional array.
4    def __init__( self, *dimensions ):
5      assert len(dimensions) > 1, "The array must have 2 or more dimensions."
6      # The variable argument tuple contains the dim sizes.
7      self._dims = dimensions
8
```

```
 9      # Compute the total number of elements in the array.
10      size = 1
11      for d in dimensions :
12        assert d > 0, "Dimensions must be > 0."
13        size *= d
14
15      # Create the 1-D array to store the elements.
16      self._elements = Array( size )
17      # Create a 1-D array to store the equation factors.
18      self._factors = Array( len(dimensions) )
19      self._computeFactors()
20
21    # Returns the number of dimensions in the array.
22    def numDims( self ):
23      return len(self._dims)
24
25    # Returns the length of the given dimension.
26    def length( self, dim ):
27      assert dim >= 1 and dim < len(self._dims),\
28          "Dimension component out of range."
29      return self._dims[dim - 1]
30
31    # Clears the array by setting all elements to the given value.
32    def clear( self, value ):
33      self._elements.clear( value )
34
35    # Returns the contents of element (i_1, i_2, ..., i_n).
36    def __getitem__( self, ndxTuple ):
37      assert len(ndxTuple) == self.numDims(), "Invalid # of array subscripts."
38      index = self._computeIndex( ndxTuple )
39      assert index is not None, "Array subscript out of range."
40      return self._elements[index]
41
42    # Sets the contents of element (i_1, i_2, ..., i_n).
43    def __setitem__( self, ndxTuple, value ):
44      assert len(ndxTuple) == self.numDims(), "Invalid # of array subscripts."
45      index = self._computeIndex( ndxTuple )
46      assert index is not None, "Array subscript out of range."
47      self._elements[index] = value
48
49    # Computes the 1-D array offset for element (i_1, i_2, ... i_n)
50    # using the equation i_1 * f_1 + i_2 * f_2 + ... + i_n * f_n
51    def _computeIndex( self, idx ):
52      offset = 0
53      for j in range( len(idx) ):
54          # Make sure the index components are within the legal range.
55        if idx[j] < 0 || idx[j] >= self._dims[j] :
56          return None
57        else : # sum the product of i_j * f_j.
58          offset += idx[j] * self._factors[j]
59      return offset
60
61    # Computes the factor values used in the index equation.
62    def _computeFactors( self ):
63      ......
```

Constructor

The constructor, which is shown in lines 4–19, defines three data fields: _dims stores the sizes of the individual dimensions; _factors stores the factor values used in the index equation; and _elements is used to store the 1-D array used as the physical storage for the multi-dimensional array.

The constructor is defined to accept a variable-length argument as required in the ADT definition. The resulting tuple will contain the sizes of the individual dimensions and is assigned to the _dims field. The dimensionality of the array must be verified at the beginning of the constructor as the MultiArray ADT is meant for use with arrays of two dimensions or more.

The elements of the multi-dimensional array will be stored in a 1-D array. The fixed size of the array can be computed as the product of the dimension lengths by traversing over the tuple containing the variable-length argument. During the traversal, the precondition requiring all dimension lengths be greater than zero is also evaluated. The **Array** class defined earlier in the chapter is used to create the storage array.

Finally, a 1-D array is created and assigned to the _factors field. The size of the array is equal to the number of dimensions in the multi-dimensional array. This array will be initialized to the factor values used in Equation 3.4 for computing the element offsets. The actual computation and initialization is performed by the _computeFactors() helper method, which is left as an exercise. A sample instance of the **MultiArray** class is illustrated in Figure 3.9.

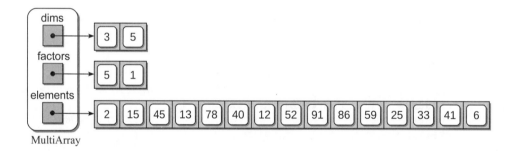

Figure 3.9: A sample **MultiArray** object for the 2-D array from Figure 3.6.

Dimensionality and Lengths

In the multi-dimensional version of the array, there is no single length value. Instead, each dimension of the array has an associated size. Python's len() function cannot be used for this task since we must specify a particular dimension to obtain its size. Instead, the length() method, as shown in lines 26–29 of Listing 3.3, is used. The method first verifies the given dimension index is between 1 and n, which is the legal range specified in the ADT definition. The size of the requested dimension is then returned using the appropriate value from the _dims tuple. The numDims() method returns the dimensionality of the array, which can be obtained from the number of elements in the _dims tuple.

Element Access

Access to individual elements within an n-D array requires an n-tuple or multi-component subscript, one for each dimension. As indicated in Section 2.3.2, when a multi-component subscript is specified (i.e., y = x[i,j]), Python automatically stores the components in a tuple in the order listed within the brackets and passes the tuple to the ndxTuple argument.

The contents of the ndxTuple are passed to the _computeIndex() helper method to compute the index offset within the 1-D storage array. The use of the helper method reduces the need for duplicate code that otherwise would be required in both element access methods. The __setitem__ operator method can be implemented in a similar fashion. The major difference is that this method requires a second argument to receive the value to which an element is set and modifies the indicated element with the new value instead of returning a value.

Computing the Offset

The _computeIndex() helper method, shown in lines 51–59 of Listing 3.3, implements Equation 3.4, which computes the offset within the 1-D storage array. The method must also verify the subscript components are within the legal range of the dimension lengths. If they are valid, the offset is computed and returned; otherwise, None is returned to flag an invalid array index. By returning None from the helper method instead of raising an exception within the method, better information can be provided to the programmer as to the exact element access operation that caused the error.

3.4   Application: Sales Reports

LazyMart, Inc. is a small regional chain department store with locations in several different cities and states. The company maintains a collection of sales records for the various items sold and would like to generate several different types of reports from this data. One such report, for example, is the yearly sales by store, as illustrated in Figure 3.10 on the next page, while others could include total sales across all stores for a specific month or a specific item.

The sales data of the current calendar year for all of LazyMart's stores is maintained as a collection of entries in a text file. For example, the following illustrates the first several lines of a sample sales data text file:

```
8
100
5   11   85    45.23
1    4   26   128.93
1    8   75    39.77
     :
```

```
                    LazyMart Sales Report
                          Store #1

Item#      Jan        Feb        Mar     . . .      Nov        Dec
  1     1237.56    1543.23    1011.00           2101.88    2532.99
  2      829.85     974.18     776.54            802.50     643.21
  3     3100.00    3218.25    3005.34           2870.50    3287.25
  4     1099.45    1573.75    1289.21           1100.00    1498.25


  :         :          :          :     . . .       :          :


 99      704.00     821.30     798.00            532.00     699.50
100      881.25     401.00     375.00            732.00     500.00
        -------    -------    -------           -------    -------
```

Figure 3.10: A sample sales report

where the first line indicates the number of stores; the second line indicates the number of individual items (both of which are integers); and the remaining lines contain the sales data. Each line of the sales data consists of four pieces of information: the store number, the month number, the item number, and the sales amount for the given item in the given store during the given month. For simplicity, the store and item numbers will consist of consecutive integer values in the range $[1 \ldots max]$, where max is the number of stores or items as extracted from the first two lines of the file. The month is indicated by an integer in the range $[1 \ldots 12]$ and the sales amount is a floating-point value.

Data Organization

While some reports, like the student report from Chapter 1, are easy to produce by simply extracting the data and writing it to the report, others require that we first organize the data in some meaningful way in order to extract the information needed. That is definitely the case for this problem, where we may need to produce many different reports from the same collection of data. The ideal structure for storing the sales data is a 3-D array, as shown in Figure 3.11, in which one dimension represents the stores, another represents the items sold in the stores, and the last dimension represents each of the 12 months in the calendar year. The 3-D array can be viewed as a collection of spreadsheets, as illustrated in Figure 3.12.

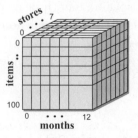

Figure 3.11: The sales data stored in a 3-D array.

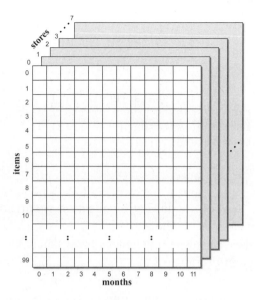

Figure 3.12: The sales data viewed as a collection of spreadsheets.

Each spreadsheet contains the sales for a specific store and is divided into rows and columns where each row contains the sales for one item and the columns contain the sales for each month.

Since the store, item, and month numbers are all composed of consecutive integer values starting from 1, we can easily represent each by a unique index that is one less than the given number. For example, the data for January will be stored in column 0, the data for February will be stored in column 1, and so on. Likewise, the data for item number 1 will be stored in row 0, the data for item number 2 will be stored in row 1, and so on. We leave the actual extraction of the data from a text file as an exercise. But for illustration purposes, we assume this step has been completed resulting in the creation and initialization of the 3-D array as shown here:

```
salesData = MultiArray( 8, 100, 12 )
```

Total Sales by Store

With the data loaded from the file and stored in a 3-D array, we can produce many different types of reports or extract various information from the sales data. For example, suppose we want to determine the total sales for a given store, which includes the sales figures of all items sold in that store for all 12 months. The following function computes this value:

```
# Compute the total sales of all items for all months in a given store.
def totalSalesByStore( salesData, store ):
    # Subtract 1 from the store # since the array indices are 1 less
    # than the given store #.
```

```
    s = store-1
    # Accumulate the total sales for the given store.
    total = 0.0

    # Iterate over item.
    for i in range( salesData.length(2) ):
      # Iterate over each month of the i item.
      for m in range( salesData.length(3) ):
        total += salesData[s, i, m]

    return total
```

Assuming our view of the data as a collection of spreadsheets, this requires traversing over every element in the spreadsheet containing the data for the given `store`.
If `store` equals 1, this is equivalent to processing every element in the spreadsheet
shown at the front of Figure 3.12. Two nested loops are required since we must sum
the values from each row and column contained in the given `store` spreadsheet.
The number of rows (dimension number 2) and columns (dimension number 3) can
be obtained using the `length()` array method.

Total Sales by Month

Next, suppose we want to compute the total sales for a given month that includes
the sales figures of all items in all stores sold during that month. This value can
be computed using the following function:

```
# Compute the total sales of all items in all stores for a given month.
def totalSalesByMonth( salesData, month ):
  # The month number must be offset by 1.
  m = month - 1
  # Accumulate the total sales for the given month.
  total = 0.0

  # Iterate over each store.
  for s in range( salesData.length(1) ):
    # Iterate over each item of the s store.
    for i in range( salesData.length(2) ):
      total += salesData[s, i, m]

  return total
```

This time, the two nested loops have to iterate over every row of every spreadsheet for the single column representing the given month. If we use this function
to compute the total sales for the month of January, the elements of the 3-D array
that will be accessed are shown by the shaded area in Figure 3.13(a).

Total Sales by Item

Another value that we can compute from the sales data in the 3-D array is the
total sales for a given item, which includes the sales figures for all 12 months and
from all 8 stores. This is computed by the following function:

```
# Compute the total sales of a single item in all stores over all months.
def totalSalesByItem( salesData, item ):
  # The item number must be offset by 1.
  m = item - 1

  # Accumulate the total sales for the given month.
  total = 0.0

  # Iterate over each store.
  for s in range( salesData.length(1) ):
    # Iterate over each month of the s store.
    for m in range( salesData.length(3) ):
      total += salesData[s, i, m]

  return total
```

The cells of the array that would be accessed when using this function to compute the total sales for item number 5 are shown by the shaded area in Figure 3.13(b). Remember, the sales for each item are stored in a specific row of the array and the index of that row is one less than the item number since the indices start at 0.

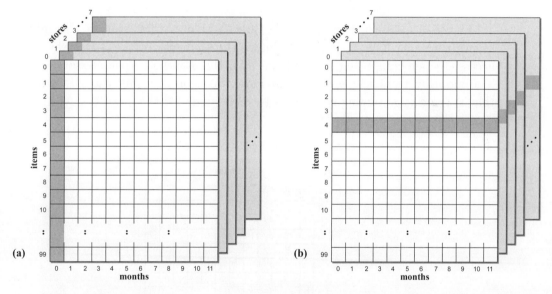

Figure 3.13: The elements of the 3-D array that must be accessed to compute the total sales: (a) for the month of January and (b) for item number 5.

Monthly Sales by Store

Finally, suppose we want to compute the total monthly sales for each of the 12 months at a given store. While the previous examples computed a single value, this task requires the computation of 12 different totals, one for each month. We can store the monthly totals in a 1-D array and return the structure, as is done in the following function:

```
# Compute the total sales per month for a given store. A 1-D array is
# returned that contains the totals for each month.

def totalSalesPerMonth( salesData, store ):
  # The store number must be offset by 1.
  s = store - 1

  # The totals will be returned in a 1-D array.
  totals = Array( 12 )

  # Iterate over the sales of each month.
  for m in range( salesData.length(3) ):
    sum = 0.0

    # Iterate over the sales of each item sold during the m month.
    for i in range( salesData.length(2) ):
      sum += salesData[s, i, m]

    # Store the result in the corresponding month of the totals array.
    totals[m] = sum

  # Return the 1-D array.
  return totals
```

Figure 3.14 illustrates the use of the 1-D array for storing the individual monthly totals. The shaded area shows the elements of the 3-D array that are accessed when computing the total sales for the month of April at store number 1. The monthly total will be stored at index position 3 within the 1-D array since that is the corresponding column in the 3-D array for the month of April.

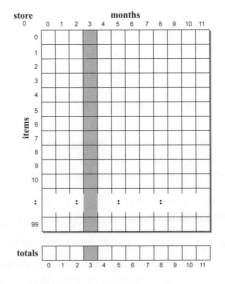

Figure 3.14: The elements the 3-D array that must be accessed to compute the monthly sales for store number 1.

Exercises

3.1 Complete the Set ADT by implementing `intersect()` and `difference()`.

3.2 Modify the `Set()` constructor to accept an optional variable argument to which a collection of initial values can be passed to initialize the set. The prototype for the new constructor should look as follows:

```
def Set( self, *initElements = None )
```

It can then be used as shown here to create a set initialized with the given values:

```
s = Set( 150, 75, 23, 86, 49 )
```

3.3 Add a new operation to the Set ADT to test for a proper subset. Given two sets, A and B, A is a proper subset of B, if A is a subset of B and A does not equal B.

3.4 Add the `_str()` method to the `Set` implementation to allow a user to print the contents of the set. The resulting string should look similar to that of a list, except you are to use curly braces to surround the elements.

3.5 Add Python operator methods to the `Set` class that can be used to perform similar operations to those already defined by named methods:

Operator Method	Current Method
__add__(setB)	union(setB)
__mul__(setB)	interset(setB)
__sub__(setB)	difference(setB)
__lt__(setB)	isSubsetOf(setB)

3.6 Add a new operation `keyArray()` to the `Map` class that returns an array containing all of the keys stored in the map. The array of keys should be in no particular ordering.

3.7 Add Python operators to the `Map` class that can be used to perform similar operations to those already defined by named methods:

Operator Method	Current Method
__setitem__(key, value)	add(key, value)
__getitem__(key)	valueOf(key)

3.8 Design and implement the iterator class `_SetIterator` for use with the Set ADT implemented using a list.

3.9 Design and implement the iterator class _MapIterator for use with the Map ADT implemented using a list.

3.10 Develop the index equation that computes the location within a 1-D array for element (i, j) of a 2-D array stored in column-major order.

3.11 The 2-D array described in Chapter 2 is a simple rectangular structure consisting of the same number of elements in each row. Other layouts are possible and sometimes required by problems in computer science. For example, the lower triangular array shown on the right is organized such that the rows are staggered with each successive row consisting of one more element than the previous row.

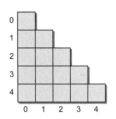

(a) Derive an equation that computes the total number of elements in the lower triangular table for a table of size $m \times n$.

(b) Derive an index equation that maps an element of the lower triangular table onto a one-dimensional array stored in row-major order.

3.12 Complete the implementation of the `MultiArray` class by implementing the helper method `_computeFactors()`.

Programming Projects

3.1 In this chapter, we implemented the Set ADT using a list. Implement the Set ADT using a bag created from the `Bag` class. In your opinion, which is the better implementation? Explain your answer.

3.2 Define a new class named `TriangleArray` to implement the lower triangular table described in Exercise 3.11.

3.3 Given a collection of items stored in a bag, design a linear time algorithm that determines the number of unique items in the collection.

3.4 Write a function that extracts the sales data from a text file and builds the 3-D array used to produce the various reports in Section 3.4. Assume the data file has the format as described in the chapter.

3.5 Write a menu-driven program that uses your function from the previous question to extract the sales data and can produce any of the following reports:

(a) Each of the four types of reports described in the chapter.

(b) The sales for a single store similar to that shown in Section 3.4 with the data sorted by total sales.

(c) The total sales for each store sorted by total sales from largest to smallest.

(d) The total sales for each item sorted by item number.

## CHAPTER 4

Algorithm Analysis

Algorithms are designed to solve problems, but a given problem can have many different solutions. How then are we to determine which solution is the most efficient for a given problem? One approach is to measure the execution time. We can implement the solution by constructing a computer program, using a given programming language. We then execute the program and time it using a wall clock or the computer's internal clock.

The execution time is dependent on several factors. First, the amount of data that must be processed directly affects the execution time. As the data set size increases, so does the execution time. Second, the execution times can vary depending on the type of hardware and the time of day a computer is used. If we use a multi-process, multi-user system to execute the program, the execution of other programs on the same machine can directly affect the execution time of our program. Finally, the choice of programming language and compiler used to implement an algorithm can also influence the execution time. Some compilers are better optimizers than others and some languages produce better optimized code than others. Thus, we need a method to analyze an algorithm's efficiency independent of the implementation details.

4.1 Complexity Analysis

To determine the efficiency of an algorithm, we can examine the solution itself and measure those aspects of the algorithm that most critically affect its execution time. For example, we can count the number of logical comparisons, data interchanges, or arithmetic operations. Consider the following algorithm for computing the sum of each row of an $n \times n$ matrix and an overall sum of the entire matrix:

```
totalSum = 0                          # Version 1
for i in range( n ) :
  rowSum[i] = 0
  for j in range( n ) :
    rowSum[i] = rowSum[i] + matrix[i,j]
    totalSum = totalSum + matrix[i,j]
```

Suppose we want to analyze the algorithm based on the number of additions performed. In this example, there are only two addition operations, making this a simple task. The algorithm contains two loops, one nested inside the other. The inner loop is executed n times and since it contains the two addition operations, there are a total of $2n$ additions performed by the inner loop for each iteration of the outer loop. The outer loop is also performed n times, for a total of $2n^2$ additions.

Can we improve upon this algorithm to reduce the total number of addition operations performed? Consider a new version of the algorithm in which the second addition is moved out of the inner loop and modified to sum the entries in the rowSum array instead of individual elements of the matrix.

```
totalSum = 0                              # Version 2
for i in range( n ) :
  rowSum[i] = 0
  for j in range( n ) :
    rowSum[i] = rowSum[i] + matrix[i,j]
  totalSum = totalSum + rowSum[i]
```

In this version, the inner loop is again executed n times, but this time, it only contains one addition operation. That gives a total of n additions for each iteration of the outer loop, but the outer loop now contains an addition operator of its own. To calculate the total number of additions for this version, we take the n additions performed by the inner loop and add one for the addition performed at the bottom of the outer loop. This gives $n + 1$ additions for each iteration of the outer loop, which is performed n times for a total of $n^2 + n$ additions.

If we compare the two results, it's obvious the number of additions in the second version is less than the first for any n greater than 1. Thus, the second version will execute faster than the first, but the difference in execution times will not be significant. The reason is that both algorithms execute on the same order of magnitude, namely n^2. Thus, as the size of n increases, both algorithms increase at approximately the same rate (though one is slightly better), as illustrated numerically in Table 4.1 and graphically in Figure 4.1.

n	$2n^2$	$n^2 + n$
10	200	110
100	20,000	10,100
1000	2,000,000	1,001,000
10000	200,000,000	100,010,000
100000	20,000,000,000	10,000,100,000

Table 4.1: Growth rate comparisons for different input sizes.

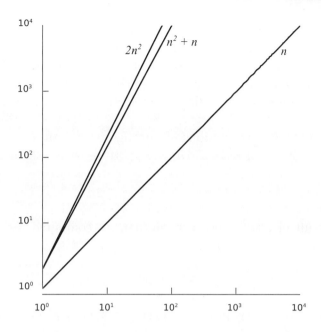

Figure 4.1: Graphical comparison of the growth rates from Table 4.1.

4.1.1 Big-O Notation

Instead of counting the precise number of operations or steps, computer scientists are more interested in classifying an algorithm based on the ***order of magnitude*** as applied to execution time or space requirements. This classification approximates the actual number of required steps for execution or the actual storage requirements in terms of variable-sized data sets. The term ***big-O***, which is derived from the expression "on the order of," is used to specify an algorithm's classification.

Defining Big-O

Assume we have a function $T(n)$ that represents the approximate number of steps required by an algorithm for an input of size n. For the second version of our algorithm in the previous section, this would be written as

$$T_2(n) = n^2 + n$$

Now, suppose there exists a function $f(n)$ defined for the integers $n \geq 0$, such that for some constant c, and some constant m,

$$T(n) \leq cf(n)$$

for all sufficiently large values of $n \geq m$. Then, such an algorithm is said to have a ***time-complexity*** of, or executes on the order of, $f(n)$ relative to the number of operations it requires. In other words, there is a positive integer m and a constant c (***constant of proportionality***) such that for all $n \geq m$, $T(n) \leq cf(n)$. The function $f(n)$ indicates the rate of growth at which the run time of an algorithm increases as the input size, n, increases. To specify the time-complexity of an algorithm, which runs on the order of $f(n)$, we use the notation

$$O(\ f(n)\ )$$

Consider the two versions of our algorithm from earlier. For version one, the time was computed to be $T_1(n) = 2n^2$. If we let $c = 2$, then

$$2n^2 \leq 2n^2$$

for a result of $O(n^2)$. For version two, we computed a time of $T_2(n) = n^2 + n$. Again, if we let $c = 2$, then

$$n^2 + n \leq 2n^2$$

for a result of $O(n^2)$. In this case, the choice of c comes from the observation that when $n \geq 1$, we have $n \leq n^2$ and $n^2 + n \leq n^2 + n^2$, which satisfies the equation in the definition of big-O.

The function $f(n) = n^2$ is not the only choice for satisfying the condition $T(n) \leq cf(n)$. We could have said the algorithms had a run time of $O(n^3)$ or $O(n^4)$ since $2n^2 \leq n^3$ and $2n^2 \leq n^4$ when $n > 1$. The objective, however, is to find a function $f(\cdot)$ that provides the tightest (lowest) **upper bound** or limit for the run time of an algorithm. The big-O notation is intended to indicate an algorithm's efficiency for large values of n. There is usually little difference in the execution times of algorithms when n is small.

Constant of Proportionality

The constant of proportionality is only crucial when two algorithms have the same $f(n)$. It usually makes no difference when comparing algorithms whose growth rates are of different magnitudes. Suppose we have two algorithms, L_1 and L_2, with run times equal to n^2 and $2n$ respectively. L_1 has a time-complexity of $O(n^2)$ with $c = 1$ and L_2 has a time of $O(n)$ with $c = 2$. Even though L_1 has a smaller constant of proportionality, L_1 is still slower and, in fact an order of magnitude slower, for large values of n. Thus, $f(n)$ dominates the expression $cf(n)$ and the run time performance of the algorithm. The differences between the run times of these two algorithms is shown numerically in Table 4.2 and graphically in Figure 4.2.

Constructing T(n)

Instead of counting the number of logical comparisons or arithmetic operations, we evaluate an algorithm by considering every operation. For simplicity, we assume that each basic operation or statement, at the abstract level, takes the same amount of time and, thus, each is assumed to cost **constant time**. The total number of

n	n^2	$2n$
10	100	20
100	10,000	200
1000	1,000,000	2,000
10000	100,000,000	20,000
100000	10,000,000,000	200,000

Table 4.2: Numerical comparison of two sample algorithms.

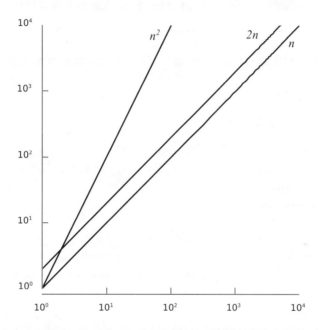

Figure 4.2: Graphical comparison of the data from Table 4.2.

operations required by an algorithm can be computed as a sum of the times required to perform each step:

$$T(n) = f_1(n) + f_2(n) + \ldots + f_k(n).$$

The steps requiring constant time are generally omitted since they eventually become part of the constant of proportionality. Consider Figure 4.3(a), which shows a markup of version one of the algorithm from earlier. The basic operations are marked with a constant time while the loops are marked with the appropriate total number of iterations. Figure 4.3(b) shows the same algorithm but with the constant steps omitted since these operations are independent of the data set size.

```
    1           totalSum = 0

          1  for i in range( n ) :
          1     rowSum[i] = 0
(a)   n
          1     for j in range( n ) :
      n   1         rowSum[i] = rowSum[i] + matrix[i,j]
          1         totalSum = totalSum + matrix[i,j]
```

```
          for i in range( n ) :
             . . .
(b)      n
      n   for j in range( n ) :
             . . .
```

Figure 4.3: Markup for version one of the matrix summing algorithm: (a) shows all operations marked with the appropriate time and (b) shows only the non-constant time steps.

Choosing the Function

The function $f(n)$ used to categorize a particular algorithm is chosen to be the **dominant term** within $T(n)$. That is, the term that is so large for big values of n, that we can ignore the other terms when computing a big-O value. For example, in the expression

$$n^2 + log_2 n + 3n$$

the term n^2 dominates the other terms since for $n \geq 3$, we have

$$n^2 + \log_2 n + 3n \quad \leq \quad n^2 + n^2 + n^2$$
$$n^2 + \log_2 n + 3n \quad \leq \quad 3n^2$$

which leads to a time-complexity of $O(n^2)$. Now, consider the function $T(n) = 2n^2 + 15n + 500$ and assume it is the polynomial that represents the exact number of instructions required to execute some algorithm. For small values of n (less than 16), the constant value 500 dominates the function, but what happens as n gets larger, say $100,000$? The term n^2 becomes the dominant term, with the other two becoming less significant in computing the final result.

Classes of Algorithms

We will work with many different algorithms in this text, but most will have a time-complexity selected from among a common set of functions, which are listed in Table 4.3 and illustrated graphically in Figure 4.4.

Algorithms can be classified based on their big-O function. The various classes are commonly named based upon the dominant term. A **logarithmic** algorithm is

$f(\cdot)$	Common Name
1	constant
$\log n$	logarithmic
n	linear
$n \log n$	log linear
n^2	quadratic
n^3	cubic
a^n	exponential

Table 4.3: Common big-O functions listed from smallest to largest order of magnitude.

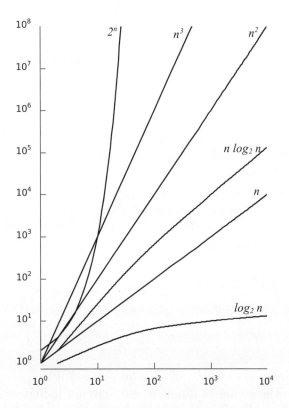

Figure 4.4: Growth rates of the common time-complexity functions.

any algorithm whose time-complexity is $O(\log_a n)$. These algorithms are generally very efficient since $\log_a n$ will increase more slowly than n. For many problems encountered in computer science a will typically equal 2 and thus we use the notation $\log n$ to imply $\log_2 n$. Logarithms of other bases will be explicitly stated. *Polynomial* algorithms with an efficiency expressed as a polynomial of the form

$$a_m n^m + a_{m-1} n^{m-1} + \ldots + a_2 n^2 + a_1 n + a_0$$

are characterized by a time-complexity of $O(n^m)$ since the dominant term is the highest power of n. The most common polynomial algorithms are **_linear_** $(m = 1)$, **_quadratic_** $(m = 2)$, and **_cubic_** $(m = 3)$. An algorithm whose efficiency is characterized by a dominant term in the form a^n is called **_exponential_**. Exponential algorithms are among the worst algorithms in terms of time-complexity.

4.1.2 Evaluating Python Code

As indicated earlier, when evaluating the time complexity of an algorithm or code segment, we assume that basic operations only require constant time. But what exactly is a basic operation? The **_basic operations_** include statements and function calls whose execution time does not depend on the specific values of the data that is used or manipulated by the given instruction. For example, the assignment statement

```
x = 5
```

is a basic instruction since the time required to assign a reference to the given variable is independent of the value or type of object specified on the righthand side of the = sign. The evaluation of arithmetic and logical expressions

```
y = x
z = x + y * 6
done = x > 0 and x < 100
```

are basic instructions, again since they require the same number of steps to perform the given operations regardless of the values of their operands. The subscript operator, when used with Python's sequence types (strings, tuples, and lists) is also a basic instruction.

Linear Time Examples

Now, consider the following assignment statement:

```
y = ex1(n)
```

An assignment statement only requires constant time, but that is the time required to perform the actual assignment and does not include the time required to execute any function calls used on the righthand side of the assignment statement.

To determine the run time of the previous statement, we must know the cost of the function call `ex1(n)`. The time required by a function call is the time it takes to execute the given function. For example, consider the `ex1()` function, which computes the sum of the integer values in the range $[0 \ldots n]$:

```python
def ex1( n ):
    total = 0
    for i in range( n ) :
        total += i
    return total
```

The time required to execute a loop depends on the number of iterations performed and the time needed to execute the loop body during each iteration. In this case, the loop will be executed n times and the loop body only requires constant time since it contains a single basic instruction. (Note that the underlying mechanism of the `for` loop and the `range()` function are both $O(1)$.) We can compute the time required by the loop as $T(n) = n * 1$ for a result of $O(n)$.

But what about the other statements in the function? The first line of the function and the `return` statement only require constant time. Remember, it's common to omit the steps that only require constant time and instead focus on the critical operations, those that contribute to the overall time. In most instances, this means we can limit our evaluation to repetition and selection statements and function and method calls since those have the greatest impact on the overall time of an algorithm. Since the loop is the only non-constant step, the function `ex1()` has a run time of $O(n)$. That means the statement `y = ex1(n)` from earlier requires linear time. Next, consider the following function, which includes two `for` loops:

```python
def ex2( n ):
    count = 0
    for i in range( n ) :
        count += 1
    for j in range( n ) :
        count += 1
    return count
```

To evaluate the function, we have to determine the time required by each loop. The two loops each require $O(n)$ time as they are just like the loop in function `ex1()` earlier. If we combine the times, it yields $T(n) = n + n$ for a result of $O(n)$.

Quadratic Time Examples

When presented with nested loops, such as in the following, the time required by the inner loop impacts the time of the outer loop.

```python
def ex3( n ):
    count = 0
    for i in range( n ) :
        for j in range( n ) :
            count += 1
    return count
```

Both loops will be executed n, but since the inner loop is nested inside the outer loop, the total time required by the outer loop will be $T(n) = n * n$, resulting in a time of $O(n^2)$ for the ex3() function. Not all nested loops result in a quadratic time. Consider the following function:

```python
def ex4( n ):
  count = 0
  for i in range( n ) :
    for j in range( 25 ) :
      count += 1
  return count
```

which has a time-complexity of $O(n)$. The function contains a nested loop, but the inner loop executes independent of the size variable n. Since the inner loop executes a constant number of times, it is a constant time operation. The outer loop executes n times, resulting in a linear run time. The next example presents a special case of nested loops:

```python
def ex5( n ):
  count = 0
  for i in range( n ) :
    for j in range( i+1 ) :
      count += 1
  return count
```

How many times does the inner loop execute? It depends on the current iteration of the outer loop. On the first iteration of the outer loop, the inner loop will execute one time; on the second iteration, it executes two times; on the third iteration, it executes three times, and so on until the last iteration when the inner loop will execute n times. The time required to execute the outer loop will be the number of times the increment statement count += 1 is executed. Since the inner loop varies from 1 to n iterations by increments of 1, the total number of times the increment statement will be executed is equal to the sum of the first n positive integers:

$$T(n) = \frac{n(n+1)}{2} = \frac{n^2 + n}{2}$$

which results in a quadratic time of $O(n^2)$.

Logarithmic Time Examples

The next example contains a single loop, but notice the change to the modification step. Instead of incrementing (or decrementing) by one, it cuts the loop variable in half each time through the loop.

```python
def ex6( n ):
  count = 0
  i = n
  while i >= 1 :
```

```
        count += 1
        i = i // 2
    return count
```

To determine the run time of this function, we have to determine the number of loop iterations just like we did with the earlier examples. Since the loop variable is cut in half each time, this will be less than n. For example, if n equals 16, variable i will contain the following five values during subsequent iterations (16, 8, 4, 2, 1).

Given a small number, it's easy to determine the number of loop iterations. But how do we compute the number of iterations for any given value of n? When the size of the input is reduced by half in each subsequent iteration, the number of iterations required to reach a size of one will be equal to

$$\lfloor \log_2 n \rfloor + 1$$

or the largest integer less than $\log_2 n$, plus 1. In our example of $n = 16$, there are $\log_2 16 + 1$, or four iterations. The logarithm to base a of a number n, which is normally written as $y = log_a n$, is the power to which a must be raised to equal n, $n = a^y$. Thus, function ex6() requires $O(\log n)$ time. Since many problems in computer science that repeatedly reduce the input size do so by half, it's not uncommon to use $\log n$ to imply $\log_2 n$ when specifying the run time of an algorithm.

Finally, consider the following definition of function ex7(), which calls ex6() from within a loop. Since the loop is executed n times and function ex6() requires logarithmic time, ex7() will have a run time of $O(n \log n)$.

```
def ex7( n ):
    count = 0
    for i in range( n )
        count += ex6( n )
    return count
```

Different Cases

Some algorithms can have run times that are different orders of magnitude for different sets of inputs of the same size. These algorithms can be evaluated for their best, worst, and average cases. Algorithms that have different cases can typically be identified by the inclusion of an event-controlled loop or a conditional statement. Consider the following example, which traverses a list containing integer values to find the position of the first negative value. Note that for this problem, the input is the collection of n values contained in the list.

```
def findNeg( intList ):
    n = len(intList)
    for i in range( n ) :
        if intList[i] < 0 :
            return i
    return None
```

At first glance, it appears the loop will execute n times, where n is the size of the list. But notice the **return** statement inside the loop, which can cause it to terminate early. If the list does not contain a negative value,

```
L = [ 72, 4, 90, 56, 12, 67, 43, 17, 2, 86, 33 ]
p = findNeg( L )
```

the **return** statement inside the loop will not be executed and the loop will terminate in the normal fashion from having traversed all n times. In this case, the function requires $O(n)$ time. This is known as the ***worst case*** since the function must examine every value in the list requiring the most number of steps. Now consider the case where the list contains a negative value in the first element:

```
L = [ -12, 50, 4, 67, 39, 22, 43, 2, 17, 28 ]
p = findNeg( L )
```

There will only be one iteration of the loop since the test of the condition by the **if** statement will be true the first time through and the **return** statement inside the loop will be executed. In this case, the **findNeg()** function only requires $O(1)$ time. This is known as the ***best case*** since the function only has to examine the first value in the list requiring the least number of steps.

The ***average case*** is evaluated for an expected data set or how we expect the algorithm to perform on average. For the **findNeg()** function, we would expect the search to iterate halfway through the list before finding the first negative value, which on average requires $n/2$ iterations. The average case is more difficult to evaluate because it's not always readily apparent what constitutes the average case for a particular problem.

In general, we are more interested in the worst case time-complexity of an algorithm as it provides an upper bound over all possible inputs. In addition, we can compare the worst case run times of different implementations of an algorithm to determine which is the most efficient for any input.

4.2   Evaluating the Python List

We defined several abstract data types for storing and using collections of data in the previous chapters. The next logical step is to analyze the operations of the various ADTs to determine their efficiency. The result of this analysis depends on the efficiency of the Python list since it was the primary data structure used to implement many of the earlier abstract data types.

The implementation details of the list were discussed in Chapter 2. In this section, we use those details and evaluate the efficiency of some of the more common operations. A summary of the worst case run times are shown in Table 4.4.

List Operation	Worst Case
v = list()	$O(1)$
v = [0] * n	$O(n)$
v[i] = x	$O(1)$
v.append(x)	$O(n)$
v.extend(w)	$O(n)$
v.insert(x)	$O(n)$
v.pop()	$O(n)$
traversal	$O(n)$

Table 4.4: Worst case time-complexities for the more common list operations.

List Traversal

A sequence traversal accesses the individual items, one after the other, in order to perform some operation on every item. Python provides the built-in iteration for the list structure, which accesses the items in sequential order starting with the first item. Consider the following code segment, which iterates over and computes the sum of the integer values in a list:

```
sum = 0
for value in valueList :
  sum = sum + value
```

To determine the order of complexity for this simple algorithm, we must first look at the internal implementation of the traversal. Iteration over the contiguous elements of a 1-D array, which is used to store the elements of a list, requires a count-controlled loop with an index variable whose value ranges over the indices of the subarray. The list iteration above is equivalent to the following:

```
sum = 0
for i in range( len(valueList) ) :
  sum = sum + valueList[i]
```

Assuming the sequence contains n items, it's obvious the loop performs n iterations. Since all of the operations within the loop only require constant time, including the element access operation, a complete list traversal requires $O(n)$ time. Note, this time establishes a minimum required for a complete list traversal. It can actually be higher if any operations performed during each iteration are worse than constant time, unlike this example.

List Allocation

Creating a list, like the creation of any object, is considered an operation whose time-complexity can be analyzed. There are two techniques commonly used to create a list:

```
temp = list()
valueList = [ 0 ] * n
```

The first example creates an empty list, which can be accomplished in constant time. The second creates a list containing n elements, with each element initialized to 0. The actual allocation of the n elements can be done in constant time, but the initialization of the individual elements requires a list traversal. Since there are n elements and a traversal requires linear time, the allocation of a vector with n elements requires $O(n)$ time.

Appending to a List

The append() operation adds a new item to the end of the sequence. If the underlying array used to implement the list has available capacity to add the new item, the operation has a best case time of $O(1)$ since it only requires a single element access. In the worst case, there are no available slots and the array has to be expanded using the steps described in Section 2.2. Creating the new larger array and destroying the old array can each be done in $O(1)$ time. To copy the contents of the old array to the new larger array, the items have to be copied element by element, which requires $O(n)$ time. Combining the times from the three steps yields a time of $T(n) = 1 + 1 + n$ and a worst case time of $O(n)$.

Extending a List

The extend() operation adds the entire contents of a source list to the end of the destination list. This operation involves two lists, each of which have their own collection of items that may be of different lengths. To simplify the analysis, however, we can assume both lists contain n items. When the destination list has sufficient capacity to store the new items, the entire contents of the source list can be copied in $O(n)$ time. But if there is not sufficient capacity, the underlying array of the destination list has to be expanded to make room for the new items. This expansion requires $O(n)$ time since there are currently n items in the destination list. After the expansion, the n items in the source list are copied to the expanded array, which also requires $O(n)$ time. Thus, in the worst case the extend operation requires $T(n) = n + n = 2n$ or $O(n)$ time.

Inserting and Removing Items

Inserting a new item into a list is very similar to appending an item except the new item can be placed anywhere within the list, possibly requiring a shift in elements. An item can be removed from any element within a list, which may also involve shifting elements. Both of these operations require linear time in the worst case, the proof of which is left as an exercise.

4.3 Amortized Cost

The `append()` operation of the list structure introduces a special case in algorithm analysis. The time required depends on the available capacity of the underlying array used to implement the list. If there are available slots, a value can be appended to the list in constant time. If the array has to be expanded to make room for the new value, however, the append operation takes linear time. When the array is expanded, extra capacity is added that can be used to add more items without having to immediately expand the array. Thus, the number of times the `append()` operation actually requires linear time in a sequence of n operations depends on the strategy used to expand the underlying array. Consider the problem in which a sequence of n append operations are performed on an initially empty list, where n is a power of 2.

```
L = list()
for i in range( 1, n+1 ) :
  L.append( i )
```

Suppose the array is doubled in capacity each time it has to be expanded and assume the size of the underlying array for an empty list has the capacity for a single item. We can tally or compute the total running time for this problem by considering the time required for each individual append operation. This approach is known as the ***aggregate method*** since it computes the total from the individual operations.

Table 4.5 illustrates the aggregate method when applied to a sequence of 16 append operations. s_i represents the time required to physically store the ith value when there is an available slot in the array or immediately after the array has been expanded. Storing an item into an array element is a constant time operation. e_i represents the time required to expand the array when it does not contain available capacity to store the item. Based on our assumptions related to the size of the array, an expansion only occurs when $i - 1$ is a power of 2 and the time incurred is based on the current size of the array $(i - 1)$. While every append operation entails a storage cost, relatively few require an expansion cost. Note that as the size of n increases, the distance between append operations requiring an expansion also increases.

Based on the tabulated results in Table 4.5, the total time required to perform a sequence of 16 append operations on an initially empty list is 31, or just under $2n$. This results from a total storage cost (s_i) of 16 and a total expansion cost (e_i) of 15. It can be shown that for any n, the sum of the storage and expansion costs, $s_i + e_i$, will never be more than $T(n) = 2n$. Since there are relatively few expansion operations, the expansion cost can be distributed across the sequence of operations, resulting in an ***amortized cost*** of $T(n) = 2n/n$ or $O(1)$ for the append operation.

Amortized analysis is the process of computing the time-complexity for a sequence of operations by computing the average cost over the entire sequence. For this technique to be applied, the cost per operation must be known and it must

i	s_i	e_i	Size	List Contents
1	1	-	1	1
2	1	1	2	1 2
3	1	2	4	1 2 3
4	1	-	4	1 2 3 4
5	1	4	8	1 2 3 4 5
6	1	-	8	1 2 3 4 5 6
7	1	-	8	1 2 3 4 5 6 7
8	1	-	8	1 2 3 4 5 6 7 8
9	1	8	16	1 2 3 4 5 6 7 8 9
10	1	-	16	1 2 3 4 5 6 7 8 9 10
11	1	-	16	1 2 3 4 5 6 7 8 9 10 11
12	1	-	16	1 2 3 4 5 6 7 8 9 10 11 12
13	1	-	16	1 2 3 4 5 6 7 8 9 10 11 12 13
14	1	-	16	1 2 3 4 5 6 7 8 9 10 11 12 13 14
15	1	-	16	1 2 3 4 5 6 7 8 9 10 11 12 13 14 15
16	1	-	16	1 2 3 4 5 6 7 8 9 10 11 12 13 14 15 16

Table 4.5: Using the aggregate method to compute the total run time for a sequence of 16 append operations.

vary in which many of the operations in the sequence contribute little cost and only a few operations contribute a high cost to the overall time. This is exactly the case with the `append()` method. In a long sequence of append operations, only a few instances require $O(n)$, while many of them are $O(1)$. The amortized cost can only be used for a long sequence of append operations. If an algorithm used a single append operation, the cost for that one operation is still $O(n)$ in the worst case since we do not know if that's the instance that causes the underlying array to be expanded.

CAUTION

⚠ Amortized Cost Is Not Average Case Time. Do not confuse amortized cost with that of average case time. In average case analysis, the evaluation is done by computing an average over all possible inputs and sometimes requires the use of statistics. Amortized analysis computes an average cost over a sequence of operations in which many of those operations are "cheap" and relatively few are "expensive" in terms of contributing to the overall time.

4.4 Evaluating the Set ADT

We can use complexity analysis to determine the efficiency of the Set ADT operations as implemented in Section 3.1. For convenience, the relevant portions of that implementation are shown again in Listing 4.1 on the next page. The evaluation is quite simple since the ADT was implemented using the list and we just evaluated the methods for that structure. Table 4.6 provides a summary of the worst case time-complexities for those operations implemented earlier in the text.

Operation	Worst Case
s = Set()	$O(1)$
len(s)	$O(1)$
x in s	$O(n)$
s.add(x)	$O(n)$
s.isSubsetOf(t)	$O(n^2)$
s == t	$O(n^2)$
s.union(t)	$O(n^2)$
traversal	$O(n)$

Table 4.6: Time-complexities for the Set ADT implementation using an unsorted list.

Simple Operations

Evaluating the constructor and length operation is straightforward as they simply call the corresponding list operation. The __contains__ method, which determines if an element is contained in the set, uses the in operator to perform a linear search over the elements stored in the underlying list. The search operation, which requires $O(n)$ time, will be presented in the next section and we postpone its analysis until that time. The add() method also requires $O(n)$ time in the worst case since it uses the in operator to determine if the element is unique and the append() method to add the unique item to the underlying list, both of which require linear time in the worst case.

Operations of Two Sets

The remaining methods of the Set class involve the use of two sets, which we label A and B, where A is the self set and B is the argument passed to the given method. To simplify the analysis, we assume each set contains n elements. A more complete analysis would involve the use of two variables, one for the size of each set. But the analysis of this more specific case is sufficient for our purposes.

The isSubsetOf() method determines if A is a subset of B. It iterates over the n elements of set A, during which the in operator is used to determine if the

| Listing 4.1 | A partial listing of the `linearset.py` module from Listing 3.1. |

```
1  class Set :
2    def __init__( self ):
3      self._theElements = list()
4
5    def __len__( self ):
6      return len( self._theElements )
7
8    def __contains__( self, element ):
9      return element in self._theElements
10
11   def add( self, element ):
12     if element not in self :
13       self._theElements.append( element )
14
15   def remove( self, element ):
16     assert element in self, "The element must be in the set."
17     self._theElements.remove( item )
18
19   def __eq__( self, setB ):
20     if len( self ) != len( setB ) :
21       return False
22     else :
23       return self.isSubsetOf( setB )
24
25   def isSubsetOf( self, setB ):
26     for element in self :
27       if element not in setB :
28         return False
29     return True
30
31   def union( self, setB ):
32     newSet = Set()
33     newSet._theElements.extend( self._theElements )
34     for element in setB :
35       if element not in self :
36         newSet._theElements.append( element )
37     return newSet
```

given element is a member of set B. Since there are n repetitions of the loop and each use of the `in` operator requires $O(n)$ time, the `isSubsetOf()` method has a quadratic run time of $O(n^2)$. The set equality operation is also $O(n^2)$ since it calls `isSubsetOf()` after determining the two sets are of equal size.

Set Union Operation

The set `union()` operation creates a new set, C, that contains all of the unique elements from both sets A and B. It requires three steps. The first step creates the new set C, which can be done in constant time. The second step fills set C with the elements from set A, which requires $O(n)$ time since the `extend()` list method is used to add the elements to C. The last step iterates over the elements of set B during which the `in` operator is used to determine if the given element is a member of set A. If the element is not a member of set A, it's added to set C by applying the `append()` list method. We know from earlier the linear search performed by the `in` operator requires $O(n)$ time and we can use the $O(1)$ amortized cost of the `append()` method since it is applied in sequence. Given that the loop is performed n times and each iteration requires $n + 1$ time, this step requires $O(n^2)$ time. Combining the times for the three steps yields a worst case time of $O(n^2)$.

4.5 Application: The Sparse Matrix

A matrix containing a large number of zero elements is called a ***sparse matrix***. Sparse matrices are very common in scientific applications, especially those dealing with systems of linear equations. A sparse matrix is formally defined to be an $m \times n$ matrix that contains k non-zero elements such that $k \ll m \times n$. The 2-D array data structure used to implement the Matrix ADT in Chapter 2 works well for general matrices. But when used to store huge sparse matrices, large amounts of memory can be wasted and the operations can be inefficient since the zero elements are also stored in the 2-D array.

Consider the sample 5×8 sparse matrix in Figure 4.5. Is there a different structure or organization we can use to store the elements of a sparse matrix that does not waste space? One approach is to organize and store the non-zero elements of the matrix within a single list instead of a 2-D array.

$$\begin{bmatrix} \cdot & 3 & \cdot & \cdot & 8 & \cdot & \cdot & \cdot \\ 2 & \cdot & \cdot & 1 & \cdot & \cdot & 5 & \cdot \\ \cdot & \cdot & 9 & \cdot & \cdot & 2 & \cdot & \cdot \\ \cdot & 7 & \cdot & \cdot & \cdot & \cdot & \cdot & 3 \\ \cdot & \cdot & \cdot & \cdot & 4 & \cdot & \cdot & \cdot \end{bmatrix}$$

Figure 4.5: A sample sparse matrix with zero elements indicated with dots.

4.5.1 List-Based Implementation

In this section, we define and implement a class for storing and working with sparse matrices in which the non-zero elements are stored in a list. The operations of a sparse matrix are the same as those for a general matrix and many of them can be implemented in a similar fashion as was done for the `Matrix` class in Listing 2.3. This would be sufficient if our only objective was to reduce the storage cost, but we can take advantage of only storing the non-zero elements to improve the efficiency of several of the sparse matrix operations. The implementation of the `SparseMatrix` class is provided in Listing 4.2 on the next page. Note the use of the new class name to distinguish this version from the original Matrix ADT and to indicate it is meant for use with sparse matrices. A sample instance of the class that corresponds to the sparse matrix from Figure 4.5 is illustrated in Figure 4.6.

Listing 4.2   The `sparsematrix.py` module.

```
1   # Implementation of the Sparse Matrix ADT using a list.
2
3   class SparseMatrix :
4     # Create a sparse matrix of size numRows x numCols initialized to 0.
5     def __init__( self, numRows, numCols ):
6       self._numRows = numRows
7       self._numCols = numCols
8       self._elementList = list()
9
10    # Return the number of rows in the matrix.
11    def numRows( self ):
12      return self._numRows
13
14    # Return the number of columns in the matrix.
15    def numCols( self ):
16      return self._numCols
17
18    # Return the value of element (i, j): x[i,j]
19    def __getitem__( self, ndxTuple ):
20      ......
21
22    # Set the value of element (i,j) to the value s: x[i,j] = s
23    def __setitem__( self, ndxTuple, scalar ):
24      ndx = self._findPosition( ndxTuple[0], ndxTuple[1] )
25      if ndx is not None :   # if the element is found in the list.
26        if scalar != 0.0 :
27          self._elementList[ndx].value = scalar
28        else :
29          self._elementList.pop( ndx )
30      else :            # if the element is zero and not in the list.
31        if scalar != 0.0 :
32          element = _MatrixElement( ndxTuple[0], ndxTuple[1], scalar )
33          self._elementList.append( element )
34
35    # Scale the matrix by the given scalar.
36    def scaleBy( self, scalar ):
37      for element in self._elementList :
38        element.value *= scalar
39
40    # The additional methods should be placed here.....
41    # def __add__( self, rhsMatrix ):
42    # def __sub__( self, rhsMatrix ):
43    # def __mul__( self, rhsMatrix ):
44
45    # Helper method used to find a specific matrix element (row,col) in the
46    # list of non-zero entries. None is returned if the element is not found.
47    def _findPosition( self, row, col ):
48      n = len( self._elementList )
49      for i in range( n ) :
50        if row == self._elementList[i].row and \
51           col == self._elementList[i].col:
52          return i        # return the index of the element if found.
53      return None       # return None when the element is zero.
54
```

```
55  # Storage class for holding the non-zero matrix elements.
56  class _MatrixElement:
57    def __init__( self, row, col, value ):
58      self.row = row
59      self.col = col
60      self.value = value
```

Constructor

The constructor defines three attributes for storing the data related to the sparse matrix. The _elementList field stores _MatrixElement objects representing the non-zero elements. Instances of the storage class contain not only the value for a specific element but also the row and column indices indicating its location within the matrix. The _numRows and _numCols fields are used to store the dimensions of the matrix. This information cannot be obtained from the element list as was done with the Array2D used in the implementation of the Matrix ADT in Chapter 2.

Helper Method

Since the element list only contains the non-zero entries, accessing an individual element is no longer as simple as directly referencing an element of the rectangular grid. Instead, we must search through the list to locate a specific non-zero element. The helper method _findPosition() performs this linear search by iterating through the element list looking for an entry with the given row and column indices. If found, it returns the list index of the cell containing the element; otherwise, None is returned to indicate the absence of the element.

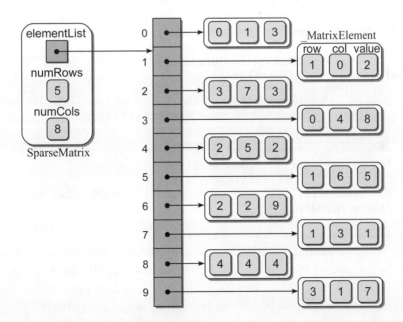

Figure 4.6: A list of _MatrixElement objects representing a sparse matrix.

Modifying an Element

The __setitem__ method for the SparseMatrix class is a bit more involved than that for the Matrix class. The value of an element cannot be directly set as was done when using the 2-D array. Instead, there are four possible conditions:

1. The element is in the list (and thus non-zero) and the new value is non-zero.

2. The element is in the list, but the new value is zero, turning the element into a zero element.

3. The element is not currently in the list and the new value is non-zero.

4. The element is not currently in the list, and the new value is zero.

The step in implementing the __setitem__ method, as shown in lines 23–33 of Listing 4.2, is to determine if the element is in the list using the _findPosition() helper method. If the entry is in the list, we either change the corresponding element to the new value if it is non-zero or we remove the entry from the list when the new value is zero. On the other hand, if there is no entry for the given element, then a new _MatrixElement object must be created and appended to the list. Of course, this is only done if the new value is non-zero.

Matrix Scaling

Scaling a matrix requires multiplying each element of the matrix by a given scale factor. Since the zero elements of the matrix are not affected by the scale factor, the implementation of this operation for the sparse matrix is as simple as traversing the list of _MatrixElement objects and scaling the corresponding value.

Matrix Addition

In the add() method of the Matrix class implemented in Chapter 2, we iterated over the 2-D array and added the values, element by element, and stored the results in the corresponding element of the new matrix. We could use the same loop structure shown here for the SparseMatrix class:

```
# Add the corresponding elements in the two matrices.
for r in range( self.numRows() ) :
  for c in range( self.numCols() ) :
    newMatrix[ r, c ] = self[ r, c ] + rhsMatrix[ r, c ]
return newMatrix
```

Given a matrix of size $n \times n$, this implementation of the add operation requires $O(n^2)$ time. If the sparse matrix contains a significant number of zero elements, this can be inefficient. Instead, only the non-zero elements contained in the two sparse matrices must be considered when adding to matrices. The nested loops can be replaced with two separate loops to reduce the number of required iterations. The new solution for sparse matrix addition requires four steps:

1. Verify the size of the two matrices to ensure they are the same as required by matrix addition.

2. Create a new `SparseMatrix` object with the same number of rows and columns as the other two.

3. Duplicate the elements of the `self` matrix and store them in the new matrix.

4. Iterate over the element list of the righthand side matrix (`rhsMatrix`) to add the non-zero values to the corresponding elements in the new matrix.

The implementation of the add operation is provided in Listing 4.3. The first two steps of the add operation are straightforward. The third step of copying the elements of the `self` matrix to the new matrix requires a list duplication, which is handled by the first loop. The second loop handles the fourth step outlined above by iterating over the list of `_MatrixElement` objects in the `rhsMatrix` and adding their values to the corresponding values in the new sparse matrix. Note the use of the `__getitem__` and `__setitem__` methods in the second loop. This is necessary since the two methods properly manage any zero elements that may currently exist in the `newMatrix` or that may result after adding corresponding elements.

Listing 4.3   Implementation of the `SparseMatrix` add operation.

```
1  class SparseMatrix :
2  # ...
3    def __add__( self, rhsMatrix ):
4      assert rhsMatrix.numRows() == self.numRows() and \
5             rhsMatrix.numCols() == self.numCols(), \
6        "Matrix sizes not compatible for the add operation."
7
8      # Create the new matrix.
9      newMatrix = SparseMatrix( self.numRows(), self.numCols() )
10
11     # Duplicate the lhs matrix. The elements are mutable, thus we must
12     # create new objects and not simply copy the references.
13     for element in self._elementList :
14       dupElement = _MatrixElement(element.row, element.col, element.value)
15       newMatrix._elementList.append( dupElement )
16
17     # Iterate through each non-zero element of the rhsMatrix.
18     for element in rhsMatrix._elementList :
19       # Get the value of the corresponding element in the new matrix.
20       value = newMatrix[ element.row, element.col ]
21       value += element.value
22       # Store the new value back to the new matrix.
23       newMatrix[ element.row, element.col ] = value
24
25     # Return the new matrix.
26     return newMatrix
```

4.5.2 Efficiency Analysis

To evaluate the various operations of the sparse matrix, we can assume a square $n \times n$ matrix since this would be the worst possible case. We begin with the _findPosition() helper method, which performs a sequential search over the list of non-zero entries. The worst case occurs when every item in the list is examined. But how many iterations does that require? It depends on the size of the element list. From the definition of a sparse matrix, we know it contains k non-zero elements such that $k \ll n^2$. Thus, the worst case run time of the helper method is $O(k)$.

The __setitem__ method calls _findPosition(), which requires k time. It then changes the value of the target entry, which is a constant time operation, or either removes an entry from the list or appends a new entry. The list operations require k time in the worst case, resulting in an overall time of $O(k)$ for the set operation. The __getitem__ method can be evaluated in the same fashion and also has a worst case time of $O(k)$.

To evaluate the operations that manipulate two SparseMatrix objects, we can specify that both matrices are of the same size or that k will represent the size of the larger of the two lists. Computing the worst case time for the new add() method requires that we first determine the complexity of the individual steps.

- The size verification and new matrix creation are constant steps.

- To duplicate the entries of the lefthand side sparse matrix requires k time since append() has an amortized cost of $O(1)$.

- The second loop iterates over the element list of the righthand side matrix, which we have assumed also contains k elements. Since the get and set element operations used within the loop each require k time in the worst case, the loop requires $2k * k$ or $2k^2$ time.

Combining this with the time for the previous steps, the add operation is $O(k^2)$ in the worst case. Is this time better than that for the add operation from the Matrix class implemented as a 2-D array? That depends on the size of k. If there were no zero elements in either matrix, then $k = n^2$, which results in a worst case time of $O(n^4)$. Remember, however, this implementation is meant to be used with a sparse matrix in which $k \ll m \times n$. In addition, the add operation only depends on the size of the element list, k. Increasing the value of m or n does not increase the size of k. For the analysis of this algorithm, m and n simply provide a maximum value for k and are not variables in the equation.

The use of a list as the underlying data structure to store the non-zero elements of a sparse matrix is a much better implementation than the use of a 2-D array as it can save significant storage space for large matrices. On the other hand, it introduces element access operations that are more inefficient than when using the 2-D array. Table 4.7 provides a comparison of the worst case time-complexities for several of the operations of the Matrix class using a 2-D array and the SparseMatrix class using a list. In later chapters, we will further explore the Sparse Matrix ADT and attempt to improve the time-complexities of the various operations.

Operation	Matrix	Sparse Matrix
constructor	$O(n^2)$	$O(1)$
s.numRows()	$O(1)$	$O(1)$
s.numCols()	$O(1)$	$O(1)$
s.scaleBy(x)	$O(n^2)$	$O(k)$
x = s[i,j]	$O(1)$	$O(k)$
s[i,j] = x	$O(1)$	$O(k)$
r = s + t	$O(n^2)$	$O(k^2)$

Table 4.7: Comparison of the worst case time-complexities for the `Matrix` class implemented using a 2-D array and the `SparseMatrix` class using a list.

Exercises

4.1 Arrange the following expressions from slowest to fastest growth rate.

$$n \log_2 n \qquad 4^n \qquad k \log_2 n \qquad 5n^2 \qquad 40 \log_2 n \qquad \log_4 n \qquad 12n^6$$

4.2 Determine the $O(\cdot)$ for each of the following functions, which represent the number of steps required for some algorithm.

(a) $T(n) = n^2 + 400n + 5$

(b) $T(n) = 67n + 3n$

(c) $T(n) = 2n + 5n \log n + 100$

(d) $T(n) = \log n + 2n^2 + 55$

(e) $T(n) = 3(2^n) + n^8 + 1024$

(f) $T(n,k) = kn + \log k$

(g) $T(n,k) = 9n + k \log n + 1000$

4.3 What is the time-complexity of the `printCalendar()` function implemented in Exercise 1.3?

4.4 Determine the $O(\cdot)$ for the following `Set` operations implemented in Chapter 1: `difference()`, `intersect()`, and `remove()`.

4.5 What is the time-complexity of the proper subset test operation implemented in Exercise 3.3?

4.6 Prove or show why the worst case time-complexity for the `insert()` and `remove()` list operations is $O(n)$.

4.7 Evaluate each of the following code segments and determine the $O(\cdot)$ for the best and worst cases. Assume an input size of n.

(a)
```python
sum = 0
for i in range( n ) :
    if i % 2 == 0 :
        sum += i
```

(b)
```python
sum = 0
i = n
while i > 0 :
    sum += i
    i = i / 2
```

(c)
```python
for i in range( n ) :
    if i % 3 == 0 :
        for j in range( n / 2 ) :
            sum += j
    elif i % 2 == 0 :
        for j in range( 5 ) :
            sum += j
    else :
        for j in range( n ) :
            sum += j
```

4.8 The slice operation is used to create a new list that contains a subset of items from a source list. Implement the `slice()` function:

```python
def slice( theList, first, last )
```

which accepts a list and creates a sublist of the values in `theList`. What is the worst case time for your implementation and what is the best case time?

4.9 Implement the remaining methods of the `SparseMatrix` class: `transpose()`, `__getitem__`, `subtract()`, and `multiply()`.

4.10 Determine the worst case time-complexities for the `SparseMatrix` methods implemented in the previous question.

4.11 Determine the worst case time-complexities for the methods of your `ReversiGameLogic` class implemented in Programming Project 2.4.

4.12 Add Python operator methods to the `SparseMatrix` class that can be used in place of the named methods for several of the operations.

Operator Method	Current Method
__add__(rhsMatrix)	add(rhsMatrix)
__mul__(rhsMatrix)	subtract(rhsMatrix)
__sub__(rhsMatrix)	multiply(rhsMatrix)

Programming Projects

4.1 The game of Life is defined for an infinite-sized grid. In Chapter 2, we defined the Life Grid ADT to use a fixed-size grid in which the user specified the width and height of the grid. This was sufficient as an illustration of the use of a 2-D array for the implementation of the game of Life. But a full implementation should allow for an infinite-sized grid. Implement the Sparse Life Grid ADT using an approach similar to the one used to implement the sparse matrix.

- **SparseLifeGrid()**: Creates a new infinite-sized game grid. All cells in the grid are initially set to dead.

- **minRange()**: Returns a 2-tuple (**minrow**, **mincol**) that contains the minimum row index and the minimum column index that is currently occupied by a live cell.

- **maxRange()**: Returns a 2-tuple (**maxrow**, **maxcol**) that contains the maximum row index and the maximum column index that is currently occupied by a live cell.

- **configure(coordList)**: Configures the grid for evolving the first generation. The **coordList** argument is a sequence of 2-tuples with each tuple representing the coordinates (r, c) of the cells to be set as alive. All remaining cells are cleared or set to dead.

- **clearCell(row, col)**: Clears the individual cell (**row**, **col**) and sets it to dead. The cell indices must be within the valid range of the grid.

- **setCell(row, col)**: Sets the indicated cell (**row**, **col**) to be alive. The cell indices must be within the valid range of the grid.

- **isLiveCell(row,col)**: Returns a boolean value indicating if the given cell (**row**, **col**) contains a live organism. The cell indices must be within the valid range of the grid.

- **numLiveNeighbors(row, col)**: Returns the number of live neighbors for the given cell (**row**, **col**). The neighbors of a cell include all of the cells immediately surrounding it in all directions. For the cells along the border of the grid, the neighbors that fall outside the grid are assumed to be dead. The cell indices must be within the valid range of the grid.

4.2 Implement a new version of the **gameoflife.py** program to use your **SparseLifeGrid** class from the previous question.

4.3 Repeat Exercise 2.5 from Chapter 2 but use your new version of the **gameoflife.py** program from the previous question.

4.4 The digital grayscale image was introduced in Programming Project 2.3 and an abstract data type was defined and implemented for storing grayscale images. A color digital image is also a two-dimensional raster image, but unlike the grayscale image, the pixels of a color image store data representing colors instead of a single grayscale value. There are different ways to specify color, but one of the most common is with the use of the discrete RGB color space. Individual colors are specified by three intensity values or components within the range $[0 \ldots 255]$, one for each of the three primary colors that represent the amount of red, green, and blue light that must be added to produce the given color. We can define the **RGBColor** class for use in storing a single color in the discrete RGB color space.

```
class RGBColor :
  def __init__( self, red = 0, green = 0, blue = 0 ):
    self.red = red
    self.green = green
    self.blue = blue
```

Given the description of the operations for the Color Image ADT, implement the abstract data type using a 2-D array that stores instances of the RGBColor class. Note when setting the initial color in the constructor or when clearing the image to a specific color, you can store aliases to one RGBColor object in each element of the array.

- ColorImage(nrows, ncols): Creates a new instance that consists of nrows and ncols of pixels each set to black.
- width(): Returns the width of the image.
- height(): Returns the height of the image.
- clear(color): Clears the entire image by setting each pixel to the given RGB color.
- getitem(row, col): Returns the RGB color of the given pixel as an RGBColor object. The pixel coordinates must be within the valid range.
- setitem(row, col, color): Set the given pixel to the given RGB color. The pixel coordinates must be within the valid range.

4.5 Color images can also be stored using three separate color channels in which the values of each color component is stored in a separate data structure. Implement a new version of the Color Image ADT using three 1-D arrays to store the red, green, and blue components of each pixel. Apply the row-major formula from Section 3.3 to map a specific pixel given by (row, col) to an entry in the 1-D arrays.

4.6 A color image can be easily converted to a grayscale image by converting each pixel of the color image, specified by the three components (R, G, B), to a grayscale value using the formula

```
gray = round( 0.299 * R + 0.587 * G + 0.114 * B )
```

The proportions applied to each color component in the formula corresponds to the levels of sensitivity with which humans see each of the three primary colors: red, green and blue. Note the result from the equation must be converted capped to an integer in the range $[0\ldots255]$. Use the equation and implement the function

```
def colorToGrayscale( colorImg ):
```

which accepts a ColorImage object as an argument and creates and returns a new GrayscaleImage that is the grayscale version of the given color image.

## CHAPTER 5

Searching and Sorting

When people collect and work with data, they eventually want to search for specific items within the collection or sort the collection for presentation or easy access. Searching and sorting are two of the most common applications found in computer science. In this chapter, we explore these important topics and study some of the basic algorithms for use with sequence structures. The searching problem will be discussed many times throughout the text as it can be applied to collections stored using many different data structures, not just sequences. We will also further explore the sorting problem in Chapters 12 and 13 with a discussion of more advanced sorting algorithms.

5.1 Searching

Searching is the process of selecting particular information from a collection of data based on specific criteria. You are familiar with this concept from your experience in performing web searches to locate pages containing certain words or phrases or when looking up a phone number in the telephone book. In this text, we restrict the term searching to refer to the process of finding a specific item in a collection of data items.

The search operation can be performed on many different data structures. The *sequence search*, which is the focus in this chapter, involves finding an item within a sequence using a *search key* to identify the specific item. A *key* is a unique value used to identify the data elements of a collection. In collections containing simple types such as integers or reals, the values themselves are the keys. For collections of complex types, a specific data component has to be identified as the key. In some instances, a key may consist of multiple components, which is also known as a *compound key*.

5.1.1 The Linear Search

The simplest solution to the sequence search problem is the sequential or *linear search* algorithm. This technique iterates over the sequence, one item at a time, until the specific item is found or all items have been examined. In Python, a target item can be found in a sequence using the `in` operator:

```
if key in theArray :
    print( "The key is in the array." )
else :
    print( "The key is not in the array." )
```

The use of the `in` operator makes our code simple and easy to read but it hides the inner workings. Underneath, the `in` operator is implemented as a linear search. Consider the unsorted 1-D array of integer values shown in Figure 5.1(a). To determine if value 31 is in the array, the search begins with the value in the first element. Since the first element does not contain the target value, the next element in sequential order is compared to value 31. This process is repeated until the item is found in the sixth position. What if the item is not in the array? For example, suppose we want to search for value 8 in the sample array. The search begins at the first entry as before, but this time every item in the array is compared to the target value. It cannot be determined that the value is not in the sequence until the entire array has been traversed, as illustrated in Figure 5.1(b).

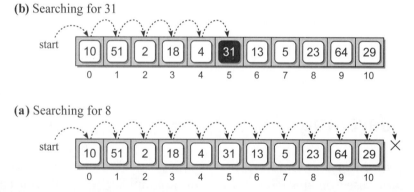

Figure 5.1: Performing a linear search on an unsorted array: (a) the target item is found and (b) the item is not in the array.

Finding a Specific Item

The function in Listing 5.1 implements the sequential search algorithm, which results in a boolean value indicating success or failure of the search. This is the same operation performed by the Python `in` operator. A count-controlled loop is used to traverse through the sequence during which each element is compared against the target value. If the item is in the sequence, the loop is terminated and `True` is returned. Otherwise, a full traversal is performed and `False` is returned after the loop terminates.

Listing 5.1   Implementation of the linear search on an unsorted sequence.

```
1  def linearSearch( theValues, target ) :
2    n = len( theValues )
3    for i in range( n ) :
4      # If the target is in the ith element, return True
5      if theValues[i] == target
6        return True
7
8    return False    # If not found, return False.
```

To analyze the sequential search algorithm for the worst case, we must first determine what conditions constitute the worst case. Remember, the worst case occurs when the algorithm performs the maximum number of steps. For a sequential search, that occurs when the target item is not in the sequence and the loop iterates over the entire sequence. Assuming the sequence contains n items, the linear search has a worst case time of $O(n)$.

Searching a Sorted Sequence

A linear search can also be performed on a sorted sequence, which is a sequence containing values in a specific order. For example, the values in the array illustrated in Figure 5.2 are in ascending or increasing numerical order. That is, each value in the array is larger than its predecessor.

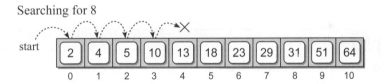

Figure 5.2: The linear search on a sorted array.

A linear search on a sorted sequence works in the same fashion as that for the unsorted sequence, with one exception. It's possible to terminate the search early when the value is not in the sequence instead of always having to perform a complete traversal. For example, suppose we want to search for 8 in the array from Figure 5.2. When the fourth item, which is value 10, is examined, we know value 8 cannot be in the sorted sequence or it would come before 10. The implementation of a linear search on a sorted sequence is shown in Listing 5.2 on the next page.

The only modification to the earlier version is the inclusion of a test to determine if the current item within the sequence is larger than the target value. If a larger value is encountered, the loop terminates and **False** is returned. With the modification to the linear search algorithm, we have produced a better version, but the time-complexity remains the same. The reason is that the worst case occurs when the value is not in the sequence and is larger than the last element. In this case, we must still traverse the entire sequence of n items.

| Listing 5.2 | Implementation of the linear search on a sorted sequence. |

```
1  def sortedLinearSearch( theValues, item ) :
2    n = len( theValues )
3    for i in range( n ) :
4      # If the target is found in the ith element, return True
5      if theValues[i] == item :
6        return True
7      # If target is larger than the ith element, it's not in the sequence.
8      elif theValues[i] > item :
9        return False
10
11   return False    # The item is not in the sequence.
```

Finding the Smallest Value

Instead of searching for a specific value in an unsorted sequence, suppose we wanted to search for the smallest value, which is equivalent to applying Python's `min()` function to the sequence. A linear search is performed as before, but this time we must keep track of the smallest value found for each iteration through the loop, as illustrated in Listing 5.3.

To prime the loop, we assume the first value in the sequence is the smallest and start the comparisons at the second item. Since the smallest value can occur anywhere in the sequence, we must always perform a complete traversal, resulting in a worst case time of $O(n)$.

| Listing 5.3 | Searching for the smallest value in an unsorted sequence. |

```
1  def findSmallest( theValues ):
2    n = len( theValues )
3    # Assume the first item is the smallest value.
4    smallest = theValues[0]
5    # Determine if any other item in the sequence is smaller.
6    for i in range( 1, n ) :
7      if theList[i] < smallest :
8        smallest = theValues[i]
9
10   return smallest        # Return the smallest found.
```

5.1.2 The Binary Search

The linear search algorithm for a sorted sequence produced a slight improvement over the linear search with an unsorted sequence, but both have a linear time-complexity in the worst case. To improve the search time for a sorted sequence, we can modify the search technique itself.

Consider an example where you are given a stack of exams, which are in alphabetical order, and are asked to find the exam for "Jessica Roberts." In performing this task, most people would not begin with the first exam and flip through one at a time until the requested exam is found, as would be done with a linear search. Instead, you would probably flip to the middle and determine if the requested exam comes alphabetically before or after that one. Assuming Jessica's paper follows alphabetically after the middle one, you know it cannot possibly be in the top half of the stack. Instead, you would probably continue searching in a similar fashion by splitting the remaining stack of exams in half to determine which portion contains Jessica's exam. This is an example of a ***divide and conquer*** strategy, which entails dividing a larger problem into smaller parts and conquering the smaller part.

Algorithm Description

The ***binary search*** algorithm works in a similar fashion to the process described above and can be applied to a sorted sequence. The algorithm starts by examining the middle item of the sorted sequence, resulting in one of three possible conditions: the middle item is the target value, the target value is less than the middle item, or the target is larger than the middle item. Since the sequence is ordered, we can eliminate half the values in the list when the target value is not found at the middle position.

Consider the task of searching for value 10 in the sorted array from Figure 5.2. We first determine which element contains the middle entry. As illustrated in Figure 5.3, the middle entry contains 18, which is greater than our target of 10. Thus, we can discard the upper half of the array from consideration since 10 cannot possibly be in that part. Having eliminated the upper half, we repeat the process on the lower half of the array. We then find the middle item of the lower half and compare its value to the target. Since that entry, which contains 5, is less than the target, we can eliminate the lower fourth of the array. The process is repeated on the remaining items. Upon finding value 10 in the middle entry from among those remaining, the process terminates successfully. If we had not found the target, the process would continue until either the target value was found or we had eliminated all values from consideration.

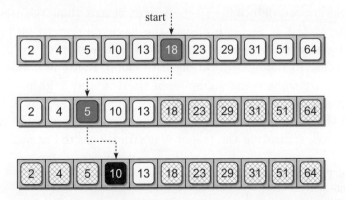

Figure 5.3: Searching for 10 in a sorted array using the binary search.

Implementation

The Python implementation of the binary search algorithm is provided in Listing 5.4. The variables `low` and `high` are used to mark the range of elements in the sequence currently under consideration. When the search begins, this range is the entire sequence since the target item can be anywhere within the sequence. The first step in each iteration is to determine the midpoint of the sequence. If the sequence contains an even number of elements, the mid point will be chosen such that the left sequence contains one less item than the right. Figure 5.4 illustrates the positioning of the `low`, `high`, and `mid` markers as the algorithm progresses.

Listing 5.4   Implementation of the binary search algorithm.

```
1  def binarySearch( theValues, target ) :
2     # Start with the entire sequence of elements.
3     low = 0
4     high = len(theValues) - 1
5
6     # Repeatedly subdivide the sequence in half until the target is found.
7     while low <= high :
8       # Find the midpoint of the sequence.
9       mid = (high + low) // 2
10      # Does the midpoint contain the target?
11      if theValues[mid] == target :
12        return True
13      # Or does the target precede the midpoint?
14      elif target < theValues[mid] :
15        high = mid - 1
16      # Or does it follow the midpoint?
17      else :
18        low = mid + 1
19
20    # If the sequence cannot be subdivided further, we're done.
21    return False
```

After computing the midpoint, the corresponding element in that position is examined. If the midpoint contains the target, we immediately return `True`. Otherwise, we determine if the target is less than the item at the midpoint or greater. If it is less, we adjust the `high` marker to be one less than the midpoint and if it is greater, we adjust the `low` marker to be one greater than the midpoint. In the next iteration of the loop, the only portion of the sequence considered are those elements between the `low` and `high` markers, as adjusted. This process is repeated until the item is found or the `low` marker becomes greater than the `high` marker. This condition occurs when there are no items left to be processed, indicating the target is not in the sorted sequence.

Run Time Analysis

To evaluate the efficiency of the the binary search algorithm, assume the sorted sequence contains n items. We need to determine the maximum number of times the

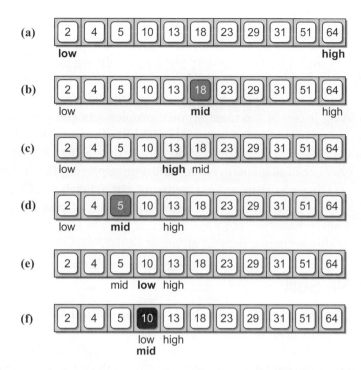

Figure 5.4: The steps performed by the binary search algorithm in searching for 10: (a) initial range of items, (b) locating the midpoint, (c) eliminating the upper half, (d) midpoint of the lower half, (e) eliminating the lower fourth, and (f) finding the target item.

`while` loop is executed. The worst case occurs when the target value is not in the sequence, the same as for the linear search. The difference with the binary search is that not every item in the sequence has to be examined before determining the target is not in the sequence, even in the worst case. Since the sequence is sorted, each iteration of the loop can eliminate from consideration half of the remaining values. As we saw earlier in Section 4.1.2, when the input size is repeatedly reduced by half during each iteration of a loop, there will be $\log n$ iterations in the worst case. Thus, the binary search algorithm has a worst case time-complexity of $O(\log n)$, which is more efficient than the linear search.

5.2 Sorting

Sorting is the process of arranging or ordering a collection of items such that each item and its successor satisfy a prescribed relationship. The items can be simple values, such as integers and reals, or more complex types, such as student records or dictionary entries. In either case, the ordering of the items is based on the value of a *sort key*. The key is the value itself when sorting simple types or it can be a specific component or a combination of components when sorting complex types.

We encounter many examples of sorting in everyday life. Consider the listings of a phone book, the definitions in a dictionary, or the terms in an index, all of which are organized in alphabetical order to make finding an entry much easier. As we saw earlier in the chapter, the efficiency of some applications can be improved when working with sorted lists. Another common use of sorting is for the presentation of data in some organized fashion. For example, we may want to sort a class roster by student name, sort a list of cities by zip code or population, rank order SAT scores, or list entries on a bank statement by date.

Sorting is one of the most studied problems in computer science and extensive research has been done in this area, resulting in many different algorithms. While Python provides a `sort()` method for sorting a list, it cannot be used with an array or other data structures. In addition, exploring the techniques used by some of the sorting algorithms for improving the efficiency of the sort problem may provide ideas that can be used with other types of problems. In this section, we present three basic sorting algorithms, all of which can be applied to data stored in a mutable sequence such as an array or list.

5.2.1   Bubble Sort

A simple solution to the sorting problem is the *bubble sort* algorithm, which re-arranges the values by iterating over the list multiple times, causing larger values to bubble to the top or end of the list. To illustrate how the bubble sort algorithm works, suppose we have four playing cards (all of the same suit) that we want to order from smallest to largest face value. We start by laying the cards out face up on a table as shown here:

The algorithm requires multiple passes over the cards, with each pass starting at the first card and ending one card earlier than on the previous iteration. During each pass, the cards in the first and second positions are compared. If the first is larger than the second, the two cards are swapped.

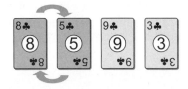

Next, the cards in positions two and three are compared. If the first one is larger than the second, they are swapped. Otherwise, we leave them as they were.

This process continues for each successive pair of cards until the card with the largest face value is positioned at the end.

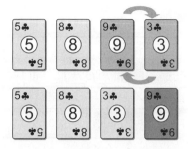

The next two passes over the cards are illustrated below. In the second pass the card with the second largest face value is positioned in the next-to-last position. In the third and final pass, the first two cards will be positioned correctly.

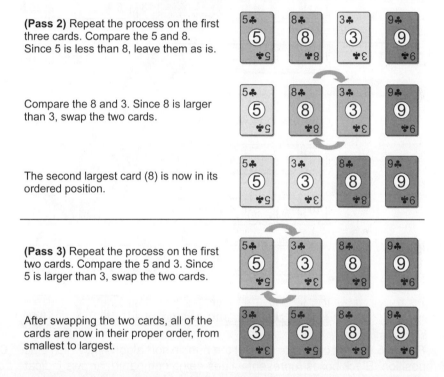

(Pass 2) Repeat the process on the first three cards. Compare the 5 and 8. Since 5 is less than 8, leave them as is.

Compare the 8 and 3. Since 8 is larger than 3, swap the two cards.

The second largest card (8) is now in its ordered position.

(Pass 3) Repeat the process on the first two cards. Compare the 5 and 3. Since 5 is larger than 3, swap the two cards.

After swapping the two cards, all of the cards are now in their proper order, from smallest to largest.

Listing 5.5 provides a Python implementation of the bubble sort algorithm. Figure 5.5 illustrates the swaps performed during the first pass of the algorithm when applied to an array containing 11 integer values. Figure 5.6 shows the ordering of the values within the array after each iteration of the outer loop.

The efficiency of the bubble sort algorithm only depends on the number of keys in the array and is independent of the specific values and the initial arrangement of those values. To determine the efficiency, we must determine the total number of iterations performed by the inner loop for a sequence containing n values. The outer loop is executed $n - 1$ times since the algorithm makes $n - 1$ passes over the sequence. The number of iterations for the inner loop is not fixed, but depends on the current iteration of the outer loop. On the first pass over the sequence, the inner loop executes $n - 1$ times; on the second pass, $n - 2$ times; on the third, $n - 3$ times, and so on until it executes once on the last pass. The total number

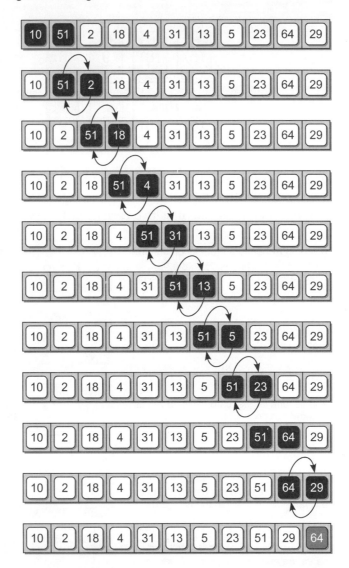

Figure 5.5: First complete pass of the bubble sort algorithm, which places 64 in its correct position. Black boxes represent values being compared; arrows indicate exchanges.

Listing 5.5   Implementation of the bubble sort algorithm.

```
1   # Sorts a sequence in ascending order using the bubble sort algorithm.
2   def bubbleSort( theSeq ):
3     n = len( theSeq )
4      # Perform n-1 bubble operations on the sequence
5     for i in range( n - 1 ) :
6        # Bubble the largest item to the end.
7       for j in range( i + n - 1 ) :
8         if theSeq[j] > theSeq[j + 1] :  # swap the j and j+1 items.
9           tmp = theSeq[j]
10          theSeq[j] = theSeq[j + 1]
11          theSeq[j + 1] = tmp
```

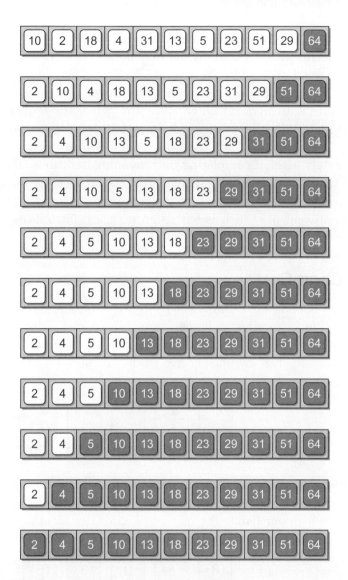

Figure 5.6: Result of applying the bubble sort algorithm to the sample sequence. The gray boxes show the values that are in order after each outer-loop traversal.

of iterations for the inner loop will be the sum of the first $n - 1$ integers, which equals

$$\frac{n(n-1)}{2} - n = \frac{1}{2}n^2 + \frac{1}{2}n$$

resulting in a run time of $O(n^2)$. Bubble sort is considered one of the most inefficient sorting algorithms due to the total number of swaps required. Given an array of keys in reverse order, a swap is performed for every iteration of the inner loop, which can be costly in practice.

The bubble sort algorithm as implemented in Listing 5.5 always performs n^2 iterations of the inner loop. But what if the sequence is already in sorted order?

In this case, there would be no need to sort the sequence. But our implementation still performs all n^2 iterations because it has no way of knowing the sequence is already sorted.

The bubble sort algorithm can be improved by having it terminate early and not require it to perform all n^2 iterations when the sequence is in sorted order. We can determine the sequence is in sorted order when no swaps are performed by the `if` statement within the inner loop. At that point, the function can return immediately without completing the remaining iterations. If a value is out of sorted order, then it will either be smaller than its predecessor in the sequence or larger than its successor at which point the condition of the `if` statement would be true. This improvement, which is left as an exercise, introduces a best case that only requires $O(n)$ time when the initial input sequence is in sorted order.

5.2.2 Selection Sort

A second sorting algorithm, which improves on the bubble sort and works in a fashion similar to what a human may use to sort a list of values, is known as the **selection sort**. We can again use the set of playing cards to illustrate the algorithm and start by placing five cards face up on a table that are to be sorted in ascending order.

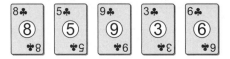

Instead of swapping the cards as was done with the bubble sort, we are going to scan through the cards and select the smallest from among those on the table and place it in our hand. For our set of cards, we identify the 3 as the smallest:

We pick up the 3 and place it in our hand, leaving the remaining cards on the table:

our hand   cards on the table

We repeat the process and identify the 5 as the next smallest face value:

cards on the table

We pick up the 5 and add it to proper sorted position, which will be on the right side since there are no cards with a smaller face value left on the table.

our hand   cards on the table

This process is continued until all of the cards have been picked up and placed in our hand in the correct sorted order from smallest to largest.

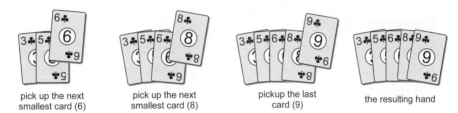

pick up the next   pick up the next   pickup the last   the resulting hand
smallest card (6)   smallest card (8)   card (9)

The process we used to sort the set of five cards is similar to the approach used by the selection sort algorithm. But when implementing insertion sort in code, the algorithm maintains both the sorted and unsorted values within the same sequence structure. The selection sort, which improves on the bubble sort, makes multiple passes over the sequence, but unlike the bubble sort, it only makes a single swap after each pass. The implementation of the selection sort algorithm is provided in Listing 5.6.

Listing 5.6   Implementation of the selection sort algorithm.

```
1  # Sorts a sequence in ascending order using the selection sort algorithm.
2  def selectionSort( theSeq ):
3    n = len( theSeq )
4    for i in range( n - 1 ):
5      # Assume the ith element is the smallest.
6      smallNdx = i
7      # Determine if any other element contains a smaller value.
8      for j in range( i + 1, n ):
9        if theSeq[j] < theSeq[smallNdx] :
10         smallNdx = j
11
12     # Swap the ith value and smallNdx value only if the smallest value is
13     # not already in its proper position. Some implementations omit testing
14     # the condition and always swap the two values.
15     if smallNdx != i :
16       tmp = theSeq[i]
17       theSeq[i] = theSeq[smallNdx]
18       theSeq[smallNdx] = tmp
```

The process starts by finding the smallest value in the sequence and swaps it with the value in the first position of the sequence. The second smallest value is then found and swapped with the value in the second position. This process continues positioning each successive value by selecting them from those not yet sorted and swapping with the values in the respective positions. Figure 5.7 shows the results after each iteration of the algorithm when applied to the sample array of integers. The grayed boxes represent those items already placed in their proper position while the black boxes show the two values that are swapped.

The selection sort, which makes $n-1$ passes over the array to reposition $n-1$ values, is also $O(n^2)$. The difference between the selection and bubble sorts is that the selection sort reduces the number of swaps required to sort the list to $O(n)$.

5.2.3   Insertion Sort

Another commonly studied sorting algorithm is the ***insertion sort***. Continuing with our analogy of sorting a set of playing cards to illustrate the sorting algorithms, consider five cards stacked in a deck face up:

the deck

We pick up the top card from the deck and place it in our hand:

our hand

the deck

Since this is the first card, there is no decision to be made as to its position. We again pick up the top card from the deck and compare it to the card already in our hand and insert it into its proper sorted position:

our hand

the deck

After placing the 8 into our hand, the process is repeated. This time, we pick up the 5 and find its position within our hand and insert it in the proper place:

our hand

the deck

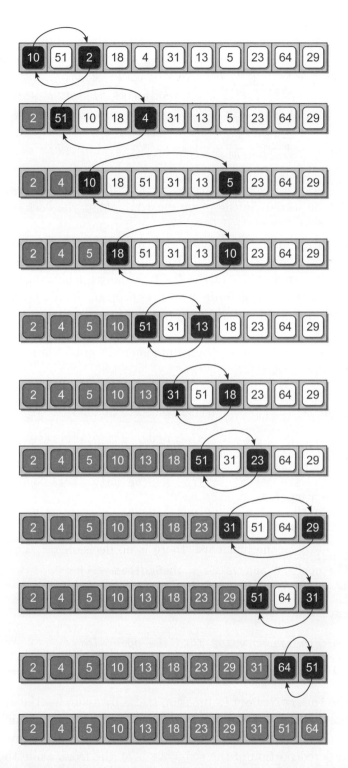

Figure 5.7: Result of applying the selection sort algorithm to our sample array. The gray boxes show the values that have been sorted; the black boxes show the values that are swapped during each iteration of the algorithm.

This process continues, one card at a time, until all of the cards have been removed from the table and placed into our hand in their proper sorted position.

pick up the next   pick up the   the resulting hand
card on top (9)   last card (6)

The insertion sort maintains a collection of sorted items and a collection of items to be sorted. In the playing card analogy, the deck represents the collection to be sorted and the cards in our hand represents those already sorted. When implementing insertion sort in a program, the algorithm maintains both the sorted and unsorted collections within the same sequence structure. The algorithm keeps the list of sorted values at the front of the sequence and picks the next unsorted value from the first of those yet to be positioned. To position the next item, the correct spot within the sequence of sorted values is found by performing a search. After finding the proper position, the slot has to be opened by shifting the items down one position. A Python implementation of the insertion sort algorithm is provided in Listing 5.7.

Listing 5.7   Implementation of the insertion sort algorithm.

```
1   # Sorts a sequence in ascending order using the insertion sort algorithm.
2   def insertionSort( theSeq ):
3     n = len( theSeq )
4     # Starts with the first item as the only sorted entry.
5     for i in range( 1, n ) :
6       # Save the value to be positioned.
7       value = theSeq[i]
8       # Find the position where value fits in the ordered part of the list.
9       pos = i
10      while pos > 0 and value < theSeq[pos - 1] :
11        # Shift the items to the right during the search.
12        theSeq[pos] = theSeq[pos - 1]
13        pos -= 1
14
15      # Put the saved value into the open slot.
16      theSeq[pos] = value
```

The insertionSort() function starts by assuming the first item is in its proper position. Next, an iteration is performed over the remaining items so each value can be inserted into its proper position within the sorted portion of the sequence. The ordered portion of the sequence is at the front while those yet to be inserted are at the end. The i loop index variable marks the separation point between the two parts. The inner loop is used to find the insertion point within the sorted sequence and at the same time, shifts the items down to make room for the next item. Thus, the inner loop starts from the end of the sorted subsequence and works its way to the front. After finding the proper position, the item is inserted. Figure 5.8 illustrates the application of this algorithm on an array of integer values.

The insertion sort is an example of a sorting algorithm in which the best and worst cases are different. Determining the different cases and the corresponding run times is left as an exercise.

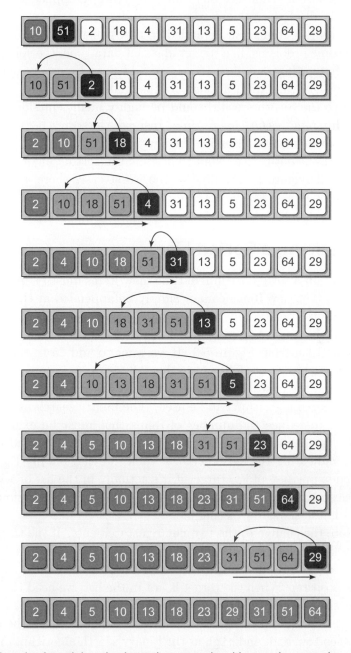

Figure 5.8: Result of applying the insertion sort algorithm to the sample array. The gray boxes show values that have been sorted; the black boxes show the next value to be positioned; and the lighter gray boxes with black text are the sorted values that have to be shifted to the right to open a spot for the next value.

5.3   Working with Sorted Lists

The efficiency of some algorithms can be improved when working with sequences containing sorted values. We saw this earlier when performing a search using the binary search algorithm on a sorted sequence. Sorting algorithms can be used to create a sorted sequence, but they are typically applied to an unsorted sequence in which all of the values are known and the collection remains static. In other words, no new items will be added to the sequence nor will any be removed.

In some problems, like the set abstract data type, the collection does not remain static but changes as new items are added and existing ones are removed. If a sorting algorithm were applied to the underlying list each time a new value is added to the set, the result would be highly inefficient since even the best sorting algorithm requires $O(n \log n)$ time. Instead, the sorted list can be maintained as the collection changes by inserting the new item into its proper position without having to re-sort the entire list. Note that while the sorting algorithms from the previous section all require $O(n^2)$ time in the worst case, there are more efficient sorting algorithms (which will be covered in Chapter 12) that only require $O(n \log n)$ time.

5.3.1   Maintaining a Sorted List

To maintain a sorted list in real time, new items must be inserted into their proper position. The new items cannot simply be appended at the end of the list as they may be out of order. Instead, we must locate the proper position within the list and use the `insert()` method to insert it into the indicated position. Consider the sorted list from Figure 5.3. If we want to add 25 to that list, then it must be inserted at position 7 following value 23.

To find the position of a new item within a sorted list, a modified version of the binary search algorithm can be used. The binary search uses a divide and conquer strategy to reduce the number of items that must be examined to find a target item or to determine the target is not in the list. Instead of returning `True` or `False` indicating the existence of a value, we can modify the algorithm to return the index position of the target if it's actually in the list or where the value should be placed if it were inserted into the list. The modified version of the binary search algorithm is shown in Listing 5.8.

Note the change to the two `return` statements. If the target value is contained in the list, it will be found in the same fashion as was done in the original version of the algorithm. Instead of returning `True`, however, the new version returns its index position. When the target is not in the list, we need the algorithm to identify the position where it should be inserted.

Consider the illustration in Figure 5.9, which shows the changes to the three variables `low`, `mid`, and `high` as the binary search algorithm progresses in searching for value 25. The `while` loop terminates when either the `low` or `high` range variable crosses the other, resulting in the condition `low > high`. Upon termination of the loop, the `low` variable will contain the position where the new value should be placed. This index can then be supplied to the `insert()` method to insert the new

Listing 5.8   Finding the location of a target value using the binary search.

```
1   # Modified version of the binary search that returns the index within
2   # a sorted sequence indicating where the target should be located.
3   def findSortedPosition( theList, target ):
4     low = 0
5     high = len(theList) - 1
6     while low <= high :
7       mid = (high + low) // 2
8       if theList[mid] == target :
9         return mid                    # Index of the target.
10      elif target < theList[mid] :
11        high = mid - 1
12      else :
13        low = mid + 1
14
15    return low            # Index where the target value should be.
```

value into the list. The findOrderedPosition() function can also be used with lists containing duplicate values, but there is no guarantee where the new value will be placed in relation to the other duplicate values beyond the proper ordering requirement that they be adjacent.

5.3.2 Merging Sorted Lists

Sometimes it may be necessary to take two sorted lists and merge them to create a new sorted list. Consider the following code segment:

```
listA = [ 2, 8, 15, 23, 37 ]
listB = [ 4, 6, 15, 20 ]
newList = mergeSortedLists( listA, listB )
print( newList )
```

which creates two lists with the items ordered in ascending order and then calls a user-defined function to create and return a new list created by merging the other two. Printing the new merged list produces

```
[2, 4, 6, 8, 15, 15, 20, 23, 37]
```

Problem Solution

This problem can be solved by simulating the action a person might take to merge two stacks of exam papers, each of which are in alphabetical order. Start by choosing the exam from the two stacks with the name that comes first in alphabetical order. Flip it over on the table to start a new stack. Again, choose the exam from the top of the two stacks that comes next in alphabetical order and flip it over and place it on top of first one. Repeat this process until one of the two original stacks is exhausted. The exams in the remaining stack can be flipped over on top of the new stack as they are already in alphabetical order and alphabetically follow the

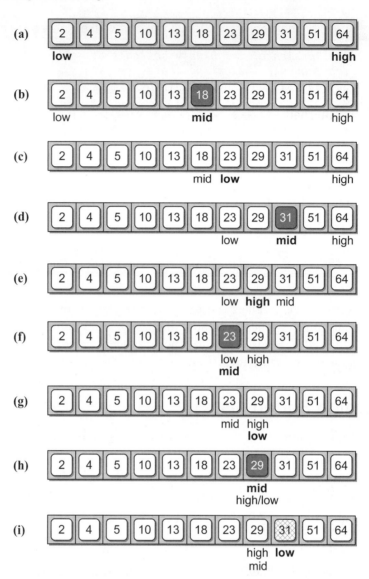

Figure 5.9: Performing a binary search on a sorted list when searching for value 25.

last exam flipped onto the new stack. You now have a single stack of exams in alphabetical order.

A similar approach can be used to merge two sorted lists. Consider the illustration in Figure 5.10, which demonstrates this process on the sample lists created in the example code segment from earlier. The items in the original list are not removed, but instead copied to the new list. Thus, there is no "top" item from which to select the smallest value as was the case in the example of merging two stacks of exams. Instead, index variables are used to indicate the "top" or next value within each list. The implementation of the `mergeSortedLists()` function is provided in Listing 5.9.

The process of merging the two lists begins by creating a new empty list and initializing the two index variables to zero. A loop is used to repeat the process

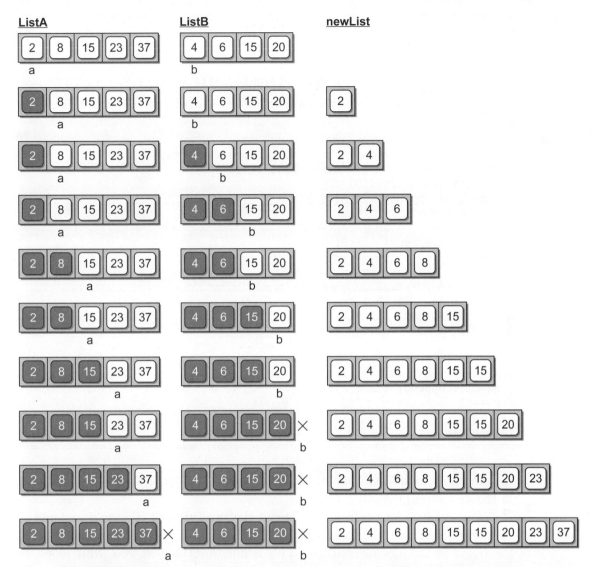

Figure 5.10: The iterative steps for merging two sorted lists into a new sorted list. a and b are index variables indicating the next value to be merged from the respective list.

of selecting the next largest value to be added to the new merged list. During the iteration of the loop, the value at listA[a] is compared to the value listB[b]. The largest of these two values is added or appended to the new list. If the two values are equal, the value from listB is chosen. As values are copied from the two original lists to the new merged list, one of the two index variables a or b is incremented to indicate the next largest value in the corresponding list.

This process is repeated until all of the values have been copied from one of the two lists, which occurs when a equals the length of listA or b equals the length of listB. Note that we could have created and initialized the new list with a sufficient number of elements to store all of the items from both listA and listB. While that works for this specific problem, we want to create a more general solution that

Listing 5.9   Merging two sorted lists.

```
1    # Merges two sorted lists to create and return a new sorted list.
2    def mergeSortedLists( listA, listB ) :
3      # Create the new list and initialize the list markers.
4      newList = list()
5      a = 0
6      b = 0
7
8      # Merge the two lists together until one is empty.
9      while a < len( listA ) and b < len( listB ) :
10       if listA[a] < listB[b] :
11         newList.append( listA[a] )
12         a += 1
13       else :
14         newList.append( listB[b] )
15         b += 1
16
17     # If listA contains more items, append them to newList.
18     while a < len( listA ) :
19       newList.append( listA[a] )
20       a += 1
21
22     # Or if listB contains more items, append them to newList.
23     while b < len( listB ) :
24       newList.append( listB[b] )
25       b += 1
26
27     return newList
```

we can easily modify for similar problems where the new list may not contain all of the items from the other two lists.

After the first loop terminates, one of the two lists will be empty and one will contain at least one additional value. All of the values remaining in that list must be copied to the new merged list. This is done by the next two while loops, but only one will be executed depending on which list contains additional values. The position containing the next value to be copied is denoted by the respective index variable a or b.

Run Time Analysis

To evaluate the solution for merging two sorted list, assume listA and listB each contain n items. The analysis depends on the number of iterations performed by each of the three loops, all of which perform the same action of copying a value from one of the two original lists to the new merged list. The first loop iterates until all of the values in one of the two original lists have been copied to the third. After the first loop terminates, only one of the next two loops will be executed, depending on which list still contains values.

- The first loop performs the maximum number of iterations when the selection of the next value to be copied alternates between the two lists. This results in all values from either `listA` or `listB` being copied to the `newList` and all but one value from the other for a total of $2n - 1$ iterations. Then, one of the next two loops will execute a single iteration in order to copy the last value to the `newList`.

- The minimum number of iterations performed by the first loop occurs when all values from one list are copied to the `newList` and none from the other. If the first loop copies the entire contents of `listA` to the `newList`, it will require n iterations followed by n iterations of the third loop to copy the values from `listB`. If the first loop copies the entire contents of `listB` to the `newList`, it will require n iterations followed by n iterations of the second loop to copy the values from `listA`.

In both cases, the three loops are executed for a combined total of $2n$ iterations. Since the statements performed by each of the three loops all require constant time, merging two lists can be done in $O(n)$ time.

5.4   The Set ADT Revisited

The implementation of the Set ADT using a list was quick and rather simple, but several of the operations require quadratic time in the worst case. This inefficiency is due to the linear search used to find an element in the unsorted list that is required by several of the operations. We saw earlier in the chapter the efficiency of the search operation can be improved by using the binary search algorithm. To use the binary search with the Set ADT, the list of elements must be in sorted order and that order must be maintained. The definition of the Set ADT, however, indicates the elements have no particular ordering. While this is true, it does not preclude us from storing the elements in sorted order. It only means there is no requirement that the items must be stored in a particular order.

5.4.1   A Sorted List Implementation

In using the binary search algorithm to improve the efficiency of the set operations, the list cannot be sorted each time a new element is added because it would increase the time-complexity of the `add()` operation. For example, suppose we used one of the sorting algorithms presented earlier in the chapter to sort the list after each element is added. Since those algorithms require $O(n^2)$ time in the worst case, the `add()` operation would then also require quadratic time. Instead, the sorted order must be maintained when new elements are added by inserting each into its proper position. A partial implementation of the Set ADT using a sorted list and the binary search algorithm is provided in Listing 5.10. There are no changes needed in the constructor or the __len__ method, but some changes are needed in the remaining methods.

Listing 5.10 The `binaryset.py` module.

```python
 1  # Implementation of the Set ADT using a sorted list.
 2  class Set :
 3      # Creates an empty set instance.
 4    def __init__( self ):
 5      self._theElements = list()
 6
 7      # Returns the number of items in the set.
 8    def __len__( self ):
 9      return len( self._theElements )
10
11      # Determines if an element is in the set.
12    def __contains__( self, element ):
13      ndx = self._findPosition( element )
14      return ndx < len( self ) and self._theElements[ndx] == element
15
16      # Adds a new unique element to the set.
17    def add( self, element ):
18      if element not in self :
19        ndx = self._findPosition( element )
20        self._theElements.insert( ndx, element )
21
22      # Removes an element from the set.
23    def remove( self, element ):
24      assert element in self, "The element must be in the set."
25      ndx = self._findPosition( element )
26      self._theElements.pop( ndx )
27
28      # Determines if this set is a subset of setB.
29    def isSubsetOf( self, setB ):
30      for element in self :
31        if element not in setB :
32          return False
33      return True
34
35      # The remaining methods go here.
36      # ......
37
38      # Returns an iterator for traversing the list of items.
39    def __iter__( self ):
40      return _SetIterator( self._theElements )
41
42      # Finds the position of the element within the ordered list.
43    def _findPosition( self, element ):
44      low = 0
45      high = len( theList ) - 1
46      while low <= high :
47        mid = (high + low) / 2
48        if theList[ mid ] == target :
49          return mid
50        elif target < theList[ mid ] :
51          high = mid - 1
52        else :
53          low = mid + 1
54      return low
```

> **NOTE**
>
> ⓘ **Short-Circuit Evaluation.** Most programming languages use *short-circuit evaluation* when testing compound logical expressions. If the result of the compound expression is known after evaluating the first component, the evaluation ends and returns the result. For example, in evaluating the logical expression a > b **and** a < c, if a > b is `False`, then there is no need to continue the evaluation of the second component since the overall expression must be `False`.

Basic Operations

Performing a binary search to locate an element in the sorted list or to find the position where an element belongs in the sorted list is needed in several methods. Instead of reimplementing the operation each time, we implement the modified version of the binary search algorithm from Listing 5.8 in the `_findPosition()` helper method. The helper method does not detect nor distinguish between unique and duplicate values. It only returns the index where the element is located within the list or where it should be placed if it were added to the list. Thus, care must be taken when implementing the various methods to check for the existence of an element when necessary.

The `__contains__` method is easily implemented using `_findPosition()`. The index value returned by the helper method indicates the location where the element should be within the sorted list, but it says nothing about the actual existence of the element. To determine if the element is in the set, we can compare the element at the `ndx` position within the list to the target element. Note the inclusion of the condition `ndx < len(self)` within the compound expression. This is needed since the value returned by `_findPosition()` can be one larger than the number of items in the list, which occurs when the target should be located at the end of the list. If this value were directly used in examining the contents of the list without making sure it was in range, an out-of-range exception could be raised. The `__contains__` method has a worst case time of $O(\log n)$ since it uses the binary search to locate the given element within the sorted list.

To implement the `add()` method, we must first determine if the element is unique since a set cannot contain duplicate values. This is done with the use of the `in` operator, which automatically calls the `__contains__` operator method. If the element is not already a member of the set, the `insert()` method is called to insert the new element in its proper position within the ordered list. Even though the `__contains__` method has a better time-complexity when using a sorted list and the binary search, the `add()` operation still requires $O(n)$ time, the proof of which is left as an exercise.

The `remove()` method requires that the target element must be a member of the set. To verify this precondition, an assertion is made using the `in` operator. After which, the `_findPosition()` helper method is called to obtain the location of the element, which can then be used with the `pop()` list method to remove the element from the underlying sorted list. Like the add operation, the `remove()` method still has a worst case time of $O(n)$, the proof of which is left as an exercise.

We can implement the `isSubsetOf()` method in the same fashion as was done in the original version that used the unsorted list as shown in lines 29–33 of Listing 5.10. To evaluate the efficiency of the method, we again assume both sets contain n elements. The `isSubsetOf()` method performs a traversal over the `self` set during which the `in` operator is applied to `setB`. Since the `in` operator requires $O(\log n)$ time and it's called n times, `isSubsetOf()` has a time-complexity of $O(n \log n)$.

A New Set Equals

We could also implement the set equals operation in the same fashion as was done in the original version when using the unsorted list:

```
def __eq__( self, setB ):
  if len( self ) != len( setB ) :
    return False
  else :
    return self.isSubsetOf( setB )
```

But that implementation would have a time-complexity of $O(n \log n)$ since it calls the `isSubsetOf()` method. A more efficient implementation of the equals operation is possible if we compare the elements in the list directly instead of using the `isSubsetOf()` method. Remember, for two sets to be equal, they must contain the exact same elements. Since the lists for both sets are sorted, not only must they contain the same elements, but those elements must be in corresponding positions within the two lists for the sets to be equal.

The new implementation of the `__eq__` method is provided in Listing 5.11. The two lists are traversed simultaneously during which corresponding elements are compared. If a single instance occurs where corresponding elements are not identical, then the two sets cannot be equal. Otherwise, having traversed the entire list and finding no mismatched items, the two sets must be equal. The new implementation only requires $O(n)$ time since it only involves one complete traversal of the lists. A similar approach can be used to improve the efficiency of the `isSubsetOf()` method to only require $O(n)$ time, which is left as an exercise.

Listing 5.11 New implementation of the Set equals method.

```
1  class Set :
2  # ...
3    def __eq__( self, setB ):
4      if len( self ) != len( setB ) :
5        return False
6      else :
7        for i in range( len(self) ) :
8          if self._theElements[i] != setB._theElements[i] :
9            return False
10       return True
```

A New Set Union

The efficiency of the set union operation can also be improved from the original version. Set union using two sorted lists is very similar to the problem of merging two sorted lists that was introduced in the previous section. In that problem, the entire contents of the two sorted lists were merged into a third list. For the Set ADT implemented using a sorted list, the result of the set union must be a new sorted list merged from the unique values contained in the sorted lists used to implement the two source sets.

The implementation of the new **union()** method, which is provided in Listing 5.12, uses a modified version of the **mergeSortedLists()** function. The only modification required is the inclusion of an additional test within the first loop to catch any duplicate values by advancing both index variables and only appending one copy to the new sorted list. The new implementation only requires $O(n)$ time since that is the time required to merge two sorted lists and the new test for duplicates does not increase that complexity. The set difference and set intersection operations can also be modified in a similar fashion and are left as an exercise.

Listing 5.12   New implementation of the Set union method.

```
 1  class Set :
 2  # ...
 3    def union( self, setB ):
 4      newSet = Set()
 5      a = 0
 6      b = 0
 7       # Merge the two lists together until one is empty.
 8      while a < len( self ) and b < len( setB ) :
 9        valueA = self._theElements[a]
10        valueB = setB._theElements[b]
11        if valueA < valueB :
12          newSet._theElements.append( valueA )
13          a += 1
14        elif valueA > valueB :
15          newSet._theElements.append( valueB )
16          b += 1
17        else :      # Only one of the two duplicates are appended.
18          newSet._theElements.append( valueA )
19          a += 1
20          b += 1
21
22      # If listA contains more items, append them to newList.
23      while a < len( self ) :
24        newSet._theElements.append( self._theElements[a] )
25        a += 1
26
27      # Or if listB contains more, append them to newList.
28      while b < len( otherSet ) :
29        newSet._theElements.append( setB._theElements[b] )
30        b += 1
31
32      return newSet
```

5.4.2   Comparing the Implementations

The implementation of the Set ADT using an unsorted list was quick and easy, but after evaluating the various operations, it became apparent many of them were time consuming. A new implementation using a sorted list to store the elements of the set and the binary search algorithm for locating elements improved the __contains__ method. This resulted in better times for the isSubsetOf() and __eq__ methods, but the set union, intersection, and difference operations remained quadratic. After observing several operations could be further improved if they were implemented to directly access the list instead of using the __contains__ method, we were able to provide a more efficient implementation of the Set ADT. Table 5.1 compares the worst case time-complexities for the Set ADT operations using an unsorted list and the improved sorted list version using the binary search and the list merging operation.

Operation	Unordered	Improved
s = Set()	$O(1)$	$O(1)$
len(s)	$O(1)$	$O(1)$
x in s	$O(n)$	$O(\log n)$
s.add(x)	$O(n)$	$O(n)$
s.isSubsetOf(t)	$O(n^2)$	$O(n)$
s == t	$O(n^2)$	$O(n)$
s.union(t)	$O(n^2)$	$O(n)$

Table 5.1: Comparison of the two Set ADT implementations using an unsorted list and the improved sorted list with binary search and list merging.

Exercises

5.1 Given an unsorted list of n values, what is the time-complexity to find the kth smallest value in the worst case? What would be the complexity if the list were sorted?

5.2 What is the $O(\cdot)$ for the findSortedPosition() function in the worst case?

5.3 Consider the new implementation of the Set class using a sorted list with the binary search.

   (a) Prove or show the worst case time for the add() method is $O(n)$.

   (b) What is the best case time for the add() method?

5.4 Determine the worst case time complexity for each method of the Map ADT implemented in Section 3.2.

5.5 Modify the binary search algorithm to find the position of the first occurrence of a value that can occur multiple times in the ordered list. Verify your algorithm is still $O(\log n)$.

5.6 Design and implement a function to find all negative values within a given list. Your function should return a new list containing the negative values. When does the worst case occur and what is the run time for that case?

5.7 In this chapter, we used a modified version of the `mergeSortedLists()` function to develop a linear time `union()` operation for our Set ADT implemented using a sorted list. Use a similar approach to implement new linear time versions of the `isSubsetOf()`, `intersect()`, and `difference()` methods.

5.8 Given the following list of keys (80, 7, 24, 16, 43, 91, 35, 2, 19, 72), show the contents of the array after each iteration of the outer loop for the indicated algorithm when sorting in ascending order.

(a) bubble sort   (b) selection sort   (c) insertion sort

5.9 Given the following list of keys (3, 18, 29, 32, 39, 44, 67, 75), show the contents of the array after each iteration of the outer loop for the

(a) bubble sort   (b) selection sort   (c) insertion sort

5.10 Evaluate the insertion sort algorithm to determine the best case and the worst case time complexities.

Programming Projects

5.1 Implement the Bag ADT from Chapter 1 to use a sorted list and the binary search algorithm. Evaluate the time complexities for each of the operations.

5.2 Implement a new version of the Map ADT from Section 3.2 to use a sorted list and the binary search algorithm.

5.3 The implementation of the Sparse Matrix ADT from Chapter 4 can be improved by storing the _MatrixElement objects in a sorted list and using the binary search to locate a specific element. The matrix elements can be sorted based on the row and column indices using an index function similar to that used with a 2-D array stored in a MultiArray. Implement a new version of the Sparse Matrix ADT using a sorted list and the binary search to locate elements.

5.4 Implement a new version of the Sparse Life Grid ADT from Chapter 4 to use a sorted list and the binary search to locate the occupied cells.

5.5 A colormap is a lookup table or color palette containing a limited set of colors. Early color graphics cards could only display up to 256 unique colors at one time. Colormaps were used to specify which 256 colors should be used to display color images on such a device. Software applications were responsible for mapping each color in the image that was to be displayed to a color in the limited color set specified by the colormap. We can define a Colormap ADT for storing a limited set of colors and for use in mapping one of the 16.7+ million colors possible in the discrete RGB color space to a color in the colormap. Given the description below of various operations, implement the Colormap ADT using a 1-D array structure.

- **ColorMap(k)**: Creates a new empty colormap that is capable of storing up to k colors.

- **length ()**: Returns the number of colors currently stored in the colormap.

- **contains (color)**: Determines if the given color is contained in the colormap.

- **add(color)**: Adds the given color to the colormap. Only one instance of each color can be added to the colormap. In addition, a color cannot be added to a full colormap.

- **remove (color)**: Removes the given color from the colormap. The color must be contained in the colormap in order to be removed.

- **map(color)**: Maps the given **color** to an entry in the colormap and returns that color. A common approach is to map the **color** to its nearest neighbor in the colormap. The nearest neighbor of a color is the entry in the colormap that has the minimum Euclidean distance squared between the two colors. If there is more than one nearest neighbor in the colormap, only one is returned. In addition, the colormap must contain at least one color in order to perform the mapping operation.

- **iterator ()**: Creates and returns an iterator object that can be used to iterate over the colors in the colormap.

5.6 Evaluate the **map()** method of your implementation of the Colormap ADT from the previous question to determine the worst case time-complexity.

5.7 Colormaps are used in color quantization, which is the process of reducing the number of colors in an image while trying to maintain the original appearance as much as possible. Part of the process recolors an original image using a reduced set of colors specified in a colormap.

(a) Implement the function **recolorImage(image, colormap)**, which produces a new **ColorImage** that results from mapping the color of each pixel in the given **image** to its nearest neighbor in the given **colormap**.

(b) What is the worst case time-complexity for your implementation?

## CHAPTER 6

Linked Structures

An array is the most basic sequence container used to store and access a collection of data. It provides easy and direct access to the individual elements and is supported at the hardware level. But arrays are limited in their functionality. The Python list, which is also a sequence container, is an abstract sequence type implemented using an array structure. It extends the functionality of an array by providing a larger set of operations than the array, and it can automatically adjust in size as items are added or removed.

The array and Python list can be used to implement many different abstract data types. They both store data in linear order and provide easy access to their elements. The binary search can be used with both structures when the items are stored in sorted order to allow for quick searches. But there are several disadvantages in the use of the array and Python list. First, insertion and deletion operations typically require items to be shifted to make room or close a gap. This can be time consuming, especially for large sequences. Second, the size of an array is fixed and cannot change. While the Python list does provide for an expandable collection, that expansion does not come without a cost. Since the elements of a Python list are stored in an array, an expansion requires the creation of a new larger array into which the elements of the original array have to be copied. Finally, the elements of an array are stored in contiguous bytes of memory, no matter the size of the array. Each time an array is created, the program must find and allocate a block of memory large enough to store the entire array. For large arrays, it can be difficult or impossible for the program to locate a block of memory into which the array can be stored. This is especially true in the case of a Python list that grows larger during the execution of a program since each expansion requires ever larger blocks of memory.

In this chapter, we introduce the linked list data structure, which is a general purpose structure that can be used to store a collection in linear order. The linked list improves on the construction and management of an array and Python list by requiring smaller memory allocations and no element shifts for insertions and deletions. But it does eliminate the constant time direct element access available with the array and Python list. Thus, it's not suitable for every data storage problem. There are several varieties of linked lists. The singly linked list is a linear structure in which traversals start at the front and progress, one element at a time, to the end. Other variations include the circularly linked, the doubly linked, and the circularly doubly linked lists.

6.1   Introduction

Suppose we have a basic class containing a single data field:

```
class ListNode :
  def __init__( self, data ) :
    self.data = data
```

We can create several instances of this class, each storing data of our choosing. In the following example, we create three instances, each storing an integer value:

```
a = ListNode( 11 )
b = ListNode( 52 )
c = ListNode( 18 )
```

the result of which is the creation of three variables and three objects :

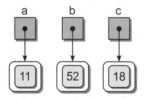

Now, suppose we add a second data field to the ListNode class:

```
class ListNode :
  def __init__( self, data ) :
    self.data = data
    self.next = None
```

The three objects from the previous example would now have a second data field initialized with a null reference, as illustrated in the following:

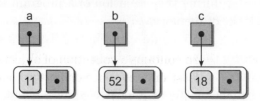

Since the `next` field can contain a reference to any type of object, we can assign to it a reference to one of the other `ListNode` objects. For example, suppose we assign b to the `next` field of object a:

```
a.next = b
```

which results in object a being linked to object b, as shown here:

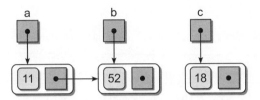

And finally, we can link object b to object c:

```
b.next = c
```

resulting in a chain of objects, as illustrated here:

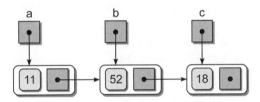

We can remove the two external references b and c by assigning `None` to each, as shown here:

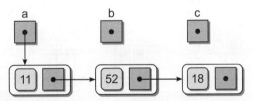

The result is a linked list structure. The two objects previously pointed to by b and c are still accessible via a. For example, suppose we wanted to print the values of the three objects. We can access the other two objects through the `next` field of the first object:

```
print( a.data )
print( a.next.data )
print( a.next.next.data )
```

A *linked structure* contains a collection of objects called *nodes*, each of which contains data and at least one reference or *link* to another node. A *linked list* is a linked structure in which the nodes are connected in sequence to form a linear list. Figure 6.1 provides an example of a linked list consisting of five nodes. The last node in the list, commonly called the **tail node**, is indicated by a null link reference. Most nodes in the list have no name and are simply referenced via the link field of the preceding node. The first node in the list, however, must be named or referenced by an external variable as it provides an entry point into the linked list. This variable is commonly known as the head pointer, or **head reference**. A linked list can also be empty, which is indicated when the head reference is null.

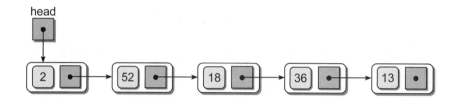

Figure 6.1: A singly linked list consisting of five nodes and a head reference.

Linked structures are built using fundamental components provided by the programming language, namely reference variables and objects. The linked list is just one of several linked structures that we can create. If more links are added to each node, as illustrated in Figure 6.2, we can connect the nodes to form any type of configuration we may need. The tree structure, which organizes the nodes in a hierarchical fashion, is another commonly used linked structure that we explore later in Chapters 13 and 14.

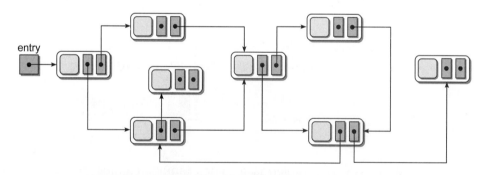

Figure 6.2: An example of a complex linked structure.

A linked list is a data structure that can be used to implement any number of abstract data types. While some languages do provide, as part of their standard library, a generic List ADT implemented using a linked list, we are going to create and work with linked lists directly. Some algorithms and abstract data types can be implemented more efficiently if we have direct access to the individual nodes within the ADT than would be possible if we created a generic linked list class.

In the next section, we explore the construction and management of a singly linked list independent of its use in the implementation of any specific ADT. In later sections we then present examples to show how linked lists can be used to implement abstract data types. We also include a number of exercises at the end of the chapter that provide practice in the construction and management of singly linked lists.

> **NOTE**
>
> ⟨i⟩ **External References.** We use the term *external reference* to indicate those reference variables that point to a node but are not themselves contained within a node as is the case with the link fields. Some external references must be permanent or exist during the lifetime of the linked list in order to maintain the collection of nodes. Others are only needed on a temporary basis in order to perform a specific operation. These temporary external references should be local variables that disappear after the function or method has completed.

6.2   The Singly Linked List

A *singly linked list* is a linked list in which each node contains a single link field and allows for a complete traversal from a distinctive first node to the last. The linked list in Figure 6.1 is an example of a singly linked list.

There are several operations that are commonly performed on a singly linked list, which we explore in this section. To illustrate the implementation of these operations, our code assumes the existence of a head reference and uses the `ListNode` class defined earlier. The data fields of the `ListNode` class will be accessed directly but this class should not be used outside the module in which it is defined as it is only intended for use by the linked list implementation.

6.2.1   Traversing the Nodes

In the earlier example, we accessed the second and third nodes of our sample list by stringing together the `next` field name off the external reference variable `a`. This may be sufficient for lists with few nodes, but it's impractical for large lists. Instead, we can use a temporary external reference to traverse through the list, moving the reference along as we access the individual nodes. The implementation is provided Listing 6.1.

The process starts by assigning a temporary external reference `curNode` to point to the first node of the list, as illustrated in Figure 6.3(a). After entering the loop, the value stored in the first node is printed by accessing the data component stored in the node using the external reference. The external reference is then advanced to the next node by assigning it the value of the current node's link field, as illustrated in Figure 6.3(b). The loop iteration continues until every node in

(a) After initializing the temporary external reference.

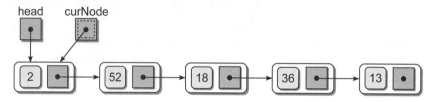

(b) Advancing the external reference after printing value 2.

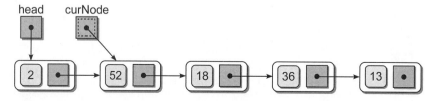

(c) Advancing the external reference after printing value 52.

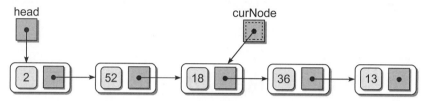

(d) Advancing the external reference after printing value 18.

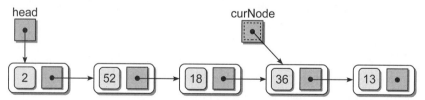

(e) Advancing the external reference after printing value 36.

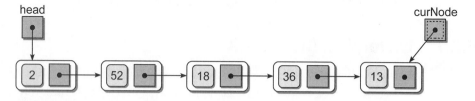

(f) The external reference is set to None after printing value 13.

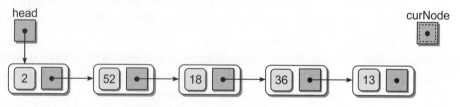

Figure 6.3: Traversing a linked list requires the initialization and adjustment of a temporary external reference variable.

Listing 6.1   Traversing a linked list.

```
1  def traversal( head ):
2    curNode = head
3    while curNode is not None :
4      print curNode.data
5      curNode = curNode.next
```

---

the list has been accessed. The completion of the traversal is determined when curNode becomes null, as illustrated in Figure 6.3(f). After accessing the last node in the list, curNode is advanced to the next node, but there being no next node, curNode is assigned None from the next field of the last node.

A correct implementation of the linked list traversal must also handle the case where the list is empty. Remember, an empty list is indicated by a null head reference. If the list were empty, the curNode reference would be set to null in line 2 of Listing 6.1 and the loop would not execute producing the correct result. A complete list traversal requires $O(n)$ time since each node must be accessed and each access only requires constant time.

6.2.2 Searching for a Node

A linear search operation can be performed on a linked list. It is very similar to the traversal demonstrated earlier. The only difference is that the loop can terminate early if we find the target value within the list. Our implementation of the linear search is illustrated in Listing 6.2.

Listing 6.2   Searching a linked list.

```
1  def unorderedSearch( head, target ):
2    curNode = head
3    while curNode is not None and curNode.data != target :
4      curNode= curNode.next
5    return curNode is not None
```

Note the order of the two conditions in the while loop. It is important that we test for a null curNode reference before trying to examine the contents of the node. If the item is not found in the list, curNode will be null when the end of the list is reached. If we try to evaluate the data field of the null reference, an exception will be raised, resulting in a run-time error. Remember, a null reference does not point to an object and thus there are no fields or methods to be referenced.

When implementing the search operation for the linked list, we must make sure it works with both empty and non-empty lists. In this case, we do not need a separate test to determine if the list is empty. This is done automatically by checking the traversal reference variable as the loop condition. If the list were empty, curNode would be set to None initially and the loop would never be entered. The linked list search operation requires $O(n)$ in the worst case, which occurs when the target item is not in the list.

6.2.3   Prepending Nodes

When working with an unordered list, new values can be inserted at any point within the list. Since we only maintain the head reference as part of the list structure, we can simply prepend new items with little effort. The implementation is provided in Listing 6.3. Prepending a node can be done in constant time since no traversal is required.

Listing 6.3   Prepending a node to the linked list.

```
1  # Given the head pointer, prepend an item to an unsorted linked list.
2  newNode = ListNode( item )
3  newNode.next = head
4  head = newNode
```

Suppose we want to add the value 96 to our example list shown in Figure 6.4(a). Adding an item to the front of the list requires several steps. First, we must create a new node to store the new value and then set its **next** field to point to the node currently at the front of the list. We then adjust **head** to point to the new node since it is now the first node in the list. These steps are represented as dashed lines in Figure 6.4(b). Note the order of the new links since it is important we first link the new node into the list before modifying the head reference. Otherwise, we lose

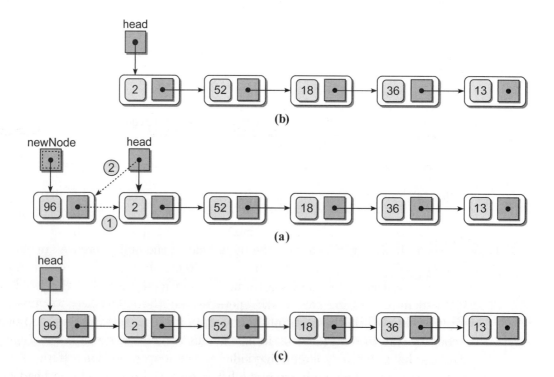

Figure 6.4: Prepending a node to the linked list: (a) the original list from Figure 6.1; (b) link modifications required to prepend the node; and (c) the result after prepending 96.

our external reference to the list and in turn, we lose the list itself. The results, after linking the new node into the list, are shown in Figure 6.4(c).

When modifying or changing links in a linked list, we must consider the case when the list is empty. For our implementation, the code works perfectly since the `head` reference will be null when the list is empty and the first node inserted needs the `next` field set to `None`.

6.2.4 Removing Nodes

An item can be removed from a linked list by removing or unlinking the node containing that item. Consider the linked list from Figure 6.4(c) and assume we want to remove the node containing 18. First, we must find the node containing the target value and position an external reference variable pointing to it, as illustrated in Figure 6.5(a). After finding the node, it has to be unlinked from the list, which entails adjusting the link field of the node's predecessor to point to its successor as shown in Figure 6.5(b). The node's link field is also cleared by setting it to `None`.

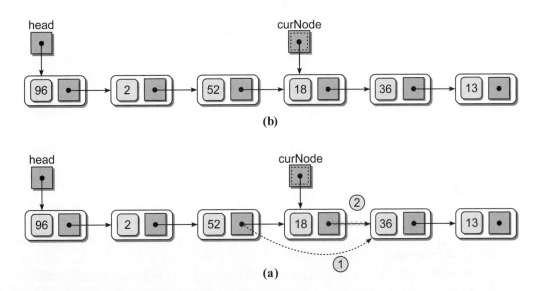

Figure 6.5: Deleting a node from a linked list: (a) finding the node to be removed and assigning an external reference variable and (b) the link modifications required to unlink and remove a node.

Accessing the node's successor is very simple using the `next` link of the node. But we must also access the node's predecessor in order to change its link. The only way we can do this is to position another external reference simultaneously during the search for the given node, as illustrated in Figure 6.6(a). The result after removing the node containing value 18 is shown in Figure 6.6(b).

Removing the first node from the list is a special case since the head pointer references this node. There is no predecessor that has to be relinked, but the head reference must be adjusted to point to the next node, as illustrated in Figure 6.7.

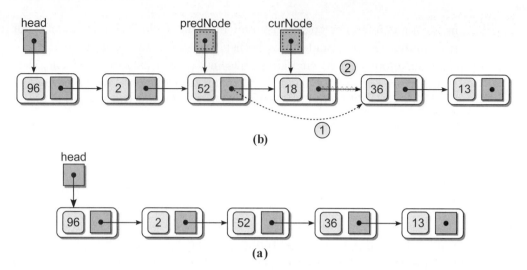

Figure 6.6: Using a second temporary reference to remove a node from a linked list: (a) positioning the second temporary reference variable `predNode`, and (b) the resulting list after removing 18 from the linked list.

We now step through the code required for deleting a node from a singly linked list, as illustrated in Listing 6.4. The `curNode` external reference is initially set to the first node in the list, the same as is done in the traversal and search operations. The `predNode` external reference is set to `None` since there is no predecessor to the first node in the list.

A loop is used to position the two temporary external reference variables as shown in lines 4–6 of Listing 6.4. As the `curNode` reference is moved along the list in the body of the loop, the `predNode` reference follows behind. Thus, `predNode` must be assigned to reference the same node as `curNode` before advancing `curNode` to reference the next node.

After positioning the two external references, there are three possible conditions: (1) the item is not in the list; (2) the item is in the first node; or (3) the item is somewhere else in the list. If the target is not in the list, `curNode` will be null, having been assigned `None` via the link field of the last node. This condition is evaluated in line 8. To determine if the target is in the first node, we can simply compare `curNode` to `head` and determine if they reference the same node. If they do, we set `head` to point to the next node in the list, as shown in lines 9–10.

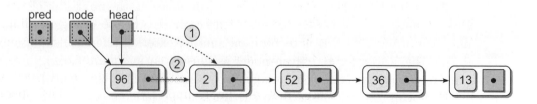

Figure 6.7: Modifications required to remove the first node of a linked list.

Listing 6.4	Removing a node from a linked list.

```
1  # Given the head reference, remove a target from a linked list.
2  predNode = None
3  curNode = head
4  while curNode is not None and curNode.data != target :
5    predNode = curNode
6    curNode = curNode.next
7
8  if curNode is not None :
9    if curNode is head :
10     head = curNode.next
11   else :
12     predNode.next = curNode.next
```

If the target is elsewhere in the list, we simply adjust the link field of the node referenced by predNode to point to the node following the one referenced by curNode. This step is performed in the else clause of the condition as shown in line 12 of Listing 6.4. If the last node is being removed, the same code can be used because the next field of the node pointed to by predNode will be set to None since curNode will be null. Removing a node from a linked list requires $O(n)$ time since the node could be at the end of the list, in which case a complete traversal is required to locate the node.

6.3 The Bag ADT Revisited

To illustrate the use of the linked list structure, we implement a new version of the Bag ADT, which we originally defined in Section 1.3. The new implementation is shown in Listing 6.5 on the next page.

6.3.1 A Linked List Implementation

We begin our discussion of the linked list implementation of the Bag ADT with the constructor. First, the _head field will store the head pointer of the linked list. The reference is initialized to None to represent an empty bag. The _size field is used to keep track of the number of items stored in the bag that is needed by the __len__ method. Technically, this field is not needed. But it does prevent us from having to traverse the list to count the number of nodes each time the length is needed. Notice we only define a head pointer as a data field in the object. Temporary references such as the curNode reference used to traverse the list are not defined as attributes, but instead as local variables within the individual methods as needed. A sample instance of the new Bag class is illustrated in Figure 6.8.

The contains() method is a simple search of the linked list as described earlier in the chapter. The add() method simply implements the prepend operation, though we must also increment the item counter (_size) as new items are added. The _BagListNode class, used to represent the individual nodes, is also defined

Listing 6.5   The `llistbag.py` module.

```python
1  # Implements the Bag ADT using a singly linked list.
2
3  class Bag :
4     # Constructs an empty bag.
5     def __init__( self ):
6       self._head = None
7       self._size = 0
8
9     # Returns the number of items in the bag.
10    def __len__( self ):
11      return self._size
12
13    # Determines if an item is contained in the bag.
14    def __contains__( self, target ):
15      curNode = self._head
16      while curNode is not None and curNode.item != target :
17        curNode = curNode.next
18      return curNode is not None
19
20    # Adds a new item to the bag.
21    def add( self, item ):
22      newNode = _BagListNode( item )
23      newNode.next = self._head
24      self._head = newNode
25      self._size += 1
26
27    # Removes an instance of the item from the bag.
28    def remove( self, item ):
29      predNode = None
30      curNode = self._head
31      while curNode is not None and curNode.item != item :
32        predNode = curNode
33        curNode = curNode.next
34
35      # The item has to be in the bag to remove it.
36      assert curNode is not None, "The item must be in the bag."
37
38      # Unlink the node and return the item.
39      self._size -= 1
40      if curNode is head :
41        self._head = curNode.next
42      else :
43        predNode.next = curNode.next
44      return curNode.item
45
46    # Returns an iterator for traversing the list of items.
47    def __iter__( self ):
48      return _BagIterator( self._head )
49
50  # Defines a private storage class for creating list nodes.
51  class _BagListNode( object ):
52    def __init__( self, item ) :
53      self.item = item
54      self.next = None
```

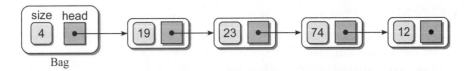

Figure 6.8: Sample instance of the Bag class.

within the same module. It is specified in lines 51–54 at the bottom of the module, but it is not intended for use outside the `Bag` class.

The `remove()` method implements the removal operation as presented in the previous section, but with a couple of modifications. The `if` statement that checked the status of the `curNode` variable has been replaced with an `assert` statement. This was necessary since the remove operation of the bag has a precondition that the item must be in the bag in order to be removed. If we make it pass the assertion, the item counter is decremented to reflect one less item in the bag, the node containing the item is unlinked from the linked list, and the item is returned as required by the ADT definition.

6.3.2 Comparing Implementations

The Python list and the linked list can both be used to manage the elements stored in a bag. Both implementations provide the same time-complexities for the various operations with the exception of the `add()` method. When adding an item to a bag implemented using a Python list, the item is appended to the list, which requires $O(n)$ time in the worst case since the underlying array may have to be expanded. In the linked list version of the Bag ADT, a new bag item is stored in a new node that is prepended to the linked structure, which only requires $O(1)$. Table 6.1 shows the time-complexities for two implementations of the Bag ADT.

In general, the choice between a linked list or a Python list depends on the application as both have advantages and disadvantages. The linked list is typically a better choice for those applications involving large amounts of *dynamic data*, data that changes quite often. If there will be a large number of insertions and/or deletions, the linked structure provides a fast implementation since large amounts

Operation	Python List	Linked List
`b = Bag()`	$O(1)$	$O(1)$
`n = len(b)`	$O(1)$	$O(1)$
`x in b`	$O(n)$	$O(n)$
`b.add(x)`	$O(n)$	$O(1)$
`b.remove(x)`	$O(n)$	$O(n)$
traversal	$O(n)$	$O(n)$

Table 6.1: Comparing the Bag ADT implemented using a Python list and a linked list.

of data do not have to be shifted as is required by the Python list. This is especially true when prepending items. On the other hand, the Python list is a better choice in those applications where individual elements must be accessed by index. This can be simulated with a linked list, but it requires a traversal of the list, resulting in a linear operation whereas the Python list only requires constant time.

6.3.3   Linked List Iterators

Suppose we want to provide an iterator for our Bag ADT implemented using a linked list as we did for the one implemented using a Python list. The process would be similar, but our iterator class would have to keep track of the current node in the linked list instead of the current element in the Python list. We define a bag iterator class in Listing 6.6, which would be placed within the `llistbag.py` module that can be used to iterate over the linked list.

Listing 6.6   An iterator for the Bag class implemented using a linked list.

```
1  # Defines a linked list iterator for the Bag ADT.
2  class _BagIterator :
3    def __init__( self, listHead ):
4      self._curNode = listHead
5
6    def __iter__( self ):
7      return self
8
9    def next( self ):
10     if self._curNode is None :
11       raise StopIteration
12     else :
13       item = self._curNode.item
14       self._curNode = self._curNode.next
15       return item
```

When iterating over a linked list, we need only keep track of the current node being processed and thus we use a single data field `_curNode` in the iterator. This reference will be advanced through the linked list as the `for` loop iterates over the nodes. As was done with our Python list-based `Bag` class, the linked list version must include the `__iter__` method (shown in lines 47–48 of Listing 6.5), which returns an instance of the `_BagIterator` class.

Figure 6.9 illustrates the `Bag` and `_BagIterator` objects at the beginning of the `for` loop. The `_curNode` pointer in the `_BagIterator` object is used just like the `curNode` pointer we used when directly performing a linked list traversal earlier in the chapter. The only difference is that we don't include a `while` loop since Python manages the iteration for us as part of the `for` loop. Note, the iterator objects can be used with any singly linked list configuration to traverse the nodes and return the data contained in each.

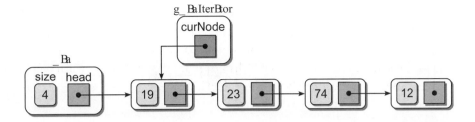

Figure 6.9: Sample `Bag` and `_BagIterator` objects at the beginning of the `for` loop.

6.4 More Ways to Build a Linked List

Earlier in the chapter, we saw that new nodes can be easily added to a linked list by prepending them to the linked structure. This is sufficient when the linked list is used to implement a basic container in which a linear order is not needed, such as with the Bag ADT. But a linked list can also be used to implement a container abstract data type that requires a specific linear ordering of its elements, such as with a Vector ADT. In addition, some implementations, such as in the case of the Set ADT, can be improved if we have access to the end of the list or if the nodes are sorted by element value.

6.4.1 Using a Tail Reference

The use of a single external reference to point to the head of a linked list is sufficient for many applications. In some instances, however, we may need to append items to the end of the list instead. Appending a new node to the list using only a head reference requires linear time since a complete traversal is required to reach the end of the list. Instead of a single external head reference, we can use two external references, one for the head and one for the tail. Figure 6.10 illustrates a sample linked list with both a head and a *tail reference*.

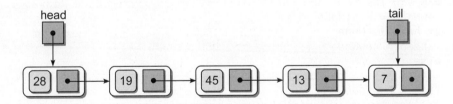

Figure 6.10: Sample linked list using both head and tail external references.

Appending Nodes

Adding the external tail reference to the linked list requires that we manage both references as nodes are added and removed. Consider the process of appending a new node to a non-empty list, as illustrated in Figure 6.11(a). First, a new node is created to store the value to be appended to the list. Then, the node is linked

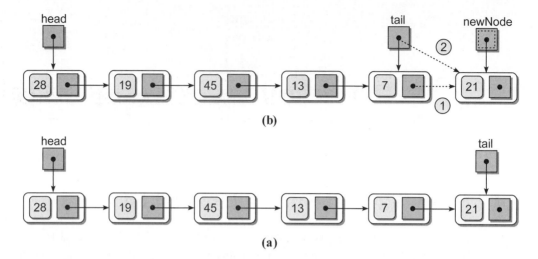

Figure 6.11: Appending a node to a linked list using a tail reference: (a) the links required to append the node, and (b) the resulting list after appending 21.

into the list following the last node. The `next` field of the node referenced by `tail` is set to point to the new node. The `tail` reference has to be adjusted to point to the new node since `tail` must always point to the last node in the list. The linked list resulting from appending 21 to the list is illustrated in Figure 6.11(b).

If the list is empty, there is no existing node in which the link field can be adjusted. Instead, both the `head` and `tail` references will be null. In this case, the new node is appended to the list by simply adjusting both external references to point to the new node. The code for appending a node to the linked list is provided in Listing 6.7. It assumes the existence of both the head and tail reference variables.

Listing 6.7 Appending a node to a linked list using a tail reference.

```
1  # Given the head and tail pointers, adds an item to a linked list.
2  newNode = ListNode( item )
3  if head is None :
4    head = newNode
5  else :
6    tail.next = newNode
7  tail = newNode
```

Removing Nodes

Removing a node from a linked list in which both head and tail references are used requires a simple modification to the code presented earlier in the chapter. Consider the sample list in Figure 6.12, in which we want to delete the node containing 21. After unlinking the node to be removed, we must check to see if it was at the end

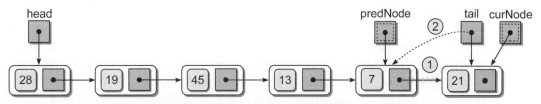

Figure 6.12: Deleting the last node in a list using a tail reference.

of the list. If it was, we must adjust the tail reference to point to the same node as predNode, which is now the last node in the list.

The code for removing an item from a linked list using a tail reference is shown in Listing 6.8. If the list contains a single node, the head reference will be assigned None when it is assigned the contents of the node's next field. The tail reference will also be set to None when it is set to predNode.

| Listing 6.8 | Removing a node from a linked list using a tail reference. |

```
1  # Given the head and tail references, removes a target from a linked list.
2  predNode = None
3  curNode = head
4  while curNode is not None and curNode.data != target :
5      predNode = curNode
6      curNode = curNode.next
7
8  if curNode is not None :
9      if curNode is head :
10         head = curNode.next
11     else :
12         predNode.next = curNode.next
13     if curNode is tail :
14         tail = predNode
```

6.4.2 The Sorted Linked List

The items in a linked list can be sorted in ascending or descending order as was done with a sequence. Consider the sorted linked list illustrated in Figure 6.13. The sorted list has to be created and maintained as items are added and removed.

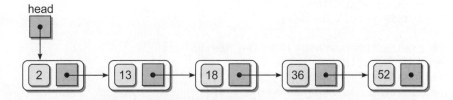

Figure 6.13: A sorted linked list with items in ascending order.

Linear Search

The linear search for use with the linked list can be modified to take advantage of the sorted items. The only change required is to add a second condition that terminates the loop early if we encounter a value larger than the target. The search routine for a sorted linked list is shown in Listing 6.9.

Listing 6.9   Searching a sorted linked list.

```
1  def sortedSearch( head, target ) :
2    curNode = head
3    while curNode is not None and curNode.data < target :
4      if curNode.data == target :
5        return True
6      else :
7        curNode = node.next
8    return False
```

Inserting Nodes

Adding a new node to an unsorted linked list is simple because we can simply add it to the front or end of the list since its placement is not important. When adding a node to a sorted list, however, the correct position for the new value must be found and the new node linked into the list at that position. The Python implementation for inserting a value into a sorted linked list is provided in Listing 6.10.

As with the removal operation for the unsorted list, we must position two temporary external references by traversing through the linked list searching for the correct position of the new value. The only difference is the loop termination condition. To insert a new node, we must terminate the loop upon finding the first value larger than the new value being added.

Listing 6.10   Inserting a value into a sorted list.

```
1  # Given the head pointer, insert a value into a sorted linked list.
2   # Find the insertion point for the new value.
3  predNode = None
4  curNode = head
5  while curNode is not None and value > curNode.data :
6    predNode = curNode
7    curNode = curNode.next
8
9   # Create the new node for the new value.
10 newNode = ListNode( value )
11 newNode.next = curNode
12  # Link the new node into the list.
13 if curNode is head :
14   head = newNode
15 else :
16   predNode.next = newNode
```

Three cases can occur when inserting a node into a sorted linked list, as illustrated in Figure 6.14: the node is inserted in the front, at the end, or somewhere in the middle. After finding the correct position, a new node is created and its `next` field is changed to point to the same node referenced by `curNode`. This link is required no matter where in the list the new node is inserted. If the new node is to be inserted in the front, then the operation is a simple prepend, as was done with an unsorted linked list, and `curNode` will be pointing to the first node. When the new value being added is the largest in the list and the new node is to be added at the end, `curNode` will be null and thus the `next` field will be null as it should be. When the new node is inserted elsewhere in the list, `curNode` will be pointing to the node that will follow the new node.

After linking the new node to the list, we must determine if it is being inserted at the front of the list, in which case the `head` reference must be adjusted. We do this by comparing the `curNode` reference with the `head` reference. If they are aliases, the new node comes first in the linked list and we must adjust the `head`

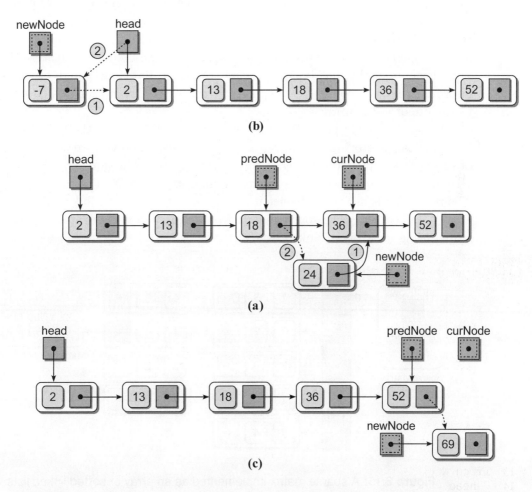

Figure 6.14: Inserting a new value into a sorted linked list: (a) inserting -7 at the front of the list; (b) inserting 24 in the middle of the list; (c) inserting 69 at the end of the list.

reference to point to the new node. If the two nodes are not aliases, then the node is inserted by setting the `next` field of the node referenced by `predNode` to point to the new node. This step is handled by lines 13–16 of Listing 6.10.

Traversing and Deleting

The traversal operation implemented for the unsorted linked list can be used with both sorted and unsorted linked lists since it is not dependent on the contents of the list itself. Deleting from a sorted linked list is the same operation used with an unsorted list with one exception. Searching for the node containing the target value can end early after encountering the first value larger than the one to be deleted.

6.5 The Sparse Matrix Revisited

In the previous chapter, we defined and implemented the Sparse Matrix ADT. Remember, a sparse matrix is a matrix containing a large number of zero elements. Instead of providing space for every element in the matrix, we need only store the non-zero elements. In our original implementation, we used a list to store the non-zero elements of the matrix, which were stored as _MatrixElement objects. This improved the time-complexity of many of the matrix operations when compared to the use of a 2-D array.

We can further improve the Sparse Matrix ADT by using the linked list structure. Instead of storing the elements in a single list, however, we can use an array of sorted linked lists, one for each row of the matrix. The non-zero elements for a given row will be stored in the corresponding linked list sorted by column index. The row index is not needed since it corresponds to a specific linked list within the array of linked lists. The sparse matrix from Figure 4.5 is illustrated in Figure 6.15 stored using an array of linked lists.

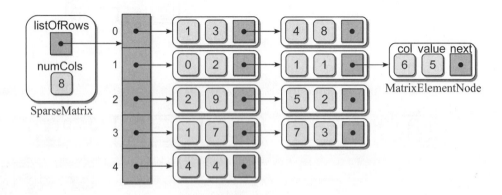

Figure 6.15: A sparse matrix implemented as an array of sorted linked lists.

6.5.1   An Array of Linked Lists Implementation

To implement the Sparse Matrix ADT using an array of sorted linked lists, we create a new `SparseMatrix` class, as shown in Listing 6.11. In the constructor, two class fields are created: one to store the number of columns in the matrix and another to store the array of head references to the linked lists in which the matrix elements will be stored. An array is created whose size is equal to the number of rows in the matrix. The individual elements are initialized to `None` to represent empty linked lists since there are no non-zero elements in the sparse matrix initially. Note we did not provide a field to store the number of rows as that information can be obtained from the length of the array. Thus, `numRows()` simply calls the array's length operation.

The `_MatrixElementNode` class, provided in lines 95–99, is a modified version of the `_MatrixElement` class used in Chapter 4. The row component has been removed while the `next` link field was added in order to use the objects as linked nodes. When elements are added to the sparse matrix, nodes will be added to the individual linked lists based on the row index of the element. Thus, the row component does not have to be stored in each node.

Changing Element Values

The `__setitem__` method is the main linked list management routine for the underlying structure. This method not only provides for the modification of element values, but it also handles node insertions for new non-zero elements and node removals when an element becomes zero. The three operations handled by this method can be combined to produce an efficient implementation.

The first step is to position the two external reference variables `predNode` and `curNode` along the linked list corresponding to the indicated row index. While only the `curNode` reference will be needed for a simple element value modification, `predNode` will be needed if we have to insert a new node or remove an existing node. After positioning the two references, we can then determine what action must be taken.

If the element corresponding to the given `row` and `col` indices is in the linked list, `curNode` will be pointing to a node and the `col` field of that node will be that of the element. In this case, either the value stored in the node is changed to the new non-zero value or the node has to be deleted when the new value is zero. Modifying the value only requires changing the `value` field of the `curNode`. Removing the element entry for a zero value is also straightforward since the two external references have been positioned correctly and the links can be changed as outlined in Section 6.2.4.

If the element is not represented by a node in the linked list of the corresponding row and the new value is non-zero, then a new node must be inserted in the proper position based on the `predNode` and `curNode` references. The only difference in the insertion operation from that used earlier in the chapter is that the head reference is stored in one of the elements of the `_listOfRows` array instead of its own variable. If the element is already a zero-entry and the new value is zero, no action is required.

Setting the value of a matrix element requires $O(n)$ time in the worst case, where n is the number of columns in the matrix. This value is obtained by observing that the most time-consuming part is the positioning of the two references, `curNode` and `predNode`, which require a complete list traversal in the worst case. Since a linked list contains a single row, we know it will contain at most n nodes.

Listing 6.11   The `llistsparse.py` module

```
1   # Implementation of the Sparse Matrix ADT using an array of linked lists.
2   from array import Array
3
4   class SparseMatrix :
5     # Creates a sparse matrix of size numRows x numCols initialized to 0.
6     def __init__( self, numRows, numCols ):
7       self._numCols = numCols
8       self._listOfRows = Array( numRows )
9
10    # Returns the number of rows in the matrix.
11    def numRows( self ):
12      return len( self._listOfRows )
13
14    # Returns the number of columns in the matrix.
15    def numCols( self ):
16      return self._numCols
17
18    # Returns the value of element (i,j): x[i,j]
19    def __getitem__( self, ndxTuple ):
20      ......
21
22    # Sets the value of element (i,j) to the value s: x[i,j] = s
23    def __setitem__( self, ndxTuple, value ):
24      predNode = None
25      curNode = self._listOfRows[row]
26      while curNode is not None and curNode.col != col :
27        predNode = curNode
28        curNode = curNode.next
29
30       # See if the element is in the list.
31      if curNode is not None and curNode.col == col :
32        if value == 0.0 :   # remove the node.
33          if curNode == self._listOfRows[row] :
34            self._listOfRows[row] = curNode.next
35          else :
36            predNode.next = curNode.next
37        else :                  # change the node's value.
38          curNode.value = value
39
40       # Otherwise, the element is not in the list.
41      elif value != 0.0 :
42        newNode = _MatrixElementNode( col, value )
43        newNode.next == curNode
44        if curNode == self._listOfRows[row] :
```

```
45              self._listOfRows[row] = newNode
46          else :
47            predNode.next = newnode
48
49    # Scales the matrix by the given scalar.
50    def scaleBy( self, scalar ):
51      for row in range( self.numRows() ) :
52        curNode = self._listOfRows[row]
53        while curNode is not None :
54          curNode.value *= scalar
55          curNode = curNode.next
56
57    # Creates and returns a new matrix that is the transpose of this matrix.
58    def transpose( self ):
59      ......
60
61    # Matrix addition: newMatrix = self + rhsMatrix.
62    def __add__( self, rhsMartrix ) :
63      # Make sure the two matrices have the correct size.
64      assert rhsMatrix.numRows() == self.numRows() and \
65             rhsMatrix.numCols() == self.numCols(), \
66             "Matrix sizes not compatable for adding."
67
68      # Create a new sparse matrix of the same size.
69      newMatrix = SparseMatrix( self.numRows(), self.numCols() )
70
71      # Add the elements of this matrix to the new matrix.
72      for row in range( self.numRows() ) :
73        curNode = self._listOfRows[row]
74        while curNode is not None :
75          newMatrix[row, curNode.col] = curNode.value
76          curNode = curNode.next
77
78      # Add the elements of the rhsMatrix to the new matrix.
79      for row in range( rhsMatrix.numRows() ) :
80        curNode = rhsMatrix._listOfRows[row]
81        while curNode is not None :
82          value = newMatrix[row, curNode.col]
83          value += curNode.value
84          newMatrix[row, curNode.col] = value
85          curNode = curNode.next
86
87      # Return the new matrix.
88      return newMatrix
89
90  # --- Matrix subtraction and multiplication ---
91  # def __sub__( self, rhsMatrix ) :
92  # def __mul__( self, rhsMatrix ) :
93
94  # Storage class for creating matrix element nodes.
95  class _MatrixElementNode :
96    def __init__( self, col, value ) :
97      self.col = col
98      self.value = value
99      self.next = None
```

Matrix Scaling

The scaleBy() method is very similar to the version used in the list implementation of the original Sparse Matrix ADT from Chapter 4. We need only traverse over each of the individual linked lists stored in the _listOfRows array, during which we scale the value stored in each node. Remember, this is sufficient as elements not represented by nodes in the linked lists have zero values and thus would not be affected by a scaling factor. The matrix scaling operation requires $O(k)$ time in the worst case since only the k non-zero elements are stored in the structure.

Matrix Addition

The __add__ method for this version of the sparse matrix, which is provided in lines 62–88 of Listing 6.11, also follows the four steps outlined in Section 4.5.1. We first create a new SparseMatrix object that will contain the new matrix resulting from the addition. Then, the contents of the self or lefthand-side matrix is copied to the new matrix, one element at a time. Finally, we traverse over the non-zero elements of the righthand-side matrix and add the values of its non-zero elements to the new matrix.

This implementation of the addition operation, which requires $O(kn)$ time in the worst case, is not the most efficient. Instead of using the __getitem__ and __setitem__ operations, we can use temporary traversal reference variables with each matrix to directly access the non-zero values in the two source matrices and to store the resulting non-zero values in the new matrix. A new implementation can be devised that only requires $O(k)$ time in the worst case.

6.5.2   Comparing the Implementations

The Sparse Matrix ADT implemented as an array of linked lists can be evaluated for any of the three cases: best, average, and worst. The analysis, which is left as an exercise, depends on the relationship between the total number of non-zero elements, k, and the number of columns, n, in the matrix.

We implemented the Matrix ADT using a 2-D array that can be used to store a sparse matrix and we implemented the Sparse Matrix ADT using two different data structures: a list of _MatrixElement objects, and an array of linked lists. Table 6.2 provides a comparison of the worst case time-complexities between the three implementations for several of the matrix operations. The 2-D array implementation offers the best advantage of quick element access with the __getitem__ and __setitem__ methods, but the other matrix operations are more costly. While both the Python list and the array of linked lists implementations provide similar times, the array of linked lists version will typically provide better times since the efficiency for many of the operations is based on the number of columns in the matrix and not the total number of non-zero elements.

Operation	2-D Array	Python List	Linked Lists
constructor	$O(1)$	$O(1)$	$O(1)$
s.numRows()	$O(1)$	$O(1)$	$O(1)$
s.numCols()	$O(1)$	$O(1)$	$O(1)$
x = s[i,j]	$O(1)$	$O(k)$	$O(n)$
s[i,j] = x	$O(1)$	$O(k)$	$O(n)$
s.scaleBy(x)	$O(n^2)$	$O(k)$	$O(k)$
r = s + t	$O(n^2)$	$O(k^2)$	$O(kn)$

Table 6.2: Comparison of the Matrix and Sparse Matrix ADT implementations.

6.6 Application: Polynomials

Polynomials, which are an important concept throughout mathematics and science, are arithmetic expressions specified in terms of variables and constants. A polynomial in one variable can be expressed in expanded form as

$$a_n x^n + a_{n-1} x^{n-1} + a_{n-2} x^{n-2} + \ldots + a_1 x^1 + a_0$$

where each $a_i x^i$ component is called a *term*. The a_i part of the term, which is a scalar that can be zero, is called the *coefficient* of the term. The exponent of the x^i part is called the *degree* of that variable and is limited to whole numbers. For example,

$$12x^2 - 3x + 7$$

consists of three terms. The first term, $12x^2$, is of degree 2 and has a coefficient of 12; the second term, $-3x$, is of degree 1 and has a coefficient of -3; the last term, while constant, is of degree 0 with a coefficient of 7.

Polynomials can be characterized by degree (i.e., all second-degree polynomials). The degree of a polynomial is the largest single degree of its terms. The example polynomial above has a degree of 2 since the degree of the first term, $12x^2$, has the largest degree.

In this section, we design and implement an abstract data type to represent polynomials in one variable expressed in expanded form. The discussion begins with a review of polynomial operations and concludes with a linked list implementation of our Polynomial ADT.

6.6.1 Polynomial Operations

A number of operations can be performed on polynomials. We review several of these operations, beginning with addition.

Addition

Two polynomials of the same variable can be summed by adding the coefficients of corresponding terms of equal degree. The result is a third polynomial. Consider the following two polynomials:

$$5x^2 + 3x - 10$$
$$2x^3 + 4x^2 + 3$$

which we can add to yield a new polynomial:

$$(5x^2 + 3x - 10) + (2x^3 + 4x^2 + 3) = 2x^3 + 9x^2 + 3x - 7$$

Subtraction is performed in a similar fashion but the coefficients are subtracted instead. Another way to view polynomial addition is to align terms by degree and add the corresponding coefficients:

$$
\begin{array}{rcccc}
 & 5x^2 & 3x & -10 \\
+ & 2x^3 & 4x^2 & & 3 \\
\hline
 & 2x^3 & 9x^2 & 3x & -7
\end{array}
$$

Multiplication

The product of two polynomials is also a third polynomial. The new polynomial is obtained by summing the result from multiplying each term of the first polynomial by each term of the second. Consider the two polynomials from the previous example:

$$(5x^2 + 3x - 10)(2x^3 + 4x^2 + 3)$$

The second polynomial has to be multiplied by each term of the first polynomial:

$$5x^2(2x^3 + 4x^2 + 3) + 3x(2x^3 + 4x^2 + 3) + -10(2x^3 + 4x^2 + 3)$$

We then distribute the terms of the first polynomial to yield three intermediate polynomials:

$$(10x^5 + 20x^4 + 15x^2) + (6x^4 + 12x^3 + 9x) + (-20x^3 - 40x^2 - 30)$$

Finally, the three polynomials are summed, resulting in

$$10x^5 + 26x^4 - 8x^3 - 25x^2 + 9x - 30$$

Evaluation

The easiest operation by far is the evaluation of a polynomial. Polynomials can be evaluated by assigning a value to the variable, commonly called the unknown. By making the variable known in specifying a value, the expression can be computed, resulting in a real value. If we assign value 3 to the variable x in the equation

$$10x^5 + 26x^4 - 8x^3 - 25x^2 + 9x - 30$$

the result will be

$$10(3)^5 + 26(3)^4 - 8(3)^3 - 25(3)^2 + 9(3) - 30 = 4092$$

6.6.2 The Polynomial ADT

Given the overview of polynomials, we now turn our attention to defining the Polynomial ADT.

Define	Polynomial ADT

A *polynomial* is a mathematical expression of a variable constructed of one or more terms. Each term is of the form $a_i x^i$ where a_i is a scalar coefficient and x^i is the unknown variable of degree i.

- Polynomial(): Creates a new polynomial initialized to be empty and thus containing no terms.

- Polynomial(degree, coefficient): Creates a new polynomial initialized with a single term constructed from the degree and coefficient arguments.

- degree(): Returns the degree of the polynomial. If the polynomial contains no terms, a value of -1 is returned.

- *getitem* (degree): Returns the coefficient for the term of the provided degree. Thus, if the expression of this polynomial is $x^3 + 4x + 2$ and a degree of 1 is provided, this operation returns 4. The coefficient cannot be returned for an empty polynomial.

- evaluate(scalar): Evaluates the polynomial at the given scalar value and returns the result. An empty polynomial cannot be evaluated.

- *add* (rhsPolynomial): Creates and returns a new Polynomial that is the result of adding this polynomial and the rhsPoly. This operation is not defined if either polynomial is empty.

- *subtract* (rhsPoly): Creates and returns a new Polynomial that is the result of subtracting this polynomial and the rhsPoly. This operation is not defined if either polynomial is empty.

- *multiply* (rhsPoly): Creates and returns a new Polynomial that is the result of multiplying this polynomial and the rhsPoly. This operation is not defined if either polynomial is empty.

Two constructors were specified for this abstract data type. Most object-oriented languages provide a mechanism to construct an object in various ways. In Python, we define a single constructor and supply default values for the arguments.

6.6.3 Implementation

To implement the Polynomial ADT, we must determine how best to represent the individual terms and how to store and manage the collection of terms. In earlier chapters, we were limited to the use of a list or dictionary. But with the introduction of the linked list in this chapter, we now have an additional option. The linked list has the advantage of requiring fewer shifts and no underlying array management as is required with the Python list. This is especially important when working with dynamic polynomials.

Linked List Structure

We are going to implement our Polynomial ADT using a singly linked list. Given this choice, we must decide how the data should be stored and organized within the linked list. Since a polynomial is constructed as the sum of one or more non-zero terms, we can simply store an individual term in each node of the list as defined by the `PolyTermNode` class, shown in lines 65–69 of Listing 6.12.

Next, we must decide whether to order the nodes within the linked list. Upon analysis of the polynomial operations, it becomes clear an ordered list would be better since many of those operations are based on the degree of the terms. For example, the degree of the polynomial is the degree of the largest term. If the list is ordered, finding the polynomial degree is rather simple. Likewise, you will soon see that ordering the terms allows for a more efficient implementation of the addition and multiplication operations. Unlike previous examples, we are going to order the nodes in descending order based on degree since polynomials are typically written with the terms ordered from largest degree to smallest. A sample linked list structure for the polynomial $5x^2 + 3x - 10$ is illustrated in Figure 6.16.

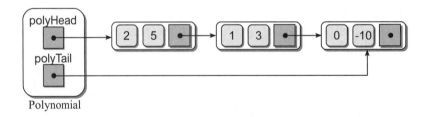

Figure 6.16: A `Polynomial` object for the polynomial $5x^2 + 3x - 10$.

Finally, we need to decide whether our implementation can benefit from the use of a tail pointer or if a head pointer alone will suffice. A rule of thumb in making this decision is whether we will be appending nodes to the list or simply inserting them in their proper position. If you need to append nodes to a linked list, you should use a tail pointer. The implementation of some of our polynomial operations can be improved if we append nodes directly to the end of the linked list. Thus, we will use and manage a tail pointer in our implementation of the Polynomial ADT.

Listing 6.12   Partial implementation of the `polynomial.py` module.

```
1  # Implementation of the Polynomial ADT using a sorted linked list.
2  class Polynomial :
3    # Create a new polynomial object.
4    def __init__(self, degree = None, coefficient = None):
5      if degree is None :
6        self._polyHead = None
7      else :
8        self._polyHead = _PolyTermNode(degree, coefficient)
9      self._polyTail = self._polyHead
10
11   # Return the degree of the polynomial.
12   def degree( self ):
13     if self._polyHead is None :
14       return -1
15     else :
16       return self._polyHead.degree
17
18   # Return the coefficient for the term of the given degree.
19   def __getitem__( self, degree ):
20     assert self.degree() >= 0,
21       "Operation not permitted on an empty polynomial."
22     curNode = self._polyHead
23     while curNode is not None and curNode.degree >= degree :
24       curNode = curNode.next
25
26     if curNode is None or curNode.degree != degree :
27       return 0.0
28     else :
29       return curNode.degree
30
31   # Evaluate the polynomial at the given scalar value.
32   def evaluate( self, scalar ):
33     assert self.degree() >= 0,
34       "Only non-empty polynomials can be evaluated."
35     result = 0.0;
36     curNode = self._polyHead
37     while curNode is not None :
38       result += curNode.coefficient * (scalar ** curNode.degree)
39       curNode = curNode.next
40     return result
41
42  # Polynomial addition: newPoly = self + rhsPoly.
43   def __add__( self, rhsPoly ):
44     ......
45
46   # Polynomial subtraction: newPoly = self - rhsPoly.
47   def __sub__( self, rhsPoly ):
48     ......
49
50   # Polynomial multiplication: newPoly = self * rhsPoly.
51   def __mul__( self, rhsPoly ):
52     ......
53
```

(Listing Continued)

Listing 6.12   Continued ...

```
54      # Helper method for appending terms to the polynomial.
55      def _appendTerm( self, degree, coefficient ) :
56        if coefficient != 0.0 :
57          newTerm = _PolyTermNode( degree, coefficient )
58          if self._polyHead is None :
59            self._polyHead = newTerm
60          else :
61            self._polyTail.next = newTerm
62          self._polyTail = newTerm
63
64  # Class for creating polynomial term nodes used with the linked list.
65  class _PolyTermNode( object ):
66    def __init__( self, degree, coefficient ):
67      self.degree = degree
68      self.coefficient = coefficient
69      self.next = None
```

Basic Operations

The Polynomial ADT calls for two constructors, one for creating an empty polynomial and the other that can be used to create a polynomial initialized with a single term supplied as an argument. In Python, we can provide multiple constructors with the use of default values. The constructor, shown in lines 4–9 of Listing 6.12, defines two data fields, the head and tail pointers, for use with the linked list implementation. These references are either initialized to None or set to point to the first node in the list depending on how the constructor was called.

The degree() method is simple to implement as it returns either the degree of the largest term that is stored in the first node or -1 if the polynomial is not defined. For our ADT, a polynomial is not defined if it does not contain any terms, which is indicated in our implementation by an empty list.

The get operation, which we implement using the subscript operator, returns the coefficient corresponding to a specific term of the polynomial identified by degree. A linear search of the linked list is required to find the corresponding term. Since the nodes are sorted by degree, we can terminate the search early if we encounter a node whose degree is smaller than the target. After the loop terminates, there are two possible conditions. If there is no non-zero term with the given degree, then curNode will either be None or pointing to a list node whose degree is smaller than the target. In this case, we must return a value of 0 since by definition a zero-term has a coefficient of 0. Otherwise, we simply return the coefficient of the corresponding term pointed to by curNode.

A polynomial is evaluated by supplying a specific value for the variable used to represent each term and then summing the terms. The evaluate() method is easily implemented as a list traversal in which a sum is accumulated, term by term. The result is a $O(n)$ time operation, where n is the degree of the polynomial.

Appending Terms

We included a tail reference in our linked list implementation for use by several of the polynomial arithmetic operations in order to perform fast append operations. While the Polynomial ADT does not define an append operation, we want to provide a helper method that implements this operation. It will be used by other methods in the class for creating efficient operations. The _appendTerm() helper method in lines 55–62 of Listing 6.12 accepts the degree and coefficient of a polynomial term, creates a new node to store the term, and appends the node to the end of the list. Since we only store the non-zero terms in the linked list, we must ensure the supplied coefficient is not zero before creating and appending the new node.

Polynomial Addition

The addition of two polynomials can be performed for our linked list implementation using a simple brute-force method, as illustrated in the code segment below:

```
class Polynomial :
# ...
  def simple_add( self, rhsPoly ):
    newPoly = Polynomial()
    if self.degree() > rhsPoly.degree() :
      maxDegree = self.degree()
    else
      maxDegree = rhsPoly.degree()

    i = maxDegree
    while i >= 0 :
      value = self[i] + rhsPoly[i]
      self._appendTerm( i, value )
      i += 1

    return newPoly
```

The new polynomial is created by iterating over the two original polynomials, term by term, from the largest degree among the two polynomials down to degree 0. The element access method is used to extract the coefficients of corresponding terms from each polynomial, which are then added, resulting in a term for the new polynomial. Since we iterate over the polynomials in decreasing degree order, we can simply append the new term to the end of the linked list storing the new polynomial.

This implementation is rather simple, but it's not very efficient. The element access method, which is used to obtain the coefficients, requires $O(n)$ time. Assuming the largest degree between the two polynomials is n, the loop will be executed n times, resulting in quadratic time in the worst case.

The polynomial addition operation can be greatly improved. Upon close examination it becomes clear this problem is similar to that of merging two sorted lists. Consider the linked lists in Figure 6.17 representing three polynomials with the nodes positioned such that corresponding terms are aligned. The top two lists represent the two polynomials $5x^2 + 3x - 10$ and $2x^3 + 4x^2 + 3$ while the bottom list is the polynomial resulting from adding the other two.

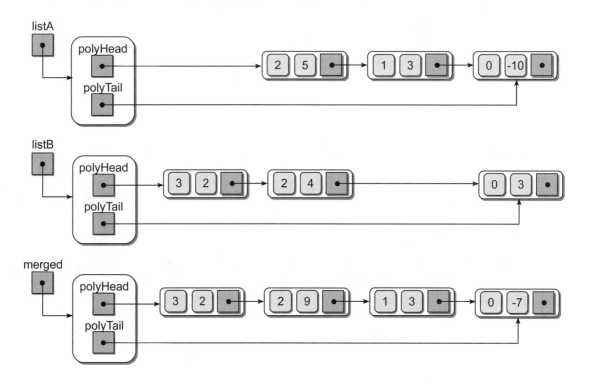

Figure 6.17: The top two linked lists store the two polynomials $5x^2 + 3x - 10$ and $2x^3 + 4x^2 + 3$. The bottom list is the resulting polynomial after adding the two original polynomials.

In Chapter 4, we discussed an efficient solution for the problem of merging two sorted lists. We also saw how that solution could be used for the set union operation, which required a new Python list containing nonduplicate items. If we use a similar approach, combining duplicate terms by adding their coefficients, we can produce a more efficient solution for our current problem of polynomial addition.

Merging two sorted arrays or Python lists, as was done in the previous chapter, is rather simple since we can refer to individual elements by index. Merging two sorted linked list requires several modifications. First, we must use temporary external references to point to the individual nodes of the two original polynomials. These references will be moved along the two linked lists as the terms are processed and merged into the new list. Next, we must utilize the _appendTerm() helper method to append new nodes to the resulting merged list. The implementation of the add() method using the list merge technique is provided in Listing 6.13.

Listing 6.13   Efficient implementation of the polynomial add operation.

```
1   class Polynomial :
2   # ...
3     def __add__( self, rhsPoly ):
4       assert self.degree() >= 0 and rhsPoly.degree() >= 0,
5           "Addition only allowed on non-empty polynomials."
6
7       newPoly = Polynomial()
8       nodeA = self._termList
9       nodeB = rhsPoly._termList
10
11       # Add corresponding terms until one list is empty.
12       while nodeA is not None and nodeB is not None :
13         if nodeA.degree > nodeB.degree :
14           degree = nodeA.degree
15           value = nodeA.coefficient
16           nodeA = nodeA.next
17         elif listA.degree < listB.degree :
18           degree = nodeB.degree
19           value = nodeB.coefficient
20           nodeB = nodeB.next
21         else :
22           degree = nodeA.degree
23           value = nodeA.coefficient + nodeB.coefficient
24           nodeA = nodeA.next
25           nodeB = nodeB.next
26         self._appendTerm( degree, value )
27
28       # If self list contains more terms append them.
29       while nodeA is not None :
30         self._appendTerm( nodeA.degree, nodeA.coefficient )
31         nodeA = nodeA.next
32
33       # Or if rhs contains more terms append them.
34       while nodeB is not None :
35         self._appendTerm( nodeB.degree, nodeB.coefficient )
36         nodeB = nodeB.next
37
38       return newPoly
```

Multiplication

Computing the product of two polynomials requires multiplying the second polynomial by each term in the first. This generates a series of intermediate polynomials, which are then added to create the final product. To aide in this operation, we create a second helper method, _termMultiply(), as shown in lines 23–39 of Listing 6.14, which creates a new polynomial from multiplying an existing polynomial by another term.

Using this helper method, we can now easily create a solution for the multiplication operation that simply implements the individual steps outlined earlier for multiplying two polynomials. As with the earlier simple_add() method, this method is quite simple but not very efficient. The implementation of the polynomial multiplication is provided in lines 3–19 of Listing 6.14. We leave as an exercise the proof that the __mul__ method requires quadratic time in the worst case as well as the development of a more efficient implementation.

Listing 6.14   Implementation of the polynomial multiply operation.

```
 1  class Polynomial :
 2  # ...
 3    def multiply( self, rhsPoly ):
 4      assert self.degree() >= 0 and rhsPoly.degree() >= 0,
 5      "Multiplication only allowed on non-empty polynomials."
 6
 7      # Create a new polynomial by multiplying rhsPoly by the first term.
 8      node = self._polyHead
 9      newPoly = rhsPoly._termMultiply( node )
10
11      # Iterate through the remaining terms of the poly computing the
12      # product of the rhsPoly by each term.
13      node = node.next
14      while node is not None :
15        tempPoly = rhsPoly._termMultiply( node )
16        newPoly = newPoly.add( tempPoly )
17        node = node.next
18
19      return newPoly
20
21    # Helper method for creating a new polynomial from multiplying an
22    # existing polynomial by another term.
23    def _termMultiply( self, termNode ):
24      newPoly = Polynomial()
25
26      # Iterate through the terms and compute the product of each term and
27      # the term in termNode.
28      curr = curr.next
29      while curr is not None :
30        # Compute the product of the term.
31        newDegree = curr.degree + termNode.degree
32        newCoeff = curr.coefficient * termNode.coefficient
33
34        # Append it to the new polynomial.
35        newPoly._appendTerm( newDegree, newCoeff )
36
37        # Advance the current pointer.
38        curr = curr.next
39      return newPoly
```

Exercises

6.1 Implement the following functions related to the singly linked list:

    (a) The `removeAll(head)` function, which accepts a head reference to a singly linked list, unlinks and remove every node individually from the list.

    (b) The `splitInHalf(head)` function, which accepts a head reference to a singly linked list, splits the list in half and returns the head reference to the head node of the second half of the list. If the original list contains a single node, `None` should be returned.

6.2 Evaluate the following code segment which creates a singly linked list. Draw the resulting list, including the external pointers.

```
box = None
temp = None
for i in range( 4 ) :
  if i % 3 != 0 :
    temp = ListNode( i )
    temp.next = box
    box = temp
```

6.3 Consider the following singly linked list. Provide the instructions to insert the new node immediately following the node containing 45. Do not use a loop or any additional external references.

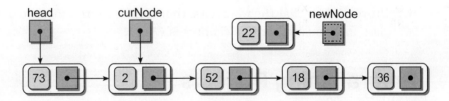

6.4 Consider the following singly linked list. Provide the instructions to remove the node containing 18. Do not use a loop or any additional external references.

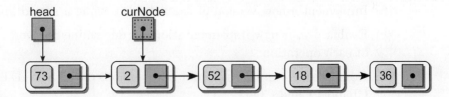

6.5 The following questions are related to the Sparse Matrix ADT.

(a) Implement the remaining methods of the `SparseMatrix` class presented in the chapter using the array of sorted linked lists: `__getitem__`, `transpose()`, `__sub__`, and `__mul__`.

(b) Determine the time-complexity for each of the `SparseMatrix` methods implemented in part (a).

(c) Prove or show that the matrix addition operation of the `SparseMatrix` class, as implemented in the chapter using an array of sorted linked lists, has a worst case run time of $O(kn)$.

(d) As you proved in part (c), the implementation of the `SparseMatrix` `__add__` method presented in the chapter is $O(kn)$. A more efficient implementation is possible without the use of the `__getitem__` and `__setitem__` methods. Design and implement a new version of the `__add__` method that has a run time of no more than $O(k)$.

(e) Show that your implementation of the `__add__` method from part(c) has a worst case run time of $O(k)$.

(f) What advantages are there to using sorted linked lists with the Sparse Matrix ADT instead of unsorted linked lists?

6.6 In Programming Project 4.1, you implemented the Sparse Life Grid ADT that creates a game grid of unlimited size for use with the game of Life. That implementation used a single Python list to store the individual live cells, which was similar to the technique we used with the Sparse Matrix ADT. Explain why the array of linked lists structure used to implement the Sparse Matrix ADT in this chapter cannot be used to implement the Sparse Life Grid ADT.

6.7 Prove or show that the worst case time for the `__mul__` method of the `Polynomial` class implemented in this chapter is $O(n^2)$.

Programming Projects

6.1 We have provided two implementations of the Set ADT in Chapter 1 and Chapter 4.

(a) Implement a new version of the Set ADT using an unsorted linked list.

(b) Implement a new version of the Set ADT using a sorted linked list.

(c) Evaluate your new implementations to determine the worst case run time of each operation.

(d) Compare the run times of your new versions of the Set ADT to those from Chapter 1 and Chapter 4.

6.2 Consider the Vector ADT from Programming Project 2.1:

(a) Implement a new version of the ADT using an unsorted linked list.

(b) Evaluate your new implementation to determine the worst case run time of each operation.

(c) Compare the run times of your new version of the Vector ADT to that of the original in Programming Project 2.1.

(d) What are the advantages and disadvantages of using a linked list to implement the Vector ADT?

6.3 Consider the Map ADT from Section 3.2:

(a) Implement a new version of the Map ADT using an unsorted linked list.

(b) Implement a new version of the Map ADT using a sorted linked list.

(c) Evaluate your new implementations to determine the worst case run time of each operation.

(d) Compare the run times of your new versions of the Map ADT to those from Section 3.2 and Programming Project 5.2.

6.4 Implement the `__sub__` method for the `Polynomial` class implemented in the chapter.

6.5 The implementation of the `Polynomial` `__mul__` method is $O(n^2)$ in the worst case. Design and implement a more efficient solution for this operation.

6.6 Provide a new implementation of the Polynomial ADT to use a Python list for storing the individual terms.

6.7 Integer values are implemented and manipulated at the hardware-level, allowing for fast operations. But the hardware does not supported unlimited integer values. For example, when using a 32-bit architecture, the integers are limited to the range -2,147,483,648 through 2,147,483,647. If you use a 64-bit architecture, this range is increased to the range -9,223,372,036,854,775,808 through 9,223,372,036,854,775,807. But what if we need more than 19 digits to represent an integer value?

In order to provide platform-independent integers and to support integers larger than 19 digits, Python implements its integer type in software. That means the storage and all of the operations that can be performed on the values are handled by executable instructions in the program and not by the hardware. Learning to implement integer values in software offers a good example of the need to provide efficient implementations. We define the Big Integer ADT below that can be used to store and manipulate integer values of any size, just like Python's built-in `int` type.

- BigInteger(initValue = "0"): Creates a new big integer that is initialized to the integer value specified by the given string.

- *toString* (): Returns a string representation of the big integer.

- *comparable* (other): Compares this big integer to the **other** big integer to determine their logical ordering. This comparison can be done using any of the logical operators: <, <=, >, >=, ==, !=.

- *arithmetic* (rhsInt): Returns a new **BigInteger** object that is the result of performing one of the arithmetic operations on the **self** and **rhsInt** big integers. Any of the following operations can be performed:

$$ + \qquad - \qquad * \qquad // \qquad \% \qquad ** $$

- *bitwise-ops* (rhsInt): Returns a new **BigInteger** object that is the result of performing one of the bitwise operators on the **self** and **rhsInt** big integers. Any of the following operations can be performed:

$$ | \qquad \& \qquad \wedge \qquad << \qquad >> $$

(a) Implement the Big Integer ADT using a singly linked list in which each digit of the integer value is stored in a separate node. The nodes should be ordered from the least-significant digit to the largest. For example, the linked list below represents the integer value 45,839:

head

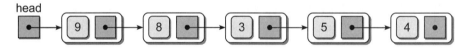

(b) Implement the Big Integer ADT using a Python list for storing the individual digits of an integer.

6.8 Modify your implementation of the Big Integer ADT from the previous question by adding the assignment combo operators that can be performed on the **self** and **rhsInt** big integers. Allow for any of the following operations to be performed:

$$ += \qquad -= \qquad *= \qquad //= \qquad \%= \qquad **= $$
$$ <<= \qquad >>= \qquad |= \qquad \&= \qquad \wedge= $$

## CHAPTER 7

Stacks

In the previous chapters, we used the Python list and linked list structures to implement a variety of container abstract data types. In this chapter, we introduce the stack, which is a type of container with restricted access that stores a linear collection. Stacks are very common in computer science and are used in many types of problems. Stacks also occur in our everyday lives. Consider a stack of trays in a lunchroom. When a tray is removed from the top, the others shift up. If trays are placed onto the stack, the others are pushed down.

7.1 The Stack ADT

A *stack* is used to store data such that the last item inserted is the first item removed. It is used to implement a *last-in first-out* (LIFO) type protocol. The stack is a linear data structure in which new items are added, or existing items are removed from the same end, commonly referred to as the ***top*** of the stack. The opposite end is known as the ***base***. Consider the example in Figure 7.1, which

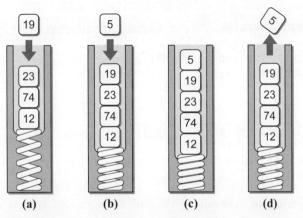

Figure 7.1: Abstract view of a stack: (a) pushing value 19; (b) pushing value 5; (c) resulting stack after 19 and 5 are added; and (d) popping top value.

illustrates new values being added to the top of the stack and one value being removed from the top.

Define   **Stack ADT**

A *stack* is a data structure that stores a linear collection of items with access limited to a last-in first-out order. Adding and removing items is restricted to one end known as the *top* of the stack. An *empty stack* is one containing no items.

- Stack(): Creates a new empty stack.

- isEmpty(): Returns a boolean value indicating if the stack is empty.

- *length*(): Returns the number of items in the stack.

- pop(): Removes and returns the top item of the stack, if the stack is not empty. Items cannot be popped from an empty stack. The next item on the stack becomes the new top item.

- peek(): Returns a reference to the item on top of a non-empty stack without removing it. Peeking, which cannot be done on an empty stack, does not modify the stack contents.

- push(item): Adds the given item to the top of the stack.

To illustrate a simple use of the Stack ADT, we apply it to the problem of reversing a list of integer values. The values will be extracted from the user until a negative value is entered, which flags the end of the collection. The values will then be printed in reverse order from how they were entered. We could use a simple list for this problem, but a stack is ideal since the values can be pushed onto the stack as they are entered and then popped one at a time to print them in reverse order. A solution for this problem follows.

```
PROMPT = "Enter an int value (<0 to end):"
myStack = Stack()
value = int(input( PROMPT ))
while value >= 0 :
  myStack.push( value )
  value = int(input( PROMPT ))

while not myStack.isEmpty() :
  value = myStack.pop()
  print( value )
```

Suppose the user enters the following values, one at a time:

```
7  13  45  19  28  -1
```

When the outer `while` loop terminates after the negative value is extracted, the contents of the stack will be as illustrated in Figure 7.2. Notice the last value entered is at the top and the first is at the base. If we pop the values from the stack, they will be removed in the reverse order from which they were pushed onto the stack, producing a reverse ordering.

Figure 7.2: Resulting stack after executing the sample application.

7.2   Implementing the Stack

The Stack ADT can be implemented in several ways. The two most common approaches in Python include the use of a Python list and a linked list. The choice depends on the type of application involved.

7.2.1   Using a Python List

The Python list-based implementation of the Stack ADT is the easiest to implement. The first decision we have to make when using the list for the Stack ADT is which end of the list to use as the top and which as the base. For the most efficient ordering, we let the end of the list represent the top of the stack and the front represent the base. As the stack grows, items are appended to the end of the list and when items are popped, they are removed from the same end. Listing 7.1 on the next page provides the complete implementation of the Stack ADT using a Python list.

The `peek()` and `pop()` operations can only be used with a non-empty stack since you cannot remove or peek at something that is not there. To enforce this requirement, we first assert the stack is not empty before performing the given operation. The `peek()` method simply returns a reference to the last item in the list. To implement the `pop()` method, we call the `pop()` method of the list structure, which actually performs the same operation that we are trying to implement. That is, it saves a copy of the last item in the list, removes the item from the list, and then returns the saved copy. The `push()` method simply appends new items to the end of the list since that represents the top of our stack.

Listing 7.1	The `pyliststack.py` module.

```
1   # Implementation of the Stack ADT using a Python list.
2   class Stack :
3      # Creates an empty stack.
4      def __init__( self ):
5        self._theItems = list()
6
7      # Returns True if the stack is empty or False otherwise.
8      def isEmpty( self ):
9        return len( self ) == 0
10
11     # Returns the number of items in the stack.
12     def __len__ ( self ):
13       return len( self._theItems )
14
15     # Returns the top item on the stack without removing it.
16     def peek( self ):
17       assert not self.isEmpty(), "Cannot peek at an empty stack"
18       return self._theItems[-1]
19
20     # Removes and returns the top item on the stack.
21     def pop( self ):
22       assert not self.isEmpty(), "Cannot pop from an empty stack"
23       return self._theItems.pop()
24
25     # Push an item onto the top of the stack.
26     def push( self, item ):
27       self._theItems.append( item )
```

The individual stack operations are easy to evaluate for the Python list-based implementation. `isEmpty()`, `__len__`, and `peek()` only require $O(1)$ time. The `pop()` and `push()` methods both require $O(n)$ time in the worst case since the underlying array used to implement the Python list may have to be reallocated to accommodate the addition or removal of the top stack item. When used in sequence, both operations have an amortized cost of $O(1)$.

7.2.2   Using a Linked List

The Python list-based implementation may not be the best choice for stacks with a large number of push and pop operations. Remember, each `append()` and `pop()` list operation may require a reallocation of the underlying array used to implement the list. A singly linked list can be used to implement the Stack ADT, alleviating the concern over array reallocations.

To use a linked list, we again must decide how to represent the stack structure. With the Python list implementation of the stack, it was most efficient to use the end of the list as the top of the stack. With a linked list, however, the front of the list provides the most efficient representation for the top of the stack. In Chapter 6, we saw how to easily prepend nodes to the linked list as well as remove the first node. The Stack ADT implemented using a linked list is provided in Listing 7.2.

Listing 7.2	The `lliststack.py` module.

```
1   # Implementation of the Stack ADT using a singly linked list.
2   class Stack :
3       # Creates an empty stack.
4       def __init__( self ):
5           self._top = None
6           self._size = 0
7
8       # Returns True if the stack is empty or False otherwise.
9       def isEmpty( self ):
10          return self._top is None
11
12      # Returns the number of items in the stack.
13      def __len__( self ):
14          return self._size
15
16      # Returns the top item on the stack without removing it.
17      def peek( self ):
18          assert not self.isEmpty(), "Cannot peek at an empty stack"
19          return self._top.item
20
21      # Removes and returns the top item on the stack.
22      def pop( self ):
23          assert not self.isEmpty(), "Cannot pop from an empty stack"
24          node = self._top
25          self.top = self._top.next
26          self._size -= 1
27          return node.item
28
29      # Pushes an item onto the top of the stack.
30      def push( self, item ) :
31          self._top = _StackNode( item, self._top )
32          self._size += 1
33
34  # The private storage class for creating stack nodes.
35  class _StackNode :
36      def __init__( self, item, link ) :
37          self.item = item
38          self.next = link
```

The class constructor creates two instance variables for each `Stack`. The `_top` field is the head reference for maintaining the linked list while `_size` is an integer value for keeping track of the number of items on the stack. The latter has to be adjusted when items are pushed onto or popped off the stack. Figure 7.3 on the next page illustrates a sample `Stack` object for the stack from Figure 7.1(b).

The `_StackNode` class is used to create the linked list nodes. Note the inclusion of the `link` argument in the constructor, which is used to initialize the `_next` field of the new node. By including this argument, we can simplify the prepend operation of the `push()` method. The two steps required to prepend a node to a linked list are combined by passing the head reference `_top` as the second argument of the `_StackNode()` constructor and assigning a reference to the new node back to `_top`.

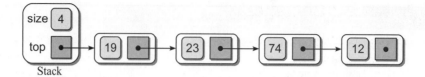

Figure 7.3: Sample object of the Stack ADT implemented as a linked list.

The peek() method simply returns a reference to the data item in the first node after verifying the stack is not empty. If the method were used on the stack represented by the linked list in Figure 7.3, a reference to 19 would be returned. The peek operation is only meant to examine the item on top of the stack. It should not be used to modify the top item as this would violate the definition of the Stack ADT.

The pop() method always removes the first node in the list. This operation is illustrated in Figure 7.4(a). This is easy to implement and does not require a search to find the node containing a specific item. The result of the linked list after popping the top item from the stack is illustrated in Figure 7.4(b).

The linked list implementation of the Stack ADT is more efficient than the Python-list based implementation. All of the operations are $O(1)$ in the worst case, the proof of which is left as an exercise.

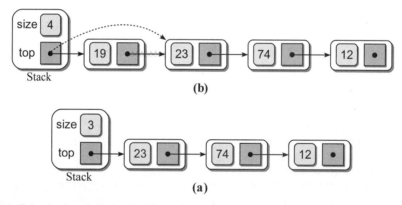

Figure 7.4: Popping an item from the stack: (a) the required link modifications, and (b) the result after popping the top item.

7.3 Stack Applications

The Stack ADT is required by a number of applications encountered in computer science. In this section, we examine several basic applications that traditionally are presented in a data structures course.

7.3.1 Balanced Delimiters

A number of applications use delimiters to group strings of text or simple data into subparts by marking the beginning and end of the group. Some common examples include mathematical expressions, programming languages, and the HTML markup language used by web browsers. There are typically strict rules as to how the delimiters can be used, which includes the requirement of the delimiters being paired and balanced. Parentheses can be used in mathematical expressions to group or override the order of precedence for various operations. To aide in reading complicated expressions, the writer may choose to use different types of symbol pairs, as illustrated here:

```
{A + (B * C) - (D / [E + F])}
```

The delimiters must be used in pairs of corresponding types: {}, [], and (). They must also be positioned such that an opening delimiter within an outer pair must be closed within the same outer pair. For example, the following expression would be invalid since the pair of braces [] begin inside the pair of parentheses () but end outside.

```
(A + [B * C)] - {D / E}
```

Another common use of the three types of braces as delimiters is in the C++ programming language. Consider the following code segment, which implements a function to compute and return the sum of integer values contained in an array:

```cpp
int sumList( int theList[], int size )
{
  int sum = 0;
  int i = 0;
  while( i < size ) {
    sum += theList[ i ];
    i += 1;
  }
  return sum;
}
```

As with the arithmetic expression, the delimiters must be paired and balanced. However, there are additional rules of the language that dictate the proper placement and use of the symbol pairs. We can design and implement an algorithm that scans an input text file containing C++ source code and determines if the delimiters are properly paired. The algorithm will need to remember not only the most recent opening delimiter but also all of the preceding ones in order to match them with closing delimiters. In addition, the opening delimiters will need to be remembered in reverse order with the most recent one available first. The Stack ADT is a perfect structure for implementing such an algorithm.

Consider the C++ code segment from earlier. As the file is scanned, we can push each opening delimiter onto the stack. When a closing delimiter is encountered, we pop the opening delimiter from the stack and compare it to the closing delimiter. For properly paired delimiters, the two should match. Thus, if the top of the stack contains a left bracket [, then the next closing delimiter should be a right bracket]. If the two delimiters match, we know they are properly paired and can continue processing the source code. But if they do not match, then we know the delimiters are not correct and we can stop processing the file. Table 7.1 shows the steps performed by our algorithm and the contents of the stack after each delimiter is encountered in our sample code segment.

Operation	Stack	Current scan line
push (	(	`int sumList(`
push	([	`int sumList( int values[`
pop & match]	(	`int sumList( int values[]`
pop & match)		`int sumList( int values[], int size )`
push {	{	`{`
	{	`    int sum = 0;`
	{	`    int i = 0;`
push (	{ (	`    while(`
pop & match)	{	`    while( i < size )`
push {	{ {	`    while( i < size ) {`
push [	{ { [	`        sum += theList[`
pop & match]	{ {	`        sum += theList[ i ]`
	{ {	`        i += 1;`
pop & match }	{	`    }`
	{	`    return sum;`
pop & match }	empty	`}`

Table 7.1: The sequence of steps scanning a valid set of delimiters: the operation performed (left column) and the contents of the stack (middle column) as each delimiter is encountered (right column) in the code.

So far, we have assumed the delimiters are balanced with an equal number of opening and closing delimiters occurring in the proper order. But what happens if the delimiters are not balanced and we encounter more opening or closing delimiters than the other? For example, suppose the programmer introduced a typographical error in the function header:

```
int sumList( int theList)], int size )
```

Our algorithm will find the first set of parentheses correct. But what happens when the closing bracket] is scanned? The result is illustrated in the top part of Table 7.2. You will notice the stack is empty since the left parenthesis was popped and matched with the preceding right parenthesis. Thus, unbalanced delimiters in which there are more closing delimiters than opening ones can be detected when trying to pop from the stack and we detect the stack is empty.

Operation	Stack	Current point of scan
push (	(	`int sumList(`
pop & match)	empty	`int sumList( int values)`
pop & match]	error	`int sumList( int values)]`

Scanning: `int sumList( int values)], int size )`

Operation	Stack	Current point of scan
push (	(	`int sumList(`
push (	((	`int sumList( int (`
push [	(([	`int sumList( int (values[`
pop & match]	((	`int sumList( int values[]`
pop & match)	(	`int sumList( int values[], int size )`

Scanning: `int sumList( int (values[], int size )`

Table 7.2: Sequence of steps scanning an invalid set of delimiters. The function header: (top) contains more closing delimiters than opening and (bottom) contains more closing delimiters than opening.

Delimiters can also be out of balance in the reverse case where there are more opening delimiters than closing ones. Consider another version of the function header, again containing a typographical error:

```
int sumList( int (theList[], int size )
```

The result of applying our algorithm to this code fragment is illustrated in the bottom chart in Table 7.2. If this were the complete code segment, you can see we would end up with the stack not being empty since there are opening delimiters yet to be paired with closing ones. Thus, in order to have a complete algorithm, we must check for both of these errors.

A Python implementation for the validation algorithm is provided in Listing 7.3. The function `isValidSource()` accepts a file object, which we assume was previously opened and contains C++ source code. The file is scanned one line at a time and each line is scanned one character at a time to determine if it contains properly paired and balanced delimiters.

A stack is used to store the opening delimiters and either implementation can be used since the implementation is independent of the definition. Here, we have chosen to use the linked list version. As the file is scanned, we need only examine

Listing 7.3	Function for validating a C++ source file.

```
1  # Implementation of the algorithm for validating balanced brackets in
2  # a C++ source file.
3  from lliststack import Stack
4
5  def isValidSource( srcfile ):
6    s = Stack()
7    for line in srcfile :
8      for token in line :
9        if token in "{[(" :
10         s.push( token )
11       elif token in "}])" :
12         if s.isEmpty() :
13           return False
14         else :
15           left = s.pop()
16           if (token == "}" and left != "{") or \
17              (token == "]" and left != "[") or \
18              (token == ")" and left != "(") :
19             return False
20
21   return s.isEmpty()
```

the characters that correspond to one of the three types of delimiter pairs. All other characters can be ignored. When an opening delimiter is encountered, we push it onto the stack. When a closing delimiter occurs, we first check to make sure the stack is not empty. If it is empty, then the delimiters are not properly paired and balanced and no further processing is needed. We terminate the function and return **False**. When the stack is not empty, the top item is popped and compared to the closing delimiter. The two delimiters do match corresponding opening and closing delimiters; we again terminate the function and return **False**. Finally, after the entire file is processed, the stack should be empty when the delimiters are properly paired and balanced. For the final test, we check to make sure the stack is empty and return either **True** or **False**, accordingly.

7.3.2   Evaluating Postfix Expressions

We work with mathematical expressions on a regular basis and they are rather easy for humans to evaluate. But the task is more difficult in a computer program when an expression is represented as a string. Given the expression

$$A * B + C / D$$

we know $A * B$ will be performed first, followed by the division and concluding with addition. When evaluating this expression stored as a string and scanning one character at a time from left to right, how do we know the addition has to wait until after the division? Your first response is probably that we know the order of the precedence for the operators. But how do we represent that in our string scanning process? Suppose we are evaluating a string containing nine non-blank characters and have scanned the first three:

A + B ▓▓▓▓▓▓

At this point, we have no way of knowing if the addition operation is to be performed on the two variables A and B or if we have to save this information for later. After moving to the the next character

A + B / ▓▓▓▓▓

we encounter the division operator and know that the addition is not the first operation to be performed. Is the division the first operation to be performed? It does have higher precedence than the addition, but it may not be the first operation since parentheses can override the order of evaluation. We will have to scan more of the string to determine which operation is the first to be performed.

A + B / (C * D)

After determining the first operation to be performed, we must then decide how to return to those previously skipped. This can become a tedious process if we have to continuously scanned forward and backward through the string in order to properly evaluate the expression. To simplify the evaluation of a mathematical expression, we need an alternative representation for the expression. A representation in which the order the operators are performed is the order they are specified would allow for a single left-to-right scan of the expression string.

Three different notations can be used to represent a mathematical expression. The most common is the traditional algebraic or *infix* notation where the operator is specified between the operands A+B. The *prefix* notation places the operator immediately preceding the two operands +AB, whereas in *postfix* notation, the operator follows the two operands AB+.

At first glance, the different notations may seem to be nothing more than different operator placement. But the postfix and prefix notations have the advantages that neither uses parentheses to override the order of precedence and both create expressions in unique form. In other words, each expression is unique and produces a specific result unlike infix notation in which the same expression can be written in multiple ways.

Converting from Infix to Postfix

Infix expressions can be easily converted by hand to postfix notation. The expression A + B - C would be written as AB+C- in postfix form. The evaluation of this expression would involve first adding A and B and then subtracting C from that result. We will examine the evaluation of postfix expressions later; for now we focus on the conversion from infix to postfix.

Short expressions can be easily converted to postfix form, even those using parentheses. Consider the expression A*(B+C), which would be written in postfix as ABC+*. Longer expressions, such as the example from earlier, A*B+C/D, are a bit more involved. To help in this conversion we can use a simple algorithm:

1. Place parentheses around every group of operators in the correct order of evaluation. There should be one set of parentheses for every operator in the infix expression.

   ((A * B) + (C / D))

2. For each set of parentheses, move the operator from the middle to the end preceding the corresponding closing parenthesis.

   ((A B *) (C D /) +)

3. Remove all of the parentheses, resulting in the equivalent postfix expression.

   A B * C D / +

Compare this result to a modified version of the expression in which parentheses are used to place the addition as the first operation:

A * (B + C) / D

Using the simple algorithm, we parenthesize the expression:

((A * (B + C)) / D)

and move the operators to the end of each parentheses pair:

((A (B C +) *) D /)

Finally, removing the parentheses yields the postfix expression:

A B C + * D /

A similar algorithm can be used for converting from infix to prefix notation. The difference is the operators are moved to the front of each group.

Postfix Evaluation Algorithm

Parentheses are used with infix expressions to change the order of evaluation. But in postfix notation, the order cannot be altered and thus there is no need for parentheses. Given the unique form or single order of evaluation, postfix notation is a good choice when evaluating a mathematical expression represented as a string. Of course the expression would have to either be given in postfix notation or first converted from infix to postfix. The latter can be easily done with an appropriate algorithm, but we limit our discussion to the evaluation of existing postfix expressions.

Evaluating a postfix expression requires the use of a stack to store the operands or variables at the beginning of the expression until they are needed. Assume we are given a valid postfix expression stored in a string consisting of operators and single-letter variables. We can evaluate the expression by scanning the string, one character or token at a time. For each token, we perform the following steps:

1. If the current item is an operand, push its value onto the stack.

2. If the current item is an operator:

   (a) Pop the top two operands off the stack.

   (b) Perform the operation. (Note the top value is the right operand while the next to the top value is the left operand.)

   (c) Push the result of this operation back onto the stack.

The final result of the expression will be the last value on the stack. To illustrate the use of this algorithm, let's evaluate the postfix expression A B C + * D / from our earlier example. Assume the existence of an empty stack and the following variable assignments have been made:

$$A = 8 \qquad\qquad C = 3$$
$$B = 2 \qquad\qquad D = 4$$

The complete sequence of algorithm steps and the contents of the stack after each operation are illustrated in Table 7.3.

Token	Alg. Step	Stack	Description
<u>A</u>BC+*D/	1	8	push value of A
A<u>B</u>C+*D/	1	8 2	push value of B
AB<u>C</u>+*D/	1	8 2 3	push value of C
ABC<u>+</u>*D/	2(a)	8	pop top two values: y = 3, x = 2
	2(b)	8	compute z = x + y or z = 2 + 3
	2(c)	8 5	push result (5) of the addition
ABC+<u>*</u>D/	2(a)		pop top two values: y = 5, x = 8
	2(b)		compute z = x * y or z = 8 * 5
	2(c)		push result (40) of the multiplication
ABC+*<u>D</u>/	1	40 4	push value of D
ABC+*D<u>/</u>	2(a)		pop top two values: y = 4, x = 40
	2(b)		compute z = x / y or z = 40 / 4
	2(c)	10	push result (10) of division

Table 7.3: The stack contents and sequence of algorithm steps required to evaluate the valid postfix expression A B C + * D.

The postfix evaluation algorithm assumes a valid expression. But what happens if the expression is invalid? Consider the following invalid expression in which there are more operands than available operators:

```
A B * C D +
```

After applying the algorithm to this expression, there are two values remaining on the stack as illustrated in Table 7.4. What happens if there are too many operators for the given number of operands? Consider such an invalid expression:

```
A B * + C /
```

In this case, there are too few operands on the stack when we encounter the addition operator, as illustrated in Table 7.5. If we attempt to perform two pops from the stack, an assertion error will be thrown since the stack will be empty on the second pop. We can modify the algorithm to detect both types of errors. In step 2(a), we must first verify the stack is not empty before popping an item. If the stack is empty, we can stop the evaluation and flag an error. The second modification occurs after the evaluation of the entire expression. We can pop the result from the stack and then verify the stack is empty. If the stack is not empty, the expression was invalid and we must flag an error.

Token	Alg. Step	Stack	Description
AB*CD+	1	8	push value of A
A**B***CD+	1	8 2	push value of B
AB*****CD+	2(a)		pop top two values: y = 2, x = 8
	2(b)		compute z = x * y or z = 8 * 2
	2(c)	16	push result (16) of the multiplication
AB***C**D+	1	16 3	push value of C
AB*C**D**+	1	16 3 4	push value of D
AB*CD**+**	2(a)	16	pop top two values: y = 4, x = 3
	2(b)	16	compute z = x + y or z = 3 + 4
	2(c)	16 7	push result (7) of the addition
Error	*xxxxxx*	*xxxxxx*	*Too many values left on stack.*

Table 7.4: The sequence of algorithm steps when evaluating the invalid postfix expression A B * C D +.

7.4 Application: Solving a Maze

A classic example of an application that requires the use of a stack is the problem of finding a path through a maze. When viewing a maze drawn on paper such

Token	Alg. Step	Stack	Description
<u>A</u>B*+C/	1	8	push value of A
A<u>B</u>*+C/	1	8 2	push value of B
AB<u>*</u>+C/	2(a)		pop top two values: y = 2, x = 8
	2(b)		compute z = x * y or z = 8 * 2
	2(c)	16	push result (16) of the multiplication
AB*<u>+</u>C/	2(a)		pop top two values: y = 16, x = ?
Error	*xxxxxx*	*xxxxxx*	*Only one value on stack, two needed.*

Table 7.5: The sequence of algorithm steps taken when evaluating the invalid postfix expression A B * + C /.

as the one illustrated in Figure 7.5, we can quickly find a path from the starting point to the exit. This usually involves scanning the entire maze and mentally eliminating dead ends. But consider a human size maze in which you are inside the maze and only have a "rat's-eye" view. You cannot see over the walls and must travel within the maze remembering where you have been and where you need to go. In this situation, it's not as easy to find the exit as compared to viewing the maze on paper.

An algorithm that can be used to find a path through a maze is likely to employ a technique similar to what you would use if you were inside the maze. In this section, we explore the backtracking technique to solving a maze and design an algorithm to implement our technique.

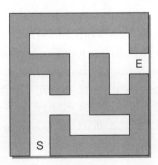

Figure 7.5: A sample maze with the indicated starting (S) and exit (E) positions.

7.4.1 Backtracking

The most basic problem-solving technique in computer science is the ***brute-force*** method. It involves searching for a solution to a given problem by systematically trying all possible candidates until either a solution is found or it can be determined there is no solution. Brute-force is time-consuming and is generally chosen as a last resort. But some problems can only be solved using this technique.

If applied to the maze problem, the brute-force method would require we start at the beginning and follow a path until we either find the exit or encounter a blocked passage. If we hit a wall instead of the exit, we would start over from the beginning and try a different path. But this would be time consuming since we would likely follow part of the same path from the beginning to some point before we encountered the blocked passage. Instead of going all the way back to the beginning, we could back up along the path we originally took until we find a passage going in a different direction. We could then follow the new passage in hopes of finding the exit. If we again encounter a blocked passage before the exit, we can back up one or more steps and try a different passage.

This process of eliminating possible contenders from the solution and partially backing up to try others is known as **backtracking** and is a refinement of the basic brute-force method. There is a broad class of algorithms that employ this technique and are known as **backtracking algorithms**. All of these algorithms attempt to find a solution to a problem by extending a partial solution one step at a time. If a "dead end" is encountered during this process, the algorithm backtracks one or more steps in an attempt to try other possibilities without having to start over from the beginning.

7.4.2   Designing a Solution

The solution to the maze problem is a classic example of backtracking. In this section, we explore the technique and design a solution to the maze problem.

Problem Details

Given a maze with indicated starting and exit positions, the objectives are (1) determine if there is a path from the starting position to the exit, and (2) specify the path with no circles or loopbacks. In designing an algorithm to solve a maze, it will be easier if we think of the maze as a collection of equal-sized cells laid out in rows and columns, as illustrated in Figure 7.6. The cells will either be filled representing walls of the maze or empty to represent open spaces. In addition, one cell will be indicated as the starting position and another as the exit.

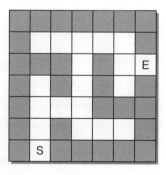

Figure 7.6: Sample maze from Figure 7.5 divided into equal-sized cells.

To further aide in the algorithm development, we place certain restrictions on movement within the maze. First, we can only move one cell at a time and only to open positions, those not blocked by a wall or previously used along the current path. The latter prevents us from reusing a cell as part of the solution since we want to find a path from the start to the exit without ever having to go in circles. Finally, we limit movement between opens cells to the horizontal and vertical directions—up, down, left, and right—as illustrated in Figure 7.7.

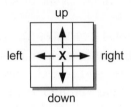

Figure 7.7: The legal moves allowed from a given cell in the maze.

During our search for the exit, we need to remember which cells have been visited. Some will be part of the final path to the exit while others will have led us to dead ends. At the end, we need to know which cells form the path from the start to the exit. But during the search for the exit, we also need to avoid cells that previously led to a dead end. To assist in remembering the cells, we can place a token in each cell visited and distinguish between the two. In our example, we will use an x to represent cells along the path and an o to represent those that led to a dead end.

Describing the Algorithm

We begin at the starting position and attempt to move from cell to cell until we find the exit. As we move between cells, we must consider what actions are available at each cell. Consider the smaller maze in Figure 7.8 in which the rows and columns have been numbered to aide in identifying the cells.

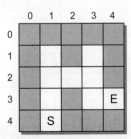

Figure 7.8: A small maze with the rows and columns labeled for easy reference.

Finding the Exit. From the starting position $(4,1)$, we can examine our surroundings or more specifically the four neighboring cells and determine if we can move from this position. We want to use a systematic or well-ordered approach in finding the path. Thus, we always examine the neighboring cells in the same order: up, down, left, and right. In the sample maze, we find the cell above, $(3,1)$, is open and prepare to move up one step. Before moving from the current position, however, we need to lay down a token to indicate the current cell is part of our path. As indicated earlier, we place a lowercase x in the cell to indicate it comprises part of the path. The complete set of steps taken to solve our sample maze are illustrated in Figure 7.9.

After placing the token, we move to the open cell above the starting position. The current position in the maze is marked in the illustration using an uppercase X. We repeat the process and find the cell above our current position is open. A token is laid in the current cell and we move up one position to cell $(2,1)$. From our vantage point above the matrix, we easily see the solution to the problem, which requires that we move to the right. But from the point of view of a mouse searching for cheese, that specific move would be unknown.

Using our systematic approach, we examine the cell above our current position. We find it open, and move up one position to cell $(1,1)$. From this position, we

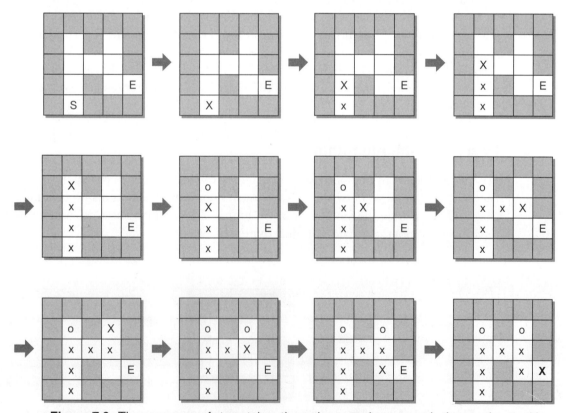

Figure 7.9: The sequence of steps taken through a sample maze. S is the starting position and E is the exit. The path is marked using the character x while the current cell is marked with X. Cells we visited but from which we had to backtrack are marked with o.

soon discover there are no legal moves since we are blocked by a wall on three sides and a cell comprising part of our path. Since we can go no further from this cell, we have no choice but to go back to our previous position in cell $(2, 1)$. When hitting a dead end, we don't simply turn around and go back over a cell previously visited as if it were part of the path since this would cause a circle. Instead, we mark the cell with a different token indicating a dead end and move back to the previous position. In our example, we use a lowercase o to represent a cell leading to a dead end.

After moving back to cell $(2, 1)$, we examine the other directions and soon find the cell to the right is open and move in that direction, placing us in cell $(2, 2)$. From this position, we find the only legal move is to the right and thus move in that direction, placing us in cell $(2, 3)$. Next, we move up one step since the cell above is open. But this move will result in a dead end, requiring us to once again back up to the previous position. After backing up to our previous position at cell $(2, 3)$, we find the cell below is open and move to position $(3, 3)$. Repeating the process we soon find the exit at position $(3, 4)$ and a path from the starting cell to the exit.

No Path to the Exit.   The exit in this example was accessible. But what happens if there is no path between the start and exit cells? Consider a modified version of our sample maze in Figure 7.10 where a wall has been placed in cell $(3, 3)$ closing the path to the exit.

When reaching position $(2, 3)$, as described earlier, we will discover this is a dead end and have to back up. But there are no other legal moves from cell $(2, 2)$ with the positions above and below blocked by a wall, the position to the right leading to a dead end and the position to the left currently part of our path. From position $(2, 2)$, we have to back up and try another direction. Ultimately, we will have to backtrack all the way to the start, having found no legal move from that position.

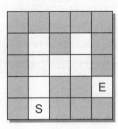

Figure 7.10: A modified version of the sample maze with the exit blocked.

7.4.3 The Maze ADT

Given the description of the maze problem and the backtracking algorithm for finding a path through the maze, we now define the Maze ADT that can be used to construct and solve a maze.

Define   Maze ADT

A *maze* is a two-dimensional structure divided into rows and columns of equal-sized cells. The individual cells can be filled representing a wall or empty representing an open space. One cell is marked as the starting position and another as the exit.

- `Maze( numRows, numCols )`: Creates a new maze with all of the cells initialized as open cells. The starting and exit positions are undefined.

- `numRows()`: Returns the number of rows in the maze.

- `numCols()`: Returns the number of columns in the maze.

- `setWall( row, col )`: Fills the indicated cell (`row`, `col`) with a wall. The cell indices must be within the valid range of rows and columns.

- `setStart( row, col )`: Sets the indicated cell (`row`, `col`) as the starting position. The cell indices must be within the valid range.

- `setExit( row, col )`: Sets the indicated cell (`row`, `col`) as the exit position. The cell indices must be within the valid range.

- `findPath()`: Attempts to the solve the maze by finding a path from the starting position to the exit. If a solution is found, the path is marked with tokens (`x`) and `True` is returned. For a maze with no solution, `False` is returned and the maze is left in its original state. The maze must contain both the starting and exit position. Cells on the perimeter of the maze can be open and it can be assumed there is an invisible wall surrounding the entire maze.

- `reset()`: Resets the maze to its original state by removing any tokens placed during the find path operation.

- `draw()`: Prints the maze in a readable format using characters to represent the walls and path through the maze, if a path has been found. Both the starting and exit positions are also indicated, if previously set.

Our ADT definition is not meant for a general purpose maze, but instead one that can be used to build a maze and then solve and print the result. A more general purpose ADT would most likely return the solution path as a list of tuples instead of simply marking the cells within the maze as is the case in our definition.

Example Use

We can use this definition of the ADT to construct a program for building and solving a maze as shown in Listing 7.4. The main routine is rather simple since we need only build the maze, determine if a path exists and print the maze if a path does exist.

| Listing 7.4 | The `solvemaze.py` program. |

```
1   # Program for building and solving a maze.
2   from maze import Maze
3
4   # The main routine.
5   def main():
6     maze = buildMaze( "mazefile.txt" )
7     if maze.findPath() :
8       print( "Path found...." )
9       maze.draw()
10    else :
11      print( "Path not found...." )
12
13  # Builds a maze based on a text format in the given file.
14  def buildMaze( filename ):
15    infile = open( filename, "r" )
16
17      # Read the size of the maze.
18    nrows, ncols = readValuePair( infile )
19    maze = Maze( nrows, ncols )
20
21      # Read the starting and exit positions.
22    row, col = readValuePair( infile )
23    maze.setStart( row, col )
24    row, col = readValuePair( infile )
25    maze.setExit( row, col )
26
27      # Read the maze itself.
28    for row in range( nrows ) :
29      line = infile.readline()
30      for col in range( len(line) ) :
31        if line[col] == "*" :
32          maze.setWall( row, col )
33
34    # Close the maze file and return the newly constructed maze.
35    infile.close()
36    return maze
37
38  # Extracts an integer value pair from the given input file.
39  def readValuePair( infile ):
40    line = infile.readline()
41    valA, valB = line.split()
42    return int(valA), int(valB)
43
44  # Call the main routine to execute the program.
45  main()
```

Maze Text File Format

Before searching for a path through the maze, we must first build a maze. The maze can be constructed directly within the program by calls to `setWall()` with literal indices or we can read a maze specification from a text file. Suppose a maze is represented in a text file using the following format:

```
5 5
4 1
3 4
*****
*.*.*
*...*
*.*..
*.***
```

The first line contains the size of the maze given as the number of rows and columns. The two subsequent lines indicate the row and column indices of the starting and exit positions. The remaining lines of text represent the maze itself, with walls represented using a hash symbol and open cells represented as blank spaces. The maze is constructed from the text file using the `buildMaze()` function as shown in lines 14–42 of Listing 7.4.

7.4.4   Implementation

The implementation of our Maze ADT will require the selection of a data structure to represent the maze and to implement the backtracking operation used to find a path. The most obvious choice of data structure for storing the maze is a 2-D array. The individual elements of the array will represent the cells of the maze. Strings containing a single character can be used to represent the walls and tokens while the open cells are easily represented as null pointers. The array representation of our sample maze is illustrated in Figure 7.11.

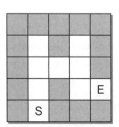 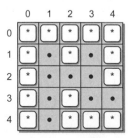

Figure 7.11: The abstract view of a maze physically represented using a 2-D array. Walls are indicated with an asterisk (∗) character, while open cells contain a null reference. The start and exit cells will be identified by cell position stored in separate data fields.

Class Definition

A partial implementation of the Maze ADT is provided in Listing 7.5. Three constant class variables are defined and initialized to store the various symbols used to mark cells within the maze. Remember, class variables are not data fields of the individual objects, but are instead variables of the class, which can be accessed by the individual methods. By using the named constants, the values used to represent the maze wall and tokens could easily be changed if we were so inclined.

Listing 7.5   The `maze.py` module.

```python
 1  # Implements the Maze ADT using a 2-D array.
 2  from array import Array2D
 3  from lliststack import Stack
 4
 5  class Maze :
 6    # Define constants to represent contents of the maze cells.
 7    MAZE_WALL = "*"
 8    PATH_TOKEN = "x"
 9    TRIED_TOKEN = "o"
10
11    # Creates a maze object with all cells marked as open.
12    def __init__( self, numRows, numCols ):
13      self._mazeCells = Array2D( numRows, numCols )
14      self._startCell = None
15      self._exitCell = None
16
17    # Returns the number of rows in the maze.
18    def numRows( self ):
19      return self._mazeCells.numRows()
20
21    # Returns the number of columns in the maze.
22    def numCols( self ):
23      return self._mazeCells.numCols()
24
25    # Fills the indicated cell with a "wall" marker.
26    def setWall( self, row, col ):
27      assert row >= 0 and row < self.numRows() and \
28             col >= 0 and col < self.numCols(), "Cell index out of range."
29      self._mazeCells.set( row, col, self.MAZE_WALL )
30
31    # Sets the starting cell position.
32    def setStart( self, row, col ):
33      assert row >= 0 and row < self.numRows() and \
34             col >= 0 and col < self.numCols(), "Cell index out of range."
35      self._startCell = _CellPosition( row, col )
36
37    # Sets the exit cell position.
38    def setExit( self, row, col ):
39      assert row >= 0 and row < self.numRows() and \
40             col >= 0 and col < self.numCols(), \
41             "Cell index out of range."
42      self._exitCell = _CellPosition( row, col )
43
44    # Attempts to solve the maze by finding a path from the starting cell
45    # to the exit. Returns True if a path is found and False otherwise.
46    def findPath( self ):
47      ......
48
```

(Listing Continued)

Listing 7.5   Continued . . .

```
49        # Resets the maze by removing all "path" and "tried" tokens.
50    def reset( self ):
51        ......
52
53        # Prints a text-based representation of the maze.
54    def draw( self ):
55        ......
56
57        # Returns True if the given cell position is a valid move.
58    def _validMove( self, row, col ):
59        return row >= 0 and row < self.numRows() \
60            and col >= 0 and col < self.numCols() \
61            and self._mazeCells[row, col] is None
62
63        # Helper method to determine if the exit was found.
64    def _exitFound( self, row, col ):
65        return row == self._exitCell.row and \
66                col == self._exitCell.col
67
68        # Drops a "tried" token at the given cell.
69    def _markTried( self, row, col ):
70        self._mazeCells.set( row, col, self.TRIED_TOKEN )
71
72        # Drops a "path" token at the given cell.
73    def _markPath( self, row, col ):
74        self._mazeCells.set( row, col, self.PATH_TOKEN )
75
76
77 # Private storage class for holding a cell position.
78 class _CellPosition( object ):
79    def __init__( self, row, col ):
80        self.row = row
81        self.col = col
```

The class constructor, shown in lines 12–15 of Listing 7.5, creates a `MultiArray` object and two fields to store the starting and exit cells. A sample `Maze` object for our maze in Figure 7.11 is illustrated in Figure 7.12. The array is created using the arguments to the constructor. The cells of the maze are automatically initialized to `None`, as specified in the previous section, since this is the default value used when creating a `MultiArray` object. The `_startCell` and `_exitCell` fields are set to `None` since they are initially undefined. Later, specific positions will have to be stored when they are defined by the respective methods. Since a cell is indicated by its position within the array, we can define the `_CellPosition` class to store a specific cell.

Maze Components

Components of the maze are specified using the various set methods, which are shown in lines 26–42 of Listing 7.5. Since the user specifies specific maze elements with each of these methods, they must first validate the cell position to ensure the

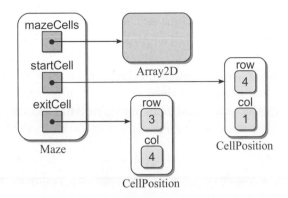

Figure 7.12: A sample Maze ADT object.

indices are within the valid range. The two methods that set the starting and exit positions simply create and store _CellPosition objects while the creation of a wall fills the indicated cell using one of the named constants defined earlier.

Helper Methods

During the actual process of finding a solution in the findPath() method, we will need to perform several routine operations that access the underlying MultiArray object. To aide in this task, we define several helper methods, as shown in lines 58–74. First, we will need to drop or place tokens as we move through the maze. The _markTried() and _markPath() methods can be used for this task. Note we do not need a "pickup token" method since the task of picking up a path token is immediately followed by dropping a tried token.

The _exitFound() method is used to determine if the exit is found based on the contents of the _exitCell object and the current position supplied as arguments. Finally, the _validMove() helper method is used to determine if we can move to a given cell. A move is valid if the destination cell is open and its indices are not outside the border of the maze. Note an assertion is not used here since we do not want to flag an error. Instead, the backtracking solution will have to try other directions when encountering an invalid move.

Finding the Path

The findPath() method implements the actual path finding algorithm described earlier, which searches through the maze for a path from the starting position to the exit. As we move through the maze, we must remember the path we took in order to backtrack when reaching a dead end. A stack provides the ideal structure we need to remember our path. As we move forward in the maze, we can push our current position onto the stack using a _CellPosition object before moving forward to the next cell. When reaching a dead end, we can backtrack by popping the previous position from the stack and backing up to that position. The implementation of this method is left as an exercise along with the reset() and draw() methods.

Exercises

7.1 Hand execute the following code segment and show the contents of the resulting stack.

```
values = Stack()
for i in range( 16 ) :
  if i % 3 == 0 :
    values.push( i )
```

7.2 Hand execute the following code segment and show the contents of the resulting stack.

```
values = Stack()
for i in range( 16 ) :
  if i % 3 == 0 :
    values.push( i )
  elif i % 4 == 0 :
    values.pop()
```

7.3 Translate each of the following infix expressions into postfix.

(a) (A * B) / C

(b) A - (B * C) + D / E

(c) (X - Y) + (W * Z) / V

(d) V * W * X + Y - Z

(e) A / B * C - D + E

7.4 Translate each of the infix expressions in Exercise 7.3 to prefix notation.

7.5 Translate each of the following postfix expressions into infix.

(a) A B C - D * +

(b) A B + C D - / E +

(c) A B C D E * + / +

(d) X Y Z + A B - * -

(e) A B + C - D E * +

7.6 Consider our implementation of the Stack ADT using the Python list, and suppose we had used the front of the list as the top of the stack and the end of the list as the base. What impact, if any, would this have on the run time of the various stack operations?

7.7 Show that all of the Stack ADT operations have a constant time in the worst case when implemented as a linked list.

7.8 Would it buy us anything to use a tail reference with the linked list structure used to implement the Stack ADT? Explain your answer.

7.9 Evaluate the run time of the `isValidSource()` function where n is the number of characters in the C++ source file.

Programming Projects

7.1 Write and test a program that extracts postfix expressions from the user, evaluates the expression, and prints the results. You may require that the user enter numeric values along with the operators and that each component of the expression be separated with white space.

7.2 The `isValidSource()` function can be used to evaluate a C++ source file, but it is incomplete. Brackets encountered inside comments and literal strings would not be paired with those found elsewhere in the program.

(a) C++ comments can be specified using `//`, which starts a comment that runs to the end of the current line, and the token pair `/* */`, which encloses a comment that can span multiple lines. Extend the function to skip over brackets found inside C++ comments.

(b) C++ literal strings are denoted by enclosing characters within double quotes (`"string"`) and literal characters are denoted by enclosing a character within single quotes (`'x'`). Extend the function to skip over brackets found inside C++ literal strings and characters.

7.3 Design and implement a function that evaluates a prefix expression stored as a text string.

7.4 Implement the `findPath()`, `reset()`, and `draw()` methods for the `Maze` class.

7.5 Implement a complete maze solving application using the components introduced earlier in the chapter. Modify the `solve()` method to return a vector containing tuples representing the path through the maze.

7.6 We can design and build a postfix calculator that can be used to perform simple arithmetic operations. The calculator consists of a single storage component that consists of an operand stack. The operations performed by the stack always use the top two values of the stack and store the result back on the top of the stack. Implement the operations of the Postfix Calculator ADT as defined here:.

- **PostfixCalculator()**: Creates a new postfix calculator with an empty operand stack.
- **value(x)**: Pushes the given operand x onto the top of the stack.
- **result()**: Returns an alias to the value currently on top of the stack. If the stack is empty, **None** is returned.
- **clear()**: Clears the entire contents of the stack.
- **clearLast()**: Removes the top entry from the stack and discards it.
- **compute(op)**: Removes the top two values from the stack and applies the given operation on those values. The first value removed from the stack is the righthand side operand and the second is the lefthand side operand. The result of the operation is pushed back onto the stack. The operation is specified as a string containing one of the operators + - * / **.

7.7 Extend the Postfix Calculator ADT as follows:

(a) To perform several unary operations commonly found on scientific calculators: absolute value, square root, sine, cosine, and tangent. The operations should be specified to the **compute()** method using the following acronyms: **abs, sqrt, sin, cos, tan**.

(b) To use a second stack on which values can be saved. Add the following two operations to the ADT:

- **store()**: Removes the top value from the operand stack and pushes it onto the save stack.
- **recall()**: Removes the top value from the save stack and pushes it onto the operand stack.

7.8 Design and implement a complete program that uses the Postfix Calculator ADT to perform various operations extracted from the user. The user enters text-based commands, one per line, that should be performed by the calculator. For example, to compute 12 * 15, the user would enter the following sequence of commands:

```
ENTER 12
ENTER 15
MUL
RESULT
```

which would result in 180 being displayed. Your program should respond to the following set of commands: ENTER, CLR, CLRLAST, RESULT, ADD, SUB, MUL, DIV, POW.

## CHAPTER 8

Queues

The term queue is commonly defined to be a line of people waiting to be served like those you would encounter at many business establishments. Each person is served based on their position within the queue. Thus, the next person to be served is the first in line. As more people arrive, they enter the queue at the back and wait their turn.

A queue structure is well suited for problems in computer science that require data to be processed in the order in which it was received. Some common examples include computer simulations, CPU process scheduling, and shared printer management. You are familiar with a printer queue if you have used a shared printer. Many people may want to use the printer, but only one thing can be printed at a time. Instead of making people wait until the printer is not being used to print their document, multiple documents can be submitted at the same time. When a document arrives, it is added to the end of the print queue. As the printer becomes available, the document at the front of the queue is removed and printed.

8.1 The Queue ADT

A *queue* is a specialized list with a limited number of operations in which items can only be added to one end and removed from the other. A queue is also known as a *first-in, first-out* (FIFO) list. Consider Figure 8.1, which illustrates an abstract view of a queue. New items are inserted into a queue at the *back* while existing items are removed from the *front*. Even though the illustration shows the individual items, they cannot be accessed directly. The definition of the Queue ADT follows.

Figure 8.1: An abstract view of a queue containing five items.

| Define | Queue ADT |

A *queue* is a data structure that a linear collection of items in which access is restricted to a first-in first-out basis. New items are inserted at the back and existing items are removed from the front. The items are maintained in the order in which they are added to the structure.

- Queue(): Creates a new empty queue, which is a queue containing no items.

- isEmpty(): Returns a boolean value indicating whether the queue is empty.

- *length*(): Returns the number of items currently in the queue.

- enqueue(item): Adds the given item to the back of the queue.

- dequeue(): Removes and returns the front item from the queue. An item cannot be dequeued from an empty queue.

Using the formal definition of the Queue ADT, we can now examine the code necessary to create the queue in Figure 8.1:

```
Q = Queue()
Q.enqueue( 28 )
Q.enqueue( 19 )
Q.enqueue( 45 )
Q.enqueue( 13 )
Q.enqueue( 7 )
```

After creating a Queue object, we simply enqueue the five values in the order as they appear in the queue. We can then remove the values or add additional values to the queue. Figure 8.2 illustrates the result of performing several additional operations on the sample queue.

8.2   Implementing the Queue

Since the queue data structure is simply a specialized list, it is commonly implemented using some type of list structure. There are three common approaches to implementing a queue: using a vector, a linked list, or an array. In the following sections, we examine and compare these three approaches.

8.2.1   Using a Python List

The simplest way to implement the Queue ADT is to use Python's list. It provides the necessary routines for adding and removing items at the respective ends. By applying these routines, we can remove items from the front of the list and append new items to the end. To use a list for the Queue ADT, the constructor must define a single data field to store the list that is initially empty. We can test for an

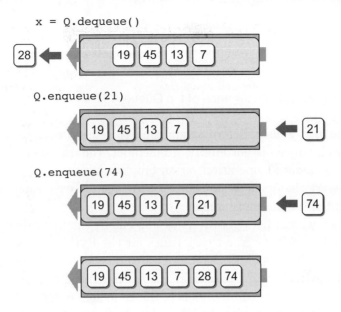

Figure 8.2: Abstract view of the queue after performing additional operations.

empty queue by examining the length of the list. The complete Python list-based implementation is provided in Listing 8.1, and an instance of the class is illustrated in Figure 8.3 on the next page.

To enqueue an item, we simply append it to the end of the list. The dequeue operation can be implemented by popping and returning the item in the first

Listing 8.1   The `pylistqueue.py` module.

```python
1  # Implementation of the Queue ADT using a Python list.
2  class Queue :
3    # Creates an empty queue.
4    def __init__( self ):
5      self._qList = list()
6
7    # Returns True if the queue is empty.
8    def isEmpty( self ):
9      return len( self ) == 0
10
11   # Returns the number of items in the queue.
12   def __len__( self ):
13     return len( self._qList )
14
15   # Adds the given item to the queue.
16   def enqueue( self, item ):
17     self._qList.append( item )
18
19   # Removes and returns the first item in the queue.
20   def dequeue( self ):
21     assert not self.isEmpty(), "Cannot dequeue from an empty queue."
22     return self._qList.pop( 0 )
```

Queue (pylist)

Figure 8.3: An instance of the Queue ADT implemented using a Python list.

element of the list. Before attempting to remove an item from the list, we must ensure the queue is not empty. Remember, the queue definition prohibits the use of the `dequeue()` operation on an empty queue. Thus, to enforce this, we must first assert the queue is not empty and raise an exception, when the operation is attempted on an empty queue.

Since we use list operations to implement the individual queue operations, we need only recall the worst case times for the Python list operations. The size and empty condition operations only require $O(1)$ time. The enqueue operation requires $O(n)$ time in the worst case since the list may need to expand to accommodate the new item. When used in sequence, the enqueue operation has an amortized cost of $O(1)$. The dequeue operation also requires $O(n)$ time since the underlying array used to implement the Python list may need to shrink when an item is removed. In addition, when an item is removed from the front of the list, the following items have to be shifted forward, which requires linear time no matter if an expansion occurs or not.

8.2.2 Using a Circular Array

The list-based implementation of the Queue ADT is easy to implement, but it requires linear time for the enqueue and dequeue operations. We can improve these times using an array structure and treating it as a circular array. A **circular array** is simply an array viewed as a circle instead of a line. An example is illustrated in Figure 8.4.

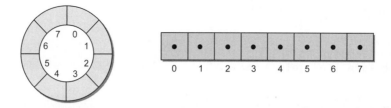

Figure 8.4: The abstract view of a circular array (left) and the physical view (right).

A circular array allows us to add new items to a queue and remove existing ones without having to shift items in the process. Unfortunately, this approach introduces the concept of a maximum-capacity queue that can become full. A circular array queue implementation is typically used with applications that only require small-capacity queues and allows for the specification of a maximum size.

Data Organization

To implement a queue as a circular array, we must maintain a count field and two markers. The count field is necessary to keep track of how many items are currently in the queue since only a portion of the array may actually contain queue items. The markers indicate the array elements containing the first and last items in the queue. Consider the following circular array:

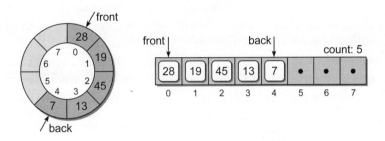

which illustrates the implementation of the queue from Figure 8.1. The figure shows the corresponding abstract and physical views of the circular array.

New items are added to the queue by inserting them in the position immediately following the **back** marker. The marker is then advanced one position and the counter is incremented to reflect the addition of the new item. For example, suppose we enqueue value 32 into the sample queue. The **back** marker is advanced to position 5 and value 32 is inserted:

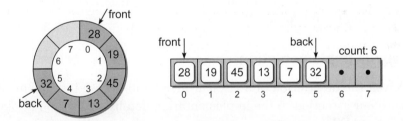

To dequeue an item, the value in the element marked by **front** will be returned and the marker is advanced one position:

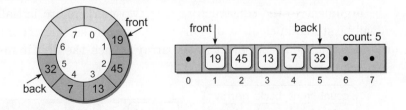

Notice the remaining items in the queue are not shifted. Instead, only the **front** marker is moved. Now, suppose we add values 8 and 23 to the queue. These values are added in the positions following the **back** marker:

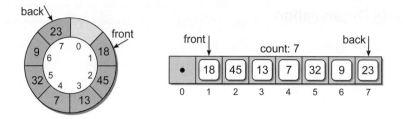

The queue now contains seven items in elements $[1 \dots 7]$ with one empty slot. What happens if value 39 is added? Since we are using a circular array, the same procedure is used and the new item will be inserted into the position immediately following the `back` marker. In this case, that position will be element 0. Thus, the queue wraps around the circular array as items are added and removed, which eliminates the need to shift items. The resulting queue is shown here:

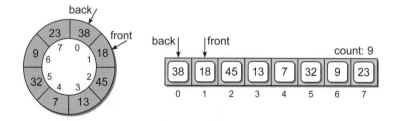

This also represents a full queue since all slots in the array are filled. No additional items can be added until existing items have been removed. This is a change from the original definition of the Queue ADT and requires an additional operation to test for a full queue.

Queue Implementation

Given the description of a circular array and its use in implementing a queue, we turn our attention to the implementation details. A Python implementation of the Queue ADT using a circular array is provided in Listing 8.2.

The constructor creates an object containing four data fields, including the counter to keep track of the number of items in the queue, the two markers, and the array itself. A sample instance of the class is illustrated in Figure 8.5.

For the circular queue, the array is created with `maxSize` elements as specified by the argument to the constructor. The two markers are initialized so the first item will be stored in element 0. This is achieved by setting `_front` to 0 and `_back` to the index of the last element in the array. When the first item is added, `_back`

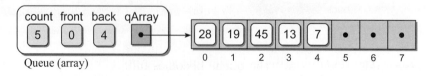

Figure 8.5: A Queue object implemented as a circular array.

Listing 8.2   The `arrayqueue.py` module.

```python
1  # Implementation of the Queue ADT using a circular array.
2  from array import Array
3
4  class Queue :
5      # Creates an empty queue.
6    def __init__( self, maxSize ) :
7      self._count = 0
8      self._front = 0
9      self._back = maxSize - 1
10     self._qArray = Array( maxSize )
11
12    # Returns True if the queue is empty.
13   def isEmpty( self ) :
14     return self._count == 0
15
16    # Returns True if the queue is full.
17   def isFull( self ) :
18     return self._count == len(self._qArray)
19
20    # Returns the number of items in the queue.
21   def __len__( self ) :
22     return self._count
23
24    # Adds the given item to the queue.
25   def enqueue( self, item ):
26     assert not self.isFull(), "Cannot enqueue to a full queue."
27     maxSize = len(self._qArray)
28     self._back = (self._back + 1) % maxSize
29     self._qArray[self._back] = item
30     self._count += 1
31
32    # Removes and returns the first item in the queue.
33   def dequeue( self ):
34     assert not self.isEmpty(), "Cannot dequeue from an empty queue."
35     item = self._qArray[ self._front ]
36     maxSize = len(self._qArray)
37     self._front = (self._front + 1) % maxSize
38     self._count -= 1
39     return item
```

---

will wrap around to element 0 and the new value will be stored in that position. Figure 8.6 illustrates the circular array when first created by the constructor.

The `size()` and `isEmpty()` methods use the value of `_count` to return the appropriate result. As indicated earlier, implementing the Queue ADT as a circular array creates the special case of a queue with a maximum capacity, which can result in a full queue. For this implementation of the queue, we must add the `isFull()` method, which can be used to test if the queue is full. Again, the `_count` field is used to determine when the queue becomes full.

To enqueue an item, as shown in lines 25–30, we must first test the precondition and verify the queue is not full. If the condition is met, the new item can be inserted

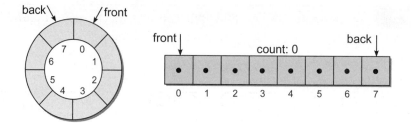

Figure 8.6: The circular array when the queue is first created in the constructor.

into the position immediately following the _back marker. But remember, we are using a circular array and once the marker reaches the last element of the actual linear array, it must wrap around to the first element. This can be done using a condition statement to test if _back is referencing the last element and adjusting it appropriately, as shown here:

```
self._back += 1
if self._back == len( self._qArray ) :
    self._back = 0
```

A simpler approach is to use the modulus operator as part of the increment step. This reduces the need for the conditional and automatically wraps the marker to the beginning of the array as follows:

```
self._back = ( self._back + 1 ) % len( self._qArray )
```

The dequeue operation is implemented in a similar fashion as enqueue() as shown in lines 33–39 of Listing 8.2. The item to be removed is taken from the position marked by _front and saved. The marker is then advanced using the modulus operator as was done when enqueueing a new item. The counter is decremented and the saved item is returned.

Run Time Analysis

The circular array implementation provides a more efficient solution than the Python list. The operations all have a worst case time-complexity of $O(1)$ since the array items never have to be shifted. But the circular array does introduce the drawback of working with a maximum-capacity queue. Even with this limitation, it is well suited for some applications.

8.2.3   Using a Linked List

A major disadvantage in using a Python list to implement the Queue ADT is the expense of the enqueue and dequeue operations. The circular array implementation improved on these operations, but at the cost of limiting the size of the queue. A better solution is to use a linked list consisting of both head and tail references. Adding the tail reference allows for quick append operations that otherwise would require a complete traversal to find the end of the list. Figure 8.7 illustrates a sample linked list with the two external references.

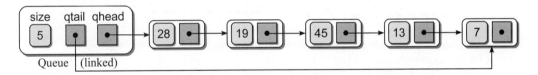

Figure 8.7: An instance of the Queue ADT implemented as a linked list.

The complete implementation of the Queue ADT using a linked list with a tail reference is provided in Listing 8.3. Remember, the individual nodes in the list contain the individual items in the queue. When dequeueing an item, we must unlink the node from the list but return the item stored in that node and not the node itself. An evaluation of the time-complexities is left as an exercise.

Listing 8.3 The `llistqueue.py` module.

```
1  # Implementation of the Queue ADT using a linked list.
2  class Queue :
3      # Creates an empty queue.
4    def __init__( self ):
5      self._qhead = None
6      self._qtail = None
7      self._count = 0
8
9     # Returns True if the queue is empty.
10   def isEmpty( self ):
11     return self._qhead is None
12
13    # Returns the number of items in the queue.
14   def __len__( self ):
15     return self._count
16
17    # Adds the given item to the queue.
18   def enqueue( self, item ):
19     node = _QueueNode( item )
20     if self.isEmpty() :
21       self._qhead = node
22     else :
23       self._qtail.next = node
24
25     self._qtail = node
26     self._count += 1
27
28    # Removes and returns the first item in the queue.
29   def dequeue( self ):
30     assert not self.isEmpty(), "Cannot dequeue from an empty queue."
31     node = self._qhead
32     if self._qhead is self._qtail :
33       self._qtail = None
```

(Listing Continued)

Listing 8.3   Continued ...

```
34
35        self._qhead = self._qhead.next
36        self._count -= 1
37        return node.item
38
39  # Private storage class for creating the linked list nodes.
40  class _QueueNode( object ):
41    def __init__( self, item ):
42      self.item = item
43      self.next = None
```

8.3   Priority Queues

Some applications require the use of a queue in which items are assigned a priority and the items with a higher priority are dequeued first. However, all items with the same priority still obey the FIFO principle. That is, if two items with the same priority are enqueued, the first in will be the first out.

8.3.1   The Priority Queue ADT

A priority queue is simply an extended version of the basic queue with the exception that a priority p must be assigned to each item at the time it is enqueued. There are two basic types of priority queues: bounded and unbounded. The **bounded priority queue** assumes a small limited range of p priorities over the interval of integers $[0 \ldots p)$. The **unbounded priority queue** places no limit on the range of integer values that can be used as priorities. The definition of the Priority Queue ADT is provided below. Note that we use one definition for both bounded and unbounded priority queues.

A *priority queue* is a queue in which each item is assigned a priority and items with a higher priority are removed before those with a lower priority, irrespective of when they were added. Integer values are used for the priorities with a smaller integer value having a higher priority. A *bounded priority queue* restricts the priorities to the integer values between zero and a predefined upper limit whereas an *unbounded priority queue* places no limits on the range of priorities.

- PriorityQueue(): Creates a new empty unbounded priority queue.

- BPriorityQueue(numLevels): Creates a new empty bounded priority queue with priority levels in the range from 0 to numLevels - 1.

- isEmpty(): Returns a boolean value indicating whether the queue is empty.

- *length* (): Returns the number of items currently in the queue.

- enqueue(item, priority): Adds the given item to the queue by inserting it in the proper position based on the given priority. The priority value must be within the legal range when using a bounded priority queue.

- dequeue(): Removes and returns the front item from the queue, which is the item with the highest priority. The associated priority value is discarded. If two items have the same priority, then those items are removed in a FIFO order. An item cannot be dequeued from an empty queue.

Consider the following code segment, which enqueues a number of items into a priority queue. The priority queue is defined with six levels of priority with a range of $[0 \ldots 5]$. The resulting queue is shown in Figure 8.8.

```
Q = BPriorityQueue( 6 )
Q.enqueue( "purple", 5 )
Q.enqueue( "black", 1 )
Q.enqueue( "orange", 3 )
Q.enqueue( "white", 0 )
Q.enqueue( "green", 1 )
Q.enqueue( "yellow", 5 )
```

Figure 8.8: Abstract view of a priority queue resulting from enqueueing several strings, along with individual priorities.

The first item to be removed will be the first item with the highest priority. Notice when items *"black"* and *"green"* are enqueued, *"green"* follows *"black"* in the queue even though they have the same priority since items with equal priority still obey the FIFO principle. The following code segment removes the items and prints them to the terminal:

```
while not Q.isEmpty() :
    item = Q.dequeue()
    print( item )
```

which results in the following output:

```
white
black
green
orange
purple
yellow
```

8.3.2 Implementation: Unbounded Priority Queue

There are a number of ways to implement an unbounded Priority Queue ADT. The most basic is to use a Python list or linked list as was done with the Queue ADT. To implement the priority queue, we must consider several facts related to the definition of the ADT:

- A priority must be associated with each item in the queue, possibly requiring the value to be stored along with the item.

- The next item to be dequeued from the priority queue is the item with the highest priority.

- If multiple items have the same priority, those items must be dequeued in the order they were originally enqueued.

Python List Implementation

We used a Python list to implement the basic queue earlier in the chapter. In that implementation, the queue items were organized within the list from front to back with new items appended directly to the end and existing items removed from the front. That simple organization worked well with the basic queue. When implementing the priority queue, however, the items cannot simply be added directly to the list, but instead we must have a way to associate a priority with each item. This can be accomplished with a simple storage class containing two fields: one for the priority and one for the queue item. For example:

```
class _PriorityQEntry :
  def __init__( self, item, priority ):
    self.item = item
    self.priority = priority
```

With the use of a storage class for maintaining the associated priorities, the next question is how should the entries be organized within the vector? We can consider two approaches, both of which satisfy the requirements of the priority queue:

- *Append new items to the end of the list.* When a new item is enqueued, simply append a new instance of the storage class (containing the item and its priority) to the end of the list. When an item is dequeued, search the vector for the item with the lowest priority and remove it from the list. If more than one item has the same priority, the first one encountered during the search will be the first to be dequeued.

- *Keep the items sorted within the list based on their priority.* When a new item is enqueued, find its proper position within the list based on its priority and insert an instance of the storage class at that point. If we order the items in the vector from lowest priority at the front to highest at the end, then the dequeue operation simply requires the removal of the last item in the list. To maintain the proper ordering of items with equal priority, the enqueue operation must ensure newer items are inserted closer to the front of the list than the other items with the same priority.

An implementation of the priority queue using a Python list in which new items are appended to the end is provided in Listing 8.4. A sample instance of the class is illustrated in Figure 8.9. Note this implementation does not use the `numLevels` argument passed to the constructor since we can store items having any number of priority levels.

Listing 8.4   The `priorityq.py` module.

```python
# Implementation of the unbounded Priority Queue ADT using a Python list
# with new items appended to the end.

class PriorityQueue :
  # Create an empty unbounded priority queue.
  def __init__( self ):
    self._qList = list()

  # Returns True if the queue is empty.
  def isEmpty( self ):
    return len( self ) == 0

  # Returns the number of items in the queue.
  def __len__( self ):
    return len( self._qList )

  # Adds the given item to the queue.
  def enqueue( self, item, priority ):
    # Create a new instance of the storage class and append it to the list.
    entry = _PriorityQEntry( item, priority )
    self._qList.append( entry )

  # Removes and returns the first item in the queue.
  def dequeue( self ) :
    assert not self.isEmpty(), "Cannot dequeue from an empty queue."

    # Find the entry with the highest priority.
    highest = self._qList[i].priority
    for i in range( self.len() ) :
      # See if the ith entry contains a higher priority (smaller integer).
      if self._qList[i].priority < highest :
        highest = self._qList[i].priority

    # Remove the entry with the highest priority and return the item.
    entry = self._qList.pop( highest )
    return entry.item

# Private storage class for associating queue items with their priority.
class _PriorityQEntry( object ):
  def __init__( self, item, prioity ):
    self.item = item
    self.priority = priority
```

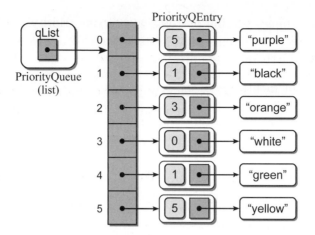

Figure 8.9: An instance of the priority queue implemented using a list.

To evaluate the efficiency, we consider the implementation of each operation. Testing for an empty queue and determining the size can be done in $O(1)$ time. The enqueue operation requires linear time in the worst case since the underlying array may have to be reallocated, but it has a $O(1)$ amortized cost. The dequeue operation is also $O(n)$ since we must search through the entire list in the worst case to find the entry with the highest priority.

Linked List Implementation

A singly linked list structure with both head and tail references can also be used to implement the priority queue as illustrated in Figure 8.10. The _QueueNode class used in the implementation of the Queue ADT using a linked list has to be modified to include the priority value. After that, the linked list can be used in a similar fashion as the Python list. When an item is enqueued, the new node is appended to the end of the linked list and when a dequeue operation is performed, the linked list is searched to find the entry with the highest priority. We leave the actual design and implementation as an exercise but examine the time-complexity of this approach.

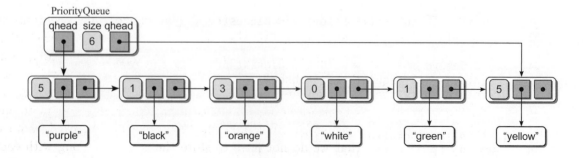

Figure 8.10: Implementation of the priority queue from Figure 8.8 using a linked list.

As with the Python list implementation of the priority queue, testing for an empty queue and determining the size can be done in $O(1)$ time. The enqueue operation can also be done in constant time since we need only append a new node to the end of the list. The dequeue operation, however, requires $O(n)$ time since the entire list must be searched in the worst case to find the entry with the highest priority. Once that entry is located, the node can be removed from the list in constant time.

8.3.3 Implementation: Bounded Priority Queue

The Python list and linked list versions are quite simple to implement and can be used to implement the bounded priority queue. But they both require linear time to dequeue an item. Since the priorities of a bounded priority queue are restricted to a finite set $[0 \ldots p)$, we can improve this worst case time with an implementation in which all of the operations only require constant time. This can be done using an array of queues, as illustrated in Figure 8.11.

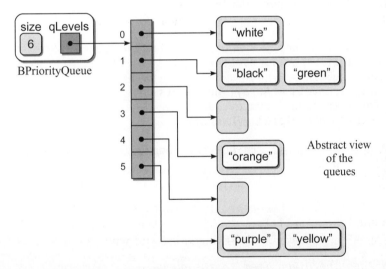

Figure 8.11: Implementation of the priority queue using an array of queues.

The implementation of the bounded Priority Queue ADT is shown in Listing 8.5. The constructor creates two data fields. The _qLevels field contains an array of p elements in which each contains an instance of the Queue ADT. The _size field maintains the number of items in the priority queue, which can also be used to determine if the queue is empty. When an item with priority k is added to the priority queue, it is added to the queue stored in the qList[k] element. To dequeue an item from the priority queue, we must iterate through the array to find the first non-empty queue, which will contain the first item to be removed from the priority queue. Note that we do not have to store the priorities along with each item since all items with a given priority will be stored in the same queue. The priority can be determined from the array indices.

The implementation of the priority queue using an array of queues is also quite simple. But can we obtain constant time operations? We begin with the `isEmpty()` and `__len__` operations. Since a data field is maintained to store the number of items in the priority queue, both can be performed in constant time. The enqueue operation also requires constant time since adding an item to a general queue can be done in constant time as can accessing an individual queue in the array. Dequeueing from a general queue implemented as a linked list can be done in constant time. But since we must iterate through the array to find the first non-empty queue, the priority dequeue operation requires $O(p)$ time. While this time is linear, it is linear with respect to the number of priorities and not to the number of elements in the queue (n). When the number of priorities is quite small,

Listing 8.5   The `bpriorityq.py` module.

```
1   # Implementation of the bounded Priority Queue ADT using an array of
2   # queues in which the queues are implemented using a linked list.
3   from array import Array
4   from llistqueue import Queue
5
6   class BPriorityQueue :
7     # Creates an empty bounded priority queue.
8     def __init__( self, numLevels ):
9       self._qSize = 0
10      self._qLevels = Array( numLevels )
11      for i in range( numLevels ) :
12        self._qLevels[i] = Queue()
13
14    # Returns True if the queue is empty.
15    def isEmpty( self ):
16      return len( self ) == 0
17
18    # Returns the number of items in the queue.
19    def __len__( self ):
20      return len( self._qSize )
21
22    # Adds the given item to the queue.
23    def enqueue( self, item, priority ):
24      assert priority >= 0 and priority < len(self._qLevels), \
25            "Invalid priority level."
26      self._qLevels[priority].enqueue( item )
27
28    # Removes and returns the next item in the queue.
29    def dequeue( self ) :
30      # Make sure the queue is not empty.
31      assert not self.isEmpty(), "Cannot dequeue from an empty queue."
32      # Find the first non-empty queue.
33      i = 0
34      p = len(self._qLevels)
35      while i < p and not self._qLevels[i].isEmpty() :
36        i += 1
37      # We know the queue is not empty, so dequeue from the ith queue.
38      return self._qLevels[i].dequeue()
```

we can safely treat p as a constant value and specify the dequeue operation as requiring constant time.

The disadvantage of this structure for the implementation of the priority queue is that the number of levels is fixed. If an application requires a priority queue with an unlimited number of priority levels, then the vector or linked-list versions are a better choice.

8.4   Application: Computer Simulations

Computers have long been used to model and simulate real-world systems and phenomena. These simulations are simply computer applications that have been designed to represent and appropriately react to the significant events occurring in the system. Simulations can allow humans to study certain behaviors or experiment with certain changes and events in a system to determine the appropriate strategy.

Some of the more common simulations include weather forecasting and flight simulators. A flight simulator, which is a mock-up of a real cockpit and controlled by software, helps train pilots to deal with real situations without having to risk the life of the pilot or loss of the aircraft. Weather forecasts today are much more reliable due to the aide of computer simulations. Mathematical models have been developed to simulate weather patterns and atmospheric conditions. These models can be solved using computer applications, which then provide information to meteorologists for use in predicting the weather.

Computer simulations are also used for less glamorous applications. Businesses can use a computer simulation to determine the number of employees needed to provide a service to its customers. For example, an airline may want to know how many ticket agents are needed at certain times of the day in order to provide timely service. Having too many agents will cost the airline money, but too few will result in angry customers. The company could simply study the customer habits at one airport and experiment with a different number of agents at different times. But this can be costly and time consuming. In addition, the results may only be valid for that one airport. To reduce the cost and allow for events that may occur at various airports, a computer simulation can be developed to model the real system.

8.4.1   Airline Ticket Counter

Simulating an airline ticket counter, or any other *queuing system* where customers stand in line awaiting service, is very common. A queue structure is used to model the queuing system in order to study certain behaviors or outcomes. Some of the typical results studied include average waiting time and average queue length. Queuing systems that use a single queue are easier to model. More complex systems like those representing a grocery store that use multiple queues, require more complex models. In this text, we limit our discussion to single-queue systems.

Queuing System Model

We can model a queuing system by constructing a *discrete event simulation*. The simulation is a sequence of significant events that cause a change in the system. For example, in our airline ticket counter simulation, these events would include customer arrival, the start or conclusion of a transaction, or customer departure.

The simulation is time driven and performed over a preset time period. The passing of time is represented by a loop, which increments a discrete time variable once for each tick of the clock. The events can only occur at discrete time intervals. Thus, the time units must be small enough such that no event can occur between units. A simulation is commonly designed to allow the user to supply parameters that define the conditions of the system. For a discrete event simulation modeling a queuing system, these parameters include:

- The length of the simulation given in number of time units. The simulation typically begins at time unit zero.

- The number of servers providing the service to the customers. We must have at least one server.

- The expected service time to complete a transaction.

- The distribution of arrival times, which is used to determine when customers arrive.

By adjusting these parameters, the user can change the conditions under which the simulation is performed. We can change the number of servers, for example, to determine the optimal number required to provide satisfactory service under the given conditions.

Finally, a set of rules are defined for handling the events during each tick of the clock. The specific rules depends on what results are being studied. To determine the average time customers must wait in line before being served, there are three rules:

Rule 1: If a customer arrives, he is added to the queue. At most, one customer can arrive during each time step.

Rule 2: If there are customers waiting, for each free server, the next customer in line begins her transaction.

Rule 3: For each server handling a transaction, if the transaction is complete, the customer departs and the server becomes free.

When the simulation completes, the average waiting time can be computed by dividing the total waiting time for all customers by the total number of customers.

Random Events

To correctly model a queuing system, some events must occur at random. One such event is customer arrival. In the first rule outlined earlier, we need to determine if a customer arrives during the current tick of the clock. In a real-world system, this event cannot be directly controlled but is a true random act. We need to model this action as close as possible in our simulation.

A simple approach would be to flip a coin and let "heads" represent a customer arrival. But this would indicate that there is a 50/50 chance a customer arrives every time unit. This may be true for some systems, but not necessarily the one we are modeling. We could change and use a six-sided die and let one of the sides represent a customer arrival. But this only changes the odds to 1 in 6 that a customer arrives.

A better approach is to allow the user to specify the odds of a customer arriving at each time step. This can be done in one of two ways. The user can enter the odds a customer arrives during the current time step as a real value between 0.0 (no chance) and 1.0 (a sure thing). If 0.2 is entered, then this would indicate there is a 1 in 5 chance a customer arrives. Instead of directly entering the odds, we can have the user enter the average time between customer arrivals. We then compute the odds within the program. If the user enters an average time of 8.0, then on average a customer arrives every 8 minutes. But customers can arrive during any minute of the simulation. The average time between arrivals simply provides the average over the entire simulation. We use the average time to compute the odds of a customer arriving as 1.0/8.0, or 0.125.

Given the odds either directly by the user or computing them based on the average arrival time, how is this value used to simulate the random act of a customer arriving? We use the *random number generator* provided by Python to generate a number between 0.0 and 1.0. We compare this result to the probability (`prob`) of an arrival. If the generated random number is between 0.0 and `prob` inclusive, the event occurs and we signal a customer arrival. On the other hand, if the random value is greater than `prob`, then no customer arrives during the current time step and no action is taken. The arrival probability can be changed to alter the number of customers served in the simulation.

8.4.2 Implementation

We can design and implement a discrete event computer simulation to analyze the average time passengers have to wait for service at an airport ticket counter. The simulation will involve multiple ticket agents serving customers who have to wait in line until they can be served. Our design will be an object-oriented solution with multiple classes.

System Parameters

The program will prompt the user for the queuing system parameters:

```
Number of minutes to simulate: 25
Number of ticket agents: 2
Average service time per passenger: 3
Average time between passenger arrival: 2
```

For simplicity we use minutes as the discrete time units. This would not be sufficient to simulate a real ticket counter as multiple passengers are likely to arrive within any given minute. The program will then perform the simulation and produce the following output:

```
Number of passengers served =   12
Number of passengers remaining in line = 1
The average wait time was 1.17 minutes.
```

We will also have the program display event information, which can be used to help debug the program. The debug information lists each event that occurs in the system along with the time the events occur. For the input values shown above, the event information displayed will be:

```
Time    2: Passenger 1 arrived.
Time    2: Agent 1 started serving passenger 1.
Time    3: Passenger 2 arrived.
Time    3: Agent 2 started serving passenger 2.
Time    5: Passenger 3 arrived.
Time    5: Agent 1 stopped serving passenger 1.
Time    6: Agent 1 started serving passenger 3.
Time    6: Agent 2 stopped serving passenger 2.
Time    8: Passenger 4 arrived.
Time    8: Agent 2 started serving passenger 4.
Time    9: Agent 1 stopped serving passenger 3.
Time   10: Passenger 5 arrived.
Time   10: Agent 1 started serving passenger 5.
Time   11: Passenger 6 arrived.
Time   11: Agent 2 stopped serving passenger 4.
Time   12: Agent 2 started serving passenger 6.
Time   13: Passenger 7 arrived.
Time   13: Agent 1 stopped serving passenger 5.
Time   14: Passenger 8 arrived.
Time   14: Agent 1 started serving passenger 7.
Time   15: Passenger 9 arrived.
Time   15: Agent 2 stopped serving passenger 6.
Time   16: Agent 2 started serving passenger 8.
Time   17: Agent 1 stopped serving passenger 7.
Time   18: Passenger 10 arrived.
Time   18: Agent 1 started serving passenger 9.
Time   19: Passenger 11 arrived.
Time   19: Agent 2 stopped serving passenger 8.
Time   20: Agent 2 started serving passenger 10.
Time   21: Agent 1 stopped serving passenger 9.
Time   22: Agent 1 started serving passenger 11.
Time   23: Passenger 12 arrived.
Time   23: Agent 2 stopped serving passenger 10.
Time   24: Agent 2 started serving passenger 12.
Time   25: Passenger 13 arrived.
Time   25: Agent 1 stopped serving passenger 11.
```

Passenger Class

First, we need a class to store information related to a single passenger. We create a Passenger class for this purpose. The complete implementation of this class is provided in Listing 8.6. The class will contain two data fields. The first is an identification number used in the output of the event information. The second field records the time the passenger arrives. This value will be needed to determine the length of time the passenger waited in line before beginning service with an agent. Methods are also provided to access the two data fields. An instance of the class is illustrated in Figure 8.12.

Listing 8.6   The Passenger class defined in the `simpeople.py` module.

```
1   # Used to store and manage information related to an airline passenger.
2   class Passenger :
3     # Creates a passenger object.
4     def __init__( self, idNum, arrivalTime ):
5       self._idNum = idNum
6       self._arrivalTime = arrivalTime
7
8     # Gets the passenger's id number.
9     def idNum( self ) :
10      return self._idNum
11
12    # Gets the passenger's arrival time.
13    def timeArrived( self ) :
14      return self._arrivalTime
```

Ticket Agent Class

We also need a class to represent and store information related to the ticket agents. The information includes an agent identification number and a timer to know when the transaction will be completed. This value is the sum of the current time and the average time of the transaction as entered by the user. Finally, we need to keep track of the current passenger being served by the agent in order to identify the specific passenger when the transaction is completed. The TicketAgent class is implemented in Listing 8.7, and an instance of the class is shown in Figure 8.12.

The _passenger field is set to a null reference, which will be used to flag a free agent. The idNum() method simply returns the id assigned to the agent when the object is created while the isFree() method examines the _passenger field to

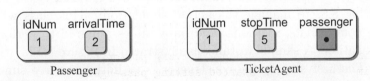

Figure 8.12: Sample Passenger and TicketAgent objects.

determine if the agent is free. The `isFinished()` method is used to determine if the passenger currently being served by this agent has completed her transaction. This method only flags the transaction as having been completed. To actually end the transaction, `stopService()` must be called. `stopService()` sets the `_passenger` field to `None` to again indicate the agent is free and returns the passenger object. To begin a transaction, `startService()` is called, which assigns the appropriate fields with the supplied arguments.

Listing 8.7   The `TicketAgent` class defined in the `simpeople.py` module.

```
1   # Used to store and manage information related to an airline ticket agent.
2   class TicketAgent :
3     # Creates a ticket agent object.
4     def __init__( self, idNum ):
5       self._idNum = idNum
6       self._passenger = None
7       self._stopTime = -1
8
9     # Gets the ticket agent's id number.
10    def idNum( self ):
11      return self._idNum
12
13    # Determines if the ticket agent is free to assist a passenger.
14    def isFree( self ):
15      return self._passenger is None
16
17    # Determines if the ticket agent has finished helping the passenger.
18    def isFinished( self, curTime ):
19      return self._passenger is not None and self._stopTime == curTime
20
21    # Indicates the ticket agent has begun assisting a passenger.
22    def startService( self, passenger, stopTime ):
23      self._passenger = passenger
24      self._stopTime = stopTime
25
26    # Indicates the ticket agent has finished helping the passenger.
27    def stopService( self ):
28      thePassenger = self._passenger
29      self._passenger = None
30      return thePassenger
```

Simulation Class

Finally, we construct the `TicketCounterSimulation` class, which is provided in Listing 8.8, to manage the actual simulation. This class will contain the various components, methods, and data values required to perform a discrete event simulation. A sample instance is illustrated in Figure 8.13.

The first step in the constructor is to initialize three simulation parameters. Note the `_arriveProb` is the probability of a passenger arriving during the current time step using the formula described earlier. A queue is created, which will be

Listing 8.8	The `simulation.py` module.

```python
1   # Implementation of the main simulation class.
2   from array import Array
3   from llistqueue import Queue
4   from people import TicketAgent, Passenger
5
6   class TicketCounterSimulation :
7     # Create a simulation object.
8     def __init__( self, numAgents, numMinutes, betweenTime, serviceTime ):
9       # Parameters supplied by the user.
10      self._arriveProb = 1.0 / betweenTime
11      self._serviceTime = serviceTime
12      self._numMinutes = numMinutes
13
14      # Simulation components.
15      self._passengerQ = Queue()
16      self._theAgents = Array( numAgents )
17      for i in range( numAgents ) :
18        self._theAgents[i] = TicketAgent(i+1)
19
20      # Computed during the simulation.
21      self._totalWaitTime = 0
22      self._numPassengers = 0
23
24    # Run the simulation using the parameters supplied earlier.
25    def run( self ):
26      for curTime in range(self._numMinutes + 1) :
27        self._handleArrival( curTime )
28        self._handleBeginService( curTime )
29        self._handleEndService( curTime )
30
31    # Print the simulation results.
32    def printResults( self ):
33      numServed = self._numPassengers - len(self._passengerQ)
34      avgWait = float( self._totalWaitTime ) / numServed
35      print( "" )
36      print( "Number of passengers served = ", numServed )
37      print( "Number of passengers remaining in line = %d" %
38             len(self._passengerQ) )
39      print( "The average wait time was %4.2f minutes." % avgWait )
40
41    # The remaining methods that have yet to be implemented.
42    # def _handleArrive( curTime ):          # Handles simulation rule #1.
43    # def _handleBeginService( curTime ):   # Handles simulation rule #2.
44    # def _handleEndService( curTime ):     # Handles simulation rule #3.
```

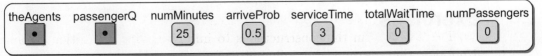

TicketCounterSimulation

theAgents	passengerQ	numMinutes	arriveProb	serviceTime	totalWaitTime	numPassengers
•	•	25	0.5	3	0	0

Figure 8.13: A sample `TicketCounterSimulation` object.

used to represent the line in which passengers must wait until they are served by a ticket agent. The ticket agents are represented as an array of **Agent** objects. The individual objects are instantiated and each is assigned an id number, starting with 1. Two data fields are needed to store data collected during the actual simulation. The first is the summation of the time each passenger has to wait in line before being served, and the second keeps track of the number of passengers in the simulation. The latter will also be used to assign an id to each passenger.

The simulation is performed by calling the **run()** method, which simulates the ticking of the clock by performing a count-controlled loop keeping track of the current time in **curTime**. The loop executes until _numMinutes have elapsed. The events of the simulation are also performed during the terminating minute, hence, the need for the _numMinutes + 1 in the **range()** function. During each iteration of the loop, the three simulation rules outlined earlier are handled by the respective _handleXYZ() helper methods. The _handleArrival() method determines if a passenger arrives during the current time step and handles that arrival. _handleBeginService() determines if any agents are free and allows the next passenger(s) in line to begin their transaction. The _handleEndService() determines which of the current transactions have completed, if any, and flags a passenger departure. The implementation of the helper methods is left as an exercise.

After running the simulation, the **printResults()** method is called to print the results. When the simulation terminates there may be some passengers remaining in the queue who have not yet been assisted. Thus, we need to determine how many passengers have exited the queue, which indicates the number of passenger wait times included in the _totalWaitTime field. The average wait time is simply the total wait time divided by the number of passengers served.

The last component of our program is the driver module, which is left as an exercise. The driver extracts the simulation parameters from the user and then creates and uses a **TicketCounterSimulation** object to perform the simulation. To produce the same results shown earlier, you will need to seed the random number generator with the value 4500 before running the simulation:

```
random.seed( 4500 )
```

In a typical experiment, a simulation is performed multiple times varying the parameters with each execution. Table 8.1 illustrates the results of a single experiment with multiple executions of the simulation. Note the significant change in the average wait time when increasing the number of ticket agents by one in the last two sets of experiments.

Exercises

8.1 Determine the worst case time-complexity for each operation defined in the TicketCounterSimulation class.

Num Minutes	Num Agents	Average Service	Time Between	Average Wait	Passengers Served	Passengers Remaining
100	2	3	2	2.49	49	2
500	2	3	2	3.91	240	0
1000	2	3	2	10.93	490	14
5000	2	3	2	15.75	2459	6
10000	2	3	2	21.17	4930	18
100	2	4	2	10.60	40	11
500	2	4	2	49.99	200	40
1000	2	4	2	95.72	400	104
5000	2	4	2	475.91	2000	465
10000	2	4	2	949.61	4000	948
100	3	4	2	0.51	51	0
500	3	4	2	0.50	240	0
1000	3	4	2	1.06	501	3
5000	3	4	2	1.14	2465	0
10000	3	4	2	1.21	4948	0

Table 8.1: Sample results of the ticket counter simulation experiment.

8.2 Hand execute the following code and show the contents of the resulting queue:

```
values = Queue()
for i in range( 16 ) :
  if i % 3 == 0 :
    values.enqueue( i )
```

8.3 Hand execute the following code and show the contents of the resulting queue:

```
values = Queue()
for i in range( 16 ) :
  if i % 3 == 0 :
    values.enqueue( i )
  elif i % 4 == 0 :
    values.dequeue()
```

8.4 Implement the remaining methods of the `TicketCounterSimulation` class.

8.5 Modify the `TicketCounterSimulation` class to use seconds for the time units instead of minutes. Run an experiment with multiple simulations and produce a table like Table 8.1.

8.6 Design and implement a function that reverses the order of the items in a queue. Your solution may only use the operations defined by the Queue ADT, but you are free to use other data structures if necessary.

Programming Projects

8.1 Implement the Priority Queue ADT using each of the following:

(a) sorted Python list   (b) sorted linked list   (c) unsorted linked list

8.2 A *deque* (pronounced "deck") is similar to a queue, except that elements can be enqueued at either end and dequeued from either end. Define a Deque ADT and then provide an implementation for your definition.

8.3 Design and implement a ToDo List ADT in which each entry can be assigned a priority and the entries with the highest priority are performed first.

8.4 Printers can be connected to the network and made available to many users. To manage multiple print jobs and to provide fair access, networked printers use print queues. Design, implement, and test a computer program to simulate a print queue that evaluates the average wait time.

8.5 Modify your simulation from Programming Project 8.4 to use a priority queue for each print job. The priorities should range from 0 to 20 with 0 being the highest priority. Use a random number generator to determine the priority of each job.

8.6 Design, implement, and test a computer program to simulate a telephone customer service center. Your simulation should evaluate the average time customers have to wait on hold.

8.7 Design, implement, and test a computer program to simulate a bank. Your simulation should evaluate the average time customers have to wait in line before they are served by a teller.

8.8 Redesign the `TicketCounterClass` to implement a generic simulation class from which a user can derive their own simulation classes.

8.9 Design, implement, and test a computer program to simulate the checkout at a grocery store. Your simulation must allow for multiple checkout lines and allow customers at the end of a line to move to another checkout line. This simulation differs from the one described in the chapter. For this simulation, you will have to accommodate the multiple checkout lines, decide how a customer chooses a line, and decide if and when a customer moves to a new checkout line.

## CHAPTER 9

Advanced Linked Lists

In Chapter 6, we introduced the linked list data structure and saw how it can be used to improve the construction and management of lists for certain types of applications. In that discussion, we limited the focus to the singly linked list in which traversals start at the front and progress, one element at a time, in a single direction. But there are a number of variations to the linked list structure based on how the nodes are linked and how many chains are constructed from those links. In this chapter, we introduce some of the more common linked list variations.

9.1 The Doubly Linked List

The singly linked list introduced in Chapter 6 consists of nodes linked in a single direction. Access and traversals begin with the first node and progress toward the last node, one node at a time. But what if we want to traverse the nodes in reverse order? With the singly linked list, this can be done but not efficiently. We would have to perform multiple traversals, with each traversal starting at the front and stopping one node earlier than on the previous traversal. Or consider the problem in which you are given a reference to a specific node and need to insert a new node immediately preceding that node. Since the predecessor of a given node cannot be directly accessed, we would have to use a modified insertion operation in which the list is traversed from the first node until the predecessor of the given node is found. Again, this is not an efficient solution. For these operations and a number of others, we need direct access to both the node following and immediately preceding a given node.

9.1.1 Organization

In a *doubly linked list*, each node contains not only the data component and a link to the next node as in the singly linked list, but also a second link that points to the preceding node, as illustrated in Figure 9.1. To create the individual nodes, we must add a third field to the node class, which we name `DListNode` to reflect its use with a doubly linked list, as shown in Listing 9.1.

Listing 9.1   Storage class for a doubly linked list node.

```
1  class DListNode :
2    def __init__( self, data ):
3      self.data = data
4      self.next = None
5      self.prev = None
```

A head reference is again used to reference the first node in the list. A tail reference, although optional, is commonly used with a doubly linked list to take advantage of the reverse chain, which allows for traversals from back to front. The last node is indicated by a null reference in the `next` link of the last node as was done in the singly linked list. But we must also indicate the first node since the list can be traversed in reverse order. This is done using a null reference in the `prev` link of the first node.

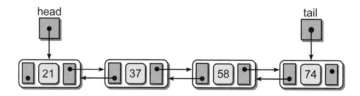

Figure 9.1: A doubly linked list with four nodes.

A doubly linked list can be sorted or unsorted depending on the specific application. The implementation of the various operations for an unsorted doubly linked list are very similar to those of the unsorted singly linked list. We leave the implementation of these operations as an exercise and only focus on the use and management of sorted doubly linked lists.

9.1.2 List Operations

The position of the nodes in a sorted doubly linked list are based on the key value of the corresponding data item stored in each node. The basic linked list operations can also be performed on a doubly linked list.

Traversals

The doubly linked list allows for traversals from front to back or back to front. The traversals are performed using a temporary external reference to mark the current node. The only difference is which node we start with and which link field is used to advance the temporary reference. Traversing the doubly linked list from beginning to end is identical to that with a singly linked list. We start at the node referenced by `head` and advance the temporary reference, `curNode`, one node at a time, using the `next` link field. The reverse traversal, provided in Listing 9.2, starts at the node referenced by `tail` and advances `curNode`, one node at a time, using the `prev` link field. In either case, the traversal terminates when `curNode` is set to null, resulting in a $O(n)$ linear time operation.

Listing 9.2   Traversing a doubly linked list in reverse order.

```
1  def revTraversal( tail ):
2    curNode = tail
3    while curNode is not None :
4      print( curNode.data )
5      curNode = curNode.prev
```

Searching

Searching for a specific item in a doubly linked list, based on key value, can be implemented in the same fashion as for a singly linked list. Start with the first node and iterate through the list until we find the target item or we encounter a node containing a key value larger than the target. But a doubly linked list provides an advantage not available in the singly linked list. Since we can move forward or backward, the search operations do not have to begin with the first node.

Suppose we perform a sequence of search operations on the list from Figure 9.1 and we begin that sequence with a search for value 58. Using the external reference `probe` to iterate through the list, the target is found in the third node. If we leave `probe` pointing to the third node, as illustrated in Figure 9.2, we can begin the next search operation where the previous search left off instead of starting over from the beginning. Suppose the next search is for value 37. We can compare this target value to the item currently referenced by `probe` and determine if the search should proceed forward or backward starting from the `probe` node. In this case, we search backward, using `probe` to traverse the list. Thus, each time a search is performed, we leave the `probe` reference where the previous search ended and use it for subsequent searches. Note that `probe` is not a temporary reference variable as `curNode` was in the normal search operation, but must be maintained between operations in the same fashion as `head` and `tail`. Given the three external

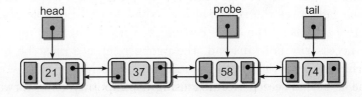

Figure 9.2: A probe reference positioned after searching for value 58.

references, `head`, `tail`, and `probe`, Listing 9.3 provides an implementation for searching a sorted doubly linked list using the probing technique.

Listing 9.3   Probing a doubly linked list.

```
 1   # Given the head, tail, and probe references, probe the list for a target.
 2
 3     # Make sure the list is not empty.
 4   if head is None :
 5     return False
 6     # If probe is null, initialize it to the first node.
 7   elif probe is None :
 8     probe = head
 9
10     # If the target comes before the probe node, we traverse backward;
11     # otherwise traverse forward.
12   if target < probe.data :
13     while probe is not None and target <= probe.data :
14       if target == probe.data :
15         return True
16       else :
17         probe = probe.prev
18   else :
19     while probe is not None and target >= probe.data :
20       if target == probe.data :
21         return True
22       else :
23         probe = probe.next
24
25     # If the target is not found in the list, return False.
26   return False
```

As with a singly linked list, all of the list operations must also work with an empty list, indicated by a null `head` reference. With the probe operation, the search simply fails if the list is empty. This can be quickly determined by examining the `head` reference.

The `probe` reference can also be null at the beginning of the search operation. This can occur when the first search is performed, since the `probe` reference has not been positioned within the list by a previous search operation. We could manage `probe` within the insert and deletion operations and make adjustments each time a new node is added or deleted. But performing this check within the search operation is just as easy, especially since this is the only operation in which `probe` is utilized. The `probe` reference can also become null when the previous search fails after the traversal has exhausted all possible nodes and the external reference "falls off the list." But unlike with a null head reference, the search does not necessarily fail. Instead, the `probe` reference must be initialized to point to the first node in the list to prepare for the current search.

The actual search is performed by either traversing forward or backward depending on the relation between the target and the key value in the node referenced by `probe`. If the target is smaller than `probe`'s key, then a reverse sorted list traversal is performed; otherwise a normal forward traversal is used. If the target is found during the iteration of the appropriate loop, the function is terminated and `True` is returned. Otherwise, the loop will terminate after exhausting all possible nodes or stopping early when it's determined the target cannot possibly be in the list. In either case, `False` is returned as the last operation of the function.

We can add a quick test to determine if the target value cannot possibly be in the list. This is done by comparing the target to the first and last nodes in the list. If the target is smaller than the first item or larger than the last, we know the search will ultimately fail since the target is not in the list. This step can be omitted as the same results can be achieved by the search traversal follow, but it can help to improve the search time on large lists.

The search operation, which maintains and uses a third external reference variable, can improve the search time for a large number of sequential searches performed on large lists. But in the worst case, it remains a linear time operation since a complete traversal may have to be performed.

Adding Nodes

Adding new nodes to a sorted doubly linked list is done similar to that for the singly linked list. The only difference is we do not need to keep track of the preceding node. Once the position for the new node is located, we can access its predecessor using the appropriate `prev` field. Consider Figure 9.3, which illustrates inserting a new node into the middle of a sorted doubly linked list. The location of the new node is found by positioning a single temporary external reference variable to point to the node containing the first value larger than the new value. After this position is found, the new node can be linked into the list using the various `prev` and `next` node fields as illustrated. The resulting list after inserting the new node is illustrated in Figure 9.4 on the next page.

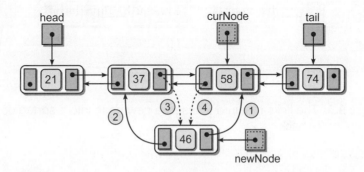

Figure 9.3: Linked modifications required to insert value 46 into the doubly linked list.

As with a singly linked list, inserting a node into a non-empty sorted doubly linked list can occur in one of three places: at the front, at the end, or somewhere in the middle. Inserting a new node into the middle of a list was illustrated above.

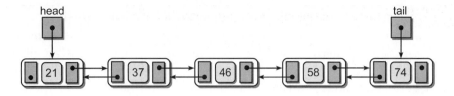

Figure 9.4: The result of inserting the new node into the doubly linked list.

Figure 9.5 illustrates the links required to insert a node at the front or end of a doubly linked list.

The code for adding a node to a sorted doubly linked list is provided in Listing 9.4. Since a tail reference is commonly used with a doubly linked list, we can provide a more efficient solution by dividing the operation into the four different cases. This reduces the need for loop traversal when the list is empty or the new node is prepended or appended to the list.

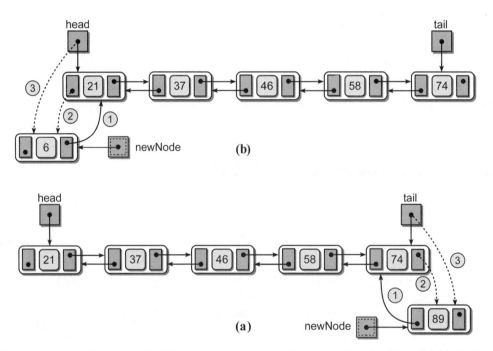

Figure 9.5: The links required to insert a new node into a sorted doubly linked list at the (a) front or (b) back.

Removing Nodes

Deleting a node from a doubly linked list is done in a similar fashion to that for a singly linked list. Again, there is no need to position a `pred` temporary external reference variable since the predecessor of a given node can be accessed using the appropriate `prev` fields. Implementation of the delete operation is left as an exercise.

| Listing 9.4 | Inserting a value into an ordered doubly linked list. |

```
1  # Given a head and tail reference and a new value, add the new value to a
2  # sorted doubly linked list.
3
4  newnode = DListNode( value )
5  if head is None :              # empty list
6    head = newnode
7    tail = head
8  elif value < head.data :  # insert before head
9    newnode.next = head
10   head.prev = newnode
11   head = newnode
12 elif value > tail.data :  # insert after tail
13   newnode.prev = tail
14   tail.next = newnode
15   tail = newnode
16 else :                        # insert in the middle
17   node = head
18   while node is not None and node.data < value :
19     node = node.next
20
21   newnode.next = node
22   newnode.prev = node.prev
23   node.prev.next = newnode
24   node.prev = newnode
```

9.2 The Circular Linked List

Another variation of the linked list structure is the *circular linked list* in which the nodes form a continuous circle. The circular linked list allows for a complete traversal of the nodes starting with any node in the list. It is also commonly used for applications in which data is processed in a round-robin fashion. For example, when scheduling the use of a CPU, the operating system must cycle through all of the processes running on a computer, allowing each an opportunity to use the processor for a short period of time. By using a circular linked list, the choice of the next process is made in a round-robin fashion.

9.2.1 Organization

The nodes in a circular linked list, as illustrated in Figure 9.6, are organized in a linear fashion the same as those in a singly or doubly linked list. In fact, a circular linked list can have single or double links. In a singly linked version, every node has a successor while in a doubly linked version every node has a successor and predecessor.

The nodes in a circular list have the same structure as those in the linear list versions. The only difference is the next field of the last node links to the first, and in the doubly linked version, the prev field of the first node links to the last.

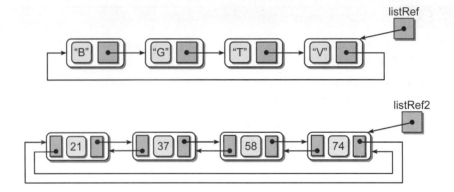

Figure 9.6: Examples of circular linked lists.

A single external reference variable is used to point to a node within the list. Technically, this could be any node in the list, but for convenience, the external reference is commonly set to the last node added to the list. By referencing that node, we have quick access to both the first node added and the last.

9.2.2   List Operations

The common set of operations performed on the linear versions of the linked list can also be performed on a circular linked list. However, some modifications are required in the algorithm for each operation to take into account the location of the external reference variable and the fact that none of the nodes have a null `next` field. In this section, we describe the various list operations for use with a sorted singly linked circular list. These operations require only slight modifications when applied to an unsorted circular list or the doubly linked version.

Traversals

Traversing a circular linked list requires a temporary external reference that is moved through the list, one node at a time, just like the linear versions. For the circular list, several modifications are required, all of which are necessary in order to perform a complete traversal while terminating the loop at the proper time. Terminating the loop is not as straightforward with the circular list since there are no nodes that have their `next` field set to `None`. Even in a single-node list, the link field of the last node always points back to the first node.

We cannot simply initialize the `curNode` reference to the first node and traverse until it "falls off" the list as was done in the linear versions. Instead, we need a way to flag the end of the traversal independent of the link fields. The algorithm for traversing a circular linked list is provided in Listing 9.5.

The traversal process begins by initializing `curNode` to reference the last node in the list, as illustrated in Figure 9.7(a). The traversal reference begins at the last node instead of the first because we are going to terminate the traversal when it again reaches the last node, after iterating over the entire list. The termination

---

Listing 9.5   Traversing a circular linked list.

```
1  def traverse( listRef ):
2      curNode = listRef
3      done = listRef is None
4      while not done :
5          curNode = curNode.next
6          print curNode.data
7          done = curNode is listRef
```

---

of the loop is handled by the boolean variable `done`, which is initialized based on the status of `listRef`. If the list is empty, `done` will be set to `False` and the loop never executes. When the list contains at least one node, `done` will be initialized to `True` and the loop is executed.

In the linear versions of the linked list, the first step in the body of the loop was to visit the current node (i.e., print the contents of the `node.data` field) and then advance the traversal reference to the next node. In this version, we must first advance `curNode`, as illustrated in Figure 9.7(b), and then perform the visit operation. Remember, `curNode` is initialized to reference the last node in the list. In order to begin the traversal with the first node, the temporary reference must be advanced to the first node in the list.

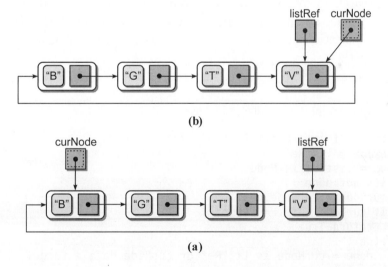

Figure 9.7: Traversing a circular linked list: (a) initial assignment of the temporary reference and (b) advancement of the temporary reference to the first node in the list.

Finally, `done` is updated by examining `curNode` to determine if it has again reached the last node in the list, as referenced by the `listRef` reference. `curNode` was initialized to be an alias of `listRef`, but it was advanced at the beginning of the loop. Thus, when `curNode` again reaches the end of the list, we know every node has been visited and the loop can terminate.

We must ensure this operation also works for a list containing a single node, as illustrated in Figure 9.8. When `curNode` is advanced to the next node, it actually still references itself. This is appropriate since the node is both the first and last node in the list. After the node is visited and the data printed in this example, `curNode` is advanced once again. When the alias test is performed at the bottom of the loop, `done` will be set to `True` and the loop will terminate properly.

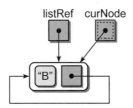

Figure 9.8: Traversing a circular linked list containing a single node.

Searching

The search operation requires a traversal through the list, although it can terminate early if we encounter the target item or reach an item larger than the target. The implementation, shown in Listing 9.6, closely follows that of the traversal operation from earlier.

Listing 9.6   Searching a circular linked list.

```
1  def searchCircularList( listRef, target ):
2    curNode = listRef
3    done = listRef is None
4    while not done :
5      curNode = curNode.next
6      if curNode.data == target :
7        return True
8      else :
9        done = curNode is listRef or curNode.data > target
10   return False
```

As with the traversal operation, the initialization of **done** handles the case where the list is empty and prevents the loop from ever being executed. The modification of the **done** flag at the bottom of the loop handles the termination of the traversal when the target is not found. A compound logical expression is used in order to test both conditions: a complete traversal was performed or we reached an item larger than the target. Finally, the condition in the **if** statement handles the case where the target item is found in the list.

Adding Nodes

Adding nodes to an ordered circular linked list is very similar to that of the ordered linear versions. The major difference is the management of the loopback link from the last node to the first. The implementation is much simpler if we divide it into four cases, as illustrated in Figure 9.9: (1) the list is empty when adding the node; (2) the new node is inserted at the front; (3) the new node is inserted at the end; or (4) the node is inserted somewhere in the middle. The first three cases are straightforward and only require a few adjustments in the links. The fourth case requires a search to find the proper location for the new node and the positioning of the two external reference variables. This requires a traversal similar to the one used earlier with the search operation. The Python code segment shown in Listing 9.7 provides the implementation of the insert operation. It should be noted again that the illustrations show the ordering in which the links should be made to avoid accidentally unlinking and destroying existing nodes in the list.

Listing 9.7   Inserting a node into an ordered circular linked list.

```
1  # Given a listRef pointer and a value, add the new value
2  # to an ordered circular linked list.
3
4  newnode = ListNode( value )
5  if listRef is None :               # empty list
6    listRef = newNode
7    newNode.next = newNode
8  elif value < listRef.next.data :   # insert in front
9    newNode.next = listRef.next
10   listRef.next = newNode
11 elif value > listRef.data :        # insert in back
12   newNode.next = listRef.next
13   listRef.next = newNode
14   listRef = newNode
15 else :                             # insert in the middle
16   # Position the two pointers.
17   predNode= None
18   curNode = listRef
19   done = listRef is None
20   while not done :
21     predNode = curNode
22     predNode = curNode.next
23     done = curNode is listRef or curNode.data > target
24
25   # Adjust links to insert the node.
26   newNode.next = curNode
27   predNode.next = newNode
```

Removing Nodes

Deleting a node from a circular linked list, for both ordered and unordered lists, closely follows the steps required for inserting a node into an ordered circular list. The implementation of this operation is left as an exercise.

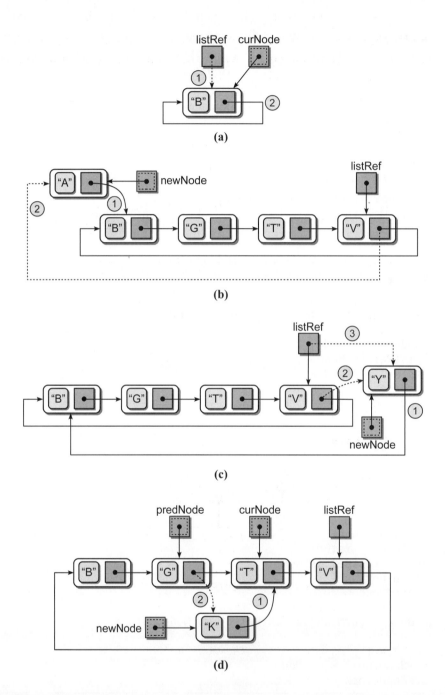

Figure 9.9: The links required to insert a new node into a circular list: (a) inserting the first node into an empty list; (b) prepending to the front; (c) appending to the end; and (d) inserting in the middle.

9.3 Multi-Linked Lists

The doubly linked list is a special instance of the more general multi-linked list. A *multi-linked list* is one in which each node contains multiple link fields which are used to create multiple chains within the same collection of nodes. In the doubly linked list, there are two chains through the collection of nodes, each using the key field to form the chains. The result is two singly linked lists in which one orders the nodes by key value in increasing order while the second orders the nodes in reverse order.

9.3.1 Multiple Chains

In a multi-linked list, chains can be created using multiple keys or different data components to create the multiple links. Consider the example of student records introduced in Chapter 1. Suppose we want to create a multi-linked list containing two chains in which the nodes are linked and sorted by id number in one chain and by name in the other, as illustrated in Figure 9.10. The first node in each chain is referenced by a separate head pointer. The `listById` reference indicates the first node in the chain sorted by id number while `listByName` indicates the first node in the chain sorted by name. For visual aid, the id chain is represented by solid lines and darker gray link fields while the name chain is represented by dashed lines and slightly lighter gray link fields.

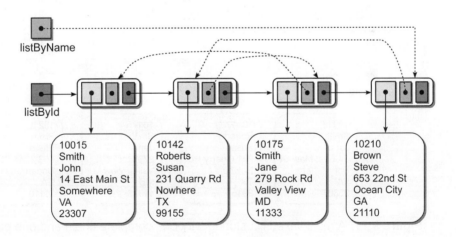

Figure 9.10: A multi-linked list storing student records with two complete chains.

The nodes in the multi-linked list can be traversed by either chain, the dashed links or the solid links, based on the desired order. It is up to the programmer to ensure he starts with the correct head node and follows the correct links. To create a multi-linked list, the nodes must contain multiple link fields, one for each chain. The `StudentMListNode` storage class in Listing 9.8 shows the definition used for the multi-linked list from Figure 9.10.

Listing 9.8   The node class for a multi-linked list.

```
1  class StudentMListNode :
2    def __init__( self, data ):
3      self.data = data
4      self.nextById = None
5      self.nextByName = None
```

When inserting nodes into the multi-linked list, a single node instance is created, but two insertions are required. After creating the new node, the multi-linked list is treated as two separate singly linked lists. Thus, the node must first be inserted into the chain ordered by id and then in the chain ordered by name. Similar action is required when deleting a node from the multi-linked list, but in this case, the node must be removed from both chains.

In the previous example, the two chains form two complete lists. That is, all of the nodes are part of both chains. The second chain could form a partial list instead. For example, suppose we wanted to create a multi-linked list of student records with one chain sorted by id and another containing only those students whose last name is "Smith," as illustrated in Figure 9.11. The former will contain all of the nodes and form a complete list, but the latter will only contain a subset of the nodes. Multi-linked lists can be organized in any number of ways with the resulting design based on the problem being solved.

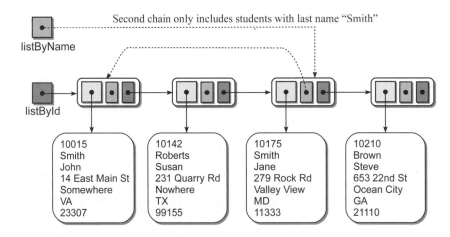

Figure 9.11: A multi-linked list storing with one complete chain and one partial chain.

9.3.2 The Sparse Matrix

A common use of a multi-linked list is an alternative implementation of the Sparse Matrix ADT, which was introduced in earlier chapters. In Chapter 4, we designed a solution for the sparse matrix using a Python list to store the non-zero elements. We improved on the original solution in Chapter 6 by using an array of linked lists to store the non-zero elements with a separate list for each row in the matrix. While both improved on the 2-D array implementation, the latter provided more efficient solutions for many of the operations since traversals could be limited to a per-row basis instead of a complete traversal of all non-zero elements. Some matrix operations and applications, however, require traversals in column order instead of row order. By organizing the non-zero elements based on the matrix rows, the time required in these cases can actually be worse than with a single linked list.

To provide convenient traversals of both rows and columns, we can use a multi-linked organization, as illustrated in Figure 9.12. The nodes are linked by two chains along the respective row and column. This requires two arrays of linked lists, one for the row lists and another for the column lists.

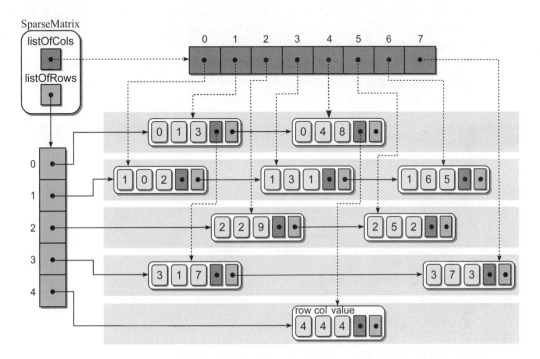

Figure 9.12: A multi-linked list implementation of the sparse matrix from Figure 4.5.

An individual element can be accessed by traversing the row chain or the column chain as needed. This dual access requires that each node contain both the row and column indices in addition to the two link fields, as shown in Listing 9.9. The implementation of the Sparse Matrix ADT using a multi-linked list is left as an exercise.

Listing 9.9   The multi-linked nodes for implementing the Sparse Matrix ADT.

```
1  class MatrixMListNode :
2    def __init__( self, row, col, value ) :
3      self.row = row
4      self.col = col
5      self.value = value
6      self.nextCol = None
7      self.nextRow = None
```

9.4   Complex Iterators

The iterators designed and used in earlier chapters were examples of simple iterators since we only needed to maintain a single traversal variable. A more complex example would be the addition of an iterator to the `SparseMatrix` class implemented as an array of linked lists in the previous chapter or the multi-linked list version defined in this chapter. Both of those implementations used an array of linked lists to store the matrix elements. To build an iterator in this case, we must keep track of the array of linked lists and both the current row within the array and the current node within the linked list for the given row. Listing 9.10 provides an implementation of an iterator for the Sparse Matrix ADT implemented using a multi-linked list.

When the iterator is first created, the constructor must initialize the `_curRow` and `_curNode` fields to reference the first node in the first non-empty row. Since

---

Listing 9.10   An iterator for the Sparse Matrix ADT implemented using a multi-linked list.

```
1   # Defines a Python iterator for the Sparse Matrix ADT implemented using
2   # an array of linked lists.
3
4   class _SparseMatrixIterator :
5     def __init__( self, rowArray ):
6       self._rowArray = rowArray
7       self._curRow = 0
8       self._curNode = None
9       self._findNextElement()
10
11    def __iter__( self ):
12      return self
13
14    def next( self ):
15      if self._curNode is None :
16        raise StopIteration
17      else :
18        value = self._curNode.value
19        self._curNode = self._curNode.next
20        if self._curNode is None :
21          self._findNextElement()
22        return value
23
24    def _findNextElement( self ):
25      i = self._curRow
26      while i < len( self._rowArray ) and
27            self._rowArray[i] is None :
28        i += 1
29
30      self._curRow = i
31      if i < len( self._rowArray ) :
32        self._currNode = self._rowVector[i]
33      else :
34        self._currNode = None
```

every row in the sparse matrix does not necessarily contain elements, we must search for the first node. This same operation will be required when advancing through the sparse matrix as we reach the end of each row, so we include the _findNextElement() helper method to find the next node in the array of linked lists.

To find the next node, the helper method starts at the current row and increments a counter until the next non-empty row is found or all rows have been processed. If the counter references a non-empty row, _curNode is set to the first node in that list. Otherwise, it is set to None, which will signal the end of the traversal loop.

The next() method of the _SparseMatrixIterator class need only examine the _curNode field to determine if the StopIteration exception should be raised or a value is to be returned. If _curNode is not null, we first save the value from the current node and then advance the reference to the next node in the list. When reaching the end of the linked list representing the current row, the _findNextElement() must be called to search for the next non-empty row in the array of linked lists. The operation concludes by returning the value saved before advancing _curNode to the next node.

9.5 Application: Text Editor

If you have used a computer, it's very likely you have used a text editor. Text editors allow us to enter text to create documents or to enter information into form fields like those found on some web pages. Editors can be very complex like a word processor or rather simple like Microsoft's *Notepad*™. No matter the complexity, all text editors must maintain and manage the text as the user enters, deletes, and manipulates characters and lines. In this section, we define an Edit Buffer ADT, which can be used by a simple text editor to store and manage the text of a document being manipulated by the actual editor. The ADT is defined independent of the text editor and only contains operations necessary for the storage and manipulation of plain text. This ADT is not meant to be used by more complex editors such as those that perform syntax highlighting or even by word processors, which must also maintain character properties like font style and size. We conclude with an implementation of our Edit Buffer ADT and discuss other alternatives.

9.5.1 Typical Editor Operations

While the design and implementation of an actual text editor is beyond the scope of this textbook, the examination of an edit storage buffer is not. We begin our discussion by examining the workings of typical text editors that will aide in the design of our ADT.

Layout

Text editors typically work with an abstract view of the text document by assuming it is organized into rows and columns as illustrated in Figure 9.13. The physical storage of a text document depends on the underlying data structure, though when stored on disk, the text file is simply a sequential stream of characters, as illustrated in Figure 9.14. The end of each line in a text document contains a newline character (\n) resulting in rows of varying sizes of unlimited length. An empty document is assumed to contain a single blank line where a blank line would consist of a single newline character. As a visual aid, the illustrations in the two diagrams use the ↩ symbol to indicate the actual location of the newline character and a small bullet (·) to indicate blank spaces.

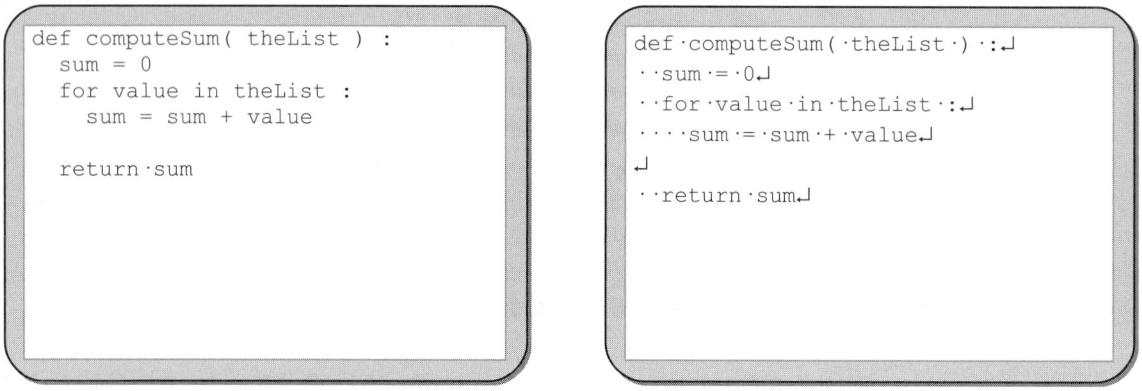

```
def computeSum( theList ) :
  sum = 0
  for value in theList :
    sum = sum + value

  return ·sum
```

```
def ·computeSum( ·theList ·) ·:↵
··sum ·= ·0↵
··for ·value ·in ·theList ·:↵
····sum ·= ·sum ·+ ·value↵
↵
··return ·sum↵
```

Figure 9.13: The abstract view of a text document as used by most text editors (top) and the same with special characters inserted for the blank spaces and newlines (bottom).

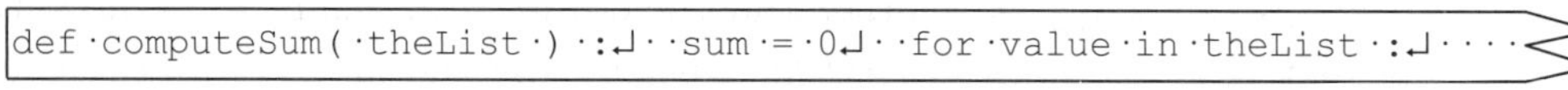

```
def ·computeSum( ·theList ·) ·:↵··sum ·= ·0↵··for ·value ·in ·theList ·:↵····
```

Figure 9.14: The file or stream view of the text document from Figure 9.13.

Text Cursor

Text editors also use the concept of a cursor to mark the current position within the document. The cursor position is identified by row and an offset or character position within the given row. All basic insertion and deletion operations are performed relative to the cursor. Note that for this example we consider the cursor to be the keyboard or text cursor and not the cursor related to the use of the mouse.

The cursor can be moved and positioned anywhere within the document, but only to a spot currently containing a character. Thus you cannot randomly place characters within a document as if you were writing on a piece of paper. To position text within a document, you must fill the document with blank lines and spaces as necessary. The minimum cursor movements available with most text editors include:

- Vertical movement in which the cursor is moved one or more lines up or down from the current line. When the cursor is moved in the vertical direction, it typically maintains the same character position on the line to which it was moved. If this line is shorter than the one from which the cursor was moved, the cursor is typically positioned at the end of the line.

- Horizontal movement along the current line in which the cursor moves either forward or backward. When the cursor reaches the beginning of the line, it wraps backward to the end of the previous line; when it reaches the end of the line, it wraps forward to the beginning of the next line. Thus, the cursor moves about the text document as if moving within a stream of text like that stored in a text file.

- Movement to the document and line extremes. The cursor can typically be moved to the front or back of the current line or to the beginning or end of the document. In the latter case, the cursor is typically moved to the front of the last row in the document.

Inserting Text

Most text editors use an entry mode of either "insert," in which new characters are inserted into the text, or "overwrite," in which new characters replace existing characters. In either mode, characters are inserted into the document at the cursor position. When using insert mode, all characters on the same line from the cursor to the end of the line are shifted down and the new character is inserted at the current position. This differs from overwrite mode, in which new characters simply replace or overwrite the character at the cursor position. In both cases, the cursor is then shifted one position to the right on the same line.

The newline characters that are used to indicate the end of a line can be treated like any other character. If new characters are inserted immediately before a newline character, the line is automatically extended. When inserting text after a newline character, you are technically inserting the text at the beginning of the next line in front of the first character on that line. When a newline character is inserted, a line break is created at the insertion point, resulting in the current line being split into two lines. The new line is always inserted immediately following the line being split.

Deleting Text

Most text editors provide both a delete and a rub-out operation for removing individual characters from a document. These are typically mapped to the Delete and Backspace keys, respectively. Both operations delete a character and shift all following characters on the same line forward one position. The difference between the two operations is which character is deleted and what happens to the cursor afterward. In the delete operation, the character at the cursor position is removed and the cursor remains at the same position. The rub-out operation, on the other hand, removes the character preceding the cursor and then moves the cursor one position to the left.

When a newline character is deleted, the current line and the one immediately following are merged. The newline character at the end of the last line in the document cannot be deleted.

Most text editors provide other text manipulation operations such as truncating a line from the cursor position to the end of the line. This operation typically does not remove the newline character at the end of the line, but instead simply deletes the non-newline characters from the cursor position to the end of the line. Some editors may also provide an operation to delete the entire line on which the cursor is positioned.

9.5.2 The Edit Buffer ADT

We are now ready to define an Edit Buffer ADT that can be used with a simple text editor. Our definition is based on the description of text editors presented in the previous section. In order to keep the example simple, we limit the operations available with our ADT.

Define   **EditBuffer ADT**

An *edit buffer* is a text buffer that can be used with a text editor for storing and manipulating the text as it is being edited. The buffer stores plain text with no special formatting or markup codes, other than the common ASCII special characters like tabs and newlines. Individual lines are terminated with a newline character. The current cursor position is maintained and all operations are performed relative to this position. The cursor can only be positioned where a character currently exists. The cursor can never be moved outside the bounds of the document. The buffer can insert characters in either insert or overwrite entry mode.

- EditBuffer(): Creates a new and empty edit buffer. An empty buffer always contains a single blank line and the cursor is placed at the first position of this blank line. The entry mode is set to insert.

- numLines(): Returns the number of lines in the text buffer.

- numChars(): Returns the length of the current line that includes the newline character.

- lineIndex(): Returns the line index of the line containing the cursor. The first line has an index of 0.

- columnIndex(): Returns the column index of the cursor within the current line. The first position in each line has an index of 0.

- setEntryMode(insert): Sets the entry mode to either insert or overwrite based on the value of the boolean argument insert.

- toggleEntryMode(): Toggles the entry mode to either insert or overwrite based on the current mode.

- inInsertMode(): Returns true if the current entry mode is set to insert and false otherwise.

- getChar(): Returns the character at the current cursor position.

- getLine(): Returns the contents of the current line as a string that includes the newline character.

- moveUp(num): Moves the cursor up num lines. The cursor is kept at the same character position unless the new line is shorter, in which case the cursor is placed at the end of the new line. The num is negative, and the cursor position is not changed.

- moveDown(num): The same as moveUp() except the cursor is moved down.

- moveDocHome(): Moves the cursor to the document's home position, which is the first line and first character position in that line.

- moveDocEnd(): Moves the cursor to the document's end position, which is the last line and first character position in that line.

- moveLeft(): Moves the cursor to the left one position. The cursor is wrapped to the end of the previous line if it is currently at the front of a line.

- moveRight(): Moves the cursor to the right one position. The cursor is wrapped to the beginning of the next line if it is currently positioned at the end of a line.

- moveLineHome(): Moves the cursor to the front of the current line at the first character position.

- moveLineEnd(): Moves the cursor to the end of the current line.

- breakLine(): Starts a new line at the cursor position. A newline character is inserted at the current position and all characters following are moved to a new line. The new line is inserted immediately following the current line and the cursor is adjusted to be at the first position of the new line.

- deleteLine(): Removes the entire line containing the cursor. The cursor is then moved to the front of the next line. If the line being deleted is the last line, the cursor is moved to the front of the previous line.

- truncateLine(): Removes all of the characters at the end of the current line starting at the cursor position. The newline character is not removed and the cursor is left at the end of the current line.

- addChar(char): Inserts the given character into the buffer at the current position. If the current entry mode is insert, the character is inserted and the following characters on that line are shifted down; in overwrite mode, the character at the current position is replaced. If the cursor is currently at a newline character and the entry mode is overwrite, the new character is inserted at the end of the line. The cursor is advanced one position. If char is the newline character, then a line break occurs, which is the same as calling breakLine().

- deleteChar(): Removes the character at the current position and leaves the cursor at the same position.

- ruboutChar(): Removes the character preceding the current position and moves the cursor left one position. If the cursor is currently at the front of the line, the newline character on the preceding line is removed and the current line and the preceding line are merged into a single line.

- deleteAll(): Deletes the entire contents of the buffer and resets it to the same state as in the constructor.

The definition of the ADT includes the operations sufficient for use with a simple text editor. All of the information needed by an editor to display or manipulate the text is available through the defined operations.

9.5.3 Implementation

Many different data structures can be used to implement the Edit Buffer ADT. The choice can depend on the type of editor with which the buffer will be used. For example, when editing a field within a dialog box or web page, the editing capabilities and the buffer size are usually limited. But a full-blown text edit like *JEdit* or *Notepad*™ requires a dynamic buffer, which can grow and shrink in size.

For our implementation, we are going to use a doubly linked list of Python lists, which provides dynamic capabilities in terms of growing and shrinking the buffer as needed while providing quick line insertions and deletions. The individual lines of text will be stored in the nodes of the doubly linked list while the individual characters within the lines will be stored in Python lists. Figure 9.15 illustrates a sample buffer using this organization.

The use of a linked list provides fast line insertions and deletions as text is added and removed. The doubly linked version allows for quick movement within the buffer both forward and backward as the user navigates among the lines of text. The choice of the vector to store the individual characters allows for quick modifications as characters are added and deleted. Existing characters can be directly modified or deleted and new characters inserted without the overhead required when using strings. Although the Python list does require resizing, it's typical for individual lines of text on average to be relatively short.

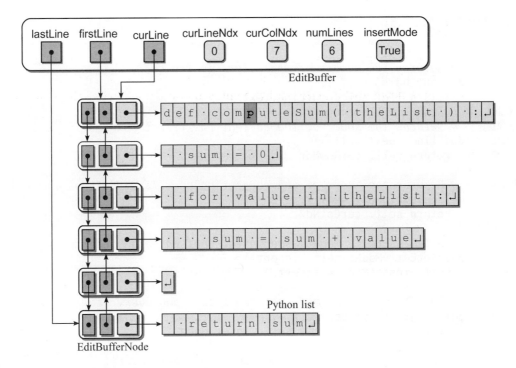

Figure 9.15: The doubly linked list of vectors used to implement the Edit Buffer ADT representing the text document from Figure 9.13.

A partial implementation of the `EditBuffer` class is provided in Listing 9.11. The implementation of some operations and helper methods, many of which can be implemented in a similar fashion to those provided, are left as exercises. Several of the operations simply provide status information and are straightforward in their implementation. These are provided in the listing without commentary. Others are more involved and require a brief discussion, which is provided the following sections.

Listing 9.11   The `editbuffer.py` module.

```
1   # Implements the Edit Buffer ADT using a doubly linked list of vectors.
2   class EditBuffer :
3     # Constructs an edit buffer containing one empty line of text.
4     def __init__( self ):
5       self._firstLine = _EditBufferNode( ['\n'] )
6       self._lastLine = self._firstLine
7       self._curLine = self._firstLine
8       self._curLineNdx = 0
9       self._curColNdx = 0
10      self._numLines = 1
11      self._insertMode = True
12
13      # Returns the number of lines in the buffer.
14    def numLines( self ):
15      return self._numLines
```

(Listing Continued)

Listing 9.11 Continued ...

```
16
17      # Returns the number of characters in the current line.
18      def numChars( self ):
19        return len( self._curLine.text )
20
21      # Returns the index of the current row (first row has index 0).
22      def lineIndex( self ):
23        return self._curRowNdx
24
25      # Returns the index of the current column (first col has index 0).
26      def columnIndex( self ):
27        return self._curColNdx
28
29      # Sets the entry mode based on the boolean value insert.
30      def setEntryMode( self, insert ):
31        self._insertMode = insert
32
33      # Toggles the entry mode between insert and overwrite.
34      def toggleEntryMode( self ):
35        self._insertMode = not self._insertMode
36
37      # Returns true if the current entry mode is insert.
38      def inInsertMode( self ):
39        return self._insertMode == True
40
41      # Returns the character at the current cursor position.
42      def getChar( self ):
43        return self._curLine.text[ self._curColNdx ]
44
45      # Returns the current line as a string.
46      def getLine( self ):
47        lineStr = ""
48        for char in self._curLine.text :
49          lineStr .= char
50        return lineStr
51
52      # Moves the cursor up num lines.
53      def moveUp( self, nlines ):
54        if nlines <= 0 :
55          return
56        elif self._curLineNdx - nlines < 0 :
57          nlines = _curLineNdx
58
59        for i in range( nlines ) :
60          self._curLine = self._curLine.prev
61
62        self._curLineNdx -= nlines
63        if self._curColNdx >= self.numChars() :
64          self.moveLineEnd()
65
66      # Moves the cursor left one position.
67      def moveLeft( self ):
68        if self._curColNdx == 0 :
69          if self._curRowNdx > 0 :
```

```
70          self.moveUp( 1 )
71          self.moveLineEnd()
72      else :
73        self._curColNdx -= 1
74
75    # Moves the cursor to the front of the current line.
76    def moveLineHome( self ) :
77      self._curColNdx = 0
78
79    # Moves the cursor to the end of the current line.
80    def moveLineEnd( self ):
81      self._curColNdx = self.numChars() - 1
82
83    # Starts a new line at the cursor position.
84    def breakLine( self ):
85        # Save the text following the cursor position.
86      nlContents = self._curLine.text[self._curColNdx:]
87        # Insert newline character and truncate the line.
88      del self._curLine.text[self.__curColNdx:]
89      self._curLine.text.append( '\n' )
90        # Insert the new line and increment the line counter.
91      self._insertNode( self._curLine, nlContents )
92        # Move the cursor.
93      self._curLine = newLine
94      self._curLineNdx += 1
95      self._curColNdx = 0
96
97    # Inserts the given character at the current cursor position.
98    def addChar( self, char ):
99      if char == '\n' :
100        self.breakLine()
101      else :
102        ndx = self._curColNdx
103        if self.inInsertMode() :
104          self._curLine.text.insert( ndx, char )
105        else :
106          if self.getChar() == '\n' :
107            self._curLine.text.insert( ndx, char )
108          else :
109            self._curLine.text[ ndx ] = char
110        self._curColNdx += 1
111
112    # Removes the character preceding the cursor; cursor remains fixed.
113    def deleteChar( self ):
114      if self.getChar() != '\n' :
115        self._curLine.text.pop( self._curColNdx )
116      else :
117        if self._curLine is self._lastLine :
118          return
119        else :
120          nextLine = self._curLine.next
121          self._curLine.text.pop()
122          self._curLine.text.extend( nextLine.text )
123          self._removeNode( nextLine )
124
```

(Listing Continued)

Listing 9.11	Continued ...

```
125  # Defines a private storage class for creating the list nodes.
126  class _EditBufferNode :
127    def __init__( self, text ):
128      self.text = text
129      self.prev = None
130      self.next = None
```

Constructor

The constructor is defined in lines 5–11 of Listing 9.11. The `_firstLine` and `_lastLine` reference variables act as the head and tail pointers for the doubly linked list. The number of lines in the buffer is maintained using `_numLines` and the current entry mode is specified by the boolean `_insertMode`. The current cursor position within the buffer must be tracked, which is done using `_curLine` and `_curColNdx`. The former is a linked list external reference since it points to a node in the doubly linked list and the latter is an index value referencing a position within the vector for the current line. The line number on which the cursor is currently positioned is also maintained since it will be needed by the `getLine()` method.

The ADT definition calls for a newly created buffer to be initially set to empty. While an empty buffer contains no visible characters, it will contain a single blank line that consists of a lone newline character. A node is created and initialized with a vector containing a single newline character. The nodes in the doubly linked list will be instances of the `EditBufferNode` class, the definition of which is provided in lines 126–130. The cursor is initially placed at the home position, which in an empty document corresponds to the newline character in the newly created blank line. Finally, the initial entry mode is set to insert mode.

Cursor Movement

A number of operations in the Edit Buffer ADT handle movement of the cursor, which allows for character manipulation at different points in the buffer. These routines modify the current cursor position by appropriately adjusting the `_curLine`, `_curLineNdx`, and `_curColNdx` fields.

Vertical movement of the cursor is handled by four methods: `moveDocHome()`, `moveDocEnd()`, `moveDown()`, and `moveUp()`. The cursor can be moved up or down one line or multiple lines at a time but it can never be moved outside the valid range. Implementation of the `moveUp()` method is provided in lines 53–64 of Listing 9.11. By definition, the number of lines the cursor is to be moved must be positive, otherwise the cursor is not moved. In addition, the cursor cannot be moved further up than the first line in the document. These conditions are evaluated by the first two logical expressions. If `nlines` would result in the cursor being moved beyond the first line, `nlines` has to be adjusted to limit the movement to the first line. Next, a `for` loop is used to move the `_curLine` reference up the indicated number of lines followed by `_curLineNdx` being adjusted appropriately. Finally, we determine if the horizontal position of the cursor must be adjusted. If the line to which the cursor has been moved is shorter than the previous line, then the cursor must be positioned at the end of the new line.

Horizontal movement of the cursor is managed by four methods: `moveLeft()`, `moveRight()`, `moveLineHome()`, and `moveLineEnd()`. Moving the cursor to the beginning or end of a line simply requires modifying the value of `_curColNdx`. Moving the cursor horizontally one space can be as simple as adjusting `_curColNdx` by one, except when the cursor is at the beginning or ending of the line when moving left or right, respectively.

Implementation of the `moveLeft()` method is provided in lines 67–73. When moving left one space and the cursor is at the beginning of the line, the cursor must be moved to the end of the previous line. This can be accomplished by moving the cursor up one line and then to the end of that line. Of course this is only done if the current line is not the first line in the buffer. Moving right one space can be implemented in a similar fashion. The implementation of the remaining cursor movement methods is left as an exercise.

Modifying the Buffer

Moving the cursor is somewhat easier than modifying the contents of the buffer. Most modifications must consider the newline character, which may require splitting a line or merging two lines depending on the specific operation. We begin our look at buffer modifications with the operation of adding a single character.

The action taken when adding a character in the `addChar()` method, shown in lines 98–110 of Listing 9.11, depends on the entry mode and what character is being added. In either mode, when adding a newline character, the result is the same as breaking a line at the current position and thus this can be done with the `breakLine()` method.

When the current entry mode is set to insert, the character is always inserted into the vector at the current cursor position, which causes the following characters on the same line to shift down one place. When inserting a character at the end of the line, we are actually inserting it immediately preceding the newline character. Thus, the newline character will always be the last character in the vector. The action taken when adding a character in overwrite mode depends on the position of the cursor. When the cursor is at the end of line, characters are inserted in the same fashion as if the entry mode was set to insert. The newline character is never overwritten. Otherwise, the new character simply replaces the character at the cursor position. After adding a new character, the cursor is always moved to the right one place. This can be done by simply adding one to `_curColNdx` since the cursor never moves to the next line during an add operation unless a newline character is being added. The latter case is handled by the `breakLine()` method.

Deleting a character from the buffer is straightforward if the character is not the newline character. It only requires removing or popping the character at the current cursor position within the vector containing the current line. The implementation of the `deleteChar()` method is provided in lines 113–123 of Listing 9.11.

Deleting a newline character requires the merging of two lines, the current line with the following one. Of course the newline character of the last line in the buffer cannot be deleted. Thus, this condition must first be checked before merging the two lines. Merging the two lines requires several steps. First, the newline character on the current line must be removed and the current line extended by appending to it the contents of the next line. Then, the node and buffer entry for the next line must be removed from the doubly linked list. This step is performed using the _removeNode() helper method, the implementation of which is left as an exercise. The helper method also handles the final step in merging the two lines, which is to decrement the line count by one.

Splitting a Line

We conclude our discussion with the breakLine() method, the implementation of which is provided in lines 84–95 of Listing 9.11. This operation splits a line into two lines at the current cursor position with the character at the cursor position becoming part of the new line. Figure 9.16 illustrates the sample buffer after splitting the third line at the letter "i" of the word "in."

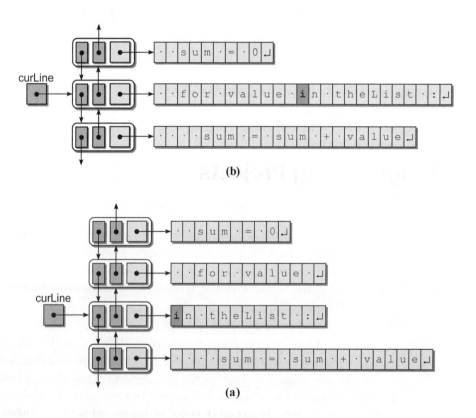

Figure 9.16: Breaking a line of text at the cursor position: (a) the sample buffer before the split and (b) the result after the split with the cursor position adjusted.

The contents at the end of the current line vector starting at the cursor position will form the new line. We first extract and save this text by creating a slice from the current line. The part of the vector from which we created the slice is then deleted and a newline character is appended. We use the `_insertNode()` helper method to then insert a new line into the buffer. The helper method inserts a new node following the one pointed to by `_curLine` and containing the supplied contents. The last step required in breaking the current line is to move the cursor to the front of the new line.

Exercises

9.1 Evaluate the four basic linked list operations for a sorted doubly linked list and indicate the worst case time-complexities of each.

9.2 Evaluate the worst case time-complexity for the search operation on a doubly linked list using a probe pointer.

9.3 Evaluate the worst case time-complexity of the Sparse Matrix ADT implemented in Programming Project 9.7.

9.4 Provide the code to implement the four basic operations — traversal, search, insertion, deletion — for an unsorted doubly linked list.

9.5 Provide the code to delete a node from a sorted doubly linked list.

9.6 Provide the code to delete a node from a sorted singly linked circular list.

Programming Projects

9.1 Complete the implementation of the `EditBuffer` class from Section 9.5.

9.2 Modify the `moveLeft()` and `moveRight()` methods to accept an integer to indicate the number of spaces to move in the respective direction.

9.3 Modify the `EditBuffer` class to include the following operations:

- `getPage( first, last )`: Returns a vector of strings consisting of the rows [first...last], which can be used for displaying a page of text.

- `insertString( str )`: Inserts a string of text within the current line starting at the current cursor position.

- `moveTo( lineNdx, colNdx )`: Moves the cursor to the indicated position within the buffer. If `lineNdx` is out of range, no action is taken. If `colNdx` is larger than the current line, then the cursor is positioned at the end of that line.

- **searchFor(str)**: Searches the buffer and returns a tuple containing the (line, col) position of the first occurrence of the given search string. `None` is returned if the buffer does not contain the search string.

- **searchForAll(str)**: The same as `searchFor()` but returns a vector of tuples indicating all occurrences of the given search string.

9.4 Modify the `EditBuffer` class to include the following file I/O operations for saving and loading the buffer:

- **save(filename)**: Saves the text in the buffer to the text file `filename`.

- **load(filename)**: Loads the text file named `filename` into the buffer. If the buffer is not empty, the original contents are deleted before the file is loaded. The given filename must refer to an existing and valid text file.

9.5 Create a line editor application that uses the `EditBuffer` class and allows a user to edit a text document in the old "line editing" style.

9.6 Define and implement a MultiChain ADT for storing and accessing student records as described in Section 9.3.1.

9.7 Implement the Sparse Matrix ADT using the multi-linked lists as described in Section 9.3.2.

9.8 Consider the Vector ADT from Programming Project 2.1:

(a) Provide a new implementation that uses a doubly linked list and a probe reference for locating a specific element.

(b) Evaluate your new implementation to determine the worst case run time of each operation.

(c) What are the advantages and disadvantages of using a doubly linked list to implement the Vector ADT? Compare this implementation to that of using a singly linked list.

9.9 Consider the Map ADT from Section 3.2:

(a) Provide a new implementation that uses a sorted doubly linked list and includes a probe reference for the search operations.

(b) Modify your `Map` class to include an iterator for use with a `for` loop.

9.10 A MultiMap ADT is similar to the Map ADT but it uses two keys that map to a single data item instead of a single key as used with the Map ADT. Define and implement a MultiMap ADT.

## CHAPTER 10

Recursion

Recursion is a process for solving problems by subdividing a larger problem into smaller cases of the problem itself and then solving the smaller, more trivial parts. Recursion is a powerful programming and problem-solving tool. It can be used with a wide range of problems from basic traditional iterations to the more advanced backtracking problems. While recursion is very powerful, recursive solutions are not always the most efficient. In some instances, however, recursion is the implementation of choice as it allows us to easily develop a solution for a complicated problem that may otherwise be difficult to solve.

10.1 Recursive Functions

A function (or method) can call any other function (or method), including itself. A function that calls itself is known as a *recursive function*. The result is a virtual loop or repetition used in a fashion similar to a `while` loop.

Consider the simple problem of printing the integer values from 1 to n in reverse order. The iterative solution for this problem is rather simple when using a loop construct. But it can also be solved recursively, that is, using a recursive function. Suppose we have implemented the following recursive function:

```
def printRev( n ):
  if n > 0 :
    print( n )
    printReverse( n-1 )
```

and we call the function with an argument of 4:

```
printRev( 4 )
```

The current sequential flow of execution is interrupted and control is transferred to the `printRev()` function with a value of 4 being assigned to argument `n`. The body of `printRev()` begins execution at the first statement. Since 4 is greater than 0, the body of the `if` statement is executed. When the flow of execution reaches the `printRev(3)` function call, the sequential flow is once again interrupted as control is transferred to another instance of the `printRev()` function. The body of this instance begins execution at the first statement, but this time with $n = 3$. Figure 10.1(a) illustrates the execution of the recursive function as a group of boxes with each box representing a single invocation of the `printRev()` function. The boxes contain the contents of local variables and only the statements of the function actually executed. Each recursive call to `printRev()` is shown inside its own box with the boxes positioned at the point where the function was invoked.

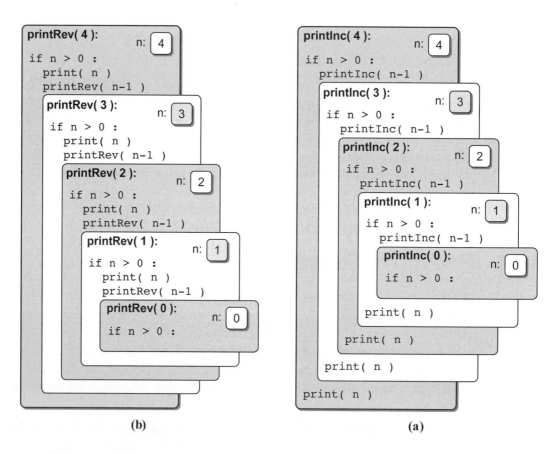

Figure 10.1: Recursive flow of execution: (a) `printRev()` and (b) `printInc()`.

These **recursive calls** continue until a value of zero is passed to the function, at which time the body of the `if` statement is skipped and execution reaches the end of the function. As with any function call, when execution reaches the end of the function or the **return** statement is encountered, execution returns to the location where the function was originally called. In this case, the call to `printRev(0)`

> **NOTE**
>
> ⓘ **Local Variables.** Like any other function, each call to a recursive function creates new instances of all local reference variables used within that function. Changing the contents of a local reference variable does not affect the contents of other instances of that variable.

was made from within the `printRev(1)` instance. Thus, execution returns to the first statement after that invocation. After execution returns to the `printRev(1)` instance, the end of that function is reached and again execution is returned to the location where that instance was invoked. The result is a chain of recursive returns or *recursive unwinding* back to the original `printRev(4)` function call.

What changes would be needed to create a recursive function to print the same integer values in increasing order instead of reverse order? We can change the location of the recursive call to change the behavior of the recursive solution. Consider a new recursive print function:

```
def printInc( n ):
  if n > 0 :
    printInc( n-1 )
    print( n )
```

In this version, the recursive call is made before the value of n is printed. The result is a series of recursive calls before any other action is performed. The actual printing of the values is performed after each instance of the function returns, as illustrated in Figure 10.1(b).

10.2 Properties of Recursion

All recursive solutions must satisfy three rules or properties:

1. A recursive solution must contain a *base case*.

2. A recursive solution must contain a *recursive case*.

3. A recursive solution must make progress toward the base case.

A recursive solution subdivides a problem into smaller versions of itself. For a problem to be subdivided, it typically must consist of a data set or a term that can be divided into smaller sets or a smaller term. This subdivision is handled by the recursive case when the function calls itself. In the `printRev()` function, the recursive case is performed for all values of $n > 0$.

The base case is the terminating case and represents the smallest subdivision of the problem. It signals the end of the virtual loop or recursive calls. In `printRev()`, the base case occurred when $n = 0$ and the function simply returned without performing any additional operations.

Finally, a recursive solution must make progress toward the base case or the recursion will never stop resulting in an infinite virtual loop. This progression typically occurs in each recursive call when the larger problem is divided into smaller parts. The larger data set is subdivided into smaller sets or the larger term is reduced to a smaller value by each recursive call. In our recursive printing solution, this progression is accomplished by subtracting one from the current value of n in each recursive function call.

10.2.1 Factorials

The factorial of a positive integer n can be used to calculate the number of permutations of n elements. The function is defined as:

$$n! = n * (n - 1) * (n - 2) * \ldots * 1$$

with the special case of $0! = 1$. This problem can be solved easily using an iterative implementation that loops through the individual values $[1 \ldots n]$ and computes a product of those values. But it can also be solved with a recursive solution and provides a simple example of recursion. Consider the factorial function on different integer values:

$$
\begin{aligned}
0! &= 1 \\
1! &= 1 \\
2! &= 2 * 1 \\
3! &= 3 * 2 * 1 \\
4! &= 4 * 3 * 2 * 1 \\
5! &= 5 * 4 * 3 * 2 * 1
\end{aligned}
$$

After careful inspection of these equations, it becomes obvious each of the successive equations, for $n > 1$, can be rewritten in terms of the previous equation:

$$
\begin{aligned}
0! &= 1 \\
1! &= 1 * (1 - 1)! \\
2! &= 2 * (2 - 1)! \\
3! &= 3 * (3 - 1)! \\
4! &= 4 * (4 - 1)! \\
5! &= 5 * (5 - 1)!
\end{aligned}
$$

Since the function is defined in terms of itself and contains a base case, a recursive definition can be produced for the factorial function as shown here. Listing 10.1 provides a recursive implementation of the factorial function.

$$
n! = \begin{cases}
1, & \text{if } n = 0 \\
n * (n - 1)!, & \text{if } n > 0
\end{cases}
$$

```
1   # Compute n!
2   def fact( n ):
3       assert n >= 0, "Factorial not defined for negative values."
4       if n < 2 :
5           return 1
6       else :
7           return n * fact(n - 1)
```

10.2.2 Recursive Call Trees

Figure 10.1 used boxes to represent function invocations and to illustrate the flow of execution for two recursive functions. The specific placement of the boxes illustrated the different results that were achieved depending on the location of the recursive call within the function. This type of illustration can be very helpful to visualize the flow of execution within and between various functions, but it's not as useful in developing and understanding recursive functions.

When developing or evaluating a recursive function, we typically use a **recursive call tree** such as the one for the factorial function illustrated in Figure 10.2. The diagram consists of small boxes and directed edges between the boxes. Each box represents a function call and is labeled with the name of the function and the actual arguments passed to the function when it was invoked. The directed edges between the boxes indicate the flow of execution. The solid edges indicate the function from which a call originated. For example, in Figure 10.2, we see the call to `fact(5)` was made from the `main()` function while the call to `fact(4)` was made during the execution of `fact(5)`. The dashed edges indicate function returns and are labeled with the return value if a value is returned to the caller.

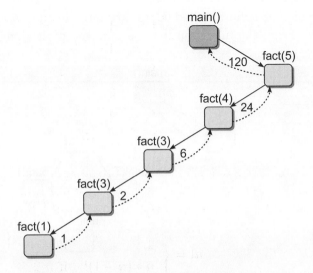

Figure 10.2: Recursive call tree for `fact(5)`.

If a function makes multiple calls to other functions, each function call is in-dicated in the tree by a box and directed edge. The edges are listed left to right in the order the calls are made. For example, suppose we execute the following simple program that consists of three functions. The resulting call tree is shown in Figure 10.3.

```
# A sample program containing three functions.
def main():
    y = foo( 3 )
    bar( 2 )

def foo( x ):
    if x % 2 != 0 :
        return 0
    else :
        return x + foo( x-1 )

def bar( n ):
    if n > 0 :
        print( n )
        bar( n-1 )

main()
```

Since the main routine makes two function calls, both are indicated as directed edges originating from the `main()` box. You will also notice the `foo()` function makes a recursive call to itself, but the second call is not indicated in the call tree. The reason is during this execution of the program, with the given arguments to `foo()`, the logical condition in the `if` statement evaluates to true and, thus, the recursive call is never made. The call tree only shows the functions actually called during a single execution, which is based on a given set of data, a specific function argument value, or specific user input.

To follow the flow of execution in Figure 10.3, we start with the top box, the one to which no solid directed edges flow into. In this case, that box is the `main()` function. From the main routine, we take the path along the leftmost solid edge

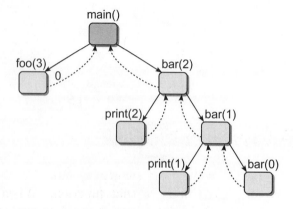

Figure 10.3: Sample call tree with multiple calls from each function.

leading to the `foo(3)` box. Since that function executes the return statement, we follow the dashed edge back to the main routine. Execution continues by following the next edge out of the main routine box, which leads us to the `bar(2)` function box. From there, we continue to follow the directed edges between the boxes and eventually return to the `main()` routine box with no further edges to follow. At that point, execution terminates.

10.2.3 The Fibonacci Sequence

The **Fibonacci sequence** is a sequence of integer values in which the first two values are both 1 and each subsequent value is the sum of the two previous values. The first 11 terms of the sequence are:

$$1, 1, 2, 3, 5, 8, 13, 21, 34, 55, 89, \ldots$$

The nth Fibonacci number can be computed by the recurrence relation (for $n > 0$):

$$fib(n) = \begin{cases} fib(n-1) + fib(n-2), & \text{if } n > 1 \\ n, & \text{if } n = 1 \text{ or } n = 0 \end{cases}$$

A recursive function for the computing the nth Fibonacci number is shown in Listing 10.2. This function illustrates the use of multiple recursive calls from within the body of the function. The call tree corresponding to the function call `fib(6)` is illustrated in Figure 10.4.

Listing 10.2   The `fib()` recursive function.

```
1  # Compute the nth number in the Fibonacci sequence.
2  def fib( n ):
3     assert n >= 1, "Fibonacci not defined for n < 1."
4     if n == 1 :
5        return 1
6     else :
7        return fib(n - 1) + fib(n - 2)
```

10.3 How Recursion Works

When a function is called, the sequential flow of execution is interrupted and execution jumps to the body of that function. When the function terminates, execution returns to the point where it was interrupted before the function was invoked. But how does it know where to return? We know for sure, it's not magic.

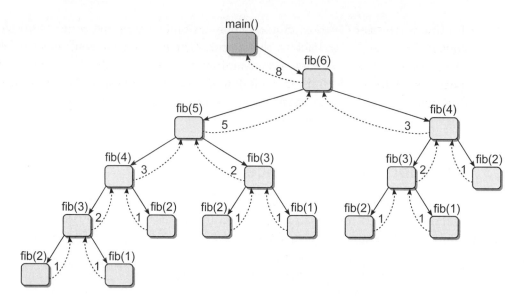

Figure 10.4: Recursive call tree for `fib(6)`.

10.3.1 The Run Time Stack

Each time a function is called, an **activation record** is automatically created in order to maintain information related to the function. One piece of information is the **return address**. This is the location of the next instruction to be executed when the function terminates. Thus, when a function returns, the address is obtained from the activation record and the flow execution can return to where it left off before the function was called.

The activation records also include storage space for the allocation of local variables. Remember, a variable created within a function is local to that function and is said to have local scope. Local variables are created when a function begins execution and are destroyed when the function terminates. The lifetime of a local variable is the duration of the function in which it was created.

An activation record is created per function call, not on a per function basis. When a function is called, an activation record is created for that call and when it terminates the activation record is destroyed. The system must manage the collection of activation records and remember the order in which they were created. The latter is necessary to allow the system to backtrack or return to the next statement in the previous function when an invoked function terminates. It does this by storing the activation records on a **run time stack**. The run time stack is just like the stack structure presented in Chapter 7 but it's hidden from the programmer and is automatically maintained. Consider the execution of the following code segment, which uses the factorial function defined earlier:

```
def main():
    y = fact( 5 )

main()
```

When the main routine is executed, the first activation record is created and pushed onto the run time stack, as illustrated in Figure 10.5(a). When the factorial function is called, the second activation record is created and pushed onto the stack, as illustrated in Figure 10.5(b), and the flow of execution is changed to that function.

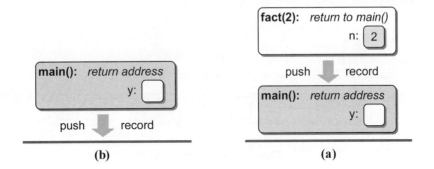

Figure 10.5: The initial run time stack for the sample code segment.

The factorial function is recursively called until the base case is reached with a value of $n = 0$. At this point, the run time stack contains four activation records, as illustrated Figure 10.6(a). When the base case statement at line 5 of Listing 10.1 is executed, the activation record for the function call `fact(0)` is popped from the stack, as illustrated in Figure 10.6(b), and execution returns to the function instance `fact(1)`. This process continues until all of the activation records have been popped from the stack and the program terminates.

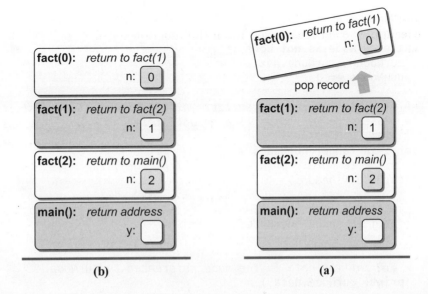

Figure 10.6: The run time stack for the sample program when the base case is reached.

10.3.2   Using a Software Stack

Using recursion in solving problems is very similar to using the software implemented stack structure. In fact, any solution that can be implemented using a stack structure can be implemented with recursion, and vice versa. Consider the problem of printing in reverse order the items stored in a singly linked list such as the one shown in Figure 10.7.

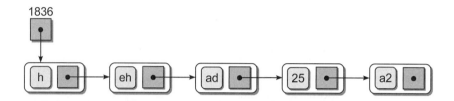

Figure 10.7: A sample singly linked list.

Since the links are in one direction, we cannot easily access the nodes in reverse order. A brute-force approach to solving this problem would be to use nested loops to iterate over the linked list multiple times with each iteration of the inner loop ending one node shorter than previous iteration. This approach is implemented by the function in Listing 10.3, but it has a run time of $O(n^2)$.

Listing 10.3   A brute-force approach for printing a singly linked list in reverse order.

```
1  # Print the contents of a singly linked list in reverse order.
2
3  def printListBF( head ):
4    # Count the number of nodes in the list.
5    numNodes = 0
6    curNode = head
7    while curNode is not None :
8      curNode = curNode.next
9      numNodes += 1
10
11   # Iterate over the linked list multiple times. The first iteration
12   # prints the last item, the second iteration prints the next to last
13   # item, and so on.
14   for i in range( numNodes ):
15     # The temporary pointer starts from the first node each time.
16     curNode = head
17
18     # Iterate one less time for iteration of the outer loop.
19     for j in range( numNodes - 1 ):
20       curNode = curNode.next
21
22     # Print the data in the node referenced by curNode.
23     print( curNode.data )
```

To provide a more efficient solution to the problem, a stack structure can be used to push the data values onto the stack, one at a time, as we traverse through the linked list. Then, the items can be popped and printed resulting in the reverse order listing. This solution is provided in Listing 10.4 and the resulting stack after the iteration over the list and before the items are popped is shown in Figure 10.8. Assuming the use of the linked list version of the stack, `printListStack()` has a run time of $O(n)$, the proof of which is left as an exercise.

Listing 10.4   Using a stack to print a linked list in reverse order.

```
1   # Print the contents of a linked list in reverse order using a stack.
2
3   from lliststack import Stack
4
5   def printListStack( head ):
6       # Create a stack to store the items.
7       s = Stack()
8
9       # Iterate through the list and push each item onto the stack.
10      curNode = head
11      while curNode is not None :
12          s.push( curNode.data )
13          curNode = curNode.next
14
15      # Repeatedly pop the items from the stack and print them until the
16      # stack is empty.
17      while not s.isEmpty() :
18          item = s.pop()
19          print item
```

A recursive solution for this problem is also possible. To design the solution, we use the divide and conquer strategy introduced in Chapter 4. With this strategy, you solve the larger problem by dividing it into smaller problems of itself and solving the smaller parts individually. A linked list is by definition a recursive structure. That is, the list can be thought of as a node linked to a sublist of nodes

Figure 10.8: The resulting stack after iterating over the linked list from Figure 10.7.

as illustrated in Figure 10.9(a). If we carry this idea further, then each link in the list can be thought of as linking the node to a sublist of nodes, as illustrated in Figure 10.9(b). With this view of the list, we can print the list in reverse order by recursively printing the sublist pointed to by the node and then printing the contents of the node itself.

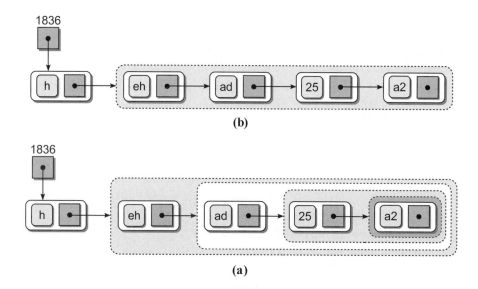

Figure 10.9: Abstract view of the linked list as a node linked to a sublist of nodes.

The solution subdivides the problem into smaller parts of itself and contains a recursive case. But what about the base case, which ends the subdivision and in turn stops the recursive calls? The recursion should stop when the next sublist is empty, which occurs when the link field of the last node is null. A simple and elegant Python implementation for the recursive solution is provided in Listing 10.5.

Listing 10.5 The `printList()` recursive function.

```
1  # Print the contents of a linked list using recursion.
2  def printList( node ):
3    if node is not None :
4      printList( node.next )
5      print( node.data )
```

To help visualize how the `printList()` function works, the call stack and the linked list are illustrated in Figure 10.10. It assumes the main routine is defined as follows:

```
def main():
  head = buildLinkedList()
  printList( head )
```

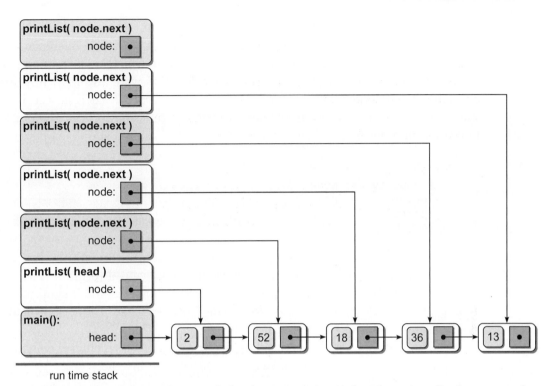

run time stack

Figure 10.10: The run time stack for the `printList()` function when the base case is reached while processing the linked list from Figure 10.7.

As the recursion progresses and more activation records are pushed onto the run time stack, the corresponding `node` argument is assigned to point to the next node in the list. When the base case is reached, the `node` argument of each of the preceding function calls will point to a different node in the list. Thus, as the recursion unwinds, the contents of each node can be printed, resulting in a listing of the values in reverse order.

Both the `printListStack()` and `printList()` functions provide an implementation to the problem of printing a linked list in reverse order. The former requires the use of an explicit loop for iterating through the list and a stack to store the data for later printing. In the recursive version the loop and stack are implicit. The loop is replaced by the recursive calls while the user-specified stack is replaced by the run time stack on which activation records are pushed for each call to the function.

10.3.3 Tail Recursion

Sometimes an algorithm is easy to visualize as a recursive operation, but when implemented as a recursive function, the solution proves to be inefficient. In these cases, it can be beneficial to use a non-recursive implementation that makes use of a basic iterative loop or the software Stack ADT from Chapter 7.

The main reason for using recursion is to push values onto the run time stack that need to be saved until the recursive operation used to solve the smaller sub-problem returns. For example, consider the function in Listing 10.5, which printed the contents of a linked list in reverse order. We had to save a reference to each node until the recursive process began unwinding, at which time the node values could be printed. By using recursion, these references were automatically pushed onto the run time stack as part of the activation record each time the function was called. Now suppose we implement a recursive function to print the items of a linked list in order from beginning to end instead of using a simple loop structure:

```python
def printInorder( node ):
  if node is not None :
    print( node.data )
    printInorder( node.next )
```

This function eliminates the need for a loop to iterate through the list, but do we have anything to save on the stack until the recursive call returns? The answer is no. When the recursive call returns, the function is finished and it simply returns. This is an example of *tail recursion*, which occurs when a function includes a single recursive call as the last statement of the function. In this case, a stack is not needed to store values to be used upon the return of the recursive call and thus a solution can be implemented using an iterative loop instead.

10.4   Recursive Applications

There are many applications that can be solved using recursion. Some in fact, can only be solved using recursion. In this section, we introduce some of the classic problems that require the use of recursion or can benefit from a recursive solution.

10.4.1   Recursive Binary Search

The binary search algorithm, which we introduced in Chapter 4, improves the search time required to locate an item in a sorted sequence. We provided an iterative implementation of the binary search algorithm in Chapter 4, but the algorithm can also be implemented recursively since it can be expressed in smaller versions of itself. In searching for a target within the sorted sequence, the middle value is examined to determine if it is the target. If not, the sequence is split in half and either the lower half or the upper half of the sequence is examined depending on the logical ordering of the target value in relation to the middle item. In examining the smaller sequence, the same process is repeated until either the target value is found or there are no additional values to be examined. A recursive implementation of the binary search algorithm is provided in Listing 10.6. As with the earlier version, this version also works with virtual subsequences instead of physically splitting the original sequence. The two arguments, `first` and `last`, indicate the range of elements within the current virtual subsequence. On the first call to the function, these values are set to the full range of the original sequence.

Listing 10.6   A recursive implementation of the binary search algorithm.

```
1   # Performs a recursive binary search on a sorted sequence.
2   def recBinarySearch( target, theSeq, first, last ):
3       # If the sequence cannot be subdivided further, we are done.
4     if first > last :     # base case #1
5         return False
6     else :
7         # Find the midpoint of the sequence.
8         mid = (last + first) // 2
9         # Does the element at the midpoint contain the target?
10        if theSeq[mid] == target :
11          return True      # base case #2
12
13        # or does the target precede the element at the midpoint?
14        elif target < theSeq[mid] :
15          return recBinarySearch( target, theSeq, first, mid - 1 )
16
17        # or does it follow the element at the midpoint?
18        else :
19          return recBinarySearch( target, theSeq, mid + 1, last )
```

We evaluated the binary search algorithm in Chapter 4 and found it required $O(\log n)$ time in the worst case. To determine the run time of a recursive implementation, we must consider the time required to execute a single invocation of the function and the number of times the function is called. In evaluating the time of a single function invocation, we use the same technique as we applied in previous chapters and sum the times of the individual statements. The recursive calls, however, are not included since their times will be computed separately. For the `recBinarySearch()` function, we can quickly determine that each non-recursive function call statement only requires $O(1)$ time.

To help determine the number of times the recursive function is called, we can use its recursive call tree. Consider the recursive call tree for the binary search algorithm, as shown at the top of Figure 10.11, which results when searching for value 8 in the sequence shown at the bottom of the figure. The number of function call boxes in the tree for a given sequence of length n will indicate the total number of times the function is called. There are two recursive calls to `recBinarySearch()` within the function body, but only one will be executed for each invocation. Thus, there will be a single function call box at each level in the call tree and we only have to determine how many levels there are in the call tree when searching a sequence of n items.

The worst case occurs when the target value is not in the sequence, which can be determined when the **first** and **last** markers cross each other with **first > last**. As with the iterative version of the algorithm, the number of elements in the sorted sequence that must be searched is reduced by half each time the function is called. We know from Chapter 4 that repeatedly reducing the input size by half requires $\log n$ reductions in order to reach the case where there are no additional elements to be searched. Thus, the recursive version of the binary search requires $O(\log n)$ time in the worst case.

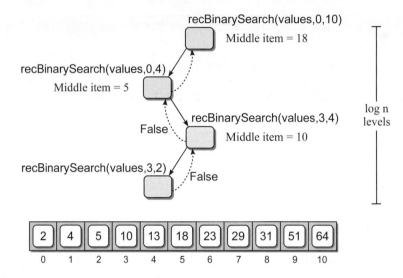

Figure 10.11: The recursive call tree for the binary search algorithm (top) when searching for value 8 in the given sequence (bottom).

10.4.2 Towers of Hanoi

The *Towers of Hanoi* puzzle, invented by the French mathematician Edouard Lucas in 1883, consists of a board with three vertical poles and a stack of disks. The diameter of the disks increases as we progress from the top to bottom, creating a tower structure. The illustration in Figure 10.12 shows the board, the three towers, and five disks. Any number of disks can be used with the puzzle, but we use five for ease of illustration.

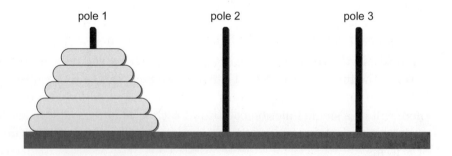

Figure 10.12: The Towers of Hanoi puzzle with five disks.

The objective is to move all of the disks from the starting pole to one of the other two poles to create a new tower. There are, however, two restrictions: (1) only one disk can be moved at a time, and (2) a larger disk can never be placed on top of a smaller disk.

How would you go about solving this problem recursively? Of course you need to think about the base case, the recursive case, and how each recursive call reduces the size of the problem. We will derive all of these in time, but the easiest way to solve this problem is to think about the problem from the bottom up. Instead of thinking about the easiest step, moving the top disk, let's start with the hardest step of moving the bottom disk.

Suppose we already know how to move the top four disks from pole A to pole B, resulting in the board shown in Figure 10.13. Moving the disk from pole A to pole C is now rather easy since it's the only disk left on pole A and there are no disks on pole C. After moving the largest disk, we then move the other four disks from pole B to pole C.

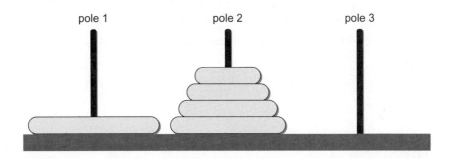

Figure 10.13: The Towers of Hanoi puzzle with four disks moved to pole 2.

Of course, we still have to figure out how to move the top four disks. There is no reason we cannot use the same technique to move the top four disks and in fact we must use the same technique, which leads to a recursive solution. Given n disks and three poles labeled source (S), destination (D), and intermediate (I), we can define the recursive operation as:

- Move the top $n - 1$ disks from pole S to pole I using pole D.

- Move the remaining disk from pole S to pole D.

- Move the $n - 1$ disks from pole I to pole D using pole S.

The first and last steps are recursive calls to the same operation but using different poles as the source, destination, and intermediate designations. The base case, which is implicit in this description, occurs when there is a single disk to move, requiring that we skip the first and last step. Finally, the solution makes progress toward the base case since the recursive calls move one less disk than the current invocation. Eventually, we will end up with a single disk to move.

The high-level solution given above for solving the Towers of Hanoi puzzle can be easily converted to a Python function, as shown in Listing 10.7. For the second step of the process where we actually move a disk, we simply print a message indicating which disk was moved and the two poles it was moved between.

Listing 10.7   Recursive solution for the Towers of Hanoi puzzle.

```
1  # Print the moves required to solve the Towers of Hanoi puzzle.
2  def move( n, src, dest, temp ):
3    if n >= 1 :
4      move( n - 1, src, temp, dest )
5      print( "Move %d -> %d" % (src, dest))
6      move( n - 1, temp, dest, src )
```

To see how this recursive solution works, consider the puzzle using three disks and the execution of the function call:

```
move( 3, 1, 3, 2 )
```

The output produced from the execution is shown here while the first four moves of the disks are illustrated graphically in Figure 10.14.

```
Move 1 -> 3
Move 1 -> 2
Move 3 -> 2
Move 1 -> 3
Move 2 -> 1
Move 2 -> 3
Move 1 -> 3
```

To evaluate the time-complexity of the `move()` function, we need to determine the cost of each invocation and the number of times the function is called for any value of n. Each function invocation only requires $O(1)$ time since there are only two non-recursive function call steps performed by the function, both of which require constant time.

Next, we need to determine how many times the function is called. Consider the recursive call tree in Figure 10.15, which results from the function invocation `move(n, 1, 3, 2)`. The first invocation of `move()` results in two recursive calls, both of which move $n-1$ disks. Both of these invocations each make two recursive calls to move $n-2$ disks. Those four invocations each make two recursive calls to move $n-3$ disks and so on until there is a single disk to be moved.

To determine the total number of times the function is called, we need to calculate the number of times the function executes at each level of the call tree and then sum those values to obtain the final result. The number of function calls at each level is double the number of calls at the previous level. If we label each level of the call tree starting with 0 at the top and going down to $n-1$ at the bottom, then the number of function calls at each level i is equal to 2^i. Summing the number of calls at each level results in the summation:

$$2^0 + 2^1 + 2^2 + \cdots + 2^{n-1} = \sum_{i=0}^{n-1} 2^i$$

or a total of $2^n - 1$ function calls. Thus, the recursive solution for solving the Towers of Hanoi problem requires exponential time of $O(2^n)$ in the worst case.

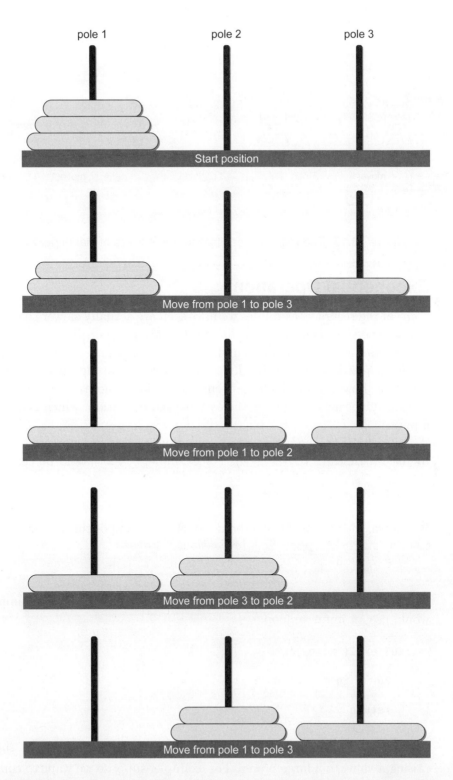

Figure 10.14: The first four moves in solving the Towers of Hanoi puzzle with three disks.

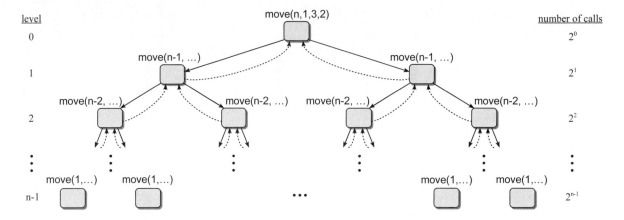

level   move(n,1,3,2)   number of calls
0 2^0

              move(n-1, ...)   move(n-1, ...)
1 2^1

    move(n-2, ...)   move(n-2, ...)   move(n-2, ...)   move(n-2, ...)
2 2^2

    move(1,...)   move(1,...)   move(1,...)   move(1,...)
n-1   ... 2^{n-1}

Figure 10.15: The recursive call tree for the Towers of Hanoi puzzle with n disks.

10.4.3 Exponential Operation

Some of the recursive examples we have seen are actually slower than an equivalent iterative version such as computing a Fibonacci number. Those were introduced to provide simple examples of recursion. Other problems such as solving the Towers of Hanoi puzzle can only be done using a recursive algorithm. There are some problems, however, in which the recursive version is more efficient than the iterative version. One such example is the exponential operation, which raises a number to a power.

By definition, the exponential operation x^n can be expressed as x multiplied by itself n times ($x * x * x \cdots x$). For example, $y = 2^8$ would be computed as:

```
2 * 2 * 2 * 2 * 2 * 2 * 2 * 2
```

Of course, in Python this can be done using the exponential operator:

```
y = 2 ** 8
```

But how is this operation actually performed in Python? A basic implementation would use an iterative loop:

```python
def exp1( x, n ):
    y = 1
    for i in range( n ):
        y *= x
    return y
```

This implementation requires linear time, which is relatively slow if we are raising a value to a large power. For example, suppose we want to compute 2^{31285}. The basic implementation requires 31,285 iterations to compute this value, but each iteration performs a multiplication, which itself is time consuming when compared to other operations. Fortunately, there is a faster way to raise a value to an integer power. Instead of computing 2^8 as 2 * 2 * 2 * 2 * 2 * 2 * 2 * 2, we can reduce the number of multiplications if we computed $(2*2)^4$ instead. Better yet, what if we just computed $16*16$? This is the idea behind a recursive definition for raising a value to an integer power. (The expression $n/2$ is integer division in which the real result is truncated.)

$$x^n = \begin{cases} 1, & \text{if } n = 0 \\ (x*x)^{n/2}, & \text{if } n \text{ is even} \\ x*(x*x)^{n/2}, & \text{if } n \text{ is odd} \end{cases}$$

Listing 10.8 provides a recursive function for raising x to the integer value of n. Since two of the expressions compute $(x*x)^{n/2}$, we go ahead and compute this value as the **result** on line 5 and then determine if n is even or odd. If n is even, then the result is returned; otherwise, we have to first multiply the result by x to include the odd factor. The run time analysis of **exp()** is left as an exercise.

Listing 10.8 The recursive implementation of exp().

```
1  # A recursive implementation for computing x ** n where n is an integer.
2  def exp( x, n ):
3    if n == 0 :
4      return 1
5    result = exp( x * x, n // 2 )
6    if n % 2 == 0 :
7      return result
8    else :
9      return x * result
```

10.4.4 Playing Tic-Tac-Toe

In this technological age, it's very likely you have played a computer game in which you are competing against the computer. For example, you may have played the game of checkers, chess, or something as simple as tic-tac-toe. In any such game, when it's the computer's turn to play, the computer must make a decision as to what play to make. Depending on the game and your level of expertise, you may sometimes think the computer is a genius or that there is some kind of magic going on behind the scenes.

So, how does the computer make its decision? One simple technique the game programmer can apply is the use of a *game tree*. A game tree provides the sequence of all possible moves that can be made in the game for both the computer and the human opponent. When the computer has to make a move, it can evaluate the game tree and determine its best move. The best move in this case is one that allows the computer to win before its human opponent in the fewest possible moves. Thus, when playing against a computer, it's not that the computer is highly intelligent, but that the computer can evaluate every possible move from the current point to the end of the game and choose the best move. Humans simply cannot visualize or evaluate this amount of information and instead must rely on experience in attempting to make the best moves.

Consider the game of tic-tac-toe in which two players use a board containing nine squares organized into three rows of three columns:

The two players take turns placing tokens of Xs and Os in the squares. One player is assigned the Xs while the other is assigned the Os. Play continues until all of the squares are filled, resulting in a draw, or one of the players wins by aligning three identical pieces vertically, diagonally, or horizontally. The following diagrams show three different game boards, two resulting in wins and one resulting in a draw:

Suppose you are playing a game of tic-tac-toe in which four moves have been played as follows:

and now it's X's turn to play, which happens to be the computer. The computer needs to evaluate all of its possible moves to determine the best move to make, which it can do by evaluating the game tree starting from this point in the game. It can use recursion and build a recursive call tree to represent all possible moves in the game for both itself and its opponent. During the recursion, the tokens are placed on the board for both the computer and its opponent as if they were both actually playing. As the recursion unwinds, the tokens are picked to return the game to its current state. This game tree shows the five possible moves the computer can make at this point:

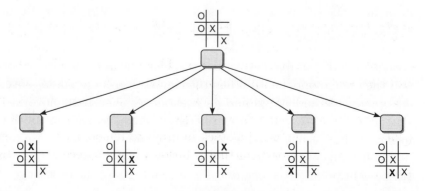

The computer would need to evaluate all of these moves to determine which would be the best. The decision would be based on which move would allow it to win before its opponent. The next figure shows the part of the game tree that is constructed while evaluating the placement of an X in the upper-right square.

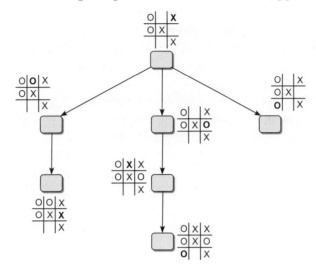

Upon evaluating this portion of the tree, the computer would soon learn it could win in two additional moves if its opponent placed their token in the upper-middle square. Following the middle branch from the top, the computer would learn that if its opponent placed their token in the middle-right square instead, it could not win in two more moves. But the opponent could win in three moves in this situation. Finally, it would be determined that the opponent could win in the next move by playing in the lower-left square if the computer made this play. While that's bad, this is only one possible move the computer could make. It still has to evaluate the other possible moves to determine if one is better. Eventually, the computer would determine that the best move would be to play in the lower-left square. This would be based on the fact it could win on the next move by playing in either of two different places before its opponent could win.

Using recursion to build a game tree can make for very interesting games in which a human competes against the computer. We leave as an exercise the implementation of a function to find the best move for the computer in playing tic-tac-toe.

10.5 Application: The Eight-Queens Problem

In Chapter 7, we explored the concept of backtracking and its use in solving certain problems such as that of finding a path through a maze. In that problem, we saw that backtracking allows us to move forward searching for a solution and, when necessary, to back up one or more steps in order to try other options. Backtracking solutions require the use of a stack in order to remember the current solution and to remove the latter parts of that solution when it's necessary to back up and try other options.

In this chapter, we have discovered that function calls and recursion are implemented internally using a run time stack. Thus, the solution to any problem that requires the use of a stack can be implemented using recursion. In this section, we explore the well-known puzzle and classic recursion example known as the Eight-Queens problem. The task is to place eight queens onto a chessboard such that no queen can attack another queen.

In the game of chess, a square board is used consisting of 64 squares arranged in eight rows of eight columns. Each player has a collection of playing pieces that move and attack in fixed ways. The queen can move and attack any playing piece of the opponent by moving any number of spaces horizontally, vertically, or diagonally, as illustrated in Figure 10.16.

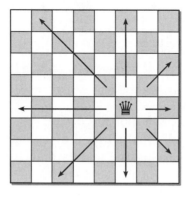

Figure 10.16: Legal moves of the queen in the game of chess.

For the eight-queens problem, we use a standard chessboard and eight queens. The objective is to place the eight queens onto the chessboard in such a way that each queen is safe from attack by the other queens. There are 92 solutions to this problem, two of which are shown in Figure 10.17.

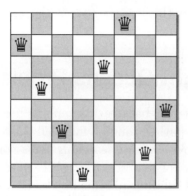 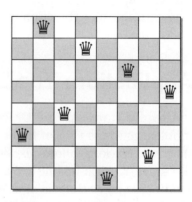

Figure 10.17: Two solutions for the eight-queens problem.

10.5.1 Solving for Four-Queens

To develop an algorithm for this problem, we can first study a smaller instance of the problem by using just four queens and a 4×4 board. How would you go about solving this smaller problem? You may attempt to randomly place the queens on the board until you find a solution that may work for this smaller case. But when attempting to solve the original eight-queens problem, this approach may lead to chaos.

Consider a more organized approach to solving this problem. Since no two queens can occupy the same column, we can proceed one column at a time and attempt to position a queen in each column. We start by placing a queen in the upper-left square or position $(0, 0)$ using the 2-D array notation:

With this move, we now eliminate all squares horizontally, vertically, and diagonally from this position for the placement of additional queens since these positions are guarded by the queen we just placed.

With the first queen placed in the first column, we now move to the second column. The first open position in this column where a queen can be placed without being attacked by the first queen we placed is at position $(2, 1)$. We can place a queen in this position and mark those squares that this queen guards, removing yet more positions for the placement of additional queens.

We are now ready to position a queen in the third column. But you may notice there are no open positions in the third column. Thus, the placement of the first two queens will not result in a valid solution. At this point, you may be tempted to remove all of the existing queens and start over. But that would be a drastic move. Instead, we can employ the backtracking strategy as introduced in Chapter 7, in which we first return to the second column and try alternate positions for that queen before possibly having to return all the way back to the first column.

The next step is to return to the second column and pick up the queen we placed at position $(2, 1)$ and remove the markers that were used to indicate the squares that queen was guarding.

We then place the queen at the next available square within the same column $(3, 1)$ and mark the appropriate squares guarded from this position, as shown here:

Now we can return to the third column and try again. This time, we place a queen at position $(1, 2)$, but this results in no open squares in the fourth column.

We could try other squares in the same column, but none are open. Thus, we must pick up the queen from the third column and again backtrack to try other combinations. We return to the second column and pick up the queen we placed earlier at position $(3, 1)$ so we can try other squares within this column.

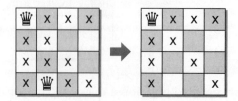

But there are no more open squares in the second column to try, so we must back up even further, returning to the first column. When returning to a column, the first step is always to pick up the queen previously placed in that column.

After picking up the queen in the first column, we place it in the next position $(1, 0)$ within that column.

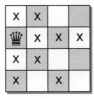

We can now repeat the process and attempt to find open positions in each of the remaining columns. These final steps, which are illustrated here, results in a solution to the four-queens problem.

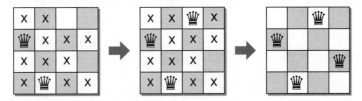

Having found a solution for the four-queens problem, we can use the same approach to solve the eight-queens problem. The only difference between the two is that there is likely to be more backtracking required to find a solution. In addition, while the four-queens problem has two solutions, the eight-queens problem has 92 solutions.

The original problem definition only considered finding a solution for a normal 8×8 chessboard. A more general problem, however, is known as the n-queens problem, which allows for the placement of n queens on a board of size $n \times n$ where $n > 3$. The same backtracking technique described earlier can be used with the n-queens problem, although finding a solution to larger-sized boards can be quite time consuming. We leave the analysis of the time-complexity as an exercise.

10.5.2 Designing a Solution

Given the description of the eight-queens problem and the high-level overview of how to find a solution to the four-queens problem, we now consider an implementation for solving this classic example of recursion and backtracking.

The Board Definition

The implementation will consist of two parts: a game board for placing the queens and a recursive function for finding a solution. We begin with the definition of the NQueens Board ADT to represent the board and the placement of the queens.

Define   NQueens Board ADT

The *n-queens board* is used for positioning queens on a square board for use in solving the *n*-queens problem. The board consists of $n \times n$ squares arranged in rows and columns, with each square identified by indices in the range $[0 \ldots n)$.

- QueensBoard(n): Creates an $n \times n$ empty board.

- size(): Returns the size of the board.

- numQueens(): Returns the number of queens currently positioned on the board.

- unguarded(row, col): Returns a boolean value indicating if the given square is currently unguarded.

- placeQueen(row,col): Places a queen on the board at position (row, col).

- removeQueen(row,col): Removes the queen from position (row, col).

- reset(): Resets the board to its original state by removing all queens currently placed on the board.

- draw(): Prints the board in a readable format using characters to represent the squares containing the queens and the empty squares.

Using the ADT

Given the ADT definition, we can now design a recursive function for solving the *n*-queens problem. The function in Listing 10.9 takes an instance of the NQueens Board ADT and the current column in which we are attempting to place a queen. When called for the first time, an index value of 0 should be passed to the function.

The function begins by testing if a solution has been found that is one of three base cases. If no solution has been found, then we must loop through the rows in the current column to find an unguarded square. If one is found, a queen is placed at that position (line 10) and a recursive call is made in an attempt to place a queen in the next column. Upon return of the recursive call, we must check to see if a solution was found with the queen placed in the square at position (row,col). If a solution was found, another base case is reached and the function returns True. If no solution was found, then the queen in the current column must be picked up (line 18) and another attempt made to place the queen within this column. If all unguarded squares within the current column have been exhausted, then there is no solution to the problem using the configuration of the queens from the previous columns. In this case, which represents the last base case, we must backtrack and allow the previous instance of the recursive function to try other squares within the previous column.

Listing 10.9 The recursive function for solving the *n*-queens problem.

```
1  def solveNQueens( board, col ):
2      # A solution was found if n-queens have been placed on the board.
3      if board.numQueens() == board.size() :
4          return True
5      else :
6          # Find the next unguarded square within this column.
7          for row in range( board.size() ):
8              if board.unguarded( row, col ):
9                  # Place a queen in that square.
10                 board.placeQueen( row, col )
11                 # Continue placing queens in the following columns.
12                 if board.solveNQueens( board, col+1 ) :
13                     # We are finished if a solution was found.
14                     return True
15                 else :
16                     # No solution was found with the queen in this square, so it
17                     # has to be removed from the board.
18                     board.removeQueen( row, col )
19
20         # If the loop terminates, no queen can be placed within this column.
21         return False
```

Implementing the ADT

Having provided the recursive function for solving the *n*-queens problem, we leave the implementation of the NQueens Board ADT as an exercise. In this section, however, we discuss possible data structures for representing the actual board.

The most obvious choice is a 2-D array of size $n \times n$. The elements of the array can contain boolean values with **True** indicating the placement of the queens. To determine if a given square is unguarded, loops can be used to iterate over all of the squares to which a queen can move from that position. If a queen is found in any of the squares searched during the loop iterations, then we know the square is currently guarded by at least one queen. The placement and removal of the queens is also quite easy to implement using the 2-D array structure.

As an alternative, we can actually use a 1-D array consisting of *n* elements. Consider the illustration in Figure 10.18 on the next page, which shows the abstract view of an 8×8 board at the top and a 1-D array at the bottom used to represent the board. Each element of the 1-D array corresponds to one column on the board. The elements of the 1-D array will contain row indices indicating the positions of the queens on the board. Since only one queen can be placed within a given column, we need only keep track of the row containing the queen in the column. When determining if a square is unguarded, we can iterate through the row and column indices for the preceding columns on the board from which the given square can be attacked by a queen. Instead of searching for a **True** value within the elements of a 2-D array, we need only determine if the elements of the 1-D array contain one of the row indices being examined. Consider the illustration in

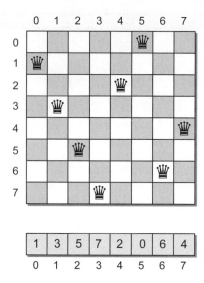

Figure 10.18: Representing an 8×8 board using a 1-D array.

Figure 10.19, in which three queens have been placed and we need to determine if the square at position $(1, 3)$ is unguarded.

When searching horizontally backward, we examine the elements of the 1-D array looking for an index equal to that of the current row. If one is found, then there is a queen already positioned on the current row as is the case in this example. If a queen was not found on the current row, then we would have to search diagonally to the upper left and to the lower left. In these two cases, we search the squares indicated by the arrows and examine the row indices of each and compare them to the entries in the 1-D array. If any of the indices match, then a queen is currently guarding the position and it is not a legal move.

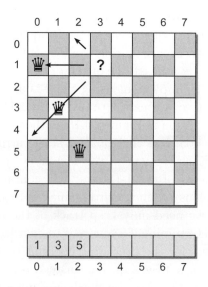

Figure 10.19: Determining if a square is unguarded using a 1-D array.

Exercises

10.1 Draw the recursive call tree for the `printRev()` function from Section 10.1 when called with a value of 5.

10.2 Determine the worst case run time of the recursive factorial function.

10.3 Determine the worst case run time of the recursive Fibonacci function.

10.4 Show or prove that the `printList()` function requires linear time.

10.5 Does the recursive implementation of the binary search algorithm from Listing 10.6 exhibit tail recursion? If not, why not?

10.6 Determine the worst case run time of the recursive exponential function `exp()`.

10.7 Determine the worst case run time of the backtracking solution for the n-queens problem.

10.8 Design and implement an iterative version of the factorial function.

10.9 Design and implement a recursive function for determining whether a string is a palindrome. A ***palindrome*** is a string of characters that is the same as the string of characters in reverse.

10.10 Design and implement a recursive function for computing the greatest common divisor of two integer values.

10.11 Design and implement a program that prints Pascal's triangle:

```
              1
           1     1
        1     2     1
     1     3     3     1
  1     4     6     4     1
1     5    10    10    5     1
```

using a recursive implementation of the binomial coefficients function:

$$a(n, r) = \frac{n!}{r!(n-r)!}$$

10.12 Implement the NQueens Board ADT using the indicated data structure to represent the chess board.

    (a) 2-D array   (b) 1-D array

Programming Projects

10.1 Design and implement a program to solve the n-queens problem. Your program should prompt the user for the size of the board, search for a solution, and print the resulting board if a solution was found.

10.2 Instead of finding a single solution to the n-queens problem, we can compute the total number of solutions for a given value of n. Modify the `solveNQueens()` function from Listing 10.9 to count the number of solutions for a given value of n instead of simply determining if a solution exists. Test your program on the following values of n (the number of solutions for the given board size is indicated in parentheses).

(a) 4 (2)   (c) 9 (352)   (e) 11 (2680)

(b) 8 (92)   (d) 10 (724)   (f) 12 (14200)

10.3 Implement a new version of the maze solving program from Chapter 7 to use recursion instead of a software stack.

10.4 Design and implement a program to play tic-tac-toe against the computer using a recursive function to build a game tree for deciding the computer's next move.

10.5 The ***Knight's tour*** problem is another chessboard puzzle in which the objective is to find a sequence of moves by the knight in which it visits every square on
the board exactly once. The legal moves of a knight are shown in the diagram to the right. Design and implement a program that uses a recursive backtracking algorithm to solve the knight's tour. Your program should extract from the user a starting position for the knight and produce a list of moves that solves the knight's tour.

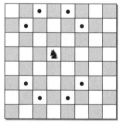

10.6 The ***knapsack problem*** is a classic problem in computer science. You are given a knapsack and a collection of items of different weights and your job is to try to fit some combination of the items into the knapsack to obtain a target weight. All of the items do not have to fit in the knapsack, but the total weight cannot exceed the target weight. For example, suppose we want to fill the knapsack to a maximum weight of 30 pounds from a collection of seven items where the weights of the seven items are 2, 5, 6, 9, 12, 14, and 20. For a small number of items, it's rather easy to solve this problem. One such solution, for example, would be to include the items that have weights 2, 5, 9, and 14. But what if we had several thousand items of varying weights and need to fit them within a large knapsack? Design and implement a recursive algorithm for solving this problem.

## CHAPTER 11

Hash Tables

The search problem, which was introduced in Chapter 4, attempts to locate an item in a collection based on its associated search key. Searching is the most common operation applied to collections of data. It's not only used to determine if an item is in the collection, but can also be used in adding new items to the collection and removing existing items. Given the importance of searching, we need to be able to accomplish this operation fast and efficiently.

If the collection is stored in a sequence, we can use a linear search to locate an item. The linear search is simple to implement but not very efficient as it requires $O(n)$ time in the worst case. We saw that the search time could be improved using the binary search algorithm as it only requires $O(\log n)$ time in the worst case. But the binary search can only be applied to a sequence in which the keys are in sorted order.

The question becomes, can we improve the search operation to achieve better than $O(\log n)$ time? The linear and binary search algorithms are both ***comparison-based searches***. That is, in order to locate an item, the target search key has to be compared against the other keys in the collection. Unfortunately, it can be shown that $O(\log n)$ is the best we can achieve for a comparison-based search. To improve on this time, we would have to use a technique other than comparing the target key against other keys in the collection. In this chapter, we explore the use of a non-comparison-based algorithm to provide a more efficient search operation. This is the same technique used in the implementation of Python's dictionary structure.

11.1 Introduction

Suppose you have a collection of products for which you need to maintain information and allow for numerous searches on that information. At the present time, you only have a small collection of products but you can envision having up to a hundred products in the future. So, you decide to assign a unique identifier or code to each product using the integer values in the range 100 . . . 199. To manage the data and allow for searches, you decide to store the product codes in an array of sufficient size for the number of products available.

Figure 11.1 illustrates the contents of the array for a collection of nine product codes. Depending on the number of searches, we can choose whether to perform a simple linear search on the array or first sort the keys and then use a binary search. Even though this example uses a small collection, in either case the searches still require at least logarithmic time and possibly even linear time in the worst case.

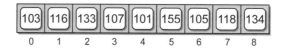

Figure 11.1: A collection of product codes stored in an array.

Given the small range of key values, this problem is a special case. The searches can actually be performed in constant time. Instead of creating an array that is only large enough to hold the products on hand, suppose we create an array with 100 elements, the size needed to store all possible product codes. We can then assign each key a specific element in the array. If the product code exists, the key and its associated data will be stored in its assigned element. Otherwise, the element will be set to None to flag the absence of that product. The search operation is reduced to simply examining the array element associated with a given search key to determine if it contains a valid key or a null reference.

To determine the element assigned to a given key, we note that the product codes are in the range [100 . . . 199] while the array indices are in the range [0 . . . 99]. There is a natural mapping between the two. Key 100 can be assigned to element 0, key 101 to element 1, key 102 to element 2, and so on. This mapping can be computed easily by subtracting 100 from the key value or with the use of the modulus operator (key % 100). Figure 11.2 illustrates the storage of our sample product collection using this approach.

This technique provides ***direct access*** to the search keys. When searching for a key, we apply the same mapping operation to determine the array element that contains the given target. For example, suppose we want to search for product 107. We compute 107 % 100 to determine the key will be in element 7 if it exists. Since

Figure 11.2: Storing a collection of product codes by direct mapping.

there is a product with code 107 and it can be directly accessed at array element 7. If the target key is not in the collection, as is the case for product code 102, the corresponding element (102 % 100 = 2) will contain a null reference. This results in a constant time search since we can directly examine a specific element of the array and not have to compare the target key against the other keys in the collection.

11.2 Hashing

We can use the direct access technique for small sets of keys that are composed of consecutive integer values. But what if the key can be any integer value? Even with a small collection of keys, we cannot create an array large enough to store all possible integer values. That's where hashing comes into play.

Hashing is the process of mapping a search key to a limited range of array indices with the goal of providing direct access to the keys. The keys are stored in an array called a *hash table* and a *hash function* is associated with the table. The function converts or maps the search keys to specific entries in the table. For example, suppose we have the following set of keys:

765, 431, 96, 142, 579, 226, 903, 388

and a hash table, T, containing $M = 13$ elements. We can define a simple hash function $h(\cdot)$ that maps the keys to entries in the hash table:

$$h(\text{key}) = \text{key} \ \% \ M$$

You will notice this is the same operation we used with the product codes in our earlier example. Dividing the integer key by the size of the table and taking the remainder ensures the value returned by the function will be within the valid range of indices for the given table.

To add keys to the hash table, we apply the hash function to determine the entry in which the given key should be stored. Applying the hash function to key 765 yields a result of 11, which indicates 765 should be stored in element 11 of the hash table. Likewise, if we apply the hash function to the next four keys in the list, we find:

h(431) => 2   h(96) => 5   h(142) => 12   h(579) => 7

all of which are unique index values. Figure 11.3 illustrates the insertion of the first five keys into the hash table.

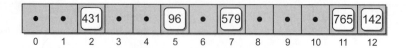

Figure 11.3: Storing the first five keys in the hash table.

11.2.1 Linear Probing

The first five keys were easily added to the table. The resulting index values were unique and the corresponding table entries contained null references, which indicated empty slots. But that's not always the case. Consider what happens when we attempt to add key 226 to the hash table. The hash function maps this key to entry 5, but that entry already contains key 96, as illustrated in Figure 11.4. The result is a **collision**, which occurs when two or more keys map to the same hash location. We mentioned earlier that the goal of hashing is to provide direct access to a collection of search keys. When the key value can be one of a wide range of values, it's impossible to provide a unique entry for all possible key values.

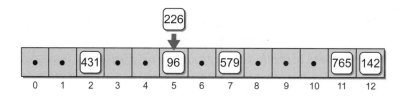

Figure 11.4: A collision occurs when adding key 226.

If two keys map to the same table entry, we must resolve the collision by **probing** the table to find another available slot. The simplest approach is to use a **linear probe**, which examines the table entries in sequential order starting with the first entry immediately following the original hash location. For key value 226, the linear probe finds slot 6 available, so the key can be stored at that position, as illustrated in Figure 11.5.

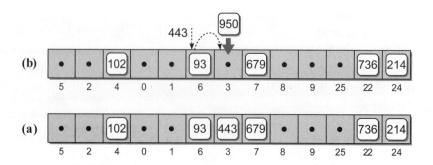

Figure 11.5: Resolving a collision for key 226 requires adding the key to the next slot.

When key 903 is added, the hash function maps the key to index 6, but we just added key 226 to this entry. Your first instinct may be to remove key 226 from this location, since 226 did not map directly to this entry, and store 903 here instead. Once a key is stored in the hash table, however, it's only removed when a delete operation is performed. This collision has to be resolved just like any other, by probing to find another slot. In the case of key 903, the linear probe leads us to slot 8, as illustrated in Figure 11.6.

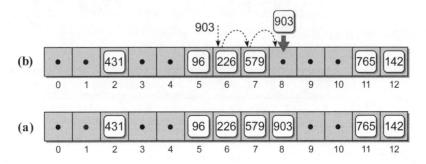

Figure 11.6: Adding key 903 to the hash table: (a) performing a linear probe; and (b) the result after adding the key.

If the end of the array is reached during the probe, we have to wrap around to the first entry and continue until either an available slot is found or all entries have been examined. For example, if we add key 388 to the hash table, the hash function maps the key to slot 11, which contains key 765. The linear probe, as illustrated in Figure 11.7, requires wrapping around to the beginning of the array.

Searching

Searching a hash table for a specific key is very similar to the add operation. The target key is mapped to an initial slot in the table and then it is determined if that entry contains the key. If the key is not at that location, the same probe used to add the keys to the table must be used to locate the target. In this case, the

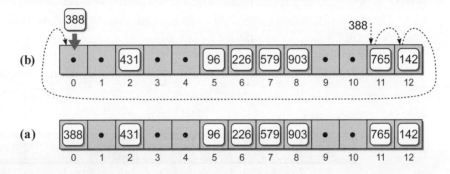

Figure 11.7: Adding key 388 to the hash table: (a) performing a linear probe; and (b) the result after adding the key.

probe continues until the target is located, a null reference is encountered, or all slots have been examined. When either of the latter two situations occurs, this indicates the target key is not in the table. Figure 11.8 illustrates the searches for key 903, which is in the table, and key 561, which is not in the table.

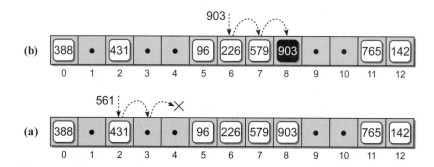

Figure 11.8: Searching the hash table: (a) a successful search for key 903 and (b) an unsuccessful search for key 561.

Deletions

We've seen how keys are added to the table with the use of the hash function and a linear probe for resolving collisions. But how are deletions handled? Deleting from a hash table is a bit more complicated than an insertion. A search can be performed to locate the key in a similar fashion as the basic search operation described earlier. But after finding the key, we cannot simply remove it by setting the corresponding table entry to `None`.

Suppose we remove key 226 from our hash table and set the entry at element 6 to `None`. What happens if we then perform a search for key 903? The `htSearch()` function will return `False`, indicating the key is not in the table, even though it's located at element 8. The reason for the unsuccessful search is due to element 6 containing a null reference from that key having been previously removed, as illustrated in Figure 11.9. Remember, key 903 maps to element 6 but when it was added, a new slot had to be found via a probe since key 226 already occupied that slot. If we simply remove key 226, there is no way to indicate we have to probe past this point when searching for other keys.

Instead of simply setting the corresponding table entry to `None`, we can use a special flag to indicate the entry is now empty but it had been previously occupied.

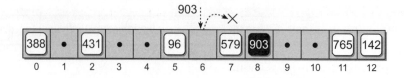

Figure 11.9: Incorrect deletion from the hash table.

Thus, when probing to add a new key or in searching for an existing key, we know the search must continue past the slot since the target may be stored beyond this point. Figure 11.10 illustrates the correct way to delete a key from the hash table. The delta Δ symbol is used to indicate a deleted entry.

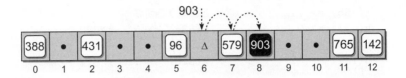

Figure 11.10: The correct way to delete a key from the hash table.

11.2.2   Clustering

As more keys are added to the hash table, more collisions are likely to occur. Since each collision requires a linear probe to find the next available slot, the keys begin to form **clusters**. As the clusters grow larger, so too does the probability that the next key added to the table will result in a collision. If our table were empty, the probability of a key being added to any of the 13 empty slots is 1 out of 13, since it is equally likely the key can hash to any of the slots. Now consider the hash table in Figure 11.8. What is the probability the next key will occupy the empty slot at position 4? If the next key hashes to this position, it can be stored directly into the slot without the need to probe. This also results in a probability of 1 out of 13. But the probability the next key will occupy slot 9 is 5 out of 13. If the next key hashes to any of the slots between 5 and 9, it will be stored in slot 9 due to the linear probe required to find the first position beyond the cluster of keys. Thus, the key is five times more likely to occupy slot 9 than slot 4.

This type of clustering is known as **primary clustering** since it occurs near the original hash position. As the clusters grow larger, so too does the length of the search needed to find the next available slot. We can reduce the amount of primary clustering by changing the technique used in the probing. In this section, we examine several different probing techniques that can be employed to reduce primary clustering.

Modified Linear Probe

When probing to find the next available slot, a loop is used to iterate through the table entries. The order in which the entries are visited form a **probe sequence**. The linear probe searches for the next available slot by stepping through the hash table entries in sequential order. The next array slot in the probe sequence can be represented as an equation:

$$slot = (home + i) \ \% \ M$$

where i is the ith probe in the sequence, $i = 1, 2, \ldots M - 1$. home is the *home position*, which is the index to which the key was originally mapped by the hash function. The modulus operator is used to wrap back around to the front of the array after reaching the end. The use of the linear probe resulted in six collisions in our hash table of size $M = 13$:

```
h(765) => 11          h(579) => 7
h(431) => 2           h(226) => 5    => 6
h(96)  => 5           h(903) => 6    => 7 => 8 => 9
h(142) => 12          h(388) => 11   => 12 => 0
```

when the keys are inserted in the order:

```
765, 431, 96, 142, 579, 226, 903, 388
```

We can improve the linear probe by skipping over multiple elements instead of probing the immediate successor of each element. This can be done by changing the step size in the probe equation to some fixed constant c:

$$slot = (home + i * c) \ \% \ M$$

Suppose we use a linear probe with $c = 3$ to build the hash table using the same set of keys. This results in only two collisions as compared to six when $c = 1$ (the resulting hash table is illustrated in Figure 11.11):

```
h(765) => 11          h(579) => 7
h(431) => 2           h(226) => 5    => 8
h(96)  => 5           h(903) => 6
h(142) => 12          h(388) => 11   => 1
```

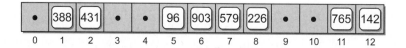

Figure 11.11: The hash table using a linear probe with $c = 3$.

Any value can be used for the constant factor, but to ensure the probe sequence includes all table entries, the constant factor c and the table size must be relatively prime. With a hash table of size $M = 13$, the linear probe with a constant factor $c = 2$ will visit every element. For example, if the key hashes to position 2, the table entries will be visited in the following order:

```
4, 6, 8, 10, 12, 1, 3, 5, 7, 9, 11, 0
```

If we use a value of $c = 3$, the probe sequence will be:

```
5, 8, 11, 1, 4, 7, 10, 0, 3, 6, 9, 12
```

Now, consider the case where the table size is $M = 10$ and the constant factor is $c = 2$. The probe sequence will only include the even numbered entries and will repeat the same sequence without possibly finding the key or an available entry to store a new key:

        4, 6, 8, 0, 2, 4, 6, 8, 0

Quadratic Probing

The linear probe with a constant factor larger than 1 spreads the keys out from the initial hash position, but it can still result in clustering. The clusters simply move equal distance from the initial hash positions. A better approach for reducing primary clustering is with the use of *quadratic probing*, which is specified by the equation:

$$\text{slot} = (\text{home} + i^2) \ \% \ M$$

Quadratic probing eliminates primary clustering by increasing the distance between each probe in the sequence. When used to build the hash table using the sample set of keys, we get seven collisions (the resulting hash table is illustrated in Figure 11.12):

```
h(765) => 11          h(579) => 7
h(431) => 2           h(226) => 5    => 6
h(96)  => 5           h(903) => 6    => 7   => 10
h(142) => 12          h(388) => 11   => 12 => 2   => 7 => 1
```

While the number of collisions has increased, the primary clustering has been reduced. In practice, quadratic probing typically reduces the number of collisions but introduces the problem of *secondary clustering*. Secondary clustering occurs when two keys map to the same table entry and have the same probe sequence. For example, if we were to add key 648 to our table, it would hash to slot 11 and follow the same probe sequence as key 388. Finally, there is no guarantee the quadratic probe will visit every entry in the table. But if the table size is a prime number, at least half of the entries will be visited.

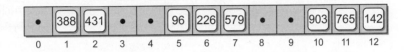

Figure 11.12: The hash table using a quadratic probe.

Double Hashing

The quadratic probe distributes the keys by increasing steps in the probe sequence. But the same sequence is followed by multiple keys that map to the same table entry, which results in the secondary clustering. This occurs because the probe equation is based solely on the original hash slot. A better approach for reducing secondary clustering is to base the probe sequence on the key itself. In **double hashing**, when a collision occurs, the key is hashed by a second function and the result is used as the constant factor in the linear probe:

$$\text{slot} = (\text{home} + i * hp(\text{key})) \ \% \ M$$

While the step size remains constant throughout the probe, multiple keys that map to the same table entry will have different probe sequences. To reduce clustering, the second hash function should not be the same as the main hash function and it should produce a valid index in the range $0 < c < M$. A simple choice for the second hash function takes the form:

$$hp(\text{key}) = 1 + \text{key} \ \% \ P$$

where P is some constant less than M. For example, suppose we define a second hash function:

$$hp(\text{key}) = 1 + \text{key} \ \% \ 8$$

and use it with double hashing to build a hash table from our sample keys. This results in only two collisions:

```
h(765) => 11          h(579) => 7
h(431) => 2           h(226) => 5    => 8
h(96)  => 5           h(903) => 6
h(142) => 12          h(388) => 11   => 3
```

The hash table resulting from the use of double hashing is illustrated in Figure 11.13. The double hashing technique is most commonly used to resolve collisions since it reduces both primary and secondary clustering. To ensure every table entry is visited during the probing, the table size must be a prime number. We leave it as an exercise to show why this is necessary.

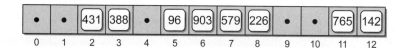

Figure 11.13: The hash table using double hashing.

11.2.3 Rehashing

We have looked at how to use and manage a hash table, but how do we decide how big the hash table should be? If we know the number of entries that will be stored in the table, we can easily create a table large enough to hold the entire collection. In many instances, however, there is no way to know up front how many keys will be stored in the hash table. In this case, we can start with a table of some given size and then grow or expand the table as needed to make room for more entries. We used a similar approach with a vector. When all available slots in the underlying array had been consumed, a new larger array was created and the contents of the vector copied to the new array.

With a hash table, we create a new array larger than the original, but we cannot simply copy the contents from the old array to the new one. Instead, we have to rebuild or **rehash** the entire table by adding each key to the new array as if it were a new key being added for the first time. Remember, the search keys were added to the hash table based on the result of the hash function and the result of the function is based on the size of the table. If we increase the size of the table, the function will return different hash values and the keys may be stored in different entries than in the original table. For example, suppose we create a hash table of size $M = 17$ and insert our set of sample keys using a simple linear probe with $c = 1$. Applying the hash function to the keys yields the following results, which includes a single collision:

```
h(765) => 0        h(579) => 1
h(431) => 6        h(226) => 5
h(96)  => 11       h(903) => 2
h(142) => 6 => 7   h(388) => 14
```

The original hash table using a linear probe is shown in Figure 11.14(a) and the new larger hash table is shown in Figure 11.14(b). You will notice the keys are stored in different locations due to the larger table size.

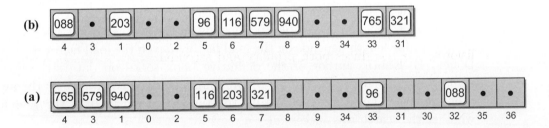

Figure 11.14: The result of enlarging the hash table from 13 elements to 17.

As the table becomes more full, the more likely it is that collisions will occur. Experience has shown that hashing works best when the table is no more than approximately three quarters full. Thus, if the hash table is to be expanded, it should be done before the table becomes full. The ratio between the number of keys in the hash table and the size of the table is called the **load factor**. In practice, a hash table should be expanded before the load factor reaches 80%.

The amount by which the table should be expanded can depend on the application, but a good rule of thumb is to at least double its size. As we indicated earlier, most of the probing techniques can benefit from a table size that is a prime number. To determine the actual size of the new table, we can first double the original size, $2m$ and then search for the first prime number greater than $2m$. Depending on the application and the type of probing used, you may be able to simply double the size and add one, $2m + 1$. Note that by adding one, the resulting size will be an odd number, which results in fewer divisors for the given table size.

11.2.4   Efficiency Analysis

The ultimate goal of hashing is to provide direct access to data items based on the search keys in the hash table. But, as we've seen, collisions routinely occur due to multiple keys mapping to the same table entry. The efficiency of the hash operations depends on the hash function, the size of the table, and the type of probe used to resolve collisions. The insertion and deletion operations both require a search to locate the slot into which a new key can be inserted or the slot containing the key to be deleted. Once the slot has been located, the insertion and deletion operations are simple and only require constant time. The time required to perform the search is the main contributor to the overall time of the three hash table operations: searching, insertions, and deletions.

To evaluate the search performed in hashing, assume there are n elements currently stored in the table of size m. In the best case, which only requires constant time, the key maps directly to the table entry containing the target and no collision occurs. When a collision occurs, however, a probe is required to find the target key. In the worst case, the probe has to visit every entry in the table, which requires $O(m)$ time.

From this analysis, it appears as if hashing is no better than a basic linear search, which also requires linear time. The difference, however, is that hashing is very efficient in the average case. The average case assumes the keys are uniformly distributed throughout the table. It depends on the average probe length and the average probe length depends on the load factor. Given the load factor $\alpha = \frac{n}{m} < 1$, Donald E. Knuth, author of the definitive book series on data structures and algorithms, *The Art of Computer Programming*, derived equations for the average probe length. The times depend on the type of probe used in the search and whether the search was successful.

When using a linear probe, the average number of comparisons required to locate a key in the hash table for a successful search is:

$$\frac{1}{2}\left(1 + \frac{1}{(1-\alpha)^2}\right)$$

and for an unsuccessful search:

$$\frac{1}{2}\left(1 + \frac{1}{(1-\alpha)}\right)$$

When using a quadratic probe or double hashing, the average number of comparisons required to locate a key for a successful search is:

$$\frac{-\log(1-\alpha)}{\alpha}$$

and for an unsuccessful search:

$$\frac{1}{(1-\alpha)}$$

Table 11.1 shows the average number of comparisons for both linear and quadratic probes when used with various load factors. As the load factor increases beyond approximately 2/3, the average number of comparisons become very large, especially for an unsuccessful search. The data in the table also shows that the quadratic and double hashing probes can allow for higher load factors than the linear probe.

Load Factor	0.25	0.5	0.67	0.8	0.99
Successful search:					
Linear Probe	1.17	1.50	2.02	3.00	50.50
Quadratic Probe	1.66	2.00	2.39	2.90	6.71
Unsuccessful search:					
Linear Probe	1.39	2.50	5.09	13.00	5000.50
Quadratic Probe	1.33	2.00	3.03	5.00	100.00

Table 11.1: Average search times for both linear and quadratic probes.

Based on experiments and the equations above, we can conclude that the hash operations only require an average time of $O(1)$ when the load factor is between 1/2 and 2/3. Compare this to the average times for the linear and binary searches ($O(n)$ and $O(\log n)$, respectively) and we find that hashing provides an efficient solution for the search operation.

11.3 Separate Chaining

When a collision occurs, we have to probe the hash table to find another available slot. In the previous section, we reviewed several probing techniques that can be used to help reduce the number of collisions. But we can eliminate collisions entirely if we allow multiple keys to share the same table entry. To accommodate multiple keys, linked lists can be used to store the individual keys that map to the same entry. The linked lists are commonly referred to as *chains* and this technique of collision resolution is known as *separate chaining*.

In separate chaining, the hash table is constructed as an array of linked lists. The keys are mapped to an individual index in the usual way, but instead of storing the key into the array elements, the keys are inserted into the linked list referenced from the corresponding entry; there's no need to probe for a different slot. New keys can be prepended to the linked list since the nodes are in no particular order. Figure 11.15 illustrates the use of separate chaining to build a hash table.

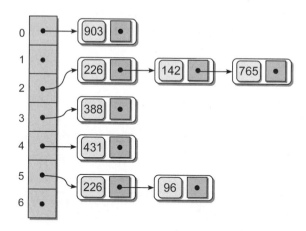

Figure 11.15: Hash table using separate chaining.

The search operation is much simpler when using separate chaining. After mapping the key to an entry in the table, the corresponding linked list is searched to determine if the key is in the table. When deleting a key, the key is again mapped in the usual way to find the linked list containing that key. After locating the list, the node containing the key is removed from the linked list just as if we were removing any other item from a linked list. Since the keys are not stored in the array elements themselves, we no longer have to mark the entry as having been filled by a previously deleted key.

Separate chaining is also known as **open hashing** since the keys are stored outside the table. The term **closed hashing** is used when the keys are stored within the elements of the table as described in the previous section. To confuse things a bit, some computer scientists also use the terms **closed addressing** to describe open hashing and **open addressing** to describe closed hashing. The use of the addressing terms refers to the possible locations of the keys in relation to the table entries. In open addressing, the keys may have been stored in an open slot different from the one to which it originally mapped while in closed addressing, the key is contained within the entry to which it mapped.

The table size used in separate chaining is not as important as in closed hashing since multiple keys can be stored in the various linked list. But it still requires attention since better key distribution can be achieved if the table size is a prime number. In addition, if the table is too small, the linked lists will grow larger with the addition of each new key. If the list become too large, the table can be rehashed just as we did when using closed hashing.

The analysis of the efficiency for separate chaining is similar to that of closed hashing. As before, the search required to locate a key is the most time consuming part of the hash operations. Mapping a key to an entry in the hash table can be done in one step, but the time to search the corresponding linked list is based on the length of that list. In the worst case, the list will contain all of the keys stored in the hash table, resulting in a linear time search. As with closed hashing, separate chaining is very efficient in the average case. The average time to locate a key within the hash table assumes the keys are uniformly distributed across the table and it depends on the average length of the linked lists. If the hash table contains n keys and m entries, the average list length is $\frac{n}{m}$, which is the same as the load factor. Deriving equations for the average number of searches in separate chaining is much easier than with closed hashing. The average number of comparisons required to locate a key in the hash table for a successful search is:

$$1 + \frac{\alpha}{2}$$

and for an unsuccessful search is:

$$1 + \alpha$$

When the load factor is less than 2 (twice the number of keys as compared to the number of table entries), it can be shown that the hash operations only require $O(1)$ time in the average case. This is a better average time than that for closed hashing, which is an advantage of separate chaining. The drawback to separate chaining, however, is the need for additional storage used by the link fields in the nodes of the linked lists.

11.4 Hash Functions

The efficiency of hashing depends in large part on the selection of a good hash function. As we saw earlier, the purpose of a hash function is to map a set of search keys to a range of index values corresponding to entries in a hash table. A "perfect" hash function will map every key to a different table entry, resulting in no collisions. But this is seldom achieved except in cases like our collection of products in which the keys are within a small range or when the keys are known beforehand. Instead, we try to design a good hash function that will distribute the keys across the range of hash table indices as evenly as possible. There are several important guidelines to consider in designing or selecting a hash function:

- The computation should be simple in order to produce quick results.
- The resulting index cannot be random. When a hash function is applied multiple times to the same key, it must always return the same index value.
- If the key consists of multiple parts, every part should contribute in the computation of the resulting index value.
- The table size should be a prime number, especially when using the modulus operator. This can produce better distributions and fewer collisions as it tends to reduce the number of keys that share the same divisor.

Integer keys are the easiest to hash, but there are many times when we have to deal with keys that are either strings or a mixture of strings and integers. When dealing with non-integer keys, the most common approach is to first convert the key to an integer value and then apply an integer-based hash function to that value. In this section, we first explore several hash functions that can be used with integers and then look at common techniques used to convert strings to integer values that can then be hashed.

Division

The simplest hash function for integer values is the one we have been using through-out the chapter. The integer key, or a mixed type key that has been converted to an integer, is divided by the size of the hash table with the remainder becoming the hash table index:

$$h(\text{key}) = \text{key} \ \% \ M$$

Computing the remainder of an integer key is the easiest way to ensure the resulting index always falls within the legal range of indices. The division technique is one of the most commonly used hash functions, applied directly to an integer key or after converting a mixed type key to an integer.

Truncation

For large integers, some columns in the key value are ignored and not used in the computation of the hash table index. In this case, the index is formed by selecting the digits from specific columns and combining them into an integer within the legal range of indices. For example, if the keys are composed of integer values that all contain seven digits and the hash table size is 1000, we can concatenate the first, third, and sixth digits (counting from right to left) to form the index value. Using this technique, key value 4873152 would hash to index 812.

Folding

In this method, the key is split into multiple parts and then combined into a single integer value by adding or multiplying the individual parts. The resulting integer value is then either truncated or the division method is applied to fit it within the range of legal table entries. For example, given a key value 4873152 consisting of seven digits, we can split it into three smaller integer values (48, 731, and 52) and then sum these to obtain a new integer: 48 + 731 + 52 = 831. The division method can then be used to obtain the hash table index. This method can also be used when the keys store data with explicit components such as social security numbers or phone numbers.

Hashing Strings

Strings can also be stored in a hash table. The string representation has to be converted to an integer value that can be used with the division or truncation methods to generate an index within the valid range. There are many different techniques available for this conversion. The simplest approach is to sum the ASCII values of the individual characters. For example, if we use this method to hash the string `'hashing'`, the result will be:

$$104 + 97 + 115 + 104 + 105 + 110 + 103 = 738$$

This approach works well with small hash tables. But when used with larger tables, short strings will not hash to the larger index values; they will only be used when probed. For example, suppose we apply this method to strings containing seven characters, each with a maximum ASCII value of 127. Summing the ASCII values will yield a maximum value of `127 * 7 = 889`. A second approach that can provide good results regardless of the string length uses a polynomial:

$$s_0 a^{n-1} + s_1 a^{n-2} + \cdots + s_{n-3} a^2 + s_{n-2} a + s_{n-1}$$

where a is a non-zero constant, s_i is the ith element of the string, and n is the length of the string. If we use this method with the string `'hashing'`, where $a = 27$, the resulting hash value will be 41746817200. This value can then be used with the division method to yield an index value within the valid range.

11.5   The HashMap Abstract Data Type

One of the most common uses of a hash table is for the implementation of a map. In fact, Python's dictionary is implemented using a hash table with closed hashing. The definition of the Map ADT from Chapter 3 allows for the use of any type of comparable key, which differs from Python's dictionary since the latter requires the keys to be hashable. That requirement can limit the efficient use of the dictionary since we must define our own hash function for any user-defined types that are to be used as dictionary keys. Our hash function must produce good results or the dictionary operations may not be very efficient.

In this section, we provide an implementation for the map that is very similar to the approach used in implementing Python's dictionary. Since this version requires the keys to be hashable, we use the name HashMap to distinguish it from the more general Map ADT. For the implementation of the HashMap ADT, we are going to use a hash table with closed hashing and a double hashing probe. The source code is provided in Listing 11.1 on the next page.

The Hash Table

In implementing the HashMap ADT, we must first decide how big the hash table should be. The HashMap ADT is supposed to be a general purpose structure that can store any number of key/value pairs. To maintain this property, we must allow the hash table to expand as needed. Thus, we can start with a relatively small table ($M = 7$) and allow it to expand as needed by rehashing each time the load factor is exceeded. The next question we need to answer is what load factor should we use? As we saw earlier, a load factor between 1/2 and 2/3 provides good performance in the average case. For our implementation we are going to use a load factor of 2/3.

Listing 11.1   The `hashmap.py` module.

```
1   # Implementation of the Map ADT using closed hashing and a probe with
2   # double hashing.
3   from arrays import Array
4
5   class HashMap :
6     # Defines constants to represent the status of each table entry.
7     UNUSED = None
8     EMPTY = _MapEntry( None, None )
9
10    # Creates an empty map instance.
11    def __init__( self ):
12      self._table = Array( 7 )
13      self._count = 0
14      self._maxCount = len(self._table) - len(self._table) // 3
15
16    # Returns the number of entries in the map.
17    def __len__( self ):
18      return self._count
19
20    # Determines if the map contains the given key.
21    def __contains__( self, key ):
22      slot = self._findSlot( key, False )
23      return slot is not None
24
25    # Adds a new entry to the map if the key does not exist. Otherwise, the
26    # new value replaces the current value associated with the key.
27    def add( self, key, value ):
28      if key in self :
29        slot = self._findSlot( key, False )
30        self._table[slot].value = value
31        return False
32      else :
33        slot = self._findSlot( key, True )
34        self._table[slot] = _MapEntry( key, value )
35        self._count += 1
36        if self._count == self._maxCount :
37          self._rehash()
38        return True
39
40    # Returns the value associated with the key.
41    def valueOf( self, key ):
42      slot = self._findSlot( key, False )
43      assert slot is not None, "Invalid map key."
44      return self._table[slot].value
45
46    # Removes the entry associated with the key.
47    def remove( self, key ):
48      ......
49
```

```
50      # Returns an iterator for traversing the keys in the map.
51    def __iter__( self ):
52      ......
53
54      # Finds the slot containing the key or where the key can be added.
55      # forInsert indicates if the search is for an insertion, which locates
56      # the slot into which the new key can be added.
57    def _findSlot( self, key, forInsert ):
58        # Compute the home slot and the step size.
59      slot = self._hash1( key )
60      step = self._hash2( key )
61
62        # Probe for the key.
63      M = len(self._table)
64      while self._table[slot] is not UNUSED :
65        if forInsert and \
66          (self._table[slot] is UNUSED or self._table[slot] is EMPTY) :
67          return slot
68        elif not forInsert and \
69          (self._table[slot] is not EMPTY and self._table[slot].key == key) :
70          return slot
71        else :
72          slot = (slot + step) % M
73
74      # Rebuilds the hash table.
75    def _rehash( self ) :
76        # Create a new larger table.
77      origTable = self._table
78      newSize = len(self._table) * 2 + 1
79      self._table = Array( newSize )
80
81        # Modify the size attributes.
82      self._count = 0
83      self._maxCount = newSize - newSize // 3
84
85        # Add the keys from the original array to the new table.
86      for entry in origTable :
87        if entry is not UNUSED and entry is not EMPTY :
88          slot = self._findSlot( key, True )
89          self._table[slot] = entry
90          self._count += 1
91
92      # The main hash function for mapping keys to table entries.
93    def _hash1( self, key ):
94      return abs( hash(key) ) % len(self._table)
95
96      # The second hash function used with double hashing probes.
97    def _hash2( self, key ):
98      return 1 + abs( hash(key) ) % (len(self._table) - 2)
99
100   # Storage class for holding the key/value pairs.
101   class _MapEntry :
102     def __init__( self, key, value ):
103       self.key = key
104       self.value = value
```

In the constructor (lines 11–14), we create three attributes: `table` stores the array used for the hash table, `count` indicates the number of keys currently stored in the table, and `maxCount` indicates the maximum number of keys that can be stored in the table before exceeding the load factor. Instead of using floating-point operations to determine if the load factor has been exceeded, we can store the maximum number of keys needed to reach that point. Each time the table is expanded, a new value of `maxCount` is computed. For the initial table size of 7, this value will be 5.

The key/value entries can be stored in the table using the same storage class `_MapEntry` as used in our earlier implementation. But we also need a way to flag an entry as having been previously used by a key but has now been deleted. The easiest way to do this is with the use of a dummy `_MapEntry` object. When a key is deleted, we simply store an alias of the dummy object reference in the corresponding table entry. For easier readability of the source code, we create two named constants in lines 7–8 to indicate the two special states for the table entries: an `UNUSED` entry, which is indicated by a null reference, is one that has not yet been used to store a key; and an `EMPTY` entry is one that had previously stored a key but has now been deleted. The third possible state of an entry, which is easily determined if the entry is not one of the other two states, is one that is currently occupied by a key.

Hash Functions

Our implementation will need two hash functions: the main function for mapping the key to a home position and the function used with the double hashing. For both functions, we are going to use the simple division method in which the key value is divided by the size of the table and the remainder becomes the index to which the key maps. The division hash functions defined earlier in the chapter assumed the search key is an integer value. But the HashMap ADT allows for the storage of any type of search key, which includes strings, floating-point values, and even user-defined types. To accommodate keys of various data types, we can use Python's built-in `hash()` function, which is automatically defined for all of the built-in types. It hashes the given key and returns an integer value that can be used in the division method. But the value returned by the Python's `hash()` function can be any integer, not just positive values or those within a given range. We can still use the function and simply take its absolute value and then divide it by the size of the table. The main hash function for our implementation is defined as:

$$h(\text{key}) = |\texttt{hash}(\text{key})| \ \% \ M$$

while the second function for use with double hashing is defined as:

$$hp(\text{key}) = 1 + |\texttt{hash}(\text{key})| \ \% \ (M - 2)$$

The size of our hash table will always be an odd number, so we subtract 2 from the size of the table in the second function to ensure the division is by an odd number. The two hash functions are implemented in lines 93–98 of Listing 11.1.

To use objects of a user-defined class as keys in the dictionary, the class must implement both the __hash__ and __eq__ methods. The __hash__ method should hash the contents of the object and return an integer that can be used by either of our two hash functions, $h()$ and $hp()$. The __eq__ is needed for the equality comparison in line 69 of Listing 11.1, which determines if the key stored in the given slot is the target key.

Searching

As we have seen, a search has to be performed no matter which hash table operation we use. To aide in the search, we create the _findSlot() helper method as shown in lines 57–72. Searching the table to determine if a key is simply contained in the table and searching for a key to be deleted require the same sequence of steps. After mapping the key to its home position, we determine if the key was found at this location or if a probe has to be performed. When probing, we step through the keys using the step size returned by the second hash function. The probe continues until the key has been located or we encounter an unused slot (contains a null reference). The search used to locate a slot for the insertion of a new key, however, has one major difference. The probe must also terminate if we encounter a table entry marked as empty from a previously deleted key since a new key can be stored in such an entry.

This minor difference between the two types of searches is handled by the forInsert argument. When True, a search is performed for the location where a new key can be inserted and the index of that location is returned. When the argument is False, a normal search is performed and either the index of the entry containing the key is returned or None is returned when the key is not in the table. When used in the __contains__ and valueOf() methods, the _findSlot() method is called with a value of False for the forInsert argument.

Insertions

The add() method also uses the _findSlot() helper method. In fact, it's called twice. First, we determine if the key is in the table that indirectly calls the __contains__ method. If the key is in the table, we have to locate the key through a normal search and modify its corresponding value. On the other, if the key is not in the table, __findSlot__ is called with a value of True passed to the forInsert argument to locate the next available slot. Finally, if the key is new and has to be added to the table, we check the count and determine if it exceeds the load factor, in which case the table has to be rehashed. The remove operation and the implementation of an iterator for use with this new version of the Map ADT are left as exercises.

Rehashing

The rehash operation is shown in lines 75–90 of Listing 11.1. The first step is to create a new larger array. For simplicity, the new size is computed to be $M*2+1$, which ensures an odd value. A more efficient solution would ensure the new size is always a prime number by searching for the next prime number larger than $M * 2 + 1$.

The original array is saved in a temporary variable and the new array is assigned to the `table` attribute. The reason for assigning the new array to the attribute at this time is that we will need to use the `_findSlot()` method to add the keys to the new array and that method works off the `table` attribute. The `count` and `maxCount` are also reset. The value of `maxCount` is set to be approximately two-thirds the size of the new table using the expression shown in line 83 of Listing 11.1.

Finally, the key/value pairs are added to the new array, one at a time. Instead of using the `add()` method, which first verifies the key is new, we perform the insertion of each directly within the `for` loop.

11.6   Application: Histograms

Graphical displays or charts of tabulated frequencies are very common in statistics. These charts, known as *histograms*, are used to show the distribution of data across discrete categories. A histogram consists of a collection of categories and counters. The number and types of categories can vary depending on the problem. The counters are used to accumulate the number of occurrences of values within each category for a given data collection. Consider the example histogram in Figure 11.16. The five letter grades are the categories and the heights of the bars represent the value of the counters.

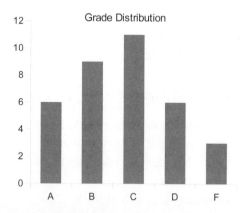

Figure 11.16: Sample histogram for a distribution of grades.

11.6.1   The Histogram Abstract Data Type

We can define an abstract data type for collecting and storing the frequency counts used in constructing a histogram. An ideal ADT would allow for building a general purpose histogram that can contain many different categories and be used with many different problems.

| Define | Histogram ADT |

A *histogram* is a container that can be used to collect and store discrete frequency counts across multiple categories representing a distribution of data. The category objects must be comparable.

- `Histogram( catSeq )`: Creates a new histogram containing the categories provided in the given sequence, `catSeq`. The frequency counts of the categories are initialized to zero.

- `getCount( category )`: Returns the frequency count for the given category, which must be valid.

- `incCount( category )`: Increments the count by 1 for the given category. The supplied category must be valid.

- `totalCount()`: Returns a sum of the frequency counts for all of the categories.

- *iterator* (): Creates and returns an iterator for traversing over the histogram categories.

Building a Histogram

The program in Listing 11.2 produces a text-based version of the histogram from Figure 11.16 and illustrates the use of the Histogram ADT. The program extracts a collection of numeric grades from a text file and assigns a letter grade to each value based on the common 10-point scale: A: 100 – 90, B: 89 – 80, C: 79 – 70, D: 69 – 60, F: 59 – 0. The frequency counts of the letter grades are tabulated and then used to produce a histogram.

| Listing 11.2 | The `buildhist.py` program. |

```
1  # Prints a histogram for a distribution of letter grades computed
2  # from a collection of numeric grades extracted from a text file.
3
4  from maphist import Histogram
5
6  def main():
7    # Create a Histogram instance for computing the frequencies.
8    gradeHist = Histogram( "ABCDF" )
9
10   # Open the text file containing the grades.
11   gradeFile = open('cs101grades.txt', "r")
12
13   # Extract the grades and increment the appropriate counter.
14   for line in gradeFile :
15     grade = int(line)
16     gradeHist.incCount( letterGrade(grade) )
17
```

(Listing Continued)

Listing 11.2   Continued …

```
18       # Print the histogram chart.
19       printChart( gradeHist )
20
21   # Determines the letter grade for the given numeric value.
22   def letterGrade( grade ):
23       if grade >= 90 :
24          return 'A'
25       elif grade >= 80 :
26          return 'B'
27       elif grade >= 70 :
28          return 'C'
29       elif grade >= 60 :
30          return 'D'
31       else :
32          return 'F'
33
34   # Prints the histogram as a horizontal bar chart.
35   def printChart( gradeHist ):
36       print( "           Grade Distribution" )
37        # Print the body of the chart.
38       letterGrades = ( 'A', 'B', 'C', 'D', 'F' )
39       for letter in letterGrades :
40          print( "   |" )
41          print( letter + " +", end = "" )
42          freq = gradeHist.getCount( letter )
43          print( '*' * freq )
44
45        # Print the x-axis.
46       print( "   |" )
47       print( "   +----+----+----+----+----+----+----+----" )
48       print( "   0    5   10   15   20   25   30   35" )
49
50   # Calls the main routine.
51   main()
```

The `buildhist.py` program consists of three functions. The `main()` function drives the program, which extracts the numeric grades and builds an instance of the Histogram ADT. It initializes the histogram to contain the five letter grades as its categories. The `letterGrade()` function is a helper function, which simply returns the letter grade for the given numeric value. The `printChart()` function prints the text-based histogram using the frequency counts computed in the main routine. Assuming the following grades are extracted from the text file:

```
77 89 53 95 68 86 91 89 60 70 80 77 73 73 93 85 83 67 75 71 94 64
79 97 59 69 61 80 73 70 82 86 70 45 100
```

the `buildhist.py` program would produce the following text-based histogram:

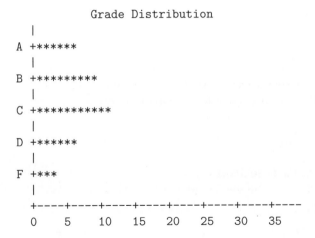

```
          Grade Distribution
       |
     A +******
       |
     B +*********
       |
     C +************
       |
     D +******
       |
     F +***
       |
       +----+----+----+----+----+----+----+----
       0    5    10   15   20   25   30   35
```

Implementation

To implement the Histogram ADT, we must select an appropriate data structure for storing the categories and corresponding frequency counts. There are several different structures and approaches that can be used, but the Map ADT provides an ideal solution since it already stores key/value mappings and allows for a full implementation of the Histogram ADT. To use a map, the categories can be stored in the key part of the key/value pairs and a counter (integer value) can be stored in the value part. When a category counter is incremented, the entry is located by its key and the corresponding value can be incremented and stored back into the entry. The implementation of the Histogram ADT using an instance of the hash table version of the Map ADT as the underlying structure is provided in Listing 11.3.

Listing 11.3 The `maphist.py` module.

```python
1  # Implementation of the Histogram ADT using a Hash Map.
2
3  from hashmap import HashMap
4
5  class Histogram :
6    # Creates a histogram containing the given categories.
7    def __init__( self, catSeq ):
8      self._freqCounts = HashMap()
9      for cat in catSeq :
10       self._freqCounts.add( cat, 0 )
11
12    # Returns the frequency count for the given category.
13    def getCount( self, category ):
14      assert category in self._freqCounts, "Invalid histogram category."
15      return self._freqCounts.valueOf( category )
16
```

(Listing Continued)

Listing 11.3	Continued ...

```
17      # Increments the counter for the given category.
18      def incCount( self, category ):
19        assert category in self._freqCounts, "Invalid histogram category."
20        value = self._freqCounts.valueOf( category )
21        self._freqCounts.add( category, value + 1 )
22
23      # Returns the sum of the frequency counts.
24      def totalCount( self ):
25        total = 0
26        for cat in self._freqCounts :
27          total += self._freqCounts.valueOf( cat )
28        return total
29
30      # Returns an iterator for traversing the categories.
31      def __iter__( self ):
32        return iter( self._freqCounts )
```

The iterator operation defined by the ADT is implemented in lines 31–32. In Section 1.4.1, we indicated the iterator method is supposed to create and return an iterator object that can be used with the given collection. Since the Map ADT already provides an iterator for traversing over the keys, we can have Python access and return that iterator as if we had created our own. This is done using the iter() function, as shown in our implementation of the __iter__ method in lines 31–32.

11.6.2 The Color Histogram

A histogram is used to tabulate the frequencies of multiple discrete categories. The Histogram ADT from the previous section works well when the collection of categories is small. Some applications, however, may deal with millions of distinct categories, none of which are known up front, and require a specialized version of the histogram. One such example is the *color histogram*, which is used to tabulate the frequency counts of individual colors within a digital image. Color histograms are used in areas of image processing and digital photography for image classification, object identification, and image manipulation.

Color histograms can be constructed for any color space, but we limit our discussion to the more common discrete RGB color space. In the RGB color space, individual colors are specified by intensity values for the three primary colors: red, green, and blue. This color space is commonly used in computer applications and computer graphics because it is very convenient for modeling the human visual system. The intensity values in the RGB color space, also referred to as color components, can be specified using either real values in the range $[0 \ldots 1]$ or discrete values in the range $[0 \ldots 255]$. The discrete version is the most commonly used for the storage of digital images, especially those produced by digital cameras and scanners. With discrete values for the three color components, more than 16.7 million colors can be represented, far more than humans are capable of distinguishing. A value of 0 indicates no intensity for the given component while

255 indicates full intensity. Thus, white is represented with all three components set to 255, while black is represented with all three components set to 0.

We can define an abstract data type for a color histogram that closely follows that of the general histogram:

Define   **Color Histogram ADT**

A *color histogram* is a container that can be used to collect and store frequency counts for multiple discrete RGB colors.

- `ColorHistogram()`: Creates a new empty color histogram.

- `getCount( red, green, blue )`: Returns the frequency count for the given RGB color, which must be valid.

- `incCount( red, green, blue )`: Increments the count by 1 for the given RGB color if the color was previously added to the histogram or the color is added to the histogram as a new entry with a count of 1.

- `totalCount()`: Returns a sum of the frequency counts for all colors in the histogram.

- *iterator* (): Creates and returns an iterator for traversing over the colors in the color histogram.

There are a number of ways we can construct a color histogram, but we need a fast and memory-efficient approach. The easiest approach would be to use a three-dimensional array of size $256 \times 256 \times 256$, where each element of the array represents a single color. This approach, however, is far too costly. It would require 256^3 array elements, most of which would go unused. On the other hand, the advantage of using an array is that accessing and updating a particular color is direct and requires no costly operations.

Other options include the use of a Python list or a linked list. But these would be inefficient when working with images containing millions of colors. In this chapter, we've seen that hashing can be a very efficient technique when used with a good hash function. For the color histogram, closed hashing would not be an ideal choice since it may require multiple rehashes involving hundreds of thousands, if not millions, of colors. Separate chaining can be used with good results, but it requires the design of a good hash function and the selection of an appropriately sized hash table.

A different approach can be used that combines the advantages of the direct access of the 3-D array and the limited memory use and fast searches possible with hashing and separate chaining. Instead of using a 1-D array to store the separate chains, we can use a 2-D array of size 256×256. The colors can be mapped to a specific chain by having the rows correspond to the red color component and the columns correspond to the green color component. Thus, all colors having the same red and green components will be stored in the same chain, with only the blue components differing. Figure 11.17 illustrates this 2-D array of linked lists.

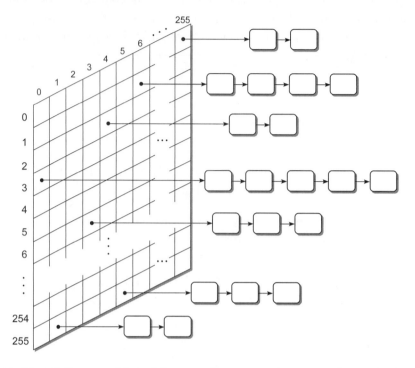

Figure 11.17: A 2-D array of linked lists used to store color counts in a color histogram.

Given a digital image consisting of n distinct pixels, all of which may contain unique colors, the histogram can be constructed in linear time. This time is derived from the fact that searching for the existence of a color can be done in constant time. Locating the specific 2-D array entry in which the color should be stored is a direct mapping to the corresponding array indices. Determining if the given color is contained in the corresponding linked list requires a linear search over the entire list. Since all of the nodes in the linked list store colors containing the same red and green components, they only differ in their blue components. Given that there are only 256 different blue component values, the list can never contain more than 256 entries. Thus, the length of the linked list is independent of the number of pixels in the image. This results in a worst case time of $O(1)$ to search for the existence of a color in the histogram in order to increment its count or to add a new color to the histogram. A search is required for each of the n distinct image pixels, resulting in a total time $O(n)$ in the worst case.

After the histogram is constructed, a traversal over the unique colors contained in the histogram is commonly performed. We could traverse over the entire 2-D array, one element at a time, and then traverse the linked list referenced from the individual elements. But this can be time consuming since in practice, many of the elements will not contain any colors. Instead, we can maintain a single separate linked list that contains the individual nodes from the various hash chains, as illustrated in Figure 11.18. When a new color is added to the histogram, a node is created and stored in the corresponding chain. If we were to include a second link within the same nodes used in the chains to store the colors and color counts, we can then easily add each node to a separate linked list. This list can then be used to provide a complete traversal over the entries in the histogram without wasting time in visiting the empty elements of the 2-D array. The implementation of the color histogram is left as an exercise.

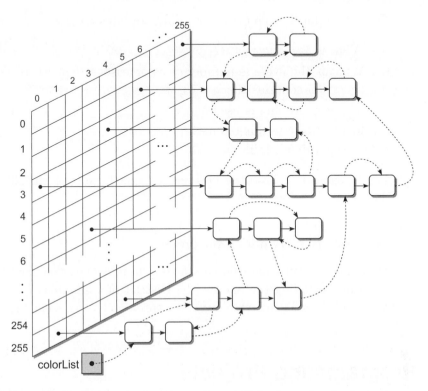

Figure 11.18: The individual chain nodes are linked together for faster traversals.

Exercises

11.1 Assume an initially empty hash table with 11 entries in which the hash function uses the division method. Show the contents of the hash table after the following keys are inserted (in the order listed), assuming the indicated type of probe is used: $67, 815, 45, 39, 2, 901, 34$.

(a) linear probe (with $c = 1$)

(b) linear probe (with $c = 3$)

(c) quadratic probe

(d) double hashing [with $hp(\text{key}) = (\text{key} * 3) \text{ \% } 7$]

(e) separate chaining

11.2 Do the same as in Exercise 11.1 but use the following hash function to map the keys to the table entries:

$$h(\text{key}) = (2 * \text{key} + 3) \ \% \ 11$$

11.3 Show the contents of the hash table from Exercise 11.1 after rehashing with a new table containing 19 entries.

11.4 Consider a hash table of size 501 that contains 85 keys.

(a) What is the load factor?

(b) What is the average number of comparisons required to determine if the collection contains the key 73, if:

    i. linear probing is used

    ii. quadratic probing is used

    iii. separate chaining is used

11.5 Do the same as in Exercise 11.4 but for a hash table of size 2031 that contains 999 keys.

11.6 Show why the table size must be a prime number in order for double hashing to visit every entry during the probe.

11.7 Design a hash function that can be used to map the two-character state abbreviations (including the one for the District of Columbia) to entries in a hash table that results in no more than three collisions when used with a table where $M < 100$.

Programming Projects

11.1 Implement the remove operation for the HashMap ADT.

11.2 Design and implement an iterator for use with the implementation of the HashMap ADT.

11.3 Modify the implementation of the HashMap ADT to:

(a) Use linear probing instead of double hashing

(b) Use quadratic probing instead of double hashing

(c) Use separate chaining instead of closed hashing

11.4 Design and implement a program that compares the use of linear probing, quadratic probing, and double hashing on a collection of string keys of varying lengths. The program should extract a collection of strings from a text file and compute the average number of collisions and the average number of probes.

11.5 Implement the Color Histogram ADT using the 2-D array of chains as described in the chapter.

CHAPTER 12

Advanced Sorting

We introduced the sorting problem in Chapter 5 and explored three basic sorting algorithms, but there are many others. Most sorting algorithms can be divided into two categories: comparison sorts and distribution sorts. In a ***comparison sort***, the data items can be arranged in either ascending (from smallest to largest) or descending (from largest to smallest) order by performing pairwise logical comparisons between the sort keys. The pairwise comparisons are typically based on either *numerical order* when working with integers and reals or *lexicographical order* when working with strings and sequences. A ***distribution sort***, on the other hand, distributes or divides the sort keys into intermediate groups or collections based on the individual key values. For example, consider the problem of sorting a list of numerical grades based on their equivalent letter grade instead of the actual numerical value. The grades can be divided into groups based on the corresponding letter grade without having to make comparisons between the numerical values.

The sorting algorithms described in Chapter 5 used nested iterative loops to sort a sequence of values. In this chapter, we explore two additional comparison sort algorithms, both of which use recursion and apply a divide and conquer strategy to sort sequences. Many of the comparison sorts can also be applied to linked lists, which we explore along with one of the more common distribution sorts.

12.1 Merge Sort

The ***merge sort*** algorithm uses the divide and conquer strategy to sort the keys stored in a mutable sequence. The sequence of values is recursively divided into smaller and smaller subsequences until each value is contained within its own subsequences. The subsequences are then merged back together to create a sorted sequence. For illustration purposes, we assume the mutable sequence is a list.

339

12.1.1   Algorithm Description

The algorithm starts by splitting the original list of values in the middle to create two sublists, each containing approximately the same number of values. Consider the list of integer values at the top of Figure 12.1. This list is first split following the element containing value 18. These two sublists are then split in a similar fashion to create four sublists and those four are split to create eight sublists.

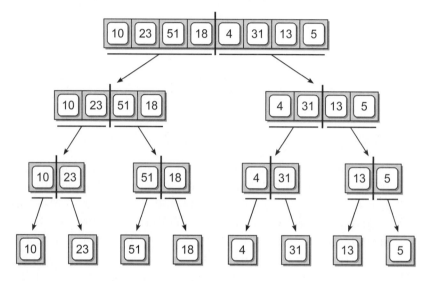

Figure 12.1: Recursively splitting a list until each element is contained within its own list.

After the list has been fully subdivided into individual sublists, the sublists are then merged back together, two at a time, to create a new sorted list. These sorted lists are themselves merged to create larger and larger lists until a single sorted list has been constructed. During the merging phase, each pair of sorted sublists are merged to create a new sorted list containing all of the elements from both sublists. This process is illustrated in Figure 12.2.

12.1.2   Basic Implementation

Given a basic description of the merge sort algorithm from an abstract view, we now turn our attention to the implementation details. There are two major steps in the merge sort algorithm: dividing the list of values into smaller and smaller sublists and merging the sublists back together to create a sorted list. The use of recursion provides a simple solution to this problem. The list can be subdivided by each recursive call and then merged back together as the recursion unwinds.

Listing 12.1 illustrates a simple recursive function for use with a Python list. If the supplied list contains a single item, it is by definition sorted and the list is simply returned, which is the base case of the recursive definition. If the list contains multiple items, it has to be split to create two sublists of approximately

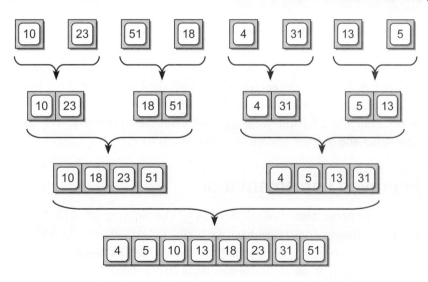

Figure 12.2: The sublists are merged back together to create a sorted list.

equal size. The split is handled by first computing the midpoint of the list and then using the slice operation to create two new sublists. The left sublist is then passed to a recursive call of the `pythonMergeSort()` function. That portion of the list will be processed recursively until it is completely sorted and returned. The right half of the list is then processed in a similar fashion. After both the left and right sublists have been ordered, the two lists are merged using the `mergeSortedLists()` function from Section 5.3.2. The new sorted list is returned.

Listing 12.1   Implementation of the merge sort algorithm for use with Python lists.

```
1    # Sorts a Python list in ascending order using the merge sort algorithm.
2    def pythonMergeSort( theList ):
3      # Check the base case - the list contains a single item.
4      if len(theList) <= 1 :
5        return theList
6      else :
7        # Compute the midpoint.
8        mid = len(theList) // 2
9
10       # Split the list and perform the recursive step.
11       leftHalf = pythonMergeSort( theList[ :mid ] )
12       rightHalf = pythonMergeSort( theList[ mid: ] )
13
14       #Merge the two ordered sublists.
15       newList = mergeOrderedLists( leftHalf, rightHalf )
16       return newList
```

The `pythonMergeSort()` function provides a simple recursive implementation of the merge sort algorithm, but it has several disadvantages. First, it relies on the use of the slice operation, which prevents us from using the function to sort an array of values since the array structure does not provide a slice operation. Second, new physical sublists are created in each recursive call as the list is subdivided. We learned in Chapter 4 that the slice operation can be time consuming since a new list has to be created and the contents of the slice copied from the original list. A new list is also created each time two sublists are merged during the unwinding of the recursion, adding yet more time to the overall process. Finally, the sorted list is not contained within the same list originally passed to the function as was the case with the sorting algorithms presented earlier in Chapter 5.

12.1.3 Improved Implementation

We can improve the implementation of the merge sort algorithm by using a technique similar to that employed with the binary search algorithm from Chapter 5. Instead of physically creating sublists when the list is split, we can use index markers to specify a subsequence of elements to create virtual sublists within the original physical list as was done with the binary search algorithm. Figure 12.3 shows the corresponding index markers used to split the sample list from Figure 12.1. The use of virtual sublists eliminates the need to repeatedly create new physical arrays or Python list structures during each recursive call.

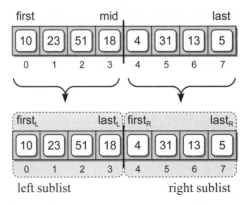

Figure 12.3: Splitting a list of values into two virtual sublists.

The new implementation of the merge sort algorithm is provided in Listing 12.2. The `recMergeSort()` function is very similar to the earlier implementation since both require the same steps to implement the merge sort algorithm. The difference is that `recMergeSort()` works with virtual sublists instead of using the slice operation to create actual sublists. This requires two index variables, `first` and `last`, for indicating the range of elements within the physical sublist that comprise the virtual sublist.

This implementation of the merge sort algorithm requires the use of a temporary array when merging the sorted virtual sublists. Instead of repeatedly creating a new array and later deleting it each time sublists are merged, we can create a single array and use it for every merge operation. Since this array is needed inside the `mergeVirtualLists()` function, it has to either be declared as a global

| Listing 12.2 | Improved implementation of the merge sort algorithm. |

```
1   # Sorts a virtual subsequence in ascending order using merge sort.
2
3   def recMergeSort( theSeq, first, last, tmpArray ):
4     # The elements that comprise the virtual subsequence are indicated
5     # by the range [first...last]. tmpArray is temporary storage used in
6     # the merging phase of the merge sort algorithm.
7
8      # Check the base case: the virtual sequence contains a single item.
9     if first == last :
10      return;
11    else :
12       # Compute the mid point.
13       mid = (first + last) // 2
14
15       # Split the sequence and perform the recursive step.
16       recMergeSort( theSeq, first, mid, tmpArray )
17       recMergeSort( theSeq, mid+1, last, tmpArray )
18
19       # Merge the two ordered subsequences.
20       mergeVirtualSeq( theSeq, first, mid+1, last+1, tmpArray )
```

variable or created and passed into the recursive function before the first call. Our implementation uses the latter approach.

The mergeVirtualSeq() function, provided in Listing 12.3 on the next page, is a modified version of mergeSortedLists() from Section 5.3.2. The original function was used to create a new list that contained the elements resulting from merging two sorted lists. This version is designed to work with two virtual mutable subsequences that are stored adjacent to each other within the physical sequence structure, theSeq. Since the two virtual subsequences are always adjacent within the physical sequence, they can be specified by three array index variables: left, the index of the first element in the left subsequence; right, the index of the first element in the right subsequence; and end, the index of the first element following the end of the right subsequence. A second difference in this version is how the resulting merged sequence is returned. Instead of creating a new list structure, the merged sequence is stored back into the physical structure within the elements occupied by the two virtual subsequences.

The tmpArray argument provides a temporary array needed for intermediate storage during the merging of the two subsequences. The array must be large enough to hold all of the elements from both subsequences. This temporary storage is needed since the resulting sorted sequence is not returned by the function but instead is copied back to the original sequence structure. During the merging operation, the elements from the two subsequences are saved into the temporary array. After being merged, the elements are copied from the temporary array back to the original structure. We could create a new array each time the function is called, which would then be deleted when the function terminates. But that requires additional overhead that is compounded by the many calls to the mergeVirtualSeq() function during the execution of the recursive recMergeSort() function. To reduce

---

Listing 12.3 | Merging two ordered virtual sublists.

```
1   # Merges the two sorted virtual subsequences: [left..right) [right..end)
2   # using the tmpArray for intermediate storage.
3
4   def mergeVirtualSeq( theSeq, left, right, end, tmpArray ):
5       # Initialize two subsequence index variables.
6       a = left
7       b = right
8       # Initialize an index variable for the resulting merged array.
9       m = 0
10      # Merge the two sequences together until one is empty.
11      while a < right and b < end :
12        if theSeq[a] < theSeq[b] :
13          tmpArray[m] = theSeq[a]
14          a += 1
15        else :
16          tmpArray[m] = theSeq[b]
17          b += 1
18        m += 1
19
20      # If the left subsequence contains more items append them to tmpArray.
21      while a < right :
22        tmpArray[m] = theSeq[a]
23        a += 1
24        m += 1
25
26      # Or if right subsequence contains more, append them to tmpArray.
27      while b < end :
28        tmpArray[m] = theSeq[b]
29        b += 1
30        m += 1
31
32      # Copy the sorted subsequence back into the original sequence structure.
33      for i in range( end - left ) :
34        theSeq[i+left] = tmpArray[i]
```

---

this overhead, implementations of the the merge sort algorithm typically allocate a single array that is of the same size as the original list and then simply pass the array into the `mergeVirtualSeq()` function. The use of the temporary array is illustrated in Figure 12.4 with the merging of the two subsequences lists formed from the second half of the original sequence.

The implementation of the earlier sorting algorithms only required the user to supply the array or list to be sorted. The `recMergeSort()` function, however,

---

NOTE

Wrapper Functions. A *wrapper function* is a function that provides a simpler and cleaner interface for another function and typically provides little or no additional functionality. Wrapper functions are commonly used with recursive functions that require additional arguments since their initial invocation may not be as natural as an equivalent sequential function.

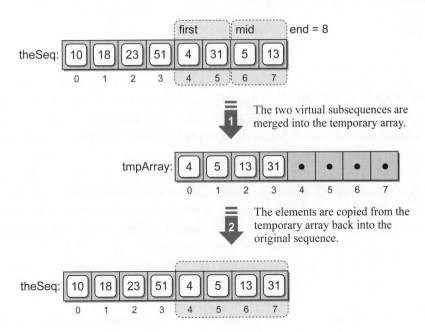

Figure 12.4: A temporary array is used to merge two virtual subsequences.

requires not only the sequence structure but also the index markers and a temporary array. These extra arguments may not be as intuitive to the user as simply passing the sequence to be sorted. In addition, what happens if the user supplies incorrect range values or the temporary array is not large enough to merge the largest subsequence? A better approach is to provide a wrapper function for `recMergeSort()` such as the one shown in Listing 12.4. The `mergeSort()` function provides a simpler interface as it only requires the array or list to be sorted. The wrapper function handles the creation of the temporary array needed by the merge sort algorithm and initiates the first call to the recursive function.

Listing 12.4 A wrapper function for the new implementation of the merge sort algorithm.

```
1  # Sorts an array or list in ascending order using merge sort.
2  def mergeSort( theSeq ):
3    n = len( theSeq )
4     # Create a temporary array for use when merging subsequences.
5    tmpArray = Array( n )
6     # Call the private recursive merge sort function.
7    recMergeSort( theSeq, 0, n-1, tmpArray )
```

12.1.4 Efficiency Analysis

We provided two implementations for the merge sort algorithm: one that can only be used with lists and employs the slice operation, and another that can be used with arrays or lists but requires the use of a temporary array in merging virtual subsequences. Both implementations run in $O(n \log n)$ time. To see how we obtain this result, assume an array of n elements is passed to `recMergeSort()` on the first invocation of the recursive function. For simplicity, we can let n be a power of 2, which results in subsequences of equal size each time a list is split.

As we saw in Chapter 10, the running time of a recursive function is computed by evaluating the time required by each function invocation. This evaluation only includes the time of the steps actually performed in the given function invocation. The recursive steps are omitted since their times will be computed separately.

We can start by evaluating the time required for a single invocation of the `recMergeSort()` function. Since each recursive call reduces the size of the problem, we let m represent the number of keys in the subsequence passed to the current instance of the function (n represents the size of the entire array). When the function is executed, either the base case or the divide and conquer steps are performed. The base case occurs when the supplied sequence contains a single item ($m = 1$), which results in the function simply returning without having performed any operations. This of course only requires $O(1)$ time. The dividing step is also a constant time operation since it only requires computing the midpoint to determine where the virtual sequence will be split. The real work is done in the conquering step by the `mergeVirtualLists()` function. This function requires $O(m)$ time in the worst case where m represents the total number of items in both subsequences. The analysis for the merging operation follows that of the `mergeSortedLists()` from Chapter 5 and is left as an exercise. Having determined the time required of the various operations, we can conclude that a single invocation of the `recMergeSort()` function requires $O(m)$ time given a subsequence of m keys.

The next step is to determine the total time required to execute all invocations of the recursive function. This analysis is best described using a recursive call tree. Consider the call tree in Figure 12.5, which represents the merge sort algorithm when applied to a sequence containing 16 keys. The values inside the function call boxes show the size of the subsequence passed to the function for that invocation. Since we know a single invocation of the `recMergeSort()` function requires $O(m)$

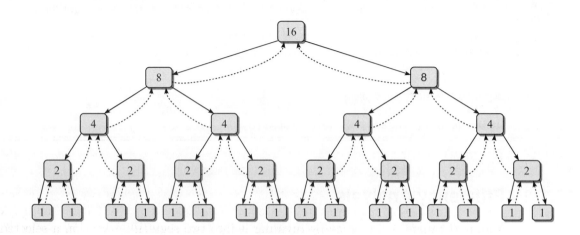

Figure 12.5: Recursive call tree for the merge sort algorithm for $n = 16$.

time, we can determine the time required for each instance of the function based on the size of the subsequence processed by that instance.

To obtain the total running time of the merge sort algorithm, we need to compute the sum of the individual times. In our sample call tree, where $n = 16$, the first recursive call processes the entire key list. This instance makes two recursive calls, each processing half $\left(\frac{n}{2}\right)$ of the original key sequence, as shown on the second level of the call tree. The two function instances at the second level of the call tree each make two recursive calls, all of which process one-fourth $\left(\frac{n}{4}\right)$ of the original key sequence. These recursive calls continue until the subsequence contains a single key value, as illustrated in the recursive call tree.

While each invocation of the function, other than the initial call, only processes a portion of the original key sequence, all n keys are processed at each level. If we can determine how many levels there are in the recursive call tree, we can multiply this value by the number of keys to obtain the final run time. When n is a power of 2, the merge sort algorithm requires $\log n$ levels of recursion. Thus, the merge sort algorithm requires $O(n \log n)$ time since there are $\log n$ levels and each level requires n time. The final analysis is illustrated graphically by the more general recursive call tree provided in Figure 12.6. When n is not a power of 2, the only difference in the analysis is that the lowest level in the call tree will not be completely full, but the call tree will still contain at most $\lceil \log n \rceil$ levels.

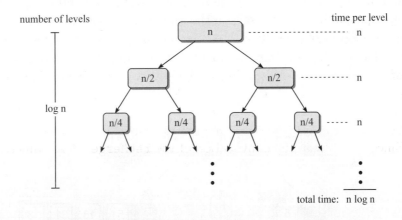

Figure 12.6: Time analysis of the merge sort algorithm.

12.2 Quick Sort

The *quick sort* algorithm also uses the divide and conquer strategy. But unlike the merge sort, which splits the sequence of keys at the midpoint, the quick sort partitions the sequence by dividing it into two segments based on a selected *pivot key*. In addition, the quick sort can be implemented to work with virtual subsequences without the need for temporary storage.

12.2.1 Algorithm Description

The quick sort is a simple recursive algorithm that can be used to sort keys stored in either an array or list. Given the sequence, it performs the following steps:

1. The first key is selected as the pivot, p. The pivot value is used to partition the sequence into two segments or subsequences, L and G, such that L contains all keys less than the p and G contains all keys greater than or equal to p.

2. The algorithm is then applied recursively to both L and G. The recursion continues until the base case is reached, which occurs when the sequence contains fewer than two keys.

3. The two segments and the pivot value are merged to produce a sorted sequence. This is accomplished by copying the keys from segment L back into the original sequence, followed by the pivot value and then the keys from segment G. After this step, the pivot key will end up in its proper position within the sorted sequence.

An abstract view of the partitioning step, in which much of the actual work is done, is illustrated in Figure 12.7. You will notice the size of the segments will vary depending on the value of the pivot. In some instances, one segment may not contain any elements. It depends on the pivot value and the relationship between that value and the other keys in the sequence. When the recursive calls return, the segments and pivot value are merged to produce a sorted sequence. This process is illustrated in Figure 12.8.

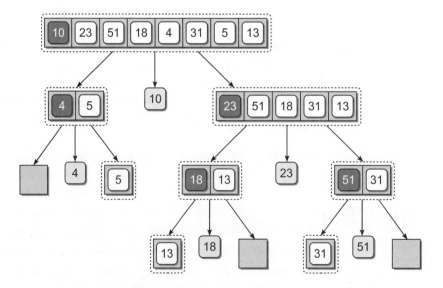

Figure 12.7: An abstract view showing how quick sort partitions the sequence into segments based on the pivot value (shown with a gray background).

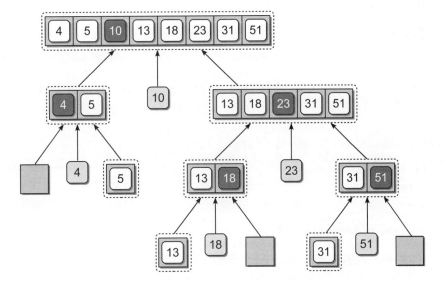

Figure 12.8: An abstract showing how quick sort merges the sorted segments and pivot value back into the original sequence.

12.2.2 Implementation

A simple implementation using the slice operation can be devised for the quick sort algorithm as was done with the merge sort but it would require the use of temporary storage. An efficient solution can be designed to work with virtual subsequences or segments that does not require temporary storage. However, it is not as easily implemented since the partitioning must be done using the same sequence structure.

A Python implementation of the quick sort algorithm is provided in Listing 12.5. The quickSort() function is a simple wrapper that is used to initiate the recursive call to recQuickSort(). The recursive function is rather simple and follows the enumerated steps described earlier. Note that first and last indicate the elements in the range [first...last] that comprise the current virtual segment.

The partitioning step is handled by the partitionSeq() function. This function rearranges the keys within the physical sequence structure by correctly positioning the pivot key within the sequence and placing all keys that are less than the pivot to the left and all keys that are greater to the right as shown here:

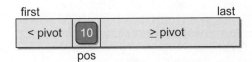

The final position of the pivot value also indicates the position at which the sequence is split to create the two segments. The left segment consists of the elements between the first element and the pos - 1 element while the right segment consists of the elements between pos + 1 and last, inclusive. The virtual segments

Listing 12.5   Implementation of the quick sort algorithm.

```python
1   # Sorts an array or list using the recursive quick sort algorithm.
2   def quickSort( theSeq ):
3     n = len( theSeq )
4     recQuickSort( theSeq, 0, n-1 )
5
6   # The recursive implementation using virtual segments.
7   def recQuickSort( theSeq, first, last ):
8       # Check the base case.
9     if first >= last :
10        return
11    else :
12        # Save the pivot value.
13      pivot = theSeq[first]
14
15        # Partition the sequence and obtain the pivot position.
16      pos = partitionSeq( theSeq, first, last )
17
18        # Repeat the process on the two subsequences.
19      recQuickSort( theSeq, first, pos - 1 )
20      recQuickSort( theSeq, pos + 1, last )
21
22  # Partitions the subsequence using the first key as the pivot.
23  def partitionSeq( theSeq, first, last ):
24      # Save a copy of the pivot value.
25    pivot = theSeq[first]
26
27      # Find the pivot position and move the elements around the pivot.
28    left = first + 1
29    right = last
30    while left <= right :
31        # Find the first key larger than the pivot.
32      while left < right and theSeq[left] < pivot :
33        left += 1
34
35        # Find the last key in the sequence that is smaller than the pivot.
36      while right >= left and theSeq[right] >= pivot :
37        right -= 1
38
39        # Swap the two keys if we have not completed this partition.
40      if left < right :
41        tmp = theSeq[left]
42        theSeq[left] =  theSeq[right]
43        theSeq[right] = tmp
44
45      # Put the pivot in the proper position.
46    if right != first :
47      theSeq[first] = theSeq[right]
48      theSeq[right] = pivot
49
50      # Return the index position of the pivot value.
51    return right
```

are passed to the recursive calls in lines 19 and 20 of Listing 12.5 using the proper index ranges.

After the recursive calls, the `recQuickSort()` function returns. In the earlier description, the sorted segments and pivot value had to be merged and stored back into the original sequence. But since we are using virtual segments, the keys are already stored in their proper position upon the return of the two recursive calls.

To help visualize the operation of the `partitionSeq()` function, we step through the first complete partitioning of the sample sequence. The function begins by saving a copy of the pivot value for easy reference and then initializes the two index markers, `left` and `right`. The `left` marker is initialized to the first position following the pivot value while the `right` marker is set to the last position within the virtual segment. The two markers are used to identify the range of elements within the sequence that will comprise the left and right segments.

The main loop is executed until one of the two markers crosses the other as they are shifted in opposite directions. The `left` marker is shifted to the right by the loop in lines 32 and 33 of Listing 12.5 until a key value larger than the pivot is found or the `left` marker crosses the `right` marker. Since the `left` marker starts at a key larger than the pivot, the body of the outer loop is not executed if `theSeq` is empty.

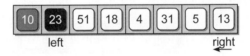

After the `left` marker is positioned, the `right` marker is then shifted to the left by the loop in lines 36 and 37. The marker is shifted until a key value less than or equal to the pivot is located or the marker crosses the `left` marker. The test for less than or equal allows for the correct sorting of duplicate keys. In our example, the `right` marker will be shifted to the position of the 5.

The two keys located at the positions marked by `left` and `right` are then swapped, which will place them within the proper segment once the location of the pivot is found.

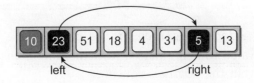

After the two keys are swapped, the two markers are again shifted starting where they left off:

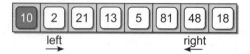

The `left` marker will be shifted to key value 51 and the `right` marker to value 4.

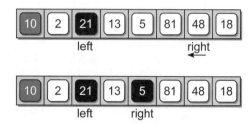

Once the two markers are shifted, the corresponding keys are swapped:

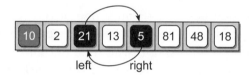

and the process is repeated. This time, the `left` marker will stop at value 18 while the `right` marker will stop at value 4.

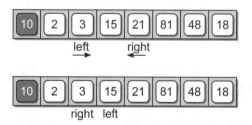

Note that the `right` marker has crossed the left such that `right < left`, resulting in the termination of the outer `while` loop. When the two markers cross, the `right` marker indicates the final position of the pivot value in the resulting sorted list. Thus, the pivot value currently located in the first element and the element marked by `right` have to be swapped:

resulting in value 10 being placed in element number 3, the final sorted position of the pivot within the original sequence:

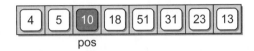

pos

The `if` statement at line 46 of Listing 12.5 is included to prevent a swap from occurring when the **right** marker is at the same position as the pivot value. This situation will occur when there are no keys in the list that are smaller than the pivot. Finally, the function returns the pivot position for use in splitting the sequence into the two segments.

We are not limited to selecting the first key within the list as the pivot, but it is the easiest to implement. We could have chosen the last key instead. But, in practice, using the first or last key as the pivot is a poor choice especially when a subsequence is already sorted that results in one of the segments being empty. Choosing a key near the middle is a better choice that can be implemented with a few modifications to the code provided. We leave these modifications as an exercise.

12.2.3 Efficiency Analysis

The quick sort algorithm has an average or expected time of $O(n \log n)$ but runs in $O(n^2)$ in the worst case, the analysis of which is left as an exercise. Even though quick sort is quadratic in the worst case, it does approach the average case in many instances and has the advantage of not requiring additional temporary storage as is the case with the merge sort. The quick sort is the commonly used algorithm to implement sorting in language libraries. Earlier versions of Python used quick sort to implement the `sort()` method of the list structure. In the current version of Python, a hybrid algorithm that combines the insertion and merge sort algorithms is used instead.

12.3 How Fast Can We Sort?

The comparison sort algorithms achieve their goal by comparing the individual sort keys to other keys in the list. We have reviewed five sorting algorithms in this chapter and Chapter 5. The first three—bubble, selection, and insertion—have a worst case time of $O(n^2)$ while the merge sort has a worst case time of $O(n \log n)$. The quick sort, the more commonly used algorithm in language libraries, is $O(n^2)$ in the worst case but it has an expected or average time of $O(n \log n)$. The natural question is can we do better than $O(n \log n)$? For a comparison sort, the answer is no. It can be shown, with the use of a decision tree and examining the permutations of all possible comparisons among the sort keys, that the worst case time for a comparison sort can be no better than $O(n \log n)$.

This does not mean, however, that the sorting operation cannot be done faster than $O(n \log n)$. It simply means that we cannot achieve this with a comparison sort. In the next section, we examine a distribution sort algorithm that works in linear time. Distribution sort algorithms use techniques other than comparisons among the keys themselves to sort the sequence of keys. While these distribution algorithms are fast, they are not general purpose sorting algorithms. In other words, they cannot be applied to just any sequence of keys. Typically, these algorithms are used when the keys have certain characteristics and for specific types of applications.

12.4   Radix Sort

Radix sort is a fast distribution sorting algorithm that orders keys by examining the individual components of the keys instead of comparing the keys themselves. For example, when sorting integer keys, the individual digits of the keys are compared from least significant to most significant. This is a special purpose sorting algorithm but can be used to sort many types of keys, including positive integers, strings, and floating-point values.

The radix sort algorithm also known as *bin sort* can be traced back to the time of punch cards and card readers. Card readers contained a number of bins in which punch cards could be placed after being read by the card reader. To sort values punched on cards the cards were first separated into 10 different bins based on the value in the ones column of each value. The cards would then be collected such that the cards in the bin representing zero would be placed on top, followed by the cards in the bin for one, and so on through nine. The cards were then sorted again, but this time by the tens column. The process continued until the cards were sorted by each digit in the largest value. The final result was a stack of punch cards with values sorted from smallest to largest.

12.4.1   Algorithm Description

To illustrate how the radix sort algorithm works, consider the array of values shown at the top of Figure 12.9. As with the card reader version, bins are used to store the various keys based on the individual column values. Since we are sorting positive integers, we will need ten bins, one for each digit.

The process starts by distributing the values among the various bins based on the digits in the ones column, as illustrated in step (a) of Figure 12.9. If keys have duplicate digits in the ones column, the values are placed in the bins in the order that they occur within the list. Thus, each duplicate is placed behind the keys already stored in the corresponding bin, as illustrated by the keys in bins 1, 3, and 8.

After the keys have been distributed based on the least significant digit, they are gathered back into the array, one bin at a time, as illustrated in step (b) of Figure 12.9. The keys are taken from each bin, without rearranging them, and inserted into the array with those in bin zero placed at the front, followed by those in bin one, then bin two, and so on until all of the keys are back in the sequence.

At this point, the keys are only partially sorted. The process must be repeated again, but this time the distribution is based on the digits in the tens column. After distributing the keys the second time, as illustrated in step (c) of Figure 12.9, they

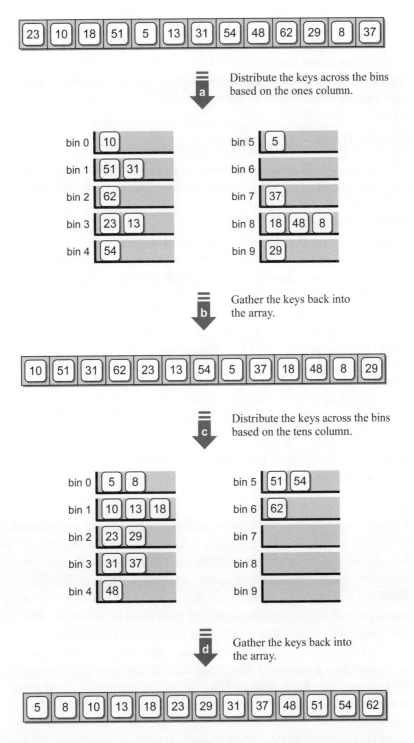

Figure 12.9: Sorting an array of integer keys using the radix sort algorithm.

are once again gathered back into the array, one bin at a time as shown in step (d). The result is a correct ordering of the keys from smallest to largest, as shown at the bottom of Figure 12.9.

In this example, the largest value (62) only contains two digits. Thus, we had to distribute and then gather the keys twice, once for the ones column and once for the tens column. If the largest value in the list had contain additional digits, the process would have to be repeated for each digit in that value.

12.4.2   Basic Implementation

The radix sort, as indicated earlier, is not a general purpose algorithm. Instead, it's used in special cases such as sorting records by zip code, Social Security number, or product codes. The sort keys can be represented as integers, reals, or strings. Different implementations are required, however, since the individual key components (digits or characters) differ based on the type of key. In addition, we must know the maximum number of digits or characters used by the largest key in order to know the number of iterations required to distribute the keys among the bins.

In this section, we implement a version of the radix sort algorithm for use with positive integer values stored in a mutable sequence. First, we must decide how to represent the bins used in distributing the values. Consider the following points related to the workings of the algorithm:

- The individual bins store groups of keys based on the individual digits.

- Keys with duplicate digits (in a given column) are stored in the same bin, but following any that are already there.

- When the keys are gathered from the bins, they have to be stored back into the original sequence. This is done by removing them from the bins in a first-in first-out ordering.

You may notice the bins sound very much like queues and in fact they can be represented as such. Adding a key to a bin is equivalent to enqueuing the key while removing the keys from the bins to put them back into the sequence is easily handled with the dequeue operation. Since there are ten digits, we will need ten queues. The queues can be stored in a ten-element array to provide easy management in the distribution and gathering of the keys. Our implementation of the radix sort algorithm is provided in Listing 12.6.

The function takes two arguments, the list of integer values to be sorted and the maximum number of digits possible in the largest key value. Instead of relying on the user to supply the number of digits, we could easily have searched for the largest key value in the sequence and then computed the number of digits in that value.

The implementation of the radix sort uses two loops nested inside an outer loop. The outer `for` loop iterates over the columns of digits with the number of iterations based on the user-supplied `numDigits` argument. The first nested loop in lines 19–21 distributes the keys across the bins. Since the queues are stored in

Listing 12.6   Implementation of the radix sort using an array of queues.

```
1   # Sorts a sequence of positive integers using the radix sort algorithm.
2
3   from llistqueue import Queue
4   from array import Array
5
6   def radixSort( intList, numDigits ):
7       # Create an array of queues to represent the bins.
8       binArray = Array( 10 )
9       for k in range( 10 ):
10          binArray[k] = Queue()
11
12      # The value of the current column.
13      column = 1
14
15      # Iterate over the number of digits in the largest value.
16      for d in range( numDigits ):
17
18          # Distribute the keys across the 10 bins.
19          for key in intList :
20              digit = (key // column) % 10
21              binArray[digit].enqueue( key )
22
23          # Gather the keys from the bins and place them back in intList.
24          i = 0
25          for bin in binArray :
26              while not bin.isEmpty() :
27                  intList[i] = bin.dequeue()
28                  i += 1
29
30          # Advance to the next column value.
31          column *= 10
```

the ten-element array, the distribution is easily handled by determining the bin or corresponding queue to which each key has to be added (based on the digit in the current column being processed) and enqueuing it in that queue. To extract the individual digits, we can use the following arithmetic expression:

```
digit = (key // columnValue) % 10
```

where `column` is the value $(1, 10, 100, \ldots)$ of the current column being processed. The variable is initialized to 1 since we work from the least-significant digit to the most significant. After distributing the keys and then gathering them back into the sequence, we can advance to the next column by simply multiplying the current value by 10, as is done at the bottom of the outer loop in line 31.

The second nested loop, in lines 24–28, handles the gathering step. To remove the keys from the queues and place them back into the sequence, we must dequeue all of the keys from each of the ten queues and add them to the sequence in successive elements starting at index position zero.

This implementation of the radix sort algorithm is straightforward, but it requires the use of multiple queues. To result in an efficient implementation, we must use the Queue ADT implemented as a linked list or have direct access to the underlying list in order to use the Python list version.

12.4.3   Efficiency Analysis

To evaluate the radix sort algorithm, assume a sequence of n keys in which each key contains d components in the largest key value and each component contains a value between 0 and $k-1$. Also assume we are using the linked list implementation of the Queue ADT, which results in $O(1)$ time queue operations.

The array used to store the k queues and the creation of the queues themselves can be done in $O(k)$ time. The distribution and gathering of the keys involves two steps, which are performed d times, one for each component:

- The distribution of the n keys across the k queues requires $O(n)$ time since an individual queue can be accessed directly by subscript.

- Gathering the n keys from the queues and placing them back into the sequence requires $O(n)$ time. Even though the keys have to be gathered from k queues, there are n keys in total to be dequeued resulting in the `dequeue()` operation being performed n times.

The distribution and gathering steps are performed d times, resulting in a time of $O(dn)$. Combining this with the initialization step we have an overall time of $O(k+dn)$. The radix sort is a special purpose algorithm and in practice both k and d are constants specific to the given problem, resulting in a linear time algorithm. For example, when sorting a list of integers, $k = 10$ and d can vary but commonly $d < 10$. Thus, the sorting time depends only on the number of keys.

12.5   Sorting Linked Lists

The sorting algorithms introduced in the previous sections and earlier in Chapter 5 can be used to sort keys stored in a mutable sequence. But what if we need to sort keys stored in an unsorted singly linked list such as the one shown in Figure 12.10? In this section, we explore that topic by reviewing two common algorithms that can be used to sort a linked list by modifying the links to rearrange the existing nodes.

The techniques employed by any of the three quadratic sorting algorithms—bubble, selection, and insertion—presented in Chapter 5 can be used to sort a linked list. Instead of swapping or shifting the values within the sequence, however, the nodes are rearranged by unlinking each node from the list and then relinking them at a different position. A linked list version of the bubble sort would rearrange the nodes within the same list by leap-frogging the nodes containing larger values over those with smaller values. The selection and insertion sorts, on the other hand, would create a new sorted linked list by selecting and unlinking nodes from the original list and adding them to the new list.

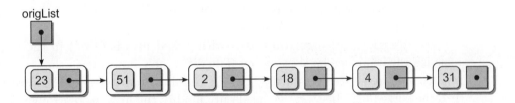

Figure 12.10: An unsorted singly linked list.

12.5.1 Insertion Sort

A simple approach for sorting a linked list is to use the technique employed by the insertion sort algorithm: take each item from an unordered list and insert them, one at a time, into an ordered list. When used with a linked list, we can unlink each node, one at a time, from the original unordered list and insert them into a new ordered list using the technique described in Chapter 6. The Python implementation is shown in Listing 12.7.

To create the sorted linked list using the insertion sort, we must unlink each node from the original list and insert them into a new ordered list. This is done in

---

Listing 12.7   Implementation of the insertion sort algorithm for use with a linked list.

```
1   # Sorts a linked list using the technique of the insertion sort. A
2   # reference to the new ordered list is returned.
3
4   def llistInsertionSort( origList ):
5     # Make sure the list contains at least one node.
6     if origList is None :
7       return None
8
9     # Iterate through the original list.
10    newList = None
11    while origList is not None :
12      # Assign a temp reference to the first node.
13      curNode = origList
14
15      # Advance the original list reference to the next node.
16      origList = origList.next
17
18      # Unlink the first node and insert into the new ordered list.
19      curNode.next = None
20      newList = addToSortedList( newList, curNode )
21
22    # Return the list reference of the new ordered list.
23    return newList
```

four steps, as illustrated in Figure 12.11 and implemented in lines 11–20. Inserting the node into the new ordered list is handled by the **addToSortedList()** function, which simply implements the operation from Listing 6.10. Figure 12.12 illustrates the results after each of the remaining iterations of the insertion sort algorithm when applied to our sample linked list.

The insertion sort algorithm used with linked lists is $O(n^2)$ in the worst case just like the sequence-based version. The difference, however, is that the items do not have to be shifted to make room for the unsorted items as they are inserted into the sorted list. Instead, we need only modify the links to rearrange the nodes.

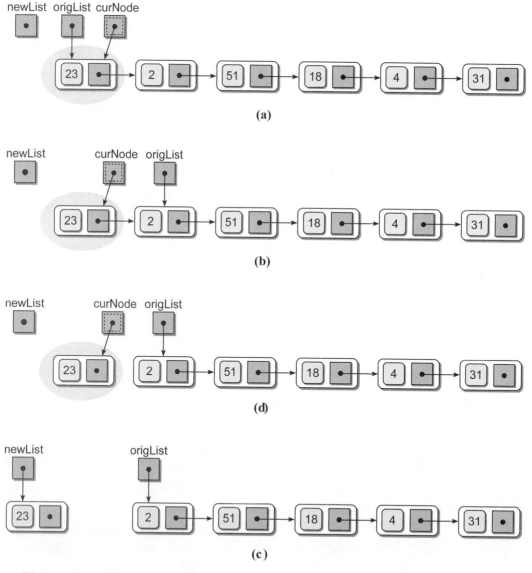

Figure 12.11: The individual steps performed in each iteration of the linked list insertion sort algorithm: (a) assign the temporary reference to the first node; (b) advance the list reference; (c) unlink the first node; and (d) insert the node into the new list.

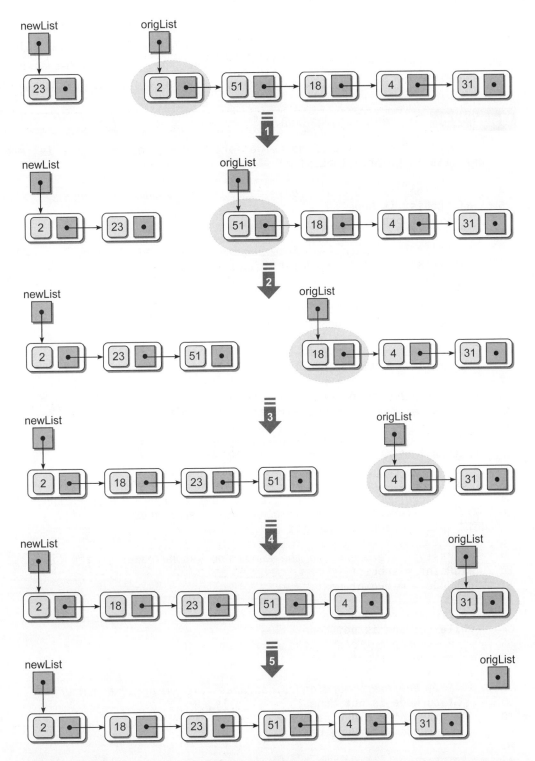

Figure 12.12: The results after each iteration of the linked list insertion sort algorithm.

12.5.2 Merge Sort

The merge sort algorithm is an excellent choice for sorting a linked list. Unlike the sequence-based version, which requires additional storage, when used with a linked list the merge sort is efficient in both time and space. The linked list version, which works in the same fashion as the sequence version, is provided in Listing 12.8.

Listing 12.8   The merge sort algorithm for linked lists.

```
1    # Sorts a linked list using merge sort. A new head reference is returned.
2    def llistMergeSort( theList ):
3
4      # If the list is empty (base case), return None.
5      if theList is None :
6        return None
7
8      # Split the linked list into two sublists of equal size.
9      rightList = _splitLinkedList( theList )
10     leftList = theList
11
12     # Perform the same operation on the left half...
13     leftList = llistMergeSort( leftList )
14
15     # ... and the right half.
16     rightList = llistMergeSort( rightList )
17
18     # Merge the two ordered sublists.
19     theList = _mergeLinkedLists( leftList, rightList )
20
21     # Return the head pointer of the ordered sublist.
22     return theList
23
24   # Splits a linked list at the midpoint to create two sublists. The
25   # head reference of the right sublist is returned. The left sublist is
26   # still referenced by the original head reference.
27   def _splitLinkedList( subList ):
28
29     # Assign a reference to the first and second nodes in the list.
30     midPoint = subList
31     curNode = midPoint.next
32
33     # Iterate through the list until curNode falls off the end.
34     while curNode is not None :
35       # Advance curNode to the next node.
36       curNode = curNode.next
37
38       # If there are more nodes, advance curNode again and midPoint once.
39       if curNode is not None :
40         midPoint = midPoint.next
41         curNode = curNode.next
42
43     # Set rightList as the head pointer to the right sublist.
44     rightList = midPoint.next
45     # Unlink the right sub list from the left sublist.
46     midPoint.next = None
```

```
47      # Return the right sub list head reference.
48    return rightList
49
50  # Merges two sorted linked list; returns head reference for the new list.
51  def _mergeLinkedLists( subListA, subListB ):
52    # Create a dummy node and insert it at the front of the list.
53    newList = ListNode( None )
54    newTail = newList
55
56      # Append nodes to the new list until one list is empty.
57    while subListA is not None and subListB is not None :
58      if subListA.data <= subListB.data :
59        newTail.next = subListA
60        subListA = subListA.next
61      else :
62        newTail.next = subListB
63        subListB = subListB.next
64
65      newTail = newTail.next
66      newTail.next = None
67
68      # If self list contains more terms, append them.
69    if subListA is not None :
70      newTail.next = subListA
71    else :
72      newTail.next = subListB
73
74      # Return the new merged list, which begins with the first node after
75      # the dummy node.
76    return newList.next
```

The linked list is recursively subdivided into smaller linked lists during each recursive call, which are then merged back into a new ordered linked list. Since the nodes are not contained within a single object as the elements of an array are, the head reference of the new ordered list has to be returned after the list is sorted. To sort a linked list using the merge sort algorithm, the sort function would be called using the statement:

```
theList = llistMergeSort( theList )
```

The implementation in Listing 12.8 includes the recursive function and two helper functions. You will note that a wrapper function is not required with this version since the recursive function only requires the head reference of the list being sorted as the single argument.

Splitting the List

The split operation is handled by the _splitLinkedList() helper function, which takes as an argument the head reference to the singly linked list to be split and returns the head reference for the right sublist. The left sublist can still be referenced by the original head reference. To split a linked list, we need to know the midpoint, or more specifically, the node located at the midpoint. An easy way to find the midpoint would be to traverse through the list and count the number of nodes and then iterate the list until the node at the midpoint is located. This is not the most efficient approach since it requires one and a half traversals through the list.

Instead, we can devise a solution that requires one complete list traversal, as shown in lines 27–48 of Listing 12.8. This approach uses two external references, `midPoint` and `curNode`. The two references are initialized with `midPoint` referencing the first node and `curNode` referencing the second node. The two references are advanced through the list using a loop as is done in a normal list traversal, but the `curNode` reference will advance twice as fast as the `midPoint` reference. The traversal continues until `curNode` becomes null, at which point the `midPoint` reference will be pointing to the last node in the left sublist. Figure 12.13 illustrates the traversal required to find the midpoint of our sample linked list.

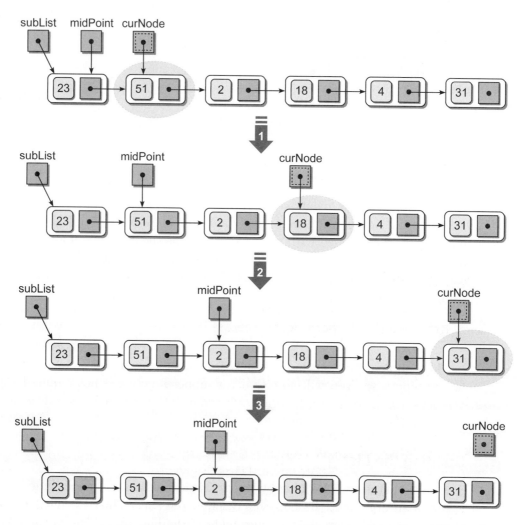

Figure 12.13: Sequence of steps for finding the midpoint in a linked list.

After the midpoint is located, the link between the node referenced by `midPoint` and its successor can be removed, creating two sublists, as illustrated in Figure 12.14. Before the link is removed, a new head reference `rightList` has to be created and initialized to reference the first node in the right sublist. The `rightList` head reference is returned by the function to provide access to the new sublist.

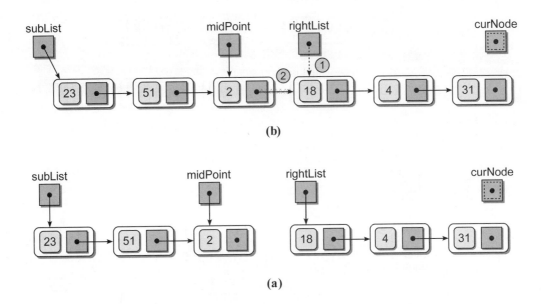

Figure 12.14: Splitting the list after finding the midpoint: (a) link modifications required to unlink the last node of the left sublist from the right sublist and (b) the two sublists resulting from the split.

Merging the Lists

The `_mergeLinkedLists()` function, provided in lines 51–76 of Listing 12.8, manages the merging of the two sorted linked lists. In Chapter 4, we discussed an efficient solution for the problem of merging two sorted Python lists, and earlier in this chapter that algorithm was adapted for use with arrays. The array and Python list versions are rather simple since we can refer to individual elements by index and easily append the values to the sequence structure.

Merging two sorted linked lists requires several modifications to the earlier algorithm. First, the nodes from the two sublists will be removed from their respective list and appended to a new sorted linked list. We can use a tail reference with the new sorted list to allow the nodes from the sublists to be appended in $O(1)$ time. Second, after all of the nodes have been removed from one of the two sublists, we do not have to iterate through the other list to append the nodes. Instead, we can simply link the last node of the new sorted list to the first node in the remaining sublist. Finally, we can eliminate the special case of appending the first node to the sorted list with the use of a ***dummy node*** at the front of the list, as illustrated in Figure 12.15. The dummy node is only temporary and will not be part of the final sorted list. Thus, after the two sublists have been merged, the function returns a reference to the second node in the list (the first real node following the dummy node), which becomes the head reference.

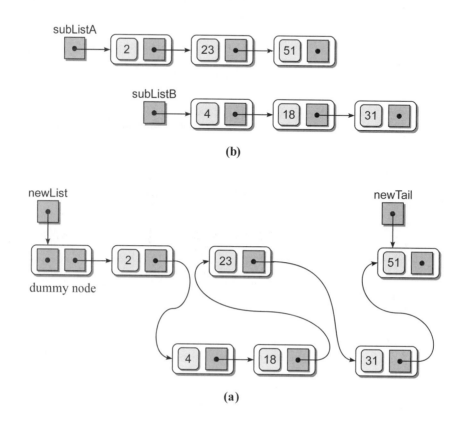

Figure 12.15: Merging two ordered linked lists using a dummy node and tail reference.

The linked list version of the merge sort algorithm is also a $O(n \log n)$ function but it does not require temporary storage to merge the sublists. The analysis of the run time is left as an exercise.

> **NOTE**
>
> ⓘ **Dummy Nodes.** A dummy node is a temporary node that is used to simplify link modifications when adding or removing nodes from a linked list. They are called dummy nodes because they contain no actual data. But they are part of the physical linked structure.

Exercises

12.1 Given the following sequence of keys (80, 7, 24, 16, 43, 91, 35, 2, 19, 72), trace the indicated algorithm to produce a recursive call tree when sorting the values in descending order.

(a) merge sort

(b) quick sort

12.2 Do the same as in Exercise 12.1 but produce a recursive call tree when sorting the values in ascending order.

12.3 Show the distribution steps performed by the radix sort when ordering the following list of keys:

(a) $135, 56, 21, 89, 395, 7, 178, 19, 96, 257, 34, 29$

(b) $1.25, 2.46, 0.34, 8.67, 3.21, 1.09, 3.33, 0.02, 5.44, 7.78, 1.93, 4.22$

(c) "MS", "VA", "AK", "LA", "CA", "AL", "GA", "TN", "WA", "DC"

12.4 Analyze the quick sort algorithm to show the worst case time is $O(n^2)$.

12.5 Analyze the `mergeVirtualSeq()` function and show that it is a linear time operation in the worst case.

12.6 Analyze the linked list version of the merge sort algorithm to show the worst case time is $O(n \log n)$.

12.7 An important property of sorting algorithms is stability. A sorting algorithm is **stable** if it preserves the original order of duplicate keys. Stability is important when sorting a collection that has already been sorted by a *primary key* that will now be sorted by a *secondary key*. For example, suppose we have a sequence of student records that have been sorted by name and now we want to sort the sequence by GPA. Since there can be many duplicate GPAs, we want to order any duplicates by name. Thus, if Smith and Green both have the same GPA, then Green would be listed before Smith. If the sorting algorithm used for this second sort is stable, then the proper ordering can be achieved since Green would appear before Smith in the original sequence.

(a) Determine which of the comparison sorts presented in this chapter and in Chapter 5 are stable sorts.

(b) For any of the algorithms that are not stable, provide a sequence containing some duplicate keys that shows the order of the duplicates is not preserved.

Programming Projects

12.1 Implement the `addToSortedList()` function for use with the linked list version of the insertion sort algorithm.

12.2 Create a linked list version of the indicated algorithm.

(a) bubble sort

(b) selection sort

12.3 Create a new version of the quick sort algorithm that chooses a different key as the pivot instead of the first element.

(a) select the middle element

(b) select the last element

12.4 Write a program to read a list of grade point averages $(0.0 - 4.0)$ from a text file and sort them in descending order. Select the most efficient sorting algorithm for your program.

12.5 Some algorithms are too complex to analyze using simple big-O notation or a representative data set may not be easily identifiable. In these cases, we must actually execute and test the algorithms on different sized data sets and compare the results. Special care must be taken to be fair in the actual implementation and execution of the different algorithms. This is known as an *empirical analysis*. We can also use an empirical analysis to verify and compare the time-complexities of a family of algorithms such as those for searching or sorting.

Design and implement a program to evaluate the efficiency of the comparison sorts used with sequences by performing an empirical analysis using random numbers. Your program should:

- Prompt the user for the size of the sequence: n.
- Generate a random list of n values (integers) from the range $[0 \ldots 4n]$.
- Sort the original list using each of the sorting algorithms, keeping track of the number of comparisons performed by each algorithm.
- Compute the average number of comparisons for each algorithm and then report the results.

When performing the empirical analysis on a family of algorithms, it is important that you use the same original sequence for each algorithm. Thus, instead of sorting the original sequence, you must make a duplicate copy of the original and sort that sequence in order to preserve the original for use with each algorithm.

## CHAPTER 13

Binary Trees

We have introduced and used several sequential structures throughout the text such as the array, Python list, linked list, stacks, and queues. These structures organize data in a linear fashion in which the data elements have a "before" and "after" relationship. They work well with many types of problems, but some problems require data to be organized in a nonlinear fashion. In this chapter, we explore the tree data structure, which can be used to arrange data in a hierarchical order. Trees can be used to solve many different problems, including those encountered in data mining, database systems, encryption, artificial intelligence, computer graphics, and operating systems.

13.1 The Tree Structure

A *tree* structure consists of nodes and edges that organize data in a hierarchical fashion. The relationships between data elements in a tree are similar to those of a family tree: "child," "parent," "ancestor," etc. The data elements are stored in **nodes** and pairs of nodes are connected by **edges**. The edges represent the relationship between the nodes that are linked with arrows or directed edges to form a **hierarchical structure** resembling an upside-down tree complete with branches, leaves, and even a root.

Formally, we can define a tree as a set of nodes that either is empty or has a node called the root that is connected by edges to zero or more subtrees to form a hierarchical structure. Each subtree is itself by definition a tree.

A classic example of a tree structure is the representation of directories and subdirectories in a file system. The top tree in Figure 13.1 illustrates the hierarchical nature of a student's home directory in the UNIX file system. Trees can be used to represent structured data, which results in the subdivision of data into smaller and smaller parts. A simple example of this use is the division of a book into its various parts of chapters, sections, and subsections, as illustrated by the bottom tree in Figure 13.1. Trees are also used for making decisions. One that you are most likely familiar with is the phone, or menu, tree. When you call customer service for most businesses today, you are greeted with an automated menu that you have to traverse. The various menus are nodes in a tree and the menu options from which you can choose are branches to other nodes.

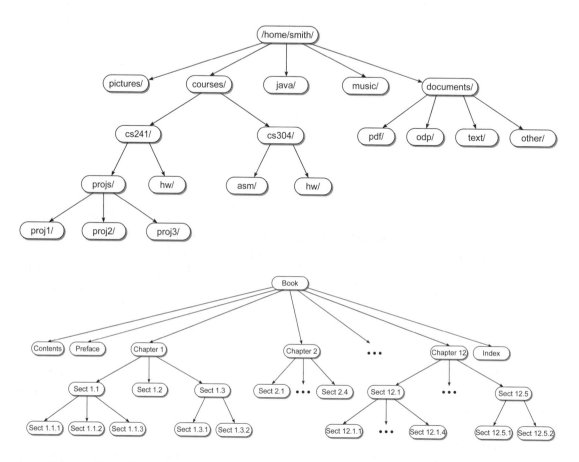

Figure 13.1: Example tree structures: a UNIX file system home directory (top) and the subdivision of a book into its parts (bottom).

We use many terms to describe the different characteristics and components of trees. Most of the terminology comes from that used to describe family relationships or botanical descriptions of trees. Knowing some of these terms will help you grasp the tree structure and its use in various applications.

Root

The topmost node of the tree is known as the ***root node***. It provides the single access point into the structure. The root node is the only node in the tree that does not have an incoming edge (an edge directed toward it). Consider the sample tree in Figure 13.2(a). The node with value T is the root of the tree. By definition, every non-empty tree must contain a root node.

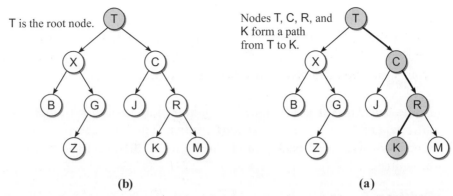

Figure 13.2: A sample tree with: (a) the root node; and (b) a path from T to K.

Path

The other nodes in the tree are accessed by following the edges starting with the root and progressing in the direction of the arrow until the destination node is reached. The nodes encountered when following the edges from a starting node to a destination form a ***path***. As shown in Figure 13.2(b), the nodes labeled T, C, R, and K form a path from node T to node K.

Parent

The organization of the nodes form relationships between the data elements. Every node, except the root, has a ***parent node***, which is identified by the incoming edge. A node can have only one parent (or incoming edge) resulting in a unique path from the root to any other node in the tree. There are a number of parent nodes in the sample tree: one is node X, which is the parent of B and G, as shown in Figure 13.3(a).

Children

Each node can have one or more ***child*** nodes resulting in a parent-child hierarchy. The children of a node are identified by the outgoing edges (directed away from the

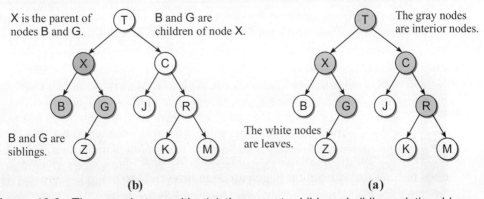

Figure 13.3: The sample tree with: (a) the parent, child, and sibling relationships; and (b) the distinction between interior and leaf nodes.

node). For example, nodes B and G are the children of X. All nodes that have the same parent are known as *siblings*, but there is no direct access between siblings. Thus, we cannot directly access node C from node X or vice versa.

Nodes

Nodes that have at least one child are known as *interior nodes* while nodes that have no children are known as *leaf nodes*. The interior nodes of the sample tree are shown with gray backgrounds in Figure 13.3(b) and the leaf nodes are shown in white.

Subtree

A tree is by definition a recursive structure. Every node can be the root of its own *subtree*, which consists of a subset of nodes and edges of the larger tree. Figure 13.4 shows the subtree with node C as its root.

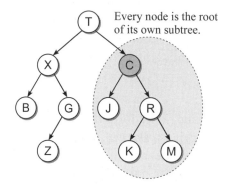

Figure 13.4: A subtree with root node C.

Relatives

All of the nodes in a subtree are *descendants* of the subtree's root. In the example tree, nodes J, R, K, and M are descendants of node C. The *ancestors* of a node include the parent of the node, its grandparent, its great-grandparent, and so on all the way up to the root. The ancestors of a node can also be identified by the nodes along the path from the root to the given node. The root node is the ancestor of every node in the tree and every node in the tree is a descendant of the root node.

> **NOTE**
>
> **Binary Tree Illustrations.** The trees illustrated above used directed edges to indicate the parent-child relationship between the nodes. But it's not uncommon to see trees drawn using straight lines or undirected edges. When a tree is drawn without arrows, we have to be able to deduce the parent-child relationship from the placement of the nodes. Thus, the parent is always placed above its children. With binary trees, the left and right children are always drawn offset from the parent in the appropriate direction in order to easily identify the specific child node.

13.2   **The Binary Tree**

Trees can come in many different shapes, and they can vary in the number of children allowed per node or in the way they organize data values within the nodes. One of the most commonly used trees in computer science is the binary tree. A *binary tree* is a tree in which each node can have at most two children. One child is identified as the *left child* and the other as the *right child*. In the remainder of the chapter, we focus on the use and construction of the binary tree. In the next chapter, we will continue our discussion of binary trees but also explore other types.

13.2.1   **Properties**

Binary trees come in many different shapes and sizes. The shapes vary depending on the number of nodes and how the nodes are linked. Figure 13.5 illustrates three different shapes of a binary tree consisting of nine nodes. There are a number of properties and characteristics associated with binary trees, all of which depend on the organization of the nodes within the tree.

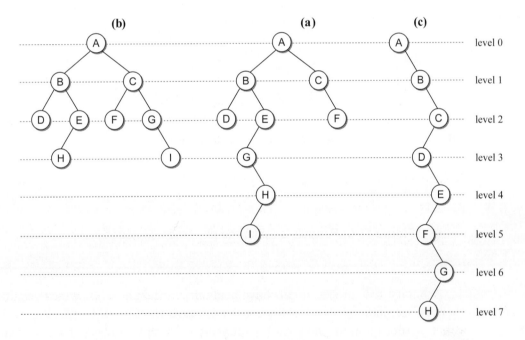

Figure 13.5: Three different arrangements of nine nodes in a binary tree.

Tree Size

The nodes in a binary tree are organized into *levels* with the root node at level 0, its children at level 1, the children of level one nodes are at level 2, and so on. In family tree terminology, each level corresponds to a generation. The binary tree in Figure 13.5(a), for example, contains two nodes at level one (B and C), four nodes at level two (D, E, F, and G), and two nodes at level three (H and I). The root node always occupies level zero.

The **depth** of a node is its distance from the root, with distance being the number of levels that separate the two. A node's depth corresponds to the level it occupies. Consider node G in the three trees of Figure 13.5. In tree (a), G has a depth of 2, in tree (b) it has a depth of 3, and in (c) its depth is 6.

The **height** of a binary tree is the number of levels in the tree. For example, the three binary trees in Figure 13.5 have different heights: (a) has a height of 4, (b) has a height of 6, and (c) has a height of 8. The **width** of a binary tree is the number of nodes on the level containing the most nodes. In the three binary trees of Figure 13.5, (a) has a width of 4, (b) has a width of 3, and (c) has a width of 1. Finally, the **size** of a binary tree is simply the number of nodes in the tree. An empty tree has a height of 0 and a width of 0, and its size is 0.

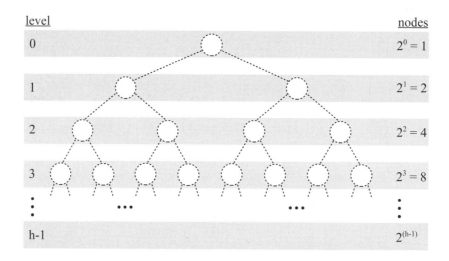

Figure 13.6: Possible slots for the placement of nodes in a binary tree.

A binary tree of size n can have a maximum height of n, which results when there is one node per level. This is the case with the binary tree in Figure 13.5(c). What is the minimum height of a binary tree with n nodes? To determine this, we need to consider the maximum number of nodes at each level since the nodes will have to be organized with each level at full capacity. Figure 13.6 illustrates the slots for the possible placement of nodes within a binary tree. Since each node can have at most two children, each successive level in the tree doubles the number of nodes contained on the previous level. This corresponds to a given tree level i having a capacity for 2^i nodes. If we sum the size of each level, when all of the levels are filled to capacity, except possibly the last one, we find that the minimum height of a binary tree of size n is $\lfloor \log_2 n \rfloor + 1$.

Tree Structure

The height of the tree will be important in analyzing the time-complexities of various algorithms applied to binary trees. The structural properties of binary trees can also play a role in the efficiency of an algorithm. In fact, some algorithms require specific tree structures.

A *full binary tree* is a binary tree in which each interior node contains two children. Full trees come in many different shapes, as illustrated in Figure 13.7.

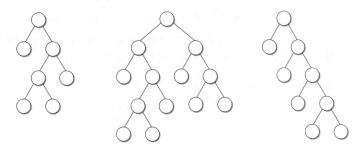

Figure 13.7: Examples of full binary trees.

A *perfect binary tree* is a full binary tree in which all leaf nodes are at the same level. The perfect tree has all possible node slots filled from top to bottom with no gaps, as illustrated in Figure 13.8.

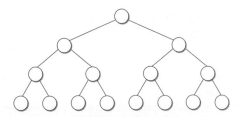

Figure 13.8: A perfect binary tree.

A binary tree of height h is a *complete binary tree* if it is a perfect binary tree down to height $h - 1$ and the nodes on the lowest level fill the available slots from left to right leaving no gaps. Consider the two complete binary trees in Figure 13.9. If any of the three leaf nodes labeled A, B, or C in the left tree were missing, that tree would not be complete. Likewise, if either leaf node labeled X or Y in the right tree were missing, it would not be complete.

13.2.2 Implementation

Binary trees are commonly implemented as a dynamic structure in the same fashion as linked lists. A binary tree is a data structure that can be used to implement many different abstract data types. Since the operations that a binary tree supports

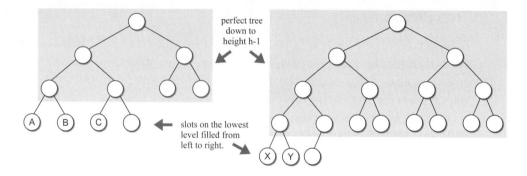

Figure 13.9: Examples of complete binary trees.

depend on its application, we are going to create and work with the trees directly instead of creating a generic binary tree class.

Trees are generally illustrated as abstract structures with the nodes represented as circles or boxes and the edges as lines or arrows. To implement a binary tree, however, we must explicitly store in each node the links to the two children along with the data stored in that node. We define the _BinTreeNode storage class, shown in Listing 13.1, for creating the nodes in a binary tree. Like other storage classes, the tree node class is meant for internal use only. Figure 13.10 illustrates the physical implementation of the sample binary tree from Figure 13.4.

Listing 13.1   The binary tree node class.

```
1  # The storage class for creating binary tree nodes.
2  class _BinTreeNode :
3    def __init__( self, data ):
4      self.data = data
5      self.left = None
6      self.right = None
```

13.2.3   Tree Traversals

The operations that can be performed on a binary tree depend on the application, especially the construction of the tree. In this section, we explore the tree traversal operation, which is one of the most common operations performed on collections of data. Remember, a traversal iterates through a collection, one item at a time, in order to access or visit each item. The actual operation performed when "visiting" an item is application dependent, but it could involve something as simple as printing the data item or saving it to a file.

With a linear structure such as a linked list, the traversal is rather easy since we can start with the first node and iterate through the nodes, one at at time, by following the links between the nodes. But how do we visit every node in a binary tree? There is no single path from the root to every other node in the tree. Remember, the links between the nodes lead us down into the tree. If we were to

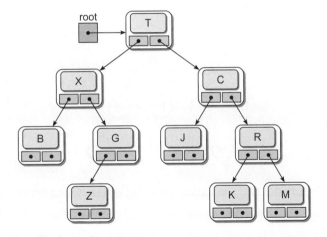

Figure 13.10: The physical implementation of a binary tree.

simply follow the links, once we reach a leaf node we cannot directly access any other node in the tree.

Preorder Traversal

A tree traversal must begin with the root node, since that is the only access into the tree. After visiting the root node, we can then traverse the nodes in its left subtree followed by the nodes in its right subtree. Since every node is the root of its own subtree, we can repeat the same process on each node, resulting in a recursive solution. The base case occurs when a null child link is encountered since there will be no subtree to be processed from that link. The recursive operation can be viewed graphically, as illustrated in Figure 13.11.

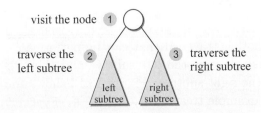

Figure 13.11: Trees are traversed recursively.

Consider the binary tree in Figure 13.12. The dashed lines show the logical order the nodes would be visited during the traversal: A, B, D, E, H, C, F, G, I, J. This traversal is known as a ***preorder traversal*** since we first visit the node followed by the subtree traversals.

The recursive function for a preorder traversal of a binary tree is rather simple, as shown in Listing 13.2. The subtree argument will either be a null reference or a reference to the root of a subtree in the binary tree. If the reference is not None, the node is first visited and then the two subtrees are traversed. By convention, the left subtree is always visited before the right subtree. The subtree argument

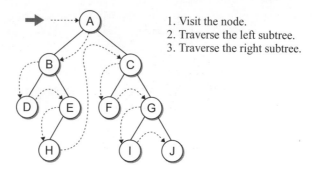

1. Visit the node.
2. Traverse the left subtree.
3. Traverse the right subtree.

Figure 13.12: The logical ordering of the nodes with a preorder traversal.

will be a null reference when the binary tree is empty or we attempt to follow a non-existent link for one or both of the children.

Given a binary tree of size n, a complete traversal of a binary tree visits each node once. If the visit operation only requires constant time, the tree traversal can be done in $O(n)$.

Listing 13.2   Preorder traversal on a binary tree.

```
1  def preorderTrav( subtree ):
2    if subtree is not None :
3      print( subtree.data )
4      preorderTrav( subtree.left )
5      preorderTrav( subtree.right )
```

Inorder Traversal

In the preorder traversal, we chose to first visit the node and then traverse both subtrees. Another traversal that can be performed is the *inorder traversal*, in which we first traverse the left subtree and then visit the node followed by the traversal of the right subtree. Figure 13.13 shows the logical ordering of the node visits in the example tree: D, B, H, E, A, F, C, I, G, J.

The recursive function for an inorder traversal of a binary tree is provided in Listing 13.3. It is almost identical to the preorder traversal function. The only difference is the visit operation is moved following the traversal of the left subtree.

Listing 13.3   Inorder traversal on a binary tree.

```
1  def inorderTrav( subtree ):
2    if subtree is not None :
3      inorderTrav( subtree.left )
4      print( subtree.data )
5      inorderTrav( subtree.right )
```

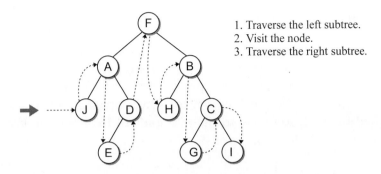

1. Traverse the left subtree.
2. Visit the node.
3. Traverse the right subtree.

Figure 13.13: The logical ordering of the nodes with an inorder traversal.

Postorder Traversal

We can also perform a *postorder traversal*, which can be viewed as the opposite of the preorder traversal. In a postorder traversal, the left and right subtrees of each node are traversed before the node is visited. The recursive function is provided in Listing 13.4.

Listing 13.4   Postorder traversal on a binary tree.

```
1  def postorderTrav( subtree ):
2    if subtree is not None :
3      postorderTrav( subtree.left )
4      postorderTrav( subtree.right )
5      print( subtree.data )
```

The example tree with the logical ordering of the node visits in a postorder traversal is shown in Figure 13.14. The nodes are visited in this order: D, H, E, B, F, I, J, G, C, A. You may notice that the root node is always visited first in a preorder traversal but last in a postorder traversal.

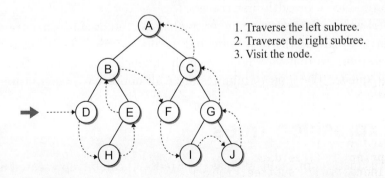

1. Traverse the left subtree.
2. Traverse the right subtree.
3. Visit the node.

Figure 13.14: The logical ordering of the nodes with a postorder traversal.

Breadth-First Traversal

The preorder, inorder, and postorder traversals are all examples of a **depth-first traversal**. That is, the nodes are traversed deeper in the tree before returning to higher-level nodes. Another type of traversal that can be performed on a binary tree is the **breadth-first traversal**. In a breadth-first traversal, the nodes are visited by level, from left to right. Figure 13.15 shows the logical ordering of the nodes in a breadth-first traversal of the example tree.

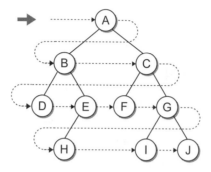

Figure 13.15: The logical ordering of the nodes with a breadth-first traversal.

Recursion cannot be used to implement a breadth-first traversal since the recursive calls must follow the links that lead deeper into the tree. Instead, we must devise another approach. Your first attempt might be to visit a node followed by its two children. Thus, in the example tree we would visit node A followed by nodes B and C, which is the correct ordering. But what happens when we visit node B? We can't visit its two children, D and E, until after we have visited node C. What we need is a way to remember or save the two children of B until after C has been visited. Likewise, when visiting node C, we will have to save its two children until after the children of B have been visited. After visiting node C, we have saved four nodes—D, E, F, and G—which are the next four to be visited, in the order they were saved. The best way to save a node's children for later access is to use a queue. We can then use an iterative loop to move across the tree in the correct node order to produce a breadth-first traversal.

Listing 13.5 uses a queue to implement the breadth-first traversal. The process starts by saving the root node and in turn priming the iterative loop. During each iteration, we remove a node from the queue, visit it, and then add its children to the queue. The loop terminates after all nodes have been visited.

13.3 Expression Trees

Arithmetic expressions such as $(9+3)*(8-4)$ can be represented using an expression tree. An **expression tree** is a binary tree in which the operators are stored in the interior nodes and the operands (the variables or constant values) are stored

---
Listing 13.5 Breadth-first traversal on a binary tree.

```
1  def breadthFirstTrav( bintree ):
2      # Create a queue and add the root node to it.
3      Queue q
4      q.enqueue( bintree )
5
6      # Visit each node in the tree.
7      while not q.isEmpty() :
8          # Remove the next node from the queue and visit it.
9          node = q.dequeue()
10         print( node.data )
11
12         # Add the two children to the queue.
13         if node.left is not None :
14             q.enqueue( node.left )
15         if node.right is not None :
16             q.enqueue( node.right )
```

---

in the leaves. Once constructed, an expression tree can be used to evaluate the expression or for converting an infix expression to either prefix or postfix notation.

The structure of the expression tree is based on the order in which the operators are evaluated. The operator in each internal node is evaluated after both its left and right subtrees have been evaluated. Thus, the lower an operator is in a subtree, the earlier it will be evaluated. The root node contains the operator to be evaluated. Figure 13.16 illustrates several expression trees.

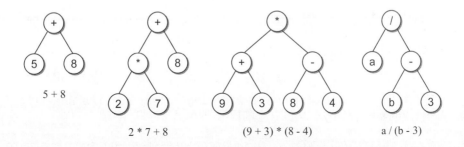

$5 + 8$

$2 * 7 + 8$

$(9 + 3) * (8 - 4)$

$a / (b - 3)$

Figure 13.16: Sample arithmetic expression trees.

While Python provides the `eval()` function for evaluating an arithmetic expression stored as a string, the string must be parsed each time it's evaluated. This means the Python interpreter has to determine the order in which the operators are evaluated and then perform each of the corresponding operations. One way it can do this is with the use of an expression tree. After the expression has been parsed and the tree constructed, the evaluation step is quite simple, as you will see later in this section. This real-time evaluation of expression strings is not commonly available in compiled languages. When using such a language and a user-supplied expression has to be evaluated, an expression tree can be constructed and evaluated to obtain the result.

13.3.1   Expression Tree Abstract Data Type

Arithmetic expressions can consist of both unary (-a, n!) and binary operators (a + b). We only consider expressions containing binary operators and leave the inclusion of unary operators as an exercise. Binary operators are stored in an expression tree with the left subtree containing the left side of the operation and the right subtree containing the right side. We define the Expression Tree ADT below for use with arithmetic expressions consisting of operands comprised of single-integer digits or single-letter variables.

Define	Expression Tree ADT

An *expression tree* is a binary tree representation of an arithmetic expression that consists of various operators (+, -, *, /, %) and operands comprised of single integer digits and single-letter variables within a fully parenthesized expression.

- ExpressionTree(expStr): Builds an expression tree for the expression given in expStr. Assume the string contains a valid, fully parenthesized expression.

- evaluate(varDict): Evaluates the expression tree and returns the numeric result. The values of the single-letter variables are extracted from the supplied dictionary structure. An exception is raised if there is a division by zero error or an undefined variable is used.

- *toString* (): Constructs and returns a string representation of the expression.

The Expression Tree ADT can be used to evaluate basic arithmetic expressions of any size. The following example illustrates the use of the ADT:

```
# Create a dictionary containing values for the one-letter variables.
vars = { 'a' : 5, 'b' : 12 }

# Build the tree for a sample expression and then evaluate it.
expTree = expressionTree( "(a/(b-3))" )
print( "The result = ", expTree.evaluate(vars) )

# We can change the value assigned to a variable and reevaluate.
vars['a'] = 22
print( "The result = ", expTree.evaluate(vars) )
```

In the following sections we develop algorithms for constructing and evaluating arithmetic expression trees in order to implement the ExpressionTree class. A partial implementation is provided in Listing 13.6. All of the operations will require a recursive algorithm that is applied to the tree structure. Thus, each will call a helper method to which the root reference will be passed in order to initiate the recursion. If the helper methods were not used, the client or user code would have to have access to the root reference in order to pass it to the recursive operation.

| Listing 13.6 | The `exptree.py` module. |

```
1   class ExpressionTree :
2      # Builds an expression tree for the expression string.
3      def __init__( self, expStr ):
4        self._expTree = None
5        self._buildTree( expStr )
6
7      # Evaluates the expression tree and returns the resulting value.
8      def evaluate( self, varMap ):
9        return self._evalTree( self._expTree, varMap )
10
11     # Returns a string representation of the expression tree.
12     def __str__( self ):
13       return self._buildString( self._expTree )
14  # ...
15
16  # Storage class for creating the tree nodes.
17  class _ExpTreeNode :
18     def __init__( self, data ):
19       self.element = data
20       self.left = None
21       self.right = None
```

The constructor creates a single data field for storing the reference to the root node of the tree. The `_buildTree()` helper method is then called to actually construct the tree. The `evaluate()` and `__str__` methods each call their own helper method and simply return the value returned by the helper. The nodes of the expression tree will be created by the `_ExpTreeNode` storage class, as shown in lines 17–21. The helper methods will be developed in the following sections.

13.3.2 String Representation

Before looking at how we create and evaluate expression trees, let's consider the results of performing the three depth-first traversals on an arithmetic expression tree. Consider the larger expression tree from Figure 13.17 and suppose we perform a postorder traversal on the tree. The order the nodes are visited is:

8 5 * 9 7 4 - / +

What does this ordering represent? If you look closely, you should notice it as the postfix representation for the expression 8 * 5 + 9 / (7 - 4). Thus, a postorder traversal can be used to convert an arithmetic expression tree to the equivalent postfix expression while a preorder traversal will produce the equivalent prefix expression. So, in what order would the nodes be visited by an inorder traversal?

8 * 5 + 9 / 7 - 4

It appears to be the infix representation, but notice the result is not correct since the parentheses around (7 - 4) were omitted. Even though this result is incorrect, we can develop an algorithm that uses a combination of all three depth-first

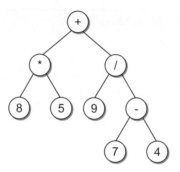

Figure 13.17: Expression tree for $8 * 5 + 9/(7 - 4)$.

traversals to produce the correct expression. Trying to determine the minimum sets of parentheses that are required can be difficult, but we can easily create a fully parenthesized expression: `((8 * 5) + (9 / (7 - 4)))`. We know an in-order traversal produces the correct ordering of operators and operands for the resulting expression. We just have to figure out how to insert the parentheses.

In a fully parenthesized expression, a pair of parentheses encloses each operator and its operands. Thus, we need to enclose each subtree within a pair of parentheses, as illustrated in Figure 13.18. A left parenthesis needs to be printed before a subtree is visited, whereas the right one needs to be printed after the subtree has been visited. We can combine all three traversals in a single recursive operation, as shown in Listing 13.7.

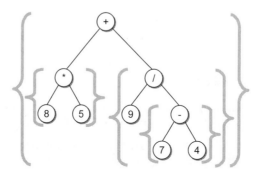

Figure 13.18: Expression tree with braces grouping the subtrees.

13.3.3 Tree Evaluation

Given an algebraic expression represented as a binary tree, we can develop an algorithm to evaluate the expression. Each subtree represents a valid subexpression with those lower in the tree having higher precedence. Thus, the two subtrees of each interior node must be evaluated before the node itself. For example, in the expression tree from Figure 13.17, the addition operation cannot be performed until both subexpressions (the multiplication and the division) have been computed as

Listing 13.7   The `_buildString` helper method.

```
1  class ExpressionTree :
2  # ...
3      # Recursively builds a string representation of the expression tree.
4      def _buildString( self, treeNode ):
5          # If the node is a leaf, it's an operand.
6      if treeNode.left is None and treeNode.right is None :
7          return str( treeNode.element )
8      else :   # Otherwise, it's an operator.
9          expStr = '('
10         expStr += self._buildString( treeNode.left )
11         expStr += str( treeNode.element )
12         expStr += self._buildString( treeNode.right )
13         expStr += ')'
14         return expStr
```

their results are needed by the operation. Further, the division cannot be evaluated until the subtraction of (7 - 4) has been computed.

We have already discussed two versions of an algorithm that processes both subtrees of a node before the node itself. Remember, this was the technique employed by both the preorder and postorder traversals. We can use one of these to evaluate an expression tree. The difference is that the visit operation is only applied to the operator (interior) nodes and a visit becomes the evaluation of the operation applied to the value of both subtrees. The recursive function for evaluating an expression tree and returning the result is provided in Listing 13.8.

Listing 13.8   Evaluate an expression tree.

```
1  class ExpressionTree :
2  # ...
3      def _evalTree( self, subtree, varDict ):
4          # See if the node is a leaf node, in which case return its value.
5      if subtree.left is None and subtree.right is None :
6          # Is the operand a literal digit?
7          if subtree.element >= '0' and subtree.element <= '9' :
8              return int(subtree.element)
9          else :   # Or is it a variable?
10             assert subtree.element in varDict, "Invalid variable."
11             return varDict[subtree.element]
12
13         # Otherwise, it's an operator that needs to be computed.
14     else :
15         # Evaluate the expression in the left and right subtrees.
16         lvalue = _evalTree( subtree.left, varDict )
17         rvalue = _evalTree( subtree.right, varDict )
18         # Evaluate the operator using a helper method.
19         return computeOp( lvalue, subtree.element, rvalue )
20
21     # Compute the arithmetic operation based on the supplied op string.
22     def _computeOp( left, op, right ):
23         ......
```

When a leaf node is encountered, we know it contains an operand. But we must determine if that operand is a single-integer digit, in which case the integer value can be returned, or if it's a single-letter variable. In the case of the latter, the value for the variable must be located and returned from the user-supplied dictionary. For interior nodes, the two subtrees are evaluated by recursively calling the _evalTree() function. After the two recursive calls return, the operation represented by the interior node can be computed. The computation is performed using the _computeOp() helper function, which performs the appropriate arithmetic operation based on the given operator. The implementation of _computeOp() is left as an exercise. The recursive call tree for the _evalStr() method is shown in Figure 13.19 when applied to the expression tree from Figure 13.17.

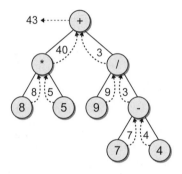

Figure 13.19: The recursive call tree for the _evalStr() function.

13.3.4 Tree Construction

You have seen how an expression tree is used; now let's look at how to construct the tree given an infix expression. For simplicity, we assume the following: (1) the expression is stored in string with no white space; (2) the supplied expression is valid and fully parenthesized; (3) each operand will be a single-digit or single-letter variable; and (4) the operators will consist of +, -, *, /, and %.

An expression tree is constructed by parsing the expression and evaluating the individual tokens. As the tokens are evaluated, new nodes are inserted into the tree for both the operators and operands. Each set of parentheses will consist of an interior node containing the operator and two children, which may be single valued or subtrees representing subexpressions. The process starts with an empty root node set as the current node:

root

current ➝

Suppose we are building the tree for the expression (8*5). The action taken depends on the value of the current token. The first token is a left parenthesis.

When a left parenthesis is encountered, a new node is created and linked into the tree as the left child of the current node. We then descend down to the new node, making the left child the new current node.

The next token is the operand: 8. When an operand is encountered, the data value of the current node is set to contain the operand. We then move up to the parent of the current node.

Next comes the plus operator. When an operator is encountered, the data value of the current node is set to the operator. A new node is then created and linked into the tree as the right child of the current node. We descend down to the new node.

The second operand, 5, repeats the same action taken with the first operand:

Finally, the right parenthesis is encountered and we move up to the parent of the current node. In this case, we have reached the end of the expression and the tree is complete.

Constructing the expression tree involves performing one of five different steps for each token in the expression. This same process can be used on larger expressions to construct each part of the tree. Consider Figure 13.20, which illustrates the steps required to build the tree for the expression ((2*7)+8). The steps illustrated in the figure are described below:

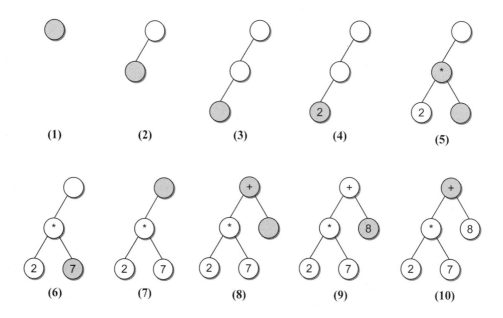

Figure 13.20: Steps for building an expression tree for $((2 * 7) + 8)$.

1. Create an empty root node and mark it as the current node.

2. Read the left parenthesis: add a new node as the left child and descend down to the new node.

3. Read the next left parenthesis: add a new node as the left child and descend down to the new node.

4. Read the operand 2: set the value of the current node to the operand and move up to the parent of the current node.

5. Read the operator *: set the value of the current node to the operator and create a new node linked as the right child. Then descend down to the new node.

6. Read the operand 7: set the value of the current node to the operand and move up to the parent of the current node.

7. Read the right parenthesis: move up to the parent of the current node.

8. Read the operator +: set the value of the current node to the operator and create a new node linked as the right child; descend down to the new node.

9. Read the operand 8: set the value of the current node to the operand and move up to the parent of the current node.

10. Read the right parenthesis: move up to the parent of the current node. Since this is the last token, we are finished and the expression tree is complete.

Having stepped through the construction of two sample expressions, we now turn our attention to the implementation of the method for building an expression tree. Throughout the process we have to descend down into the tree to construct each side of an operator and then back up when a right parenthesis is encountered. But how do we remember where we were in order to back up? There are two approaches we can use. One involves the use of a stack and the other recursion. In Chapter 10, you saw that backtracking is automatically handled by the recursion as the recursive calls unwind. Given this simplicity, we implement a recursive function to build an expression tree, as shown in Listing 13.9.

Listing 13.9   Constructing an expression tree.

```
 1  class ExpressionTree :
 2  # ...
 3    def _buildTree( self, expStr ):
 4      # Build a queue containing the tokens in the expression string.
 5      expQ = Queue()
 6      for token in expStr :
 7        expQ.enqueue( token )
 8
 9      # Create an empty root node.
10      self._expTree = _ExpTreeNode( None )
11      # Call the recursive function to build the expression tree.
12      self._recBuildTree( self._expTree, expQ )
13
14    # Recursively builds the tree given an initial root node.
15    def _recBuildTree( self, curNode, expQ ):
16      # Extract the next token from the queue.
17      token = expQ.dequeue()
18
19      # See if the token is a left paren: '('
20      if token == '(' :
21        curNode.left = _ExpTreeNode( None )
22        buildTreeRec( curNode.left, expQ )
23
24        # The next token will be an operator: + - / * %
25        curNode.data = expQ.dequeue()
26        curNode.right = _ExpTreeNode( None )
27        self._buildTreeRec( curNode.right, expQ )
28
29        # The next token will be a ), remove it.
30        expQ.dequeue()
31
32      # Otherwise, the token is a digit that has to be converted to an int.
33      else :
34        curNode.element = token
```

The _recBuildTree() method takes two arguments, a reference to the current node and a queue containing the tokens that have yet to be processed. The use of the queue is the easiest way to keep track of the tokens throughout the recursive process. We indicated earlier that the expression will be supplied as a string, but strings in Python are immutable, which makes it difficult to remove the tokens as they are processed. The queue, which was introduced in Chapter 8, is the best choice since the tokens will be processed in a FIFO order.

The non-recursive _buildTree() method creates a queue and fills it with the tokens from the expression, as shown in lines 5–7 of Listing 13.9. The code in this method can actually be placed within the constructor. We only used this helper method in order to hide the tree construction details in the initial presentation of the ExpressionTree class in Listing 13.6 until the actual operation was presented. The recursive function assumes the root node has been created before the first invocation. Thus, after building the token queue in _buildTree(), an empty root node is created and the two structures are passed to the recursive function.

The _recBuildTree() method implements the five operations for building the expression tree as described earlier. If you review those steps, you will notice the only times we descend down the tree is after encountering a left parenthesis or an operator. After moving down to either the left or right child node, the next token encountered must be either a left parenthesis or an operand. Thus, the function extracts the next token to be processed and then evaluates it to see if it is either a (or an operand. If the token is an operand, we can set the data field of the current node with the integer value of the token and then return. This takes us back to the parent of the current node.

The bulk of the work is done when a left parenthesis is encountered. The same sequence of steps, as shown in lines 20–30, is always performed since we are only working with binary operators. First, a new left child is created and we descend down to the new node by making a recursive call. Upon returning to this invocation of the function, which represents the parent of the new node, the next token must contain an operator. It is removed from the queue and assigned to the current node's data field. A new right child is then created and again we descend down to the new node to process the right side of the operator. Finally, when the second recursive call returns, the next token will be a right parenthesis, which can removed from the queue and discarded.

13.4 Heaps

A *heap* is a complete binary tree in which the nodes are organized based on their data entry values. There are two variants of the heap structure. A *max-heap* has the property, known as the *heap order property*, that for each non-leaf node V, the value in V is greater than the value of its two children. The largest value in a max-heap will always be stored in the root while the smallest values will be stored in the leaf nodes. The *min-heap* has the opposite property. For each non-leaf node V, the value in V is smaller than the value of its two children. Figure 13.21 illustrates an example of a max-heap and a min-heap.

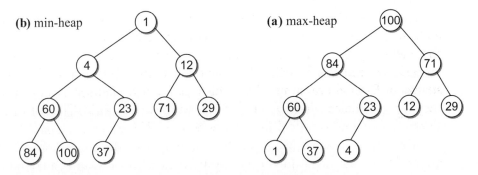

Figure 13.21: Examples of a heap.

13.4.1 Definition

The heap is a specialized structure with limited operations. We can insert a new value into a heap or extract and remove the root node's value from the heap. In this section, we explore these operations for use with a max-heap. Their application to a min-heap is identical except for the logical relationship between each node and its children.

Insertions

When a new value is inserted into a heap, the heap order property and the **heap shape property** (a complete binary tree) must be maintained. Suppose we want to add value 90 to the max-heap in Figure 13.21(b). If we are to maintain the property of the max-heap, there are only two places in the tree where 90 can be inserted, as shown in Figure 13.22(a). Contrast this to the possible locations if we were to add value 41 to the max-heap, shown in Figure 13.22(b).

Knowing the possible locations is only part of the problem. What happens to the values in the nodes where the new value must be stored in order to maintain the heap order property? In other words, if we insert 90 into the heap, it must be placed into either the node currently containing 84 or 71. Suppose we choose to place it in the node containing value 84, what becomes of value 84? It will have to

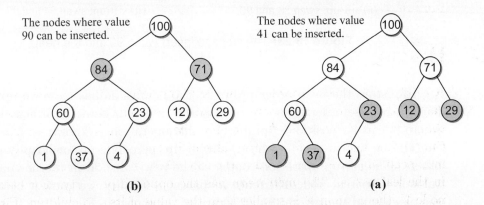

Figure 13.22: Candidate locations in a heap for new values.

be moved to another node where it can be legally placed, and the value displaced by 84 will have to be moved, and so on until a new leaf node is created for the last value displaced.

Instead of starting from the top and searching for a node in the tree where the new value can be properly placed, we can start at the bottom and work our way up. This involves several steps, which we outline using Figure 13.23. First, we create a new node and fill it with the new value as shown in part (a). The node is then attached as a leaf node at the only spot in the tree where the heap shape property can be maintained (part (b)). Remember, a heap is a complete tree and in such a tree, the leaf nodes on the lowest level must be filled from left to right. As you will notice, the heap order property has been violated since the parent of node 90 is smaller but in a max-heap it is supposed to be larger.

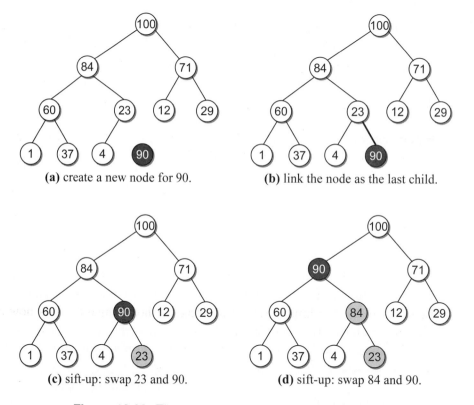

Figure 13.23: The steps to insert value 90 into the heap.

To restore the heap order property, the new value has to move up along the path in reverse order from the root to the insertion point until a node is found where it can be positioned properly. This operation is known as a *sift-up*. It can also be known as an up-heap, bubble-up, percolate-up, or heapify-up, among others. The sift-up operation compares the new value 90 in the new node to the value in its parent node, 23. Since its parent is smaller, we know it belongs above the parent and the two values are swapped, as shown in Figure 13.23(c). Value 90 is then compared to the value in its new parent node. Again, we find the parent is smaller and the two values have to be swapped, as shown in part (d). The comparison is repeated again, but this time we find value 90 is less than or equal to its parent and the process ends.

Now, suppose we add value 41 to the heap, as illustrated in Figure 13.24. The new node is created and filled with value 41 and linked into the tree as the left child of node 12. When the new value is sifted up, we find values 12 and 41 have to be swapped, resulting in the final placement of the new value.

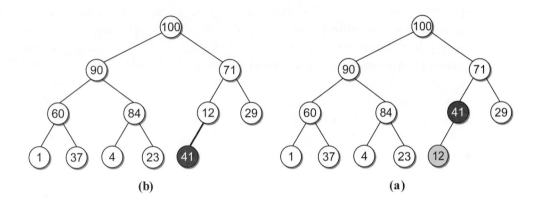

(b)   **(a)**

Figure 13.24: Inserting value 41 into the heap: (a) create the new node and link it into the tree; and (b) sift the new value up the tree.

Extractions

When a value is extracted and removed from the heap, it can only come from the root node. Thus, in a max-heap, we always extract the largest value and in a min-heap, we always extract the smallest value. After the value in the root has been removed, the binary tree is no longer a heap since there is now a gap in the root node, as illustrated in Figure 13.25.

To restore the tree to a heap, another value will have to take the place of the value extracted from the root and a node has to be removed from the tree since

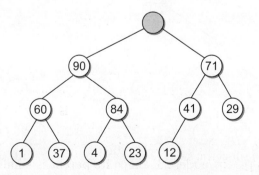

Figure 13.25: Extracting a value from the max-heap leaves a hole at the root node.

there is one less value in the heap. Since a heap requires a complete tree, there is only one leaf that can be removed: the rightmost node on the lowest level.

To maintain a complete tree and the heap order property, an extraction requires several steps. First, we copy and save the value from the root node, which will be returned after the extraction process has been completed. Next, the value from the rightmost node on the lowest level is copied to the root and that leaf node is removed from the tree, as shown in Figure 13.26(a). This maintains the heap structure property requiring a complete tree, but it violates the heap order property since 12 is smaller than its children. To restore the heap order property, value 12 has to be sifted-down the tree. The **sift-down** works in the same fashion as the sift-up used with an insertion. Starting at the root node, the node's value is compared to its children and swapped with the larger of the two. The sift-down is then applied to the node into which the smaller value was copied. This process continues until the smaller value is copied into a leaf node or a node whose children are even smaller. Parts (b - d) of Figure 13.26 show the sift-down operation applied to value 12 in the root node: value 12 is swapped with 90, then with 84, and finally with 23, resulting in a proper heap.

The code in this method can be placed within the constructor. We only used this helper method in order to hide the tree construction details in the initial presentation of the `ExpressionTree` class in Listing 13.6 until the actual operation was presented.

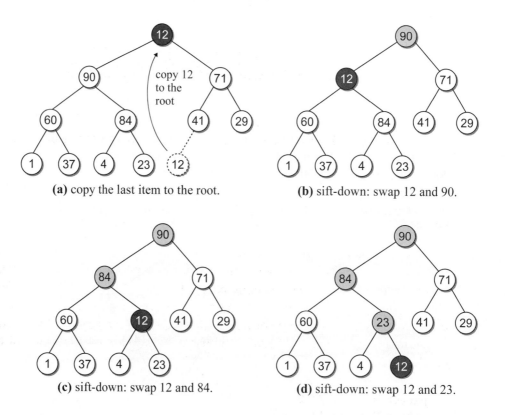

Figure 13.26: The steps in restoring a max-heap after extracting the root value.

13.4.2   Implementation

Throughout our discussion, we have used the abstract view of a binary tree with nodes and edges to illustrate the heap structure. While a heap is a binary tree, it's seldom, if ever, implemented as a dynamic linked structure due to the need of navigating the tree both top-down and bottom-up. Instead, we can implement a heap using an array or vector to physically store the individual nodes with implicit links between the nodes. Suppose we number the nodes in the heap left to right by level starting with zero, as shown in Figure 13.27(a). We can then place the heap values within an array using these node numbers as indices into the array, as shown in Figure 13.27(b).

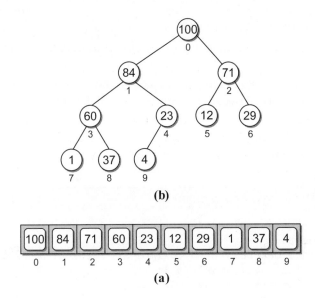

Figure 13.27: A heap can be implemented using an array or vector.

Node Access

Since a heap is a complete tree, it will never contain holes resulting from missing internal nodes. Thus, the root will always be at position 0 within the array and its two children will always occupy elements 1 and 2. In fact, the children of any given node will always occupy the same elements within the array. This allows us to quickly locate the parent of any node or the left and right child of any node. Given the array index i of a node, the index of the parent or children of that node can be computed as:

```
parent = (i-1) // 2
left = 2 * i + 1
right = 2 * i + 2
```

Determining if a node's child link is null is simply a matter of computing the index of the appropriate child and testing to see if the index is out of range. For example, suppose we want to test if node 29 in the tree from Figure 13.27 has a left child. Since the node is stored at index position 6, we plug this value into the equation for computing the left child index, which yields 13. This tells us that if node 29 had a left child it would be located within the array at index position 13. But there are only 10 items in the heap, stored in positions 0 . . . 9, and 13 would be outside the range of valid node positions. This indicates node 29 does not have a left child.

Class Definition

We define the `MaxHeap` class for our array-based implementation of the max-heap in Listing 13.10. An array-based version of the heap structure is commonly used when the maximum capacity of the heap is known beforehand. If the maximum capacity is not known, then a Python list structure can be used instead. The array is created with a size equal to the `maxSize` argument supplied to the constructor and assigned to `_elements`. Since we will be adding one item at a time to the heap, the items currently in the heap will only use a portion of the array, with the remaining elements available for new items. The `_count` attribute keeps track of how many items are currently in the heap.

Listing 13.10 The `arrayheap.py` module.

```
1   # An array-based implementation of the max-heap.
2   class MaxHeap :
3     # Create a max-heap with maximum capacity of maxSize.
4     def __init__( self, maxSize ):
5       self._elements = Array( maxSize )
6       self._count = 0
7
8     # Return the number of items in the heap.
9     def __len__( self ):
10      return self._count
11
12    # Return the maximum capacity of the heap.
13    def capacity( self ):
14      return len( self._elements )
15
16    # Add a new value to the heap.
17    def add( self, value ):
18      assert self._count < self.capacity(), "Cannot add to a full heap."
19      # Add the new value to the end of the list.
20      self._elements[ self._count ] = value
21      self._count += 1
22      # Sift the new value up the tree.
23      self._siftUp( self._count - 1 )
24
25    # Extract the maximum value from the heap.
26    def extract( self ):
27      assert self._count > 0, "Cannot extract from an empty heap."
```

```
28        # Save the root value and copy the last heap value to the root.
29        value = self._elements[0]
30        self._count -= 1
31        self._elements[0] = self._elements[ self._count ]
32        # Sift the root value down the tree.
33        self._siftDown( 0 )
34
35    # Sift the value at the ndx element up the tree.
36    def _siftUp( self, ndx ):
37      if ndx > 0 :
38        parent = ndx // 2
39        if self._elements[ndx] > self._elements[parent] :  # swap elements
40          tmp = self._elements[ndx]
41          self._elements[ndx] = self._elements[parent]
42          self._elements[parent] = tmp
43          self._siftUp( parent )
44
45    # Sift the value at the ndx element down the tree.
46    def _siftDown( self, ndx ):
47      left = 2 * ndx + 1
48      right = 2 * ndx + 2
49      # Determine which node contains the larger value.
50      largest = ndx
51      if left < count and self._elements[left] >= self._elements[largest] :
52        largest = left
53      elif right < count and self._elements[right] >= self._elements[largest]:
54        largest = right
55      # If the largest value is not in the current node (ndx), swap it with
56      # the largest value and repeat the process.
57      if largest != ndx :
58        swap( self._elements[ndx], self._elements[largest] )
59        _siftDown( largest )
```

The first step when adding a new item to a heap is to link a new leaf node in the rightmost position on the lowest level. In the array implementation, this will always be the next position following the last heap item in the array. After inserting the new item into the array (lines 20–21) it has to be sifted up the tree to find its correct position. Figure 13.28 illustrates the modifications to the heap and the storage array when adding 90 to the sample heap.

To extract the maximum value from a max-heap, we first have to copy and save the value in the root node, which we know is in index position 0. Next, the root value has to be replaced with the value from the leaf node that is in the rightmost position on the lowest level of the tree. In the array implementation, that leaf node will always be the last item of the heap stored in linear order within the array. After copying the last heap item to the root node (lines 30–31), the new value in the root node has to be sifted down the tree to find its correct position.

The implementation of the sift-down operation is straightforward. After determining the indices of the nodes left and right child, we determine which of the three values is larger: the value in the node, the value in the node's left child, or the value in the node's right child. If one of the two children contains a value greater than or equal to the value in the node: (1) it has to be swapped with the

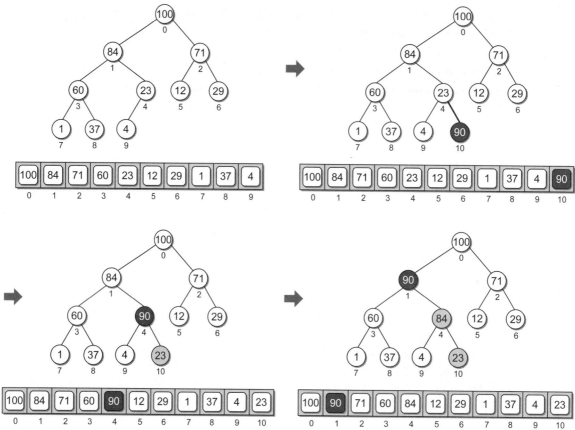

Figure 13.28: Inserting value 90 into the heap implemented as an array.

value in the current node and (2) the sift-down operation has to be repeated on that child. Otherwise, the proper position of the value being sifted down has been located and the base case of the recursive operation is reached.

Analysis

Inserting an item into a heap implemented as an array requires $O(\log n)$ time in the worst case. Inserting the new item at the end of the sequence of heap items can be done in $O(1)$ time. After the new item is inserted, it has to be sifted up the tree. The worst case time of the sift-up operation is the maximum number of levels the new item can move up the tree. A new item always begins in a leaf node and may end up in the root node, which is a distance equal to the height of the tree. Since a heap is a complete binary tree, we know its height is always $\log n$. Extracting an item from a heap implemented as an array also requires $O(\log n)$ time in the worst case, the analysis of which we leave as an exercise.

13.4.3   The Priority Queue Revisited

A priority queue, which was introduced in Chapter 8, works like a normal queue except each item is assigned a priority and the items with a higher priority are dequeued first. The bounded priority queue, in which the number of priorities is fixed, allows for an efficient implementation with the use of an array of queues (Section 8.3.3). The unbounded priority queue does not place any restriction on the maximum positive integer value that can be used as the priority values. With an unlimited number of priorities, the array of queues implementation would not be very efficient and could waste a lot of space. Instead, we would have to use either the Python list (Section 8.3.2) or linked list (Section 8.3.2) based implementation of the priority queue.

A min-heap can also be used to implement the general priority queue. The ordering of the heap nodes is based on the priority associated with each item in the queue. For example, Figure 13.29 illustrates the contents of the heap for the example priority queue from Figure 8.8. Since lower values indicate a higher priority, the item with the highest priority will always be in the root of the min-heap. When that item is dequeued, the item with the next highest priority will work its way to the top as the sift-down operation is performed.

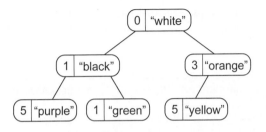

Figure 13.29: Contents of the heap used in the implementation of a priority queue.

When using a heap implemented as an array, the operations of the general priority queue are very efficient: both the enqueue and dequeue operations have worst case times of $O(\log n)$. An array-based version of the heap is sufficient in applications where the maximum capacity of the queue is known beforehand. If the heap is implemented using a Python list, the enqueue and dequeue operations have worst case times of $O(n)$ since the underlying array may have to expand or shrink, but amortized cost of $O(\log n)$. Table 13.1 compares the worst case times and amortized cost for various implementations of the unbounded priority queue.

Implementation	Worst Case		Amortized	
	Enqueue	Dequeue	Enqueue	Dequeue
Python List	$O(n)$	$O(n)$	$O(1)$	$O(n)$
Linked List	$O(1)$	$O(n)$	-	-
Heap (array)	$O(\log n)$	$O(\log n)$	-	-
Heap (list)	$O(n)$	$O(n)$	$O(\log n)$	$O(\log n)$

Table 13.1: Time-complexities for various implementations of the bounded priority queue.

13.5 Heapsort

The simplicity and efficiency of the heap structure can be applied to the sorting problem. The *heapsort* algorithm builds a heap from a sequence of unsorted values and then extracts the items from the heap to create a sorted sequence.

13.5.1 Simple Implementation

Consider the function in Listing 13.11. We create a max-heap with enough capacity to store all of the values in `theSeq`. Each value from the sequence is then inserted into the heap. After that, the values are then extracted from the heap, one at a time, and stored back into the original sequence structure in reverse order. Since we are using a max-heap, each time a value is extracted, we get the next largest value in sorted order.

The heapsort algorithm is very efficient and only requires $O(n \log n)$ time in the worst case. The construction of the heap requires $O(n \log n)$ time since there are n items in the sequence and each call to `add()` requires $\log n$ time. Extracting the values from the heap and storing them into the sequence structure also requires $O(n \log n)$ time.

Listing 13.11 A simple implementation of the heapsort algorithm.

```
 1  def simpleHeapSort( theSeq ):
 2      # Create an array-based max-heap.
 3      n = len(theSeq)
 4      heap = MaxHeap( n )
 5
 6      # Build a max-heap from the list of values.
 7      for item in theSeq :
 8        heap.add( item )
 9
10      # Extract each value from the heap and store them back into the list.
11      for i in range( n, 0, -1 ) :
12        theSeq[i] = heap.extract()
```

13.5.2 Sorting In Place

The implementation of the heapsort algorithm provided in Listing 13.11 has one drawback: it requires the use of additional storage to build the heap structure. But we don't actually need a second array. The entire process of building the heap and extracting the values can be done in place—that is, within the same sequence in which the original values are supplied.

Suppose we are given the array of values shown at the bottom of Figure 13.30(a) and want to sort them using the heapsort algorithm. The first step is to construct a heap from this sequence of values. As you will see, we can do this within the same array without the need for additional storage. Remember, the nodes in the heap occupy the elements of the array from front to back. We can keep the heap items at the front of the array and those values that have yet to be added to the

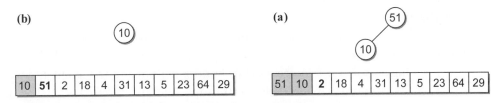

Figure 13.30: Adding the first two values to the heap.

heap at the end of the array. All we have to do is keep track of where the heap ends and the sequence of remaining values begin.

If we consider the first value in the array, it constitutes a max-heap of one item, as shown in Figure 13.30(a). When adding a value to a heap, it's copied to the first element in the array immediately following the last heap item and sifted up the tree. The next value, 51, from our sequence that is to be added to the heap is already in this position. Thus, all we have to do is apply the sift-up operation to the value, resulting in a max-heap with two items, as illustrated in Figure 13.30(b). We can repeat this process on each value in the array to create a max-heap consisting of all the values from the array. This process is illustrated in Figure 13.31 and includes both the abstract view of the heap and the contents

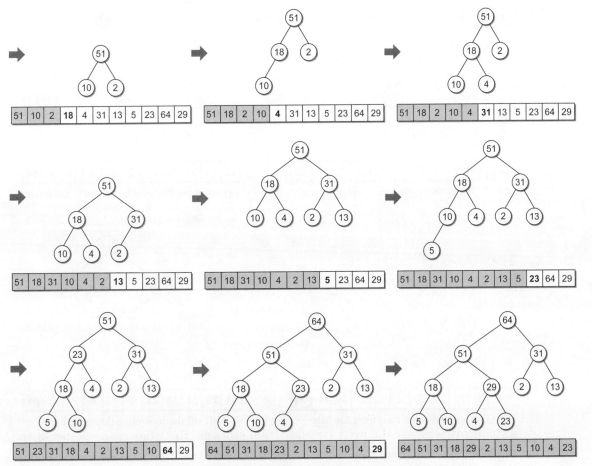

Figure 13.31: Adding the remaining values to the heap.

of the corresponding array. The shaded part of the array indicates the items that are currently part of the array. The boldfaced value indicates the next item to be sifted up the tree.

We have shown it is quite easy to build a heap using the same array containing the values that are to be added to the heap. A similar approach can be used to extract the values from the heap and create a sorted array using the array containing the heap. Remember, when the root value is extracted from a heap, the value from the rightmost leaf at the lowest level is copied to the root node and then sifted down the tree. Consider the completed heap in Figure 13.32(a). When value 64 is extracted from the heap, the last value in the array, 23, would be copied to the root node since it corresponds to the rightmost leaf node at the lowest level. Instead of simply copying this leaf value to the root, we can swap the two values, as shown in Figure 13.32(b).

The next step in the process of extracting a value from the heap is to remove the leaf node from the heap. In an array representation, we do this by reducing a counter indicating the number of items in the heap. In Figure 13.32(c), the elements comprising the heap are shown with a white background and the value

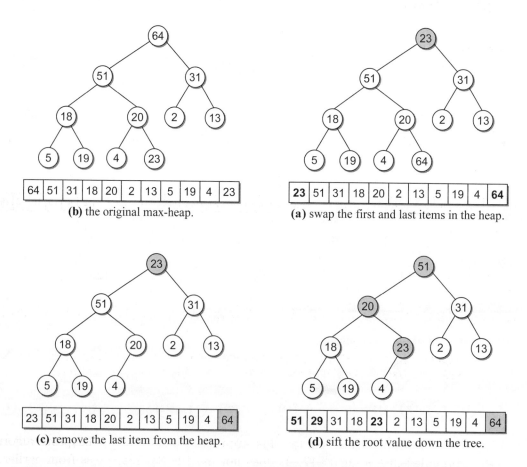

(b) the original max-heap.

(a) swap the first and last items in the heap.

(c) remove the last item from the heap.

(d) sift the root value down the tree.

Figure 13.32: The three steps performed to extract in place a single value from the heap.

just swapped with the root is shown in a gray background. Notice that value 64 is the largest value in the original array of unsorted values and when sorted belongs in this exact position at the end of the array. Finally, the value copied from the leaf to the root has to be sifted down, as illustrated in Figure 13.32(d).

If we repeat this same process, swapping the root value with the last item in the subarray that comprises the heap, for each item in the heap we end up with a sorted array of values in ascending order. Figure 13.33 illustrates the remaining steps in extracting each value from the heap and storing them in the same array. The shaded part of the array shows the values that have been removed from the heap and placed in sorted order while the elements with a white background show those that comprise the heap are currently part of the array. The boldfaced values indicate those that were affected by the sift-down operation.

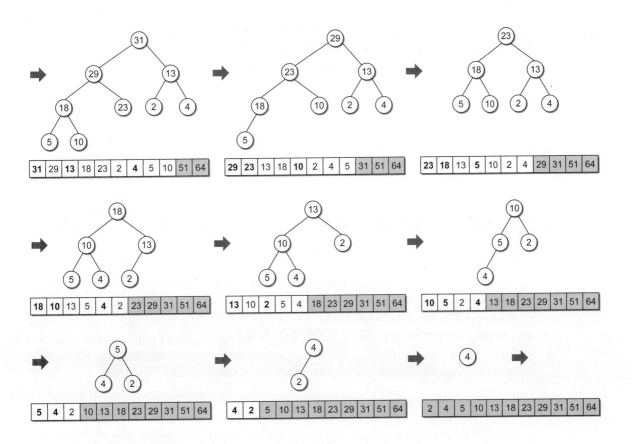

Figure 13.33: The steps in extracting the values from the heap into the same array that will store the resulting sequence.

The implementation for this improved version of the heapsort algorithm is provided in Listing 13.12. It does not use the `MaxHeap` class from earlier, but it does rely on `siftUp()` and `siftDown()` functions like those used with the class.

| Listing 13.12 | Improved implementation of the heapsort algorithm. |

```
1   # Sorts a sequence in ascending order using the heapsort.
2   def heapsort( theSeq ):
3     n = len(theSeq)
4       # Build a max-heap within the same array.
5     for i in range( n ) :
6       siftUp( theSeq, i )
7
8       # Extract each value and rebuild the heap.
9     for j in range( n-1, 0, -1 ) :
10      tmp = theSeq[j]
11      theSeq[j] = theSeq[0]
12      theSeq[0] = tmp
13      siftDown( theSeq, j-1, 0 )
```

13.6 Application: Morse Code

Morse Code is a type of character encoding originally designed in the late 1830s by Samuel Morse for use with his telegraph system. Morse Code allowed messages to be transmitted long distances across telegraph wires and was extensively used by the American railroad companies. It was first used in 1844 to transmit messages between Washington and Baltimore. The original code used various patterns of dots and spaces to represent the letters of the alphabet. While this was sufficient for use in the United States, the code could not be used in Europe to transmit non-English text, which contains diacritic marks. To remedy this shortcoming, Friedrich Clemens Gerke improved on the original Morse Code and developed a new version that was first used in 1848 to transmit messages in Germany. Gerke's version of the code, with minor changes, was standardized in 1851 and became known as International Morse Code. The original code developed by Samuel Morse became known as American Morse Code.

The modern International Morse Code represents various letters, symbols, and digits using sequences of dots (or dits), dashes (or dahs), short gaps, and long gaps. The short gaps are used to break the sequence between letters and the long gaps are used to separate words. The most famous is the sequence for SOS:

    ... --- ...

At this point, you might be wondering why we are discussing Morse Code and what it has to do with binary trees. Suppose you are given the following sequence:

    - .-. . . ...   .- .-. .   ..-. ..- -.

and would like to know what it means. The most obvious way to decode this message is to look through a table for each part of the sequence and find the corresponding letter. When decoded the message reads:

    TREES ARE FUN

13.6.1 Decision Trees

Another way to translate the message is with the use of a decision tree. A **decision tree** models a sequence of decisions or choices in which selections are made in stages from among multiple alternatives at each stage. The stages in the decision are represented as nodes while the branches indicate the decisions that can be made at each stage.

A common use of the decision tree with which you should be familiar is the dreaded automated phone menu. When the automated system answers your call, it starts at the root of the tree and offers several choices from which you can choose. After making your initial selection, you are presented with a submenu from which you must make a second selection, and then possibly a third selection, and so on. The presentation of the menu options by the automated system are the stages in the decision and represented in the tree as nodes. The menu choices from which you can select at each stage are indicated by branches from those nodes.

This same idea can be used to decode a Morse Code sequence. While each code sequence is unique, they do not have unique prefixes. For example, the sequences for the letters R and S both begin with a dot. To distinguish between the two, we have to examine more of the sequence. The second symbol in the sequence for R is a dash, while the sequence for S has a dot. It's not until the third component of the sequence that we can fully distinguish between the R and the S. To confuse the situation even more, the letter A is indicated by the two-symbol sequence of (.-), which is the sequence prefix for R. A subset of the International Morse Code is shown here:

A	.-	F	..-.	K	-.-	P	.--.	U	..-
B	-...	G	--.	L	.-..	Q	--.-	V	...-
C	-.-.	H	....	M	--	R	.-.	W	.--
D	-..	I	..	N	-.	S	...	X	-..-
E	.	J	.---	O	---	T	-	Y	-.--
								Z	--..

To help decode a sequence, we can build a decision tree that models Morse Code, as illustrated in Figure 13.34. The nodes represent the letters and symbols that are part of Morse Code and the branches provide a selection of either a dot (left branch) or a dash (right branch). The root node is empty and indicates the starting position when decoding a sequence.

To decode a given sequence, we start at the root and follow the left or right branch to the next node based on the current symbol in our sequence. For example, to decode (.-.), we start at the root and examine the first symbol. Since the first symbol is a dot, we have to follow the left branch to the next node, which leads us to node E. Each time we move to a node, we examine the next character in the sequence. Since the second symbol is a dash, we take the right branch from node E leading us to node A. From that node, we take the left branch since the third symbol is a dot. This leads us to node R. After exhausting all of the symbols in the sequence, the last node visited will contain the character corresponding to the

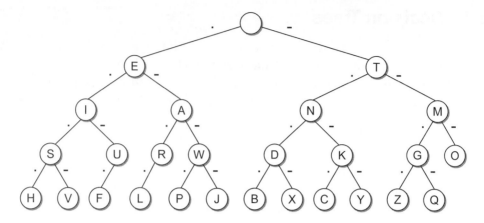

Figure 13.34: Morse Code modeled as a binary decision tree.

given sequence. In this case, the sequence (.-.) represents the letter R. The path of the steps through the tree to decode the sequence is shown in Figure 13.35.

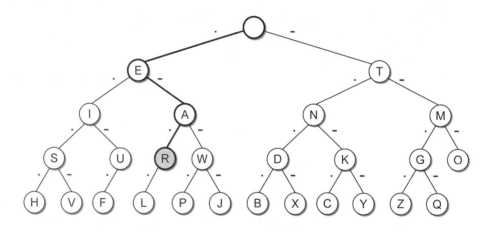

Figure 13.35: Decoding the Morse Code sequence (.-.).

What happens if we try to decode an invalid sequence? For example, try decoding the sequence (-.-..). This will take us from the root node, right to node T, left to node N, right to node K, and left to node C. The last symbol in the sequence is a dot, which indicates we are supposed to take the left branch at node C, but it has no left child, as illustrated in Figure 13.36. If a null child link is encountered during the navigation of the tree, we know the sequence is invalid.

13.6.2   The ADT Definition

We can define an abstract data type that can be used to store a Morse Code tree for use in decoding Morse Code sequences. The ADT only includes two operations: the constructor and the translate operations.

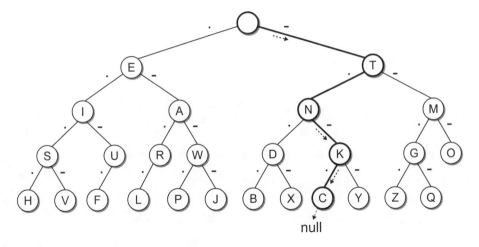

Figure 13.36: Decoding an invalid Morse Code sequence (-.-..).

| Define | Morse Code Tree ADT |

A *Morse Code tree* is a decision tree that contains the letters of the alphabet and other special symbols in its nodes. The nodes are organized based on the Morse Code sequence corresponding to each letter and symbol.

- `MorseCodeTree()`: Builds the Morse Code tree consisting of the letters of the alphabet and other special symbols.

- `translate( codeSeq )`: Translates and returns the given Morse Code sequence to its equivalent character if the sequence is valid or returns `None` otherwise.

We leave the implementation of the ADT as an exercise. The tree has to be built as part of the constructor. Start with an empty root node and then add one letter at a time. When adding a letter, follow the branches corresponding to the code sequence representing the given letter. If a null child link is encountered, simply add a new empty node and continue following the branches. After reaching the end of the sequence, the letter being added to the tree is assigned to the last node visited.

Exercises

13.1 Given a binary tree of size 76, what is the minimum number of levels it can contain? What is the maximum number of levels?

13.2 Draw all possible binary trees that contain 12 nodes.

13.3 What is the maximum number of nodes possible in a binary tree with 5 levels?

13.4 Given the following binary trees:

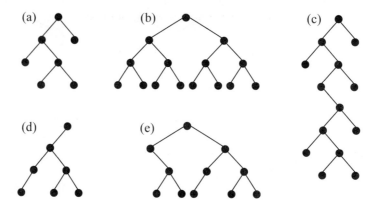

(a) Indicate all of the structure properties that apply to each tree: *full, perfect, complete.*

(b) Determine the size of each tree.

(c) Determine the height of each tree.

(d) Determine the width of each tree.

13.5 Consider the following binary tree:

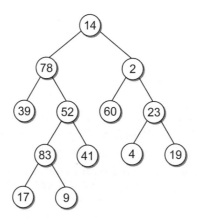

(a) Show the order the nodes will be visited in a:

    i. preorder traversal   iii. postorder traversal

    ii. inorder traversal   iv. breadth-first traversal

(b) Identify all of the leaf nodes.

(c) Identify all of the interior nodes.

(d) List all of the nodes on level 4.

(e) List all of the nodes in the path to each of the following nodes:

    i. 83   ii. 39   iii. 4   iv. 9

(f) Consider node 52 and list the node's:

    i. descendants   ii. ancestors   iii. siblings

(g) Identify the depth of each of the following nodes:

    i. 78   ii. 41   iii. 60   iv. 19

13.6 Determine the arithmetic expression represented by each of the following expression trees:

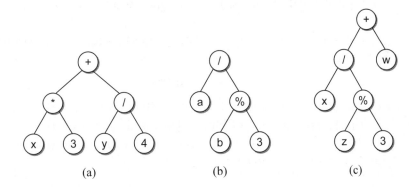

          (a)   (b)   (c)

13.7 Build the expression tree for each of the following arithmetic expressions:

(a) (A * B) / C

(b) A - (B * C) + D / E

(c) (X - Y) + (W * Z) / V

(d) V * W % X + Y - Z

(e) A / B * C - D + E

13.8 Consider the following set of values and use them to build a heap by adding one value at a time in the order listed:

    30 63 2 89 16 24 19 52 27 9 4 45

(a) min-heap   (b) max-heap

13.9 Prove or show that the worst case time of the extraction operation on a heap implemented as an array is $O(\log n)$.

13.10 Prove or show that the insertion and extraction operations on a heap implemented as a Python list is $O(n)$ in the worst case. Also show that each operation has an amortized cost of $O(\log n)$.

Programming Projects

13.1 Implement the function `treeSize(root)`, which computes the number of nodes in a binary tree.

13.2 Implement the function `treeHeight(root)`, which computes the height of a binary tree.

13.3 Implement the `_computeOp(lvalue, operator, rvalue)` helper method used to compute the value of a binary operator when evaluating an expression tree. Assume all operands in the expression tree are single digits.

13.4 Modify the `ExpressionTree` class from the chapter to handle the unary operator − and unary mathematical function `n!`.

13.5 Implement the general Priority Queue ADT using the min-heap implemented as an array. Instead of having the number of priority levels as an argument of the constructor, specify the maximum capacity of the queue. In addition, define the `isFull()` method that returns `True` when the queue is full and `False` otherwise.

13.6 Implement the general Priority Queue ADT using the min-heap implemented as a vector. Instead of having the number of priority levels as an argument of the constructor, specify the maximum capacity of the queue.

13.7 Complete the implementation of the Morse Code Tree ADT.

13.8 Add the operation `getCodeSeq(symbol)` to the Morse Code Tree ADT, which accepts a single-character symbol and returns the corresponding Morse Code sequence for that symbol. `None` should be returned if the supplied symbol is invalid.

13.9 Design and implement a program that uses the Morse Code Tree ADT to decode Morse Code sequences extracted from standard input. Your program should detect and report any invalid code sequences.

## CHAPTER 14

Search Trees

Searching, which has been discussed throughout the text, is a very common operation and has been studied extensively. A linear search of an array or Python list is very slow, but that can be improved with a binary search. Even with the improved search time, arrays and Python lists have a disadvantage when it comes to the insertion and deletion of search keys. Remember, a binary search can only be performed on a sorted sequence. When keys are added to or removed from an array or Python list, the order must be maintained. This can be time consuming since keys have to be shifted to make room when adding a new key or to close the gap when deleting an existing key. The use of a linked list provides faster insertions and deletions without having to shift the existing keys. Unfortunately, the only type of search that can be performed on a linked list is a linear search, even if the list is sorted. In this chapter, we explore some of the many ways the tree structure can be used in performing efficient searches.

The tree structure, which was introduced in the last chapter, can be used to organize dynamic data in a hierarchical fashion. Trees come in various shapes and sizes depending on their application and the relationship between the nodes. When used for searching, each node contains a search key as part of its data entry (sometimes called the *payload*) and the nodes are organized based on the relationship between the keys. There are many different types of search trees, some of which are simply variations of others, and some that can be used to search data stored externally. But the primary goal of all search trees is to provide an efficient search operation for quickly locating a specific item contained in the tree.

Search trees can be used to implement many different types of containers, some of which may only need to store the search keys within each node of the tree. More commonly, however, applications associate data or a payload with each search key and use the structure in the same fashion as a Map ADT would be used. The Map ADT was introduced in Chapter 3, at which time we implemented it using a list structure. Exercises in several chapters offered the opportunity to provide new implementations using various data structures. In Chapter 11, we implemented a hash table version of the Map ADT that improved the search times. But its efficiency depends on the type of keys stored in the map, since the choice of hash function can greatly impact the search operation. Throughout the chapter, we explore several different search trees, each of which we will use to implement new versions of the Map ADT. To help avoid confusion between the various implementations, we use a different class name for each implementation.

14.1   The Binary Search Tree

A *binary search tree* (BST) is a binary tree in which each node contains a search key within its payload and the tree is structured such that for each interior node V:

- All keys less than the key in node V are stored in the left subtree of V.
- All keys greater than the key in node V are stored in the right subtree of V.

Consider the binary search tree in Figure 14.1, which contains integer search keys. The root node contains key value 60 and all keys in the root's left subtree are less than 60 and all of the keys in the right subtree are greater than 60. If you examine every node in the keys, you will notice the same key relationship applies to every node in the tree. Given the relationship between the nodes, an inorder traversal will visit the nodes in increasing search key order. For the example binary search tree, the order would be   1 4 12 23 29 37 41 60 71 84 90 100.

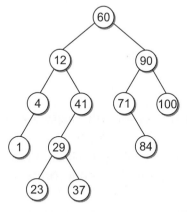

Figure 14.1: A binary search tree storing integer search keys.

Our definition of the binary search tree precludes the storage of duplicate keys in the tree, which makes the implementation of the various operations much easier. It's also appropriate for some applications, but the restriction can be changed to allow duplicate keys, if needed. In addition, for illustration purposes, we only show the key within each node of our search trees. You should assume the corresponding data value is also stored in the nodes.

A partial implementation of the binary search tree version of the Map ADT is shown in Listing 14.1. The remaining code will be added as each operation is

---

Listing 14.1   Partial implementation of the Map ADT using a binary search tree.

```
1   class BSTMap :
2       # Creates an empty map instance.
3       def __init__( self ):
4           self._root = None
5           self._size = 0
6
7       # Returns the number of entries in the map.
8       def __len__( self ):
9           return self._size
10
11      # Returns an iterator for traversing the keys in the map.
12      def __iter__( self ):
13          return _BSTMapIterator( self._root )
14
15  # Storage class for the binary search tree nodes of the map.
16  class _BSTMapNode :
17      def __init__( self, key, value ):
18          self.key = key
19          self.value = value
20          self.left = None
21          self.right = None
```

---

discussed throughout the section. As with any binary tree, a reference to the root node must also be maintained for a binary search tree. The constructor defines the _root field for this purpose and also defines the _size field to keep track of the number of entries in the map. The latter is needed by the __len__ method. The definition of the private storage class used to create the tree nodes is shown in lines 16–21.

14.1.1 Searching

Given a binary search tree, you will eventually want to search the tree to determine if it contains a given key or to locate a specific element. In the last chapter, we saw that there is a single path from the root to every other node in a tree. If the binary search tree contains the target key, then there will be a unique path from the root to the node containing that key. The only question is, how do we know which path to take?

Since the root node provides the single access point into any binary tree, our search must begin there. The target value is compared to the key in the root node as illustrated in Figure 14.2. If the root contains the target value, our search is over with a successful result. But if the target is not in the root, we must decide which of two possible paths to take. From the definition of the binary search tree, we know the key in the root node is larger than the keys in its left subtree and smaller than the keys in its right subtree. Thus, if the target is less than the root's key, we move left and we move right if it's greater. We repeat the comparison on the root node of the subtree and take the appropriate path. This process is repeated until target is located or we encounter a null child link.

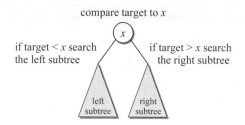

Figure 14.2: The structure of a binary search tree is based on the search keys.

Suppose we want to search for key value 29 in the binary search tree from Figure 14.1. We begin by comparing the target to 60. Since the target is less than 60, we move left. The target is then compared to 12. This time we move right since the target is larger than 12. Next, the target is compared to 41, resulting in a move to the left. Finally, when we examine the left child of node 41, we find the target and report a successful search. The path taken to find key 29 in the example tree is illustrated in Figure 14.3(a) by the dashed directed lines.

What if the target is not in the tree? For example, suppose we want to search for key 68. We would repeat the same process used to find key 29, as illustrated in Figure 14.3(b). The difference is what happens when we reach node 71 and compare it to the target. If 68 were in the the binary search tree, it would have to be in the left subtree of node 71. But you will notice node 71 does not have a left child. If we continue in that direction, we will "fall" off the tree. Thus, reaching a null child link during the search for a target key indicates an unsuccessful search.

The binary search tree operations can be implemented iteratively or with the use of recursion. We implement recursive functions for each operation and leave the iterative versions as exercises. The _bstSearch() helper method, provided in lines 14–22 of Listing 14.2, recursively navigates a binary search tree to find the node containing the target key. The method has two base cases: the target is contained in the current node or a null child link is encountered. When a base case is reached, the method returns either a reference to the node containing the key or None, back through all of the recursive calls. The latter indicates the key was not

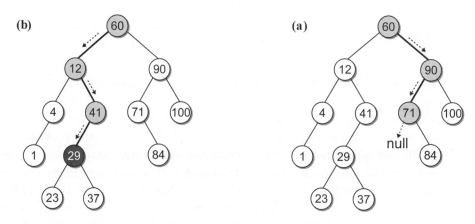

Figure 14.3: Searching a binary search tree: (a) successful search for 29 and (b) unsuccessful search for 68.

Listing 14.2   Searching for a target key in a binary search tree.

```
1   class BSTMap :
2   # ...
3       # Determines if the map contains the given key.
4       def __contains__( self, key ):
5           return self._bstSearch( self._root, key ) is not None
6
7       # Returns the value associated with the key.
8       def valueOf( self, key ):
9           node = self._bstSearch( self._root, key )
10          assert node is not None, "Invalid map key."
11          return node.value
12
13      # Helper method that recursively searches the tree for a target key.
14      def _bstSearch( self, subtree, target ):
15          if subtree is None :          # base case
16              return None
17          elif target < subtree.key :  # target is left of the subtree root.
18              return self._bstSearch( subtree.left )
19          elif target > subtree.key :  # target is right of the subtree root.
20              return self._bstSearch( subtree.right )
21          else :                        # base case
22              return subtree
```

---

found in the tree. The recursive call is made by passing the link to either the left or right subtree depending on the relationship between the target and the key in the current node.

You may be wondering why we return a reference to the node and not just a boolean value to indicate the success or failure of the search. This allows us to use the same helper method to implement both the __contains__ and valueOf() methods of the Map class. Both call the recursive helper method to locate the node containing the target key. In doing so, the root node reference has to be passed to the helper to initiate the recursion. The value returned from _bstSearch() can be evaluated to determine if the key was found in the tree and the appropriate action can be taken for the corresponding Map ADT operation.

A binary search tree can be empty, as indicated by a null root reference, so we must ensure any operation performed on the tree also works when the tree is empty. In the _bstSearch() method, this is handled by the first base case on the first call to the method.

14.1.2 Min and Max Values

Another operation similar to a search that can be performed on a binary search tree is finding the minimum or maximum key values. Given the definition of the binary search tree, we know the minimum value is either in the root or in a node to its left. But how do we know if the root is the smallest value and not somewhere in its left subtree? We could compare the root to its left child, but if you think about it, there is no need to compare the individual keys. The reason has to do with the relationship between the keys. If the root node contains keys in its left subtree, then it cannot possibly contain the minimum key value since all of the keys to the left of the root are smaller than the root. What if the root node does not have a left child? In this case, the root would contain the smallest key value since all of the keys to the right are larger than the root.

If we applied the same logic to the left child of the root node (assuming it has a left child) and then to that node's left child and so on, we will eventually find the minimum key value. That value will be found in a node that is either a leaf or an interior node with no left child. It can be located by starting at the root and following the left child links until a null link is encountered, as illustrated in Figure 14.4. The maximum key value can be found in a similar fashion.

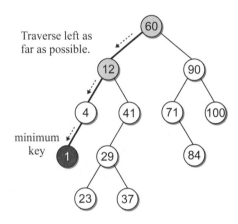

Figure 14.4: Finding the minimum or maximum key in a binary search tree.

Listing 14.3 provides a recursive helper method for finding the node that contains the minimum key value in the binary search tree. The method requires the root of the tree or of a subtree as an argument. It returns either a reference to the node containing the smallest key value or **None** when the tree is empty.

Listing 14.3   Find the element with the minimum key value in a binary search tree.

```
1  class BSTMap :
2  # ...
3    # Helper method for finding the node containing the minimum key.
4    def _bstMinumum( self, subtree ):
5      if subtree is None :
6        return None
7      elif subtree.left is None :
8        return subtree
9      else :
10       return self._bstMinimum( subtree.left )
```

14.1.3 Insertions

When a binary search tree is constructed, the keys are added one at a time. As the keys are inserted, a new node is created for each key and linked into its proper position within the tree. Suppose we want to build a binary search tree from the key list [60, 25, 100, 35, 17, 80] by inserting the keys in the order they are listed. Figure 14.5 illustrates the steps in building the tree, which you can follow as we describe the process.

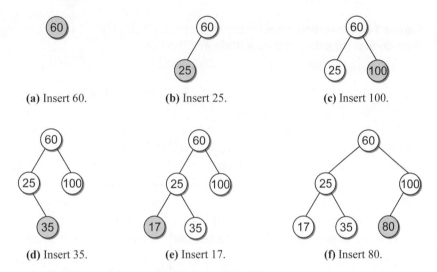

(a) Insert 60.   (b) Insert 25.   (c) Insert 100.

(d) Insert 35.   (e) Insert 17.   (f) Insert 80.

Figure 14.5: Building a binary tree by inserting the keys [60, 25, 100, 35, 17, 80].

We start by inserting value 60. A node is created and its data field set to that value. Since the tree is initially empty, this first node becomes the root of the tree (part a). Next, we insert value 25. Since it is smaller than 60, it has to be inserted to the left of the root, which means it becomes the left child of the root (part b). Value 100 is then inserted in a node linked as the right child of the root since it is larger than 60 (part c). What happens when value 35 is inserted? The root already has both its left and right children. When new keys are inserted, we do not modify the data fields of existing nodes or the links between existing nodes. Thus, there is only one location in which key value 35 can be inserted into our current tree and still maintain the search tree property. It has to be inserted as the right child of node 25 (part d). You may have noticed the pattern that is forming as new nodes are added to the binary tree. The new nodes are always inserted as a leaf node in its proper position such that the binary search tree property is maintained. We conclude this example by inserting the last two keys, 35 and 80, into the tree (parts e and f).

Working through this example by hand, it was easy to see where each new node had to be linked into the tree. But how do we insert the new keys in program code? Suppose we want to insert key 30 into the tree we built by hand. What happens if we use the _bstSearch() method and search for key 30? The search will lead us to node 35 and we then fall off the tree when attempting to follow its left child

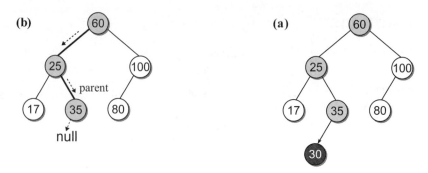

Figure 14.6: Inserting a new node into a binary search tree: (a) searching for the node's location and (b) linking the new node into the tree.

link, as illustrated in Figure 14.6(a). Notice that this is the exact location where the new key needs to be inserted.

We can use a modified version of the search operation to insert new keys into a binary search tree, as shown in Listing 14.4. To describe how the recursive method works, suppose we want to insert key value 30 into the tree we built by hand in Figure 14.5. Figure 14.7 illustrates the method's view of the tree in each invocation and shows the changes to the tree as the specific instructions are executed.

Remember, given the recursive definition of a binary tree, each node is itself the root of a subtree. As the _bstInsert() recursive method navigates through

Listing 14.4   Insert a key into a binary tree.

```
1  class BSTMap :
2  # ...
3    # Adds a new entry to the map or replaces the value of an existing key.
4    def add( self, key, value ):
5      # Find the node containing the key, if it exists.
6      node = self._bstSearch( key )
7      # If the key is already in the tree, update its value.
8      if node is not None :
9        node.value = value
10       return False
11     # Otherwise, add a new entry.
12     else :
13       self._root = self._bstInsert( self._root, key, value )
14       self._size += 1
15       return True
16
17     # Helper method that inserts a new item, recursively.
18     def _bstInsert( self, subtree, key, value ):
19       if subtree is None :
20         subtree = _BSTMapNode( key, value )
21       elif key < subtree.key :
22         subtree.left = self._bstInsert( subtree.left, key, value )
23       elif key > subtree.key :
24         subtree.right = self._bstInsert( subtree.right, key, value )
25       return subtree
```

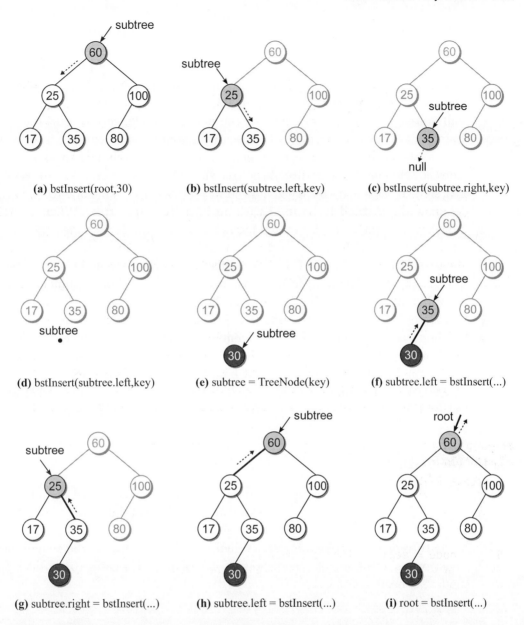

(a) bstInsert(root,30)   (b) bstInsert(subtree.left,key)   (c) bstInsert(subtree.right,key)

(d) bstInsert(subtree.left,key)   (e) subtree = TreeNode(key)   (f) subtree.left = bstInsert(...)

(g) subtree.right = bstInsert(...)   (h) subtree.left = bstInsert(...)   (i) root = bstInsert(...)

Figure 14.7: The recursive steps of the _bstInsert() method when inserting 30 into the binary search tree. Each tree shows the results after performing the indicated instruction.

the tree, the root of the current subtree will be the node of interest. To insert key value 30, the method must search for its ultimate location by recursively navigating deeper into the tree following either the left or right branch at each node as appropriate. These recursive steps are shown in parts (a – c) of Figure 14.7. The gray nodes indicate the root of the subtree currently being processed by the current invocation of the method. The dashed lines indicate the direction we must follow to find the correct path through the tree and then the path followed during the unwinding of the recursion.

The base case is reached when the empty subtree is encountered after taking the left child link from node 35, as shown in (part d). At this point, a new tree node is created and its data field set to the new key 30 (part e). A reference to this new node is then returned and the recursion begins unwinding. The first step in the unwinding takes us back to node 35. The reference returned by the recursive call is assigned to the `left` field of the `subtree` node, resulting in the new node being linked into the tree. As the recursion continues unwinding, shown in parts (f – i), the current `subtree` reference is returned and relinked to its parent. This does not change the structure of the tree since the same references are simply being reassigned. This is necessary given the way we link the new node to its parent and to allow the method to be used with an initially empty tree. When inserting the first key into the tree, the root reference will be null. If we called the method on an empty tree with `self._bstInsert( self._root, 30 )`, the new node will be created within the method, but the reference to the new node is not assigned to the `_root` field and the tree remains empty. Since method arguments are passed by value in Python, we have to return the reference and explicitly assign it to the `_root` field as is done in the `add()` method. Finally, after the new item is added to the tree, the `_size` field is incremented by one to reflect this change.

You may have noticed the insertion method lacks a final `else` clause on the conditional statement, which would handle the case when the new key equals an existing key. If a duplicate key is encountered during the search phase, we simply return the subtree reference to stop the recursion and allow for a proper unwinding.

14.1.4 Deletions

Removing an element from a binary search tree is a bit more complicated than searching for an element or inserting a new element into the tree. A deletion involves searching for the node that contains the target key and then unlinking the node to remove it from the tree. When a node is removed, the remaining nodes must preserve the search tree property. There are three cases to consider once the node has been located:

1. The node is a leaf.

2. The node has a single child.

3. The node has two children.

The first step in removing an element is to find the node that contains the key. This can be done in a manner similar to that used when searching for the location to insert a new element. Once the node is located, it has to be unlinked to remove it from the tree. We consider the three cases separately and then provide a complete listing of the recursive `_bstRemove()` method and its use in implementing the `remove()` method.

Removing a Leaf Node

Removing a leaf node is the easiest among the three cases. Suppose we want to delete key value 23 from the binary search tree in Figure 14.1. After finding the node, it has to be unlinked, which can be done by setting the left child field of its parent, node 29, to `None`, as shown in Figure 14.8(a).

Removing a leaf node in our recursive method is as simple as returning a null reference. The `_bstRemove()` method uses the same technique of returning a reference from each recursive call as the insertion operation. By returning `None` back to the parent node, a null reference will be assigned to the appropriate link field in the parent, thus unlinking it from the tree, as shown in Figure 14.8(b).

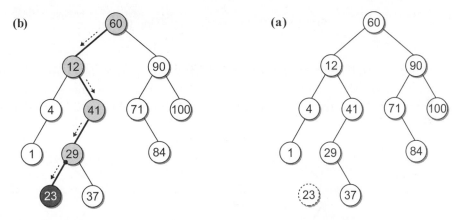

Figure 14.8: Removing a leaf node from a binary search tree: (a) finding the node and unlinking it from its parent; and (b) the tree after removing 23.

Removing an Interior Node with One Child

If the node to be removed has a single child, it can be either the left or right child. Suppose we want to delete key value 41 from the binary search tree in Figure 14.1. The node containing 41 has a subtree linked as the left child. If we were to simply return `None` back to the parent (12) as we did for a leaf node, not only would node 41 be removed, but we would also lose all of its descendants, as illustrated in Figure 14.9.

To remove node 41, we will have to do something with its descendants. But don't worry, we don't have to unlink each descendant and add them back to the tree. Since node 41 contains a single child, all of its descendants will either have keys that are smaller than 41 or all of them will be larger. In addition, given that node 41 is the right child of node 12, all of the descendants of node 41 must also be larger than 12. Thus, we can set the link in the right child field of node 12 to reference node 29, as illustrated in Figure 14.10. Node 29 now becomes the right child of node 12 and all of the descendants of node 41 will be properly linked without losing any nodes.

To accomplish this removal in the recursive method, we need only change the link in the appropriate child field of the parent to reference the child of the node

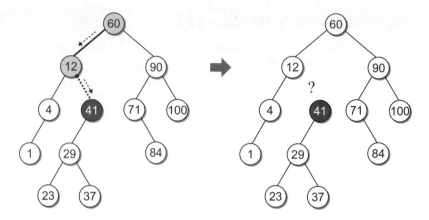

Figure 14.9: Incorrectly unlinking the interior node.

being deleted. Selecting the child field of the parent to change is automatically handled by the assignment performed upon return of the recursive call. All we have to do is return the appropriate child link in the node being deleted.

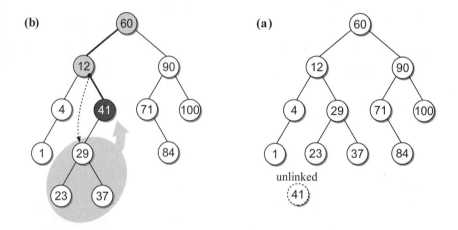

Figure 14.10: Removing an interior node (41) with one child: (a) redirecting the link from the node's parent to its child subtree; and (b) the tree after removing 41.

Removing an Interior Node with Two Children

The most difficult case is when the node to be deleted has two children. For example, suppose we want to remove node 12 from the binary search tree in Figure 14.1. Node 12 has two children, both of which are the roots of their own subtrees. If we were to apply the same approach used with removing an interior node containing one child, which child do we choose to replace the parent and what happens to the other child and its subtree? Figure 14.11 illustrates the result of replacing node 12 with its right child. This leaves the left subtree unlinked and thus removed from the tree. It would be possible to link the left child and its subtree as the left child of node 23. But this will increase the height of the tree, which we will see later causes the tree operations to be less efficient.

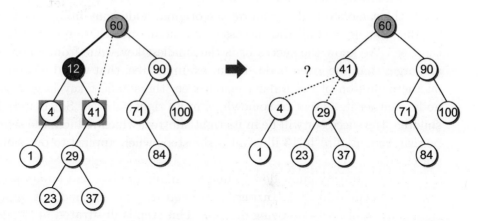

Figure 14.11: Attempting to remove an interior node with two children by replacing the node with one of its children.

The keys in a binary search tree are arranged such that an inorder traversal produces a sorted key sequence. Thus, each node has a logical predecessor and successor. For node 12, its predecessor is node 4 and its successor is node 23, as illustrated in Figure 14.12. Instead of attempting to replace the node with one of its two children, we can replace it with one of these nodes, both of which will either be a leaf or an interior node with one child. Since we already know how to remove a leaf and a one-child interior node, the one selected to replace node 12 can then easily be removed from the tree. Removing an interior node with two children requires three steps:

1. Find the logical successor, S, of the node to be deleted, N.

2. Copy the key from node S to node N.

3. Remove node S from the tree.

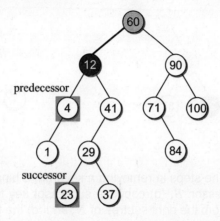

Figure 14.12: The logical successor and predecessor of node 12.

The latter two steps are straightforward. Once we have found the successor, we can simply copy the data from one node to the other. In addition, since we already know how to remove a leaf node or an interior node with one child we can apply the same method to remove the original node containing the successor.

But how do we find the successor of a node and where might it be located in the tree? We know the successor is the smallest key value from among those that are larger than the given node. In our example tree, that would be node 23. Based on the definition of the binary search tree, the smallest key larger than a given node is either its parent or somewhere in its right subtree. Since node 12 has two children, the successor will be in its right subtree, which reduces the set of nodes to be searched. Figure 14.13 illustrates the steps when applied to our sample binary search tree.

Since we already know how to find the minimum key in a binary search tree as was implemented in _bstMinimum(), we can use this method but apply it to the right subtree of the node being deleted. This step is illustrated in Figure 14.13(a). After finding the element that contains the successor key, we copy it to the node containing the element being removed, as shown in Figure 14.13(b).

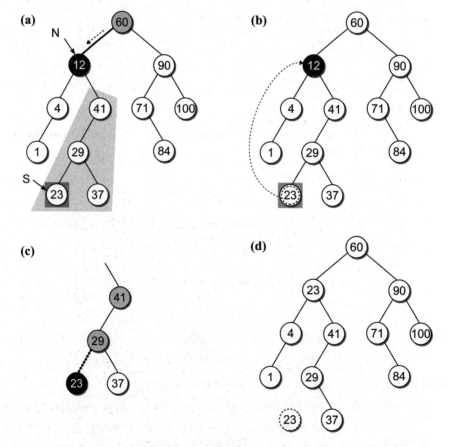

Figure 14.13: The steps in removing a key from a binary search tree: (a) find the node, N, and its successor, S; (b) copy the successor key from node N to S; (c) remove the successor key from the right subtree of N; and (d) the tree after removing 12.

After copying the element containing the successor key, the node originally containing the successor has to be removed from the right subtree, as shown in Figure 14.13(c). This can be done by calling the _bstRemove() method and passing it the root of the subtree. The result of removing the successor node is illustrated in Figure 14.13(d).

The _bstRemove() method is shown in Listing 14.5 along with the remove() map operation, which uses the recursive helper method to remove an entry from the tree. The _size field is decremented to reflect the change.

Listing 14.5   Delete a key from the binary search tree.

```
1  class BSTMap :
2  # ...
3    # Removes the map entry associated with the given key.
4    def remove( self, key ):
5      assert key in self, "Invalid map key."
6      self._root = self._bstRemove( self._root, key )
7      self._size -= 1
8
9    # Helper method that removes an existing item recursively.
10   def _bstRemove( self, subtree, target ):
11     # Search for the item in the tree.
12     if subtree is None :
13       return subtree
14     elif target < subtree.key :
15       subtree.left = self._bstRemove( subtree.left, target )
16       return subtree
17     elif target > subtree.key :
18       subtree.right = self._bstRemove( subtree.right, target )
19       return subtree
20     # We found the node containing the item.
21     else :
22       if subtree.left is None and subtree.right is None :
23         return None
24       elif subtree.left is None or subtree.right is None :
25         if subtree.left is not None :
26           return subtree.left
27         else :
28           return subtree.right
29       else
30         successor = self._bstMinimum( subtree.right )
31         subtree.key = successor.key
32         subtree.value = successor.value
33         subtree.right = self._bstRemove( subtree.right, successor.key )
34         return subtree
```

14.1.5 Efficiency of Binary Search Trees

The time-complexities for the binary search tree operations are listed in Table 14.1. This evaluation assumes the tree contains n nodes. We begin with the _bstSearch()

method. In searching for a target key, the function starts at the root node and works its way down into the tree until either the key is located or a null link is encountered. The worst case time for the search operation depends on the number of nodes that have to be examined.

In the previous chapter, we saw that the worst case time of a tree traversal was linear since it visited every node in the tree. When a null child link is encountered, the tree traversal backtracks to follow the other branches. During a search, however, the function never backtracks; it only moves down the tree, following one branch or the other at each node. Note that the recursive function does unwind in order to return to the location in the program where it was first invoked, but during the unwinding other branches are not examined. The search follows a single path from the root down to the target node or to the node at which the search falls off the tree.

The worst case occurs when the longest path in the tree is followed in search of the target and the longest path is based on the height of the tree. Binary trees come in many shapes and sizes and their heights can vary. But, as we saw in the previous chapter, a tree of size n can have a minimum height of roughly $\log n$ when the tree is complete and a maximum height of n when there is one node per level. If we have no knowledge about the shape of the tree and its height, we have to assume the worst and in this case that would be a tree of height n. Thus, the time required to find a key in a binary search tree is $O(n)$ in the worst case.

Searching for the minimum key in a binary search tree is also a linear time operation. Even though it does not compare keys, it does have to navigate through the tree by always taking the left branch starting from the root. In the worst case, there will be one node per level with each node linked to its parent via the left child link.

The _bstInsert() method, which implements the algorithm for inserting a new element into the tree, performs a search to find where the new key belongs in the tree. We know from our earlier analysis the search operation requires linear time in the worst case. How much work is done after locating the parent of the node that will contain the new element? The only work done is the creation of a new node and returning its link to the parent, which can be done in constant time. Thus, the insertion operation requires $O(n)$ time in the worst case. The _bstRemove() method also requires $O(n)$ time, the analysis of which is left as an exercise.

Operation	Worst Case
_bstSearch(root, k)	$O(n)$
_bstMinimum(root)	$O(n)$
_bstInsert(root, k)	$O(n)$
_bstDelete(root, k)	$O(n)$
traversal	$O(n)$

Table 14.1: Time-complexities for the binary search tree operations.

14.2 Search Tree Iterators

The definition of the Search Tree ADT specifies an iterator that can be used to traverse through the keys contained in the tree. The implementation of the iterators for use with the linear list structures were rather simple. For the sequence types, we were able to initialize an index variable for accessing the elements that was incremented after each iteration of the **for** loop. With a linked list, the iterator can define and use an external reference that is initialized to the head node and then advanced through the list with each iteration of the loop.

Traversals can be performed on a binary search tree, but this requires a recursive solution. We cannot easily advance to the next key without moving down into the tree and then backing up each time a leaf is encountered. One solution is to have the iterator build an array of elements by recursively traversing the tree, which we can then step through as the iterator progresses just as we did with the linear structures. An iterator using this approach is provided in Listing 14.6.

While this approach works, it requires the allocation of additional storage space, which can be significant if the tree contains a large number of elements. As an alternative, we can perform a recursive traversal with the use of a stack. Remember, recursion simulates the use of a stack without having to directly perform the push and pop operations. Any recursive function or method can be implemented using a

---

Listing 14.6   An iterator for the binary search tree using an array.

```
 1  class _BSTMapIterator :
 2    def __init__( self, root, size ):
 3      # Creates the array and fills it with the keys.
 4      self._theKeys = Array( size )
 5      self._curItem = 0     # Keep track of the next location in the array.
 6      self._bstTraversal( root )
 7      self._curItem = 0     # Reset the current item index.
 8
 9    def __iter__( self ):
10      return self
11
12    # Returns the next key from the array of keys
13    def __next__( self ):
14      if self._curItem < len( self._theKeys ) :
15        key = self._theKeys[ self._curItem ]
16        self._curItem += 1
17        return key
18      else :
19        raise StopIteration
20
21    # Performs an inorder traversal used to build the array of keys.
22    def _bstTraversal( self, subtree ):
23      if subtree is not None :
24        self._bstTraversal( subtree.left )
25        self._theKeys[ self._curItem ] = subtree.key
26        self._curItem += 1
27        self._bstTraversal( subtree.right )
```

software stack. For the tree traversal, node references are pushed onto the stack as it moves down into the tree and the references are popped as the process backtracks. Listing 14.7 shows the implementation of the iterator using a software stack.

Listing 14.7   An iterator for the binary search tree using a software stack.

```
 1  class _BSTMapIterator :
 2    def __init__( self, root ):
 3      # Create a stack for use in traversing the tree.
 4      self._theStack = Stack()
 5      # We must traverse down to the node containing the smallest key
 6      # during which each node along the path is pushed onto the stack.
 7      self._traverseToMinNode( root )
 8
 9    def __iter__( self ):
10      return self
11
12    # Returns the next item from the BST in key order.
13    def __next__( self ):
14      # If the stack is empty, we are done.
15      if self._theStack.isEmpty() :
16        raise StopIteration
17      else :
18        # The top node on the stack contains the next key.
19        node = self._theStack.pop()
20        key = node.key
21        # If this node has a subtree rooted as the right child, we must
22        # find the node in that subtree that contains the smallest key.
23        # Again, the nodes along the path are pushed onto the stack.
24        if node.right is not None :
25          self._traverseToMinNode( node.right )
26
27    # Traverses down the subtree to find the node containing the smallest
28    # key during which the nodes along that path are pushed onto the stack.
29    def _traverseToMinNode( self, subtree ):
30      if subtree is not None :
31        self._theStack.push( subtree )
32        self._traverseToMinNode( subtree.left )
```

14.3 AVL Trees

The binary search tree provides a convenient structure for storing and searching data collections. The efficiency of the search, insertion, and deletion operations depend on the height of the tree. In the best case, a binary tree of size n has a height of $\log n$, but in the worst case, there is one node per level, resulting in a height of n. Thus, it would be to our advantage to try to build a binary search tree that has height $\log n$.

If we were constructing the tree from the complete set of search keys, this would be easy to accomplish. The keys can be sorted in ascending order and then using a technique similar to that employed with the linked list version of the merge sort, the interior nodes can be easily identified. But this requires knowing all of the keys up front, which is seldom the case in real applications where keys are routinely being added and removed. We could rebuild the binary search tree each time a new key is added or an existing one is removed. But the time to accomplish this would be extreme in comparison to using a simple brute-force search on one of the sequential list structures. What we need is a way to maintain the optimal tree height in real time, as the entries in the tree change.

The **AVL tree**, which was invented by G. M. **A**del'son-**V**elskii and Y. M. **L**andis in 1962, improves on the binary search tree by always guaranteeing the tree is height balanced, which allows for more efficient operations. A binary tree is **balanced** if the heights of the left and right subtrees of every node differ by at most 1. Figure 14.14 illustrates two examples of AVL trees.

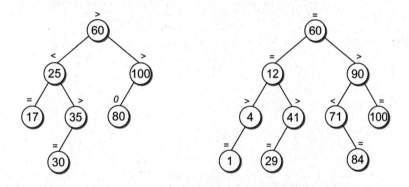

Figure 14.14: Examples of balanced binary search trees.

With each node in an AVL tree, we associate a **balance factor**, which indicates the height difference between the left and right branch. The balance factor can be one of three states:

left high: When the left subtree is higher than the right subtree.

equal high: When the two subtrees have equal height.

right high: When the right subtree is higher than the left subtree.

The balance factors of the tree nodes in our illustrations are indicated by symbols: > for a left high state, = for the equal high state, and < for a right high state. When a node is out of balance, we will use either << or >> to indicate which subtree is higher.

The search and traversal operations are the same with an AVL tree as with a binary search tree. The insertion and deletion operations have to be modified in order to maintain the balance property of the tree as new keys are inserted and existing ones removed. By maintaining a balanced tree, we ensure its height never exceeds $1.44 \log n$. This height is sufficient for providing $O(\log n)$ time operations even in the worst case.

14.3.1   Insertions

Inserting a key into an AVL tree begins with the same process used with a binary search tree. We search for the new key in the tree and add a new node at the child link where we fall off the tree. When a new key is inserted into an AVL tree, the balance property of the tree must be maintained. If the insertion of the new key causes any of the subtrees to become unbalanced, they will have to be rebalanced.

Some insertions are simpler than others. For example, suppose we want to add key 120 to the sample AVL tree from Figure 14.14(a). Following the insertion operation of the binary search tree, the new key will be inserted as the right child of node 100, as illustrated in Figure 14.15(a). The tree remains balanced since the insertion does not change the height of any subtree, but it does cause a change in the balance factors. After the key is inserted, the balance factors have to be adjusted in order to determine if any subtree is out of balance. There is a limited set of nodes that can be affected when a new key is added. This set is limited to the nodes along the path to the insertion point. Figure 14.15(b) shows the new balance factors after key 120 is added.

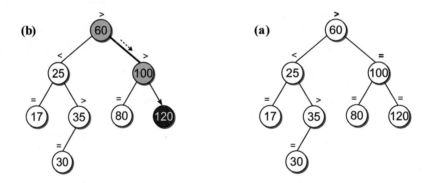

Figure 14.15: A simple insertion into an AVL tree: (a) with key 120 inserted; and (b) the new balance factors.

What happens if we add key 28 to the AVL? The new node is inserted as the left child of node 30, as illustrated in Figure 14.16(a). When the balance factors are recalculated, as in Figure 14.16(b), we can see all of the subtrees along the path that are above node 30 are now out of balance, which violates the AVL balance property. For this example, we can correct the imbalance by rearranging the subtree rooted at node 35, as illustrated in Figure 14.16(c).

Rotations

Multiple subtrees can become unbalanced after inserting a new key, all of which have roots along the insertion path. But only one will have to be rebalanced: the one deepest in the tree and closest to the new node. After inserting the key, the balance factors are adjusted during the unwinding of the recursion. The first

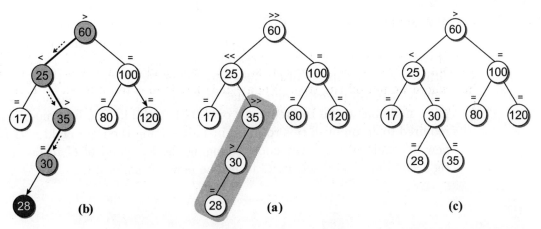

Figure 14.16: An insertion that causes the AVL tree to become unbalanced: (a) the new key is inserted; (b) the balance factors showing an out-of-balance tree; and (c) the subtree after node 35 is rearranged.

subtree encountered that is out of balance has to be rebalanced. The root node of this subtree is known as the ***pivot node***.

An AVL subtree is rebalanced by performing a ***rotation*** around the pivot node. This involves rearranging the links of the pivot node, its children, and possibly one of its grandchildren. The actual modifications depend on which descendant's subtree of the pivot node the new key was inserted into and the balance factors. There are four possible cases:

- *Case 1:* This case, as illustrated in Figure 14.17, occurs when the balance factor of the pivot node (P) is left high before the insertion and the new key is inserted into the left child (C) of the pivot node. To rebalance the subtree, the pivot node has to be rotated right over its left child. The rotation is accomplished by changing the links such that P becomes the right child of C and the right child of C becomes the left child of P.

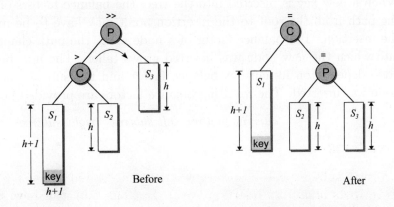

Figure 14.17: Case 1: a right rotation of the pivot node over its left child.

- *Case 2:* This case involves three nodes: the pivot (P), the left child of the pivot (C), and the right child (G) of C. For this case to occur, the balance factor of the pivot is left high before the insertion and the new key is inserted into either the right subtree of C. This case, which is illustrated in Figure 14.18, requires two rotations. Node C has to be rotated left over node V and the pivot node has to be rotated right over its left child. The link modifications required to accomplish this rotation include setting the right child of G as the new left child of the pivot node, changing the left child of G to become the right child of C, and setting C to be the new left child of G.

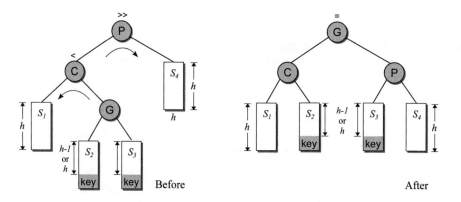

Figure 14.18: Case 2: a double rotation with the pivot's left child rotated left over its right child and the pivot rotated right over its left child.

- *Cases 3 and 4:* The third case is a mirror image of the first case and the fourth case is a mirror image of the second case. The difference is the new key is inserted in the right subtree of the pivot node or a descendant of its right subtree. The two cases are illustrated in Figure 14.19.

New Balance Factors

When a new key is inserted into the tree, the balance factors of the nodes along the path from the root to the insertion point may have to be modified to reflect the insertion. The balance factor of a node along the path changes if the subtree into which the new node was inserted grows taller. The new balance factor of a node depends on its current balance factor and the subtree into which the new node was inserted. The resulting balance factors are provided here:

current factor	left subtree	right subtree
>	>>	=
=	>	<
<	=	<<

Modifications to the balance factors are made in reverse order as the recursion unwinds. When a node has a left high balance and the new node is inserted into

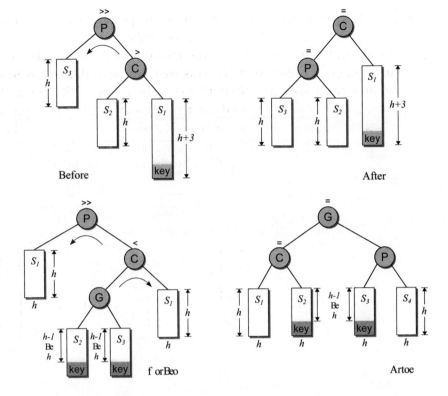

Figure 14.19: Cases 3 (top) and 4 (bottom) are mirror images of cases 1 and 2.

its left child or it has a right high balance and the new node is inserted into its right child, the node is out of balance and its subtree has to be rebalanced. After rebalancing, the subtree will shrink by one level, which results in the balance factors of its ancestors remaining the same. The balance factors of the ancestors will also remain the same when the balance factor changes to equal high.

After a rotation is performed, the balance factor of the impacted nodes have to be changed to reflect the new node heights. The changes required depend on which of the four cases triggered the rotation. The balance factor settings in cases 2 and 4 depend on the balance factor of the original pivot nodes grandchild (the right child of node L or the left child of node R). The new balance factors for the nodes involved in a rotation are provided in Table 14.2.

Figure 14.20 illustrates the construction of an AVL tree by inserting the keys from the list [60, 25, 35, 100, 17, 80], one key at a time. Each tree in the figure shows the results after performing the indicate operation. Two double rotations are required to construct the tree: one after node 35 is inserted and one after node 80 is inserted.

14.3.2 Deletions

When an entry is removed from an AVL tree, we must ensure the balance property is maintained. As with the insert operation, deletion begins by using the corre-

original G	new P	new L	new R	new G
case 1	·	=	=	·	·
case 2	>	<	=	·	=
	=	=	=	·	=
	<	=	>	·	=
case 3	·	=	·	=	·
case 4	>	=	·	=	<
	=	=	·	=	=
	<	=	·	=	>

Table 14.2: The new balance factors for the nodes after a rotation.

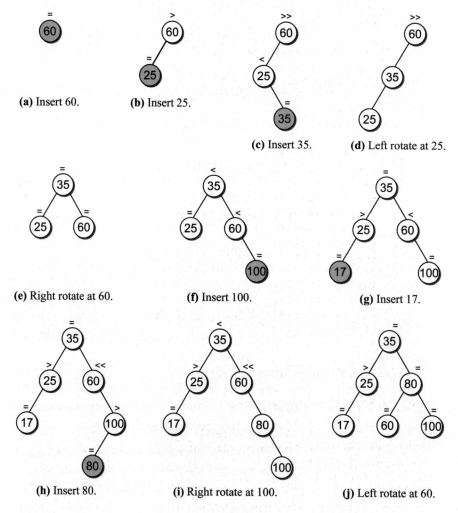

Figure 14.20: Building an AVL tree from the list of keys [60, 25, 35, 100, 17, 80]. Each tree shows the results after performing the indicated operation.

sponding operation from the binary search tree. After removing the targeted entry, subtrees may have to be rebalanced. For example, suppose we want to remove key 17 from the AVL tree in Figure 14.21(a). After removing the leaf node, the subtree rooted at node 25 is out of balance, as shown in Figure 14.21(b). A left rotation has to be performed pivoting on node 25 to correct the imbalance, as shown in Figure 14.21(c).

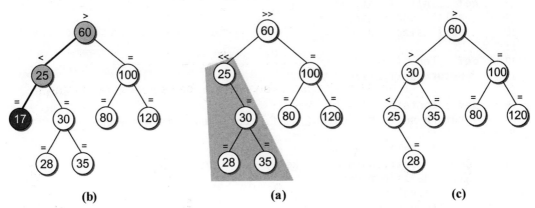

(b)   (a)   (c)

Figure 14.21: A deletion that causes the AVL tree to become unbalanced: (a) the node is located; (b) the balance factors change showing an out-of-balance tree; and (c) the tree after a left rotation.

As with an insertion, the only subtrees that can become unbalanced are those along the path from the root to the original node containing the target. Remember, if the key being removed is in an interior node, its successor is located and copied to the node and the successor's original node is removed. In the insertion operation, at most one subtree can become unbalanced. After the appropriate rotation is performed on the subtree, the balance factors of the node's ancestors do not change. Thus, it restores the **_height-balance property_** both locally at the subtree and globally for the entire tree. This is not the case with a deletion. When a subtree is rebalanced due to a deletion, it can cause the ancestors of the subtree to then become unbalanced. This effect can ripple up all the way to the root node. So, all of the nodes along the path have to be evaluated and rebalanced if necessary.

14.3.3 Implementation

A partial implementation of the Map ADT using a balanced binary search tree is provided in Listing 14.8. The implementation of the non-helper methods is very similar to that of the binary search tree version. Since the traversal and search operations of the AVL tree are identical to those of the binary search tree, the `valueOf()` method can use the `_bstSearch()` helper method and the `__iter__` method can create an instance of the `_BSTMapIterator`. Of course, we assume the implementation of these components are included within the `AVLMap` class. The

Listing 14.8   Partial implementation of the `avltree.py` module.

```python
1  # Constants for the balance factors.
2  LEFT_HIGH =  1
3  EQUAL_HIGH = 0
4  RIGHT_HIGH = -1
5
6  # Implementation of the Map ADT using an AVL tree.
7  class AVLMap :
8    def __init__( self ):
9      self._root = None
10     self._size = 0
11
12   def __len__( self ):
13     return self._size
14
15   def __contains__( self, key ):
16     return self._bstSearch( self._root, key ) is not None
17
18   def add( self, key, value ):
19     node = self._bstSearch( key )
20     if node is not None :
21       node.value = value
22       return False
23     else :
24       (self._root, tmp) = self._avlInsert( self._root, key, value )
25       self._size += 1
26       return True
27
28   def valueOf( self, key ):
29     node = self._bstSearch( self._root, key )
30     assert node is not None, "Invalid map key."
31     return node.value
32
33   def remove( self, key ):
34     assert key in self, "Invalid map key."
35     (self._root, tmp) = self._avlRemove( self._root, key )
36     self._size -= 1
37
38   def __iter__( self ):
39     return _BSTMapIterator( self._root )
40
41  # Storage class for creating the AVL tree node.
42  class _AVLMapNode :
43    def __init__( self, key, value ):
44      self.key = key
45      self.value = value
46      self.bfactor = EQUAL_HIGH
47      self.left = None
48      self.right = None
```

only change required to the add() and remove() methods is that each method must call an AVL specific helper method. We provide the implementation for adding a new element to an AVL tree and leave the removal as an exercise.

The nodes in an AVL tree must store their balance factor in addition to the key, data, and two child links. The _AVLTreeNode is provided in lines 42–48 of Listing 14.8. We also create and initialize three named constants to represent the three balance factor values. By using named constants, we avoid possible confusion in having to remember what value represents which of the possible balance factors.

The implementation of the insertion operation is divided into several helper methods for a better modular solution. First, we provide helper methods for performing the left and right rotations, as shown in Listing 14.9. A right rotation on a given pivot node is performed using _avlRotateRight(). The operation is illustrated in Figure 14.17. The _avlRotateLeft() function handles a left rotation, as illustrated in the top of Figure 14.19. Both methods return a reference to the new root node of the subtree after the rotation.

Listing 14.9   Helper functions for performing the AVL tree rotations.

```
1   class AVLMap :
2   # ...
3     # Rotates the pivot to the right around its left child.
4     def _avlRotateRight( self, pivot ):
5       C = pivot.left
6       pivot.left = C.right
7       C.right = pivot
8       return C
9
10    # Rotates the pivot to the left around its right child.
11    def _avlRotateLeft( self, pivot ):
12      C = pivot.right
13      pivot.right = C.left
14      C.left = pivot
15      return C
```

When a subtree becomes unbalanced, we have to determine which of the four possible cases caused the event. Cases 1 and 3 occur when the left subtree of the pivot node is two levels higher than the right subtree, whereas cases 2 and 4 occur when the right subtree becomes two levels higher than the left. We divide the cases into two groups based on which subtree of the pivot node is higher.

The _avlLeftBalance() method, provided in Listing 14.10, handles the rotations when the left subtree is higher. To distinguish between the two cases, we have to examine the balance factor of the pivot node's left child. Case one occurs when the left child has a factor of left high (its left child is higher). For this case, the balance factors are adjusted appropriately and a right rotation is performed using the _avlRightRotate() method, as shown in lines 9–13. Case 3 occurs when the balance factor of the left child of the pivot node is right high. Note that the case of the pivot's left child having equal balance can never occur, so we do not have to check for this condition. After setting the balance factors, case 3 requires a double rotation, as shown in lines 16–34. We first perform a left rotation on the right child (C) of the pivot node. The root node of the subtree resulting from this rotation becomes the new left child of the pivot node. A right rotation is then performed on

Listing 14.10 Helper functions used to rebalance AVL subtrees.

```
1   class AVLMap :
2   # ...
3       # Rebalance a node when its left subtree is higher.
4       def _avlLeftBalance( self, pivot ):
5           # Set L to point to the left child of the pivot.
6           C = pivot.left
7
8           # See if the rebalancing is due to case 1.
9           if C.bfactor == LEFT_HIGH :
10              pivot.bfactor = EQUAL_HIGH
11              C.bfactor = EQUAL_HIGH
12              pivot = _avlRotateRight( pivot )
13              return pivot
14
15          # Otherwise, a balance from the left is due to case 3.
16          else :
17              # Change the balance factors.
18              if G.bfactor == LEFT_HIGH :
19                  pivot.bfactor = RIGHT_HIGH
20                  C.bfactor = EQUAL_HIGH
21              elif G.bfactor == EQUAL_HIGH :
22                  pivot.bfactor = EQUAL_HIGH
23                  C.bfactor = EQUAL_HIGH
24              else : # G.bfactor == RIGHT_HIGH
25                  pivot.bfactor = EQUAL_HIGH
26                  C.bfactor = LEFT_HIGH
27
28              # All three cases set G's balance factor to equal high.
29              G.bfactor = EQUAL_HIGH
30
31              # Perform the double rotation.
32              pivot.left = _avlRotateLeft( L )
33              pivot = _avlRotateRight( pivot )
34              return pivot
```

the pivot node, resulting in the grandchild (G) of the original pivot node becoming the new root node. The _avlRightBalance() method can be implemented in a similar fashion. The actual implementation is left as an exercise.

The insert operation for the binary search tree returned a reference to the existing subtree or the new node, depending on the current invocation of the recursive function. When inserting into an AVL tree, the method must also return a boolean flag indicating if the subtree grew taller. In order to return both values, the _avlInsert() function, shown in Listing 14.11, returns a tuple with the first element containing the node reference and the second containing the boolean flag.

Finding the location of the new key and linking its node into the tree uses the same navigation technique as in the binary search tree. The real difference between the insertions into a BST and an AVL tree occurs during the unwinding of the recursion. We have to check to see if the subtree we just visited has grown taller. A taller child subtree means we have to check to see if the current subtree

Listing 14.11 Inserting an entry into an AVL tree.

```
1   class AVLMap :
2   # ...
3       # Recursive method to handle the insertion into an AVL tree. The
4       # function returns a tuple containing a reference to the root of the
5       # subtree and a boolean to indicate if the subtree grew taller.
6       def _avlInsert( self, subtree, key, newitem ):
7         # See if we have found the insertion point.
8         if subtree is None :
9           subtree = _AVLTreeNode( key, newitem )
10          taller = True
11
12          # Is the key already in the tree?
13        elif key == subtree.data :
14          return (subtree, False)
15
16          # See if we need to navigate to the left.
17        elif key < subtree.data :
18          (subtree, taller) = _avlInsert( subtree.left, key, newitem )
19          # If the subtree grew taller, see if it needs rebalancing.
20          if taller :
21            if subtree.bfactor == LEFT_HIGH :
22              subtree.right = _avlLeftBalance( subtree )
23              taller = False
24            elif subtree.bfactor == EQUAL_HIGH :
25              subtree.bfactor = LEFT_HIGH
26              taller = True
27            else :      # RIGHT_HIGH
28              subtree.bfactor = EQUAL_HIGH
29              taller = False
30
31          # Otherwise, navigate to the right.
32        else key > subtree.data :
33          (node, taller) = _avlInsert( subtree.right, key, newitem )
34          # If the subtree grew taller, see if it needs rebalancing.
35          if taller :
36            if subtree.bfactor == LEFT_HIGH :
37              subtree.bfactor = EQUAL_HIGH
38              taller = False
39            elif subtree.bfactor == EQUAL_HIGH :
40              subtree.bfactor = RIGHT_HIGH
41              taller = True
42            else :      # RIGHT_HIGH
43              subtree.right = _avlRightBalance( subtree )
44              taller = False
45
46          # Return the results.
47        return (subtree, taller)
```

is out of balance and needs to be rebalanced. Regardless if the subtree is out of balance, the balance factor of the current subtree's root node has to be modified as discussed in the previous section. If a subtree did not grow taller, nothing needs to be done.

As the recursion unwinds, the growth status has to be passed back to the parent of each subtree. There are only three circumstances when a subtree grows taller. The first is when a new node is created and linked into the tree. Since the child link in the parent of the new node was originally null, the new node grows from an empty subtree to a subtree of height one. A subtree can also grow taller when its children were originally of equal height and one of the child subtrees has grown taller. In all other instances, the subtree does not grow. Indicating the growth of a subtree is spread throughout the _avlInsert() method as appropriate.

14.4   The 2-3 Tree

The binary search tree and the AVL tree are not the only two tree structures that can be used when implementing abstract data types that require fast search operations. The 2-3 tree is a multi-way search tree that can have up to three children. It provides fast operations that are easy to implement. The tree gets its name from the number of keys and children each node can contain. Figure 14.22 provides an abstract view of a simple 2-3 tree.

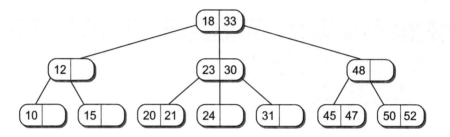

Figure 14.22: A 2-3 tree with integer search keys.

A *2-3 tree* is a search tree that is always balanced and whose shape and structure is defined as follows:

- Every node has capacity for one or two keys (and their corresponding payload), which we term key one and key two.

- Every node has capacity for up to three children, which we term the left, middle, and right child.

- All leaf nodes are at the same level.

- Every internal node must contains two or three children. If the node has one key, it must contain two children; if it has two keys, it must contain three children.

In addition, the 2-3 tree has a search property similar to the binary search tree, as illustrated in Figure 14.23. For each interior node, V:

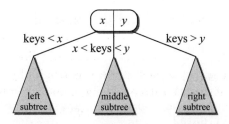

Figure 14.23: A search property of a 2-3 tree.

- All keys less than the first key of node V are stored in the left subtree of V.

- If the node has two children, all keys greater than the first key of node V are stored in the middle subtree of V.

- If the node has three children: (1) all keys greater than the first key of node V but less than the second key are stored in the middle subtree of V; and (2) all keys greater than the second key are stored in the right subtree.

The implementation of 2-3 tree assumes the nodes are constructed from the _23TreeNode class as defined in Listing 14.12.

Listing 14.12 Storage class for creating the 2-3 tree nodes.

```
1   class _23TreeNode( object ):
2     def __init__( self, key, data ):
3       self.key1 = key
4       self.key2 = None
5       self.data1 = data
6       self.data2 = None
7       self.left = None
8       self.middle = None
9       self.right = None
10
11      # Is this a leaf node?
12    def isALeaf( self ):
13      return self.left is None and self.middle is None and self.right is None
14
15      # Are there two keys in this node?
16    def isFull( self ):
17      return self.key2 is not None
18
19      # Does the node contain the given target key?
20    def hasKey( self, target ):
21      if (target == self.key1) or
22         (self.key2 is not None and target == self.key2) :
23        return True
24      else :
25        return False
26
```

(Listing Continued)

Listing 14.12   Continued . . .

```
27      # Returns the data associated with the target key or None.
28    def getData( self, target ):
29      if target == self.key1 :
30        return self.data1
31      elif self.key2 is not None and target == self.key2 :
32        return self.data2
33      else :
34        return None
35
36      # Chooses the appropriate branch for the given target.
37    def getBranch( self, target ):
38      if target < self.key1 :
39        return self.left
40      elif self.key2 is None :
41        return self.middle
42      elif target < self.key2 :
43        return self.middle
44      else :
45        return self.right
```

The node class contains seven fields, one for each of the two keys and corresponding data and one for each of the three child links. It also defines three accessor methods that compute information related to the given node. The `isLeaf()` method determines if the node is a leaf, `isFull()` determines if the node contains two keys, `hasKey()` determines if the target key is contained in the node, `getData()` returns the data associated with the given key or `None` if the key is not in the node, and `getBranch()` compares a target key to the nodes key(s) and returns a reference to the appropriate branch that must be followed to find the target. These methods are included to provide meaningful names for those common operations.

14.4.1 Searching

Searching a 2-3 tree is very similar to that of a binary search tree. We start at the root and follow the appropriate branch based on the value of the target key. The only difference is that we have to compare the target against both keys if the node contains two keys, and we have to choose from among possibly three branches. As in a binary search tree, a successful search will lead to a key in one of the nodes while an unsuccessful search will lead to a null link. That null link will always be in a leaf node. The reason for this is that if an interior node contains one key, it always contains two child links, one for the keys less than its key and one for the keys greater than its key. In a similar fashion, if the node contains two keys, it will always contain three child links that direct us to one of the value ranges: (1) keys less than the node's first key, (2) keys greater than the node's first key but less than its second key, and (3) keys greater than the node's second key. Thus, there is never an opportunity to take a null link from an interior node as there was in a binary search tree. Figure 14.24 illustrates two searches, one that is successful and one that is not. The search operation for the 2-3 tree is implemented in Listing 14.13.

Listing 14.13 Searching a 2-3 tree.

```
 1  class Tree23Map :
 2  # ...
 3    def _23Search( subtree, target ):
 4      # If we encounter a null pointer, the target is not in the tree.
 5      if subtree is None :
 6        return None
 7      # See if the node contains the key. If so, return the data.
 8      elif subtree.hashKey( target ) :
 9        return subtree.getData( target )
10      # Otherwise, take the appropriate branch.
11      else :
12        branch = subtree.getBranch( target )
13        return _23Search( branch, target )
```

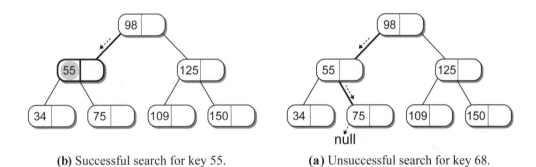

(b) Successful search for key 55.   (a) Unsuccessful search for key 68.

Figure 14.24: Searching a 2-3 tree.

14.4.2 Insertions

The process of inserting a key into a 2-3 tree is similar to that of a binary search tree, although it's more complicated. The first step is to search for the key as if it were in the tree. As we saw in the previous section, the search for a non-existent key will lead us to a leaf node. The next step is to determine if there is space in the leaf for the new key. If the leaf contains a single key, we can easily insert the key into the node. Consider the partial 2-3 tree illustrated in Figure 14.25 and suppose we want to insert key value 84. In searching for 84, we end up at the node containing value 75. Since there is space in this node, 84 can be added as the node's second key.

But what if the new key is less than the key stored in the leaf node? Suppose we want to add key 26 to the tree, as shown in Figure 14.26. The search leads us to the leaf node containing value 34. When the new key is smaller than the existing key, the new key is inserted as the first key and the existing one is moved to become the second key.

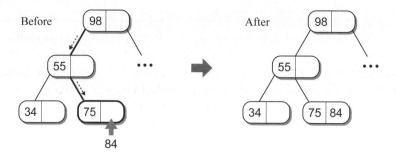

Figure 14.25: Inserting key 84 into a 2-3 tree with space available in the leaf node.

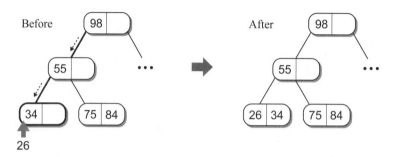

Figure 14.26: Inserting key 26 into a 2-3 tree with space available in the leaf node.

Splitting a Leaf Node

Things become more complicated when the leaf node is full. Suppose we want to insert value 80 into our sample tree. The search for the node leads to the leaf node containing keys 75 and 84, as shown in Figure 14.27. Based on the search property of the 2-3 tree, the new key belongs in this leaf node, but it's full. You might be tempted to create a new leaf node and attach it to the full node as a child. This cannot be done, however, since all leaf nodes must be at the same level and all interior nodes must have at least two children. Instead, the node has to be split, resulting in a new node being created at the same level.

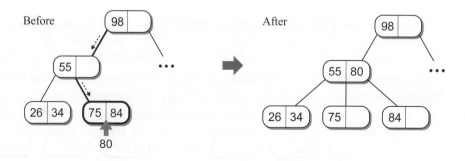

Figure 14.27: Inserting a key into a 2-3 tree with a full leaf node.

The splitting process involves two steps. First, a new node is created, then the new key is compared to the two keys (75 and 84) in the original node. The smallest among the three is inserted into the original node and the largest is inserted into the new node. The middle value is *promoted* to the parent along with a reference to the newly created node. The promoted key and reference are then inserted into the parent node. Figure 14.28 illustrates the three possible cases when splitting a leaf node. k_1 and k_2 are the two keys in the original node and x is the new key that we are trying to insert into the node.

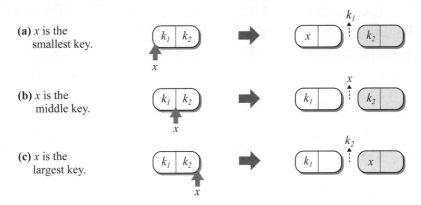

Figure 14.28: Splitting a leaf node into two nodes: each node gets one key and one key is promoted to the parent.

When a key is promoted to the parent, it has to be inserted into the parent's node in a similar fashion to that of a leaf node. The difference is that a reference to the newly created node is also passed up to the parent that has to be inserted into one of the link fields of the parent. Inserting the promoted key and reference into the parent node is simple if the parent contains a single key. The placement of the key and reference depends on which child node was split, as illustrated in Figure 14.29.

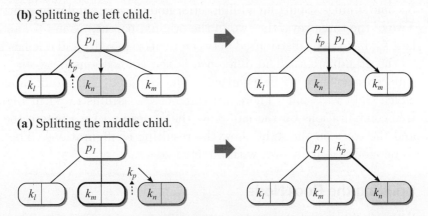

Figure 14.29: Inserting the promoted key and reference into a parent with one key.

There are two cases:

1. *The left child is split*: The existing key p_1 in the parent node becomes the second key and the middle child is moved to become the right child. The promoted key k_p becomes the first key in the parent and the reference to the new node becomes the middle child. Links that have to be modified are shown by directed edges in the figure.

2. *The middle child is split*: The promoted key k_p becomes the second key of the parent and the newly created node becomes the right child.

Splitting a Parent Node

What happens if the node is split and its parent contains three children? For example, suppose we want to insert key 42 into the sample tree shown in Figure 14.30. The node containing keys 26 and 34 has to be split with 34 being promoted to the parent. But the parent also contains two keys (55 and 80). When the parent node is full, it has to be split in a similar fashion as a leaf node, resulting in a key and node reference being promoted to its parent, the grandparent of the child that was split. The splitting process can continue up the tree until either a non-full parent node or the root is located.

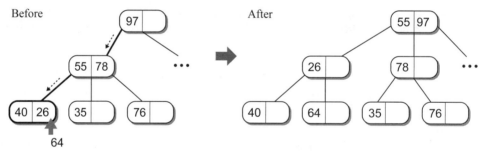

Figure 14.30: A full parent node has to be split to accommodate a promoted key.

When the parent node is split, a new parent node is created and the two will become siblings. Splitting a full interior node is very similar to splitting a leaf node. Two of the three keys, the two in the original parent, p_1 and p_2, and the promoted key, k_p, have to be distributed between the two parents and one has to be promoted to the grandparent. The difference is the connections between the parents and children also have to be changed. The required link modifications depends on which child was split. There are three cases, as illustrated in Figure 14.31. The tree configurations on the left show the nodes and keys before the parent is split and the trees on the right show the resulting configurations. The links that have to be modified are shown with directed edges.

Splitting the Root Node

When the root node has to be split, as illustrated in Figure 14.32, a new root node is created into which the promoted key is stored. The original root becomes the

(b) Splitting the left child.

(a) Splitting the middle child.

(c) Splitting the right child.

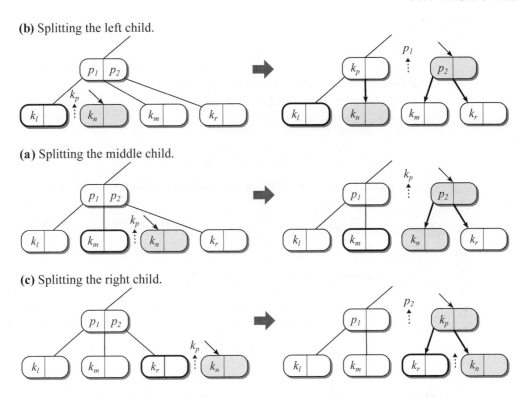

Figure 14.31: Inserting the promoted key and reference into a full parent node.

left child and new child node becomes its middle child. Splitting the root node results in a new level being added to the tree.

Implementation

The 2-3 tree insertion is best implemented recursively. Remember, to insert a new item, not only do we have to navigate down into the tree to find a leaf node, but we may also have to split the nodes along the path as we backtrack to the root node.

The implementation of the 2-3 tree insertion is provided in Listing 14.14. The _23Insert() method handles the two special cases involving the root node: the insertion of the first key, resulting in the creation of the first node, and splitting the root node, resulting in a new tree level. If the tree is not initially empty, the

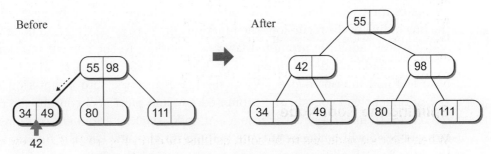

Figure 14.32: Splitting the root node is a special case.

Listing 14.14   Insert a new key into a 2-3 tree.

```
1   class Tree23Map :
2   # ...
3     def _23Insert( self, key, newitem ):
4       # If the tree is empty, a node has to be created for the first key.
5       if self._root is None :
6         self._root = _23TreeNode( key, newitem )
7
8       # Otherwise, find the correct leaf and insert the key.
9       else :
10        (pKey, pData, pRef) = _23Insert( self._root, key, newitem )
11
12        # See if the node was split.
13        if pKey is not None :
14          newRoot = _23TreeNode( pKey, pData )
15          newRoot.left = self._root
16          newRoot.middle = pRef
17          self._root = newRoot
18
19    # Recursive function to insert a new key into the tree.
20    def _23RecInsert( subtree, key, newitem ):
21      # Make sure the key is not already in the tree.
22      if subtree.hasKey( key ) :
23        return (None, None, None)
24
25      # Is this a leaf node?
26      elif subtree.isALeaf() :
27        return _23AddToNode( subtree, key, newitem, None )
28
29      # Otherwise, it's an interior node.
30      else :
31        # Which branch do we take?
32        branch = subtree.getBranch( key )
33        (pKey, pData, pRef) = _23Insert( branch, key, newitem )
34        # If the child was split, the promoted key and reference have to be
35        # added to the interior node.
36        if pKey is None :
37          return (None, None, None)
38        else :
39          return _23AddToNode( subtree, pKey, pData, pRef )
```

recursive _23RecInsert() method is called to insert the new key. This method navigates the tree to find the leaf node into which the key is to be inserted. During the unwinding of the recursion, the function checks to see if the child node was split, and if it was, adds the promoted key and reference to the current interior node.

The _23AddToNode(), provided in Listing 14.15, is used to insert a key into both leaf and interior nodes. When the key is inserted into an interior node, the key argument will contain the promoted key and pRef will contain the promoted reference. To insert a new key into a leaf node, the key argument contains the new key and pRef will be None. If there is room for the new key, the function arranges the keys and the links in the proper order and null references are returned in a

Listing 14.15 Helper function for inserting a key into a node of the 2-3 tree.

```
1   # Handles the insertion of a key into a node. If pRef != None, then
2   # the insertion is into an interior node.
3   class Tree23Map :
4   # ...
5     def _23AddToNode( self, subtree, key, data, pRef ):
6       # If the leaf is full, it has to be split.
7       if subtree.isFull() :
8         return self._23SplitNode( subtree, key, data,  None )
9       # Otherwise, add the new key in its proper order.
10      else :
11        if key < subtree.key1 :
12          subtree.key2 = subtree.key1
13          subtree.data2 = subtree.data1
14          subtree.key1 = key
15          subtree.data1 = data
16          if pRef is not None :  # If interior node, set the links.
17            subtree.right = subtree.middle
18            subtree.middle = pRef
19        else :
20          subtree.key2 = key
21          subtree.data2 = data
22          if pRef is not None :  # If interior node, set the links.
23            subtree.right = pRef
24
25        return (None, None, None)
```

tuple to indicate the node was not split. Otherwise, the node has to be split by calling _23SplitNode() and the resulting tuple is returned to the parent.

The _23SplitNode(), provided in Listing 14.16, handles the creation of the new tree node and the distribution of the keys and links to the proper location. The pRef argument is again used to indicate if we are working with a leaf node or an interior node. When an interior node is split, the links have to be rearranged in order to maintain the tree property. The three cases that can occur, which depends on the child node into which the key is inserted, are all handled by the function. The promoted key and reference are returned in a tuple for use by the _23TreeInsert() function.

14.4.3 Efficiency of the 2-3 Tree

By definition, a 2-3 tree is height balanced with all leaf nodes at the same level. In the worst case, all nodes in the 2-3 tree will contain a single key and all interior nodes will only have two children. From the discussion of the binary search tree, we know such a structure results in a height of $\log n$ for a tree of size n. The traversal operation must visit every node in the 2-3 tree resulting in a worst case time of $O(n)$. The search operation used with 2-3 tree is identical to that of the binary search tree, which we know depends on the height of the tree. Since the maximum height of a 2-3 tree is $\log n$, the search operation will take no more $\log n$ comparisons, resulting in a worst case time of $O(\log n)$.

Listing 14.16 Helper function that splits a full node.

```
1   # Splits a non-root node and returns a tuple with the promoted key and ref.
2   class Tree2dMap :
3   # ...
4       # If pRef != None, then an interior node is being split so the new
5       # node N created in the function will also be an interior node. In that
6       # case, the links of the interior node have to be set appropriately.
7
8       def _23SplitNode( self, node, key, data, pRef ):
9           # Create the new node, the reference to which will be promoted.
10          newnode = _23TreeNode( None, None )
11          # See where the key belongs.
12          if key < node.key1 :        # left
13              pKey = node.key1
14              pData = node.data1
15              node.key1 = key
16              node.data1 = data
17              newnode.key1 = node.key2
18              newnode.data1 = node.data2
19              if pRef is not None :  # If interior node, set its links.
20                  newnode.left = node.middle
21                  newnode.middle = node.right
22                  node.middle = pRef
23          elif key < node.key2 :     # middle
24              pKey = key
25              pData = data
26              newnode.key1 = node.key2
27              newnode.data1 = node.data2
28              if pRef is not None :  # If interior node, set its links.
29                  newnode.left = pRef
30                  newnode.middle = node.right
31          else :                     # right
32              pKey = node.key2
33              pData = node.data2
34              newnode.key1 = key
35              newnode.data1 = data
36              if pRef is not None :  # If interior node, set its links.
37                  newnode.left = node.right
38                  newnode.middle = pRef
39
40          # The second key of the original node has to be set to null.
41          node.key2 = None
42          node.data2 = None
43          # Return the promoted key and reference to the new node.
44          return (pKey, pData, newnode)
```

The insertion operation, and the deletion which we leave as an exercise, also works very similarly to that of the binary search tree. The search down the tree to find a leaf into which the new key can be inserted takes logarithmic time. If the leaf is full, it has to be split. A node can be split and the keys distributed between the original node, the new node, and the parent node in constant time. In the worst case, a node split is required at each level of the tree during the unwinding of the recursion. Since the tree can be no higher than $\log n$ and each split is a constant time operation, the worst case time of an insertion is also $O(\log n)$.

Exercises

14.1 Prove or explain why the `_bstRemove()` method requires $O(n)$ time in the worst case.

14.2 Why can new keys not be inserted into the interior nodes of a 2-3 tree?

14.3 Consider the following set of values and use them to build the indicated type of tree by adding one value at a time in the order listed:

> 30   63   2   89   16   24   19   52   27   9   4   45

(a) binary search tree   (b) AVL tree   (c) 2-3 tree

14.4 Repeat Exercise 14.3, but for the following set of keys:

> T   I   P   A   F   W   Q   X   E   N   S   B   Z

14.5 Given the following binary trees, indicate which trees are height balanced.

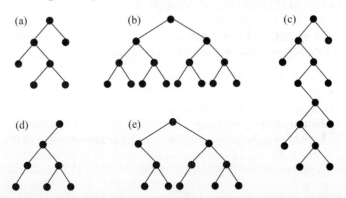

14.6 Consider the binary search tree below and show the resulting tree after deleting each of the following keys: 14, 52, and 39.

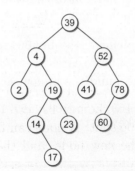

14.7 Consider AVL tree below and show the resulting tree after deleting key values 1, 78, and 41.

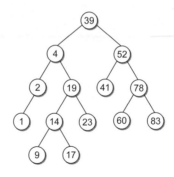

14.8 Given the 2-3 tree below, show the resulting tree after inserting key values 112, 80, 90, 41, and 20.

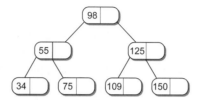

Programming Projects

14.1 The binary search tree operations can also be implemented iteratively. Design and implement an iterative solution for each operation:

    (a) search   (b) find minimum (c) insert   (d) delete

14.2 Design and implement the function `_bstMaximum()`, which finds and returns the maximum key value in a binary search tree.

14.3 Implement the delete operation for the AVL and 2-3 trees.

14.4 Implement the Set ADT using an AVL search tree and evaluate the time-complexity of each operation.

14.5 Implement a new version of the Color Histogram ADT (from Chapter 11) to use a binary search tree for the chains instead of a linked list.

14.6 Design and implement the `bstBuild()` function, which takes a sequence of keys and builds a new search tree from those keys. For example, the function could be used to build the binary search tree in Figure 14.5.

```
keyList = [60, 25, 100, 35, 17, 80]
buildBST( keyList )
```

Python Review

Python is a modern interpreted programming language that can be used to construct programs using either a procedural or object-oriented paradigm. It provides many built-in features and has a simple syntax that is easy to learn. In this appendix, we review the basics of Python in order to provide a refresher of the material you learned in your first introductory Python course. This is not a complete coverage of the language, but it focuses on those concepts that will be important to the coverage of the material in this text. Python has evolved over the years with various modifications and the addition of new features with each new version. In this text, we assume the use of Python version 3.2, which includes some important differences from the popular earlier versions 2.5 and 2.6. In order to aide those who learned Python using the earlier versions, we note the major differences throughout the review.

A.1 The Python Interpreter

Python programs are executed using the Python interpreter, which is a program that reads and executes instructions written in the Python language. The interpreter can execute Python programs in either interactive mode or script mode. Interactive mode is useful for testing single statements or small code segments. To use interactive mode, start the interpreter by entering the command:

```
python
```

at the prompt in a command-line terminal. The interpreter will display an informational message similar to the following:

```
Python 3.1.1 (r311:74480, Oct 26 2009, 21:59:21)
[GCC 4.3.0 20080428 (Red Hat 4.3.0-8)] on linux2
Type "help", "copyright", "credits" or "license" for more information.
>>>
```

The >>> at the bottom of the output is the interactive mode prompt that is used to enter Python statements to the interpreter. For example, if you enter the statement:

```
print( "Hello World" )
```

the interpreter will respond by executing the `print()` function and displaying the contents of the string to the terminal window, followed by another prompt:

```
>>> print( "Hello World" )
Hello World
>>>
```

Script mode is used to execute Python programs that are stored in text files. The source files containing Python programs can be created with any text editor or integrated development environment (IDE) of your choosing.

```
total = 0
i = 1
while i <= 100 :
    total += i
    i += 1
print( "The sum of the first 100 integers is", total )
```

To execute the program, you would change to the directory containing the file and enter the command:

```
python summation.py
```

at the command-line prompt. This causes the Python interpreter to run in script mode, which reads the text file and executes the statements contained within the file. When the `summation.py` program is executed, the following output is displayed to the terminal:

```
The sum of the first 100 integers is 5050
```

The first statement to be executed in script mode is the first statement in the text file at global scope, which include all statements not enclosed within a function, class, or method. In the summation example, the assignment statement `total = 0` will be the first statement executed.

A.2   The Basics of Python

A programming language is defined by its syntax and semantics, which vary from one language to the next. But all languages require the use of specific instructions for expressing algorithms as a program in the given language. The Python language consists of many different instructions, including those for sequential, selection, and repetition constructs. In this section, we review the basic syntax used in the construction of simple sequential instructions.

Identifiers are used to name things in a programming language. In Python, identifiers are case sensitive and may be of any length but they may only contain letters, digits, or the underscore, and they may not begin with a digit. Some identifiers are reserved and cannot be used by the programmer. The following is a list of Python's reserved words:

and	as	assert	break	class	continue	def
del	elif	else	except	finally	for	from
global	if	import	in	is	lambda	nonlocal
not	or	pass	raise	return	try	while
with	yield	False	None	True		

A.2.1 Primitive Types

A primitive type is a built-in type that is part of the language itself. Python defines several primitive data types, as described in the following bullets along with sample *literals* of each type:

- **integer** — Numeric values with no fractional part:

    -9   50   0x4F   077

- **floating-point** — Numeric values with a fractional part:

    25.45   -17.4   0.34   17.045E-03

- **boolean** — Logical values of true or false:

    True   False

- **string** — An ordered sequence of alphanumeric characters:

    'string'   "another string"   "c"

- **list** — An ordered sequence of objects in which each element is identified by an integer subscript:

    [0, 1, 2, 3]   ['abc', 1, 4.5]   []

- **tuple** — Similar to a list type but the contents of a tuple cannot be changed once it has been created:

    ('a', 'b', 'c')   (1, 4, 5, 8)

- **dictionary** – a collection of items in which each item contains a key and a corresponding value:

    {123 : "bob",   456 : "sally"}

Python also has a literal block string in which white space (spaces and newlines) is maintained.

    """This is a string which
       can continue onto a new line. When printed, it will appear
       exactly as written between the triple quotes."""

Python inserts newline characters at the end of each line of the text block and adds blank spaces everywhere they appear within the literal, including at the front of each line. Single or double quotes can be used for string block literals.

A.2.2 Statements

The Python syntax, as with all languages, is very specific when it comes to statement structure. The interpreter expects a statement to be contained on a single line of the text file. Sometimes, however, we need to split a single statement across several lines in order to produce easily readable code or when following the specifications of a programming style guide. A backslash (\) can be used at the end of the line to continue the statement onto the next line.

```
result = (someValue * 5 + anotherValue * 12) \
           - (originalValue * 2)
```

For function calls and method invocations that require pairs of parentheses, the line can be broken without the use of backslashes. The interpreter will parse the instructions across lines until the closing parenthesis is encountered. For example, the following will parse without error:

```
myFunction( a, b,
            "name", avg )
```

Some constructs in Python are *compound statements*, which span multiple lines and consist of a header and a *statement block*. A statement block, sometimes simply referred to as a block, is a group of one or more statements, all of which are indented to the same indentation level, as illustrated by the following code segment:

```
while i <= 100 :
    total += i
    i += 1
```

Compound statements are easily identified by the requirement of a colon (:) as part of their syntax. Statement blocks, which can be nested inside other blocks, begin on the next line following the header of the compound statement. Statement blocks end at the next blank line or the first statement whose indentation level is shorter than those in the block. Only statements within a block or the parts of a statement continued from a previous line may be indented. The number of spaces used to indent statements within a block is irrelevant, but all statements within the block must have the same indentation level. Finally, the top-level statements of a file can have no indentation.

> **⚠ Statement Block Indentation.** All statements within a given block must be indented with either blank spaces or tab characters, but not a mixture of the two. The alignment of statements as displayed by some text editors can be misleading. It's best to use an editor that can insert "soft tabs" when the Tab key is pressed.
>
> **CAUTION**

> **NOTE**
>
> ⓘ **Variable Terminology.** Even though a variable in Python stores a reference to an object, it is quite common in programming to use phrases such as "The value is assigned to x", "idNum contains 42", and "name contains a string". In all such cases, these phases should be understood as referring to the object referenced by the variable and not the variable itself.

A.2.3 Variables

Computers manipulate and process data. In Python, all data is stored in objects, which are created from various class definitions. Objects can store a single value or multiple values. But no matter the size, we must have some means to access the object after it's been created. A **_variable_** is a named storage location that associates a name with an object. Variables do not store data themselves, but instead store references to the objects that contain the data. A _reference_ is simply the memory address of the location where the object is stored.

Assignments

Variables in Python are created when they are first assigned an object reference. Consider the following assignment statements:

```
name = "John Smith"
idNum = 42
avg = 3.45
```

which creates three variables and assigns references to each of the given literal values. Note that a reference to an object is commonly illustrated as a directed edge leading from the variable to the object:

In Python, objects are automatically created for literals and initialized with the given value. Each unique literal within a program results in a unique object. A variable itself does not have a type and thus can store a reference to any type of object. It is the object, that has a data type. A variable cannot be used before it has been created by an assignment of a reference to some object. Attempting to do so will generate an error.

As shown in the previous code segment, Python uses a single equal sign (=) for assigning an object reference to a variable. When an assignment statement is used, the righthand side is evaluated and a reference to the resulting value is stored in the variable on the lefthand side. When a new reference is assigned to an existing variable, the old reference is replaced. For example, suppose we assign a new value to variable idNum using the assignment statement idNum = 70, which results in the original reference to value 42 being replaced by a reference to value 70:

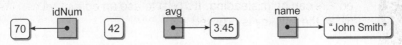

If all references to an object are removed—that is, no variable contains a reference to the object—it is automatically destroyed as part of Python's garbage collection.

Aliases

When one variable is assigned to another (`student = name`), the reference contained in the variable on the righthand side is copied to the variable on the lefthand side, resulting in an ***alias*** since both variables refer to the same object:

Null References

A variable can be set such that it does not reference any object, in which case it's called a ***null reference***. In Python, the special object `None` is used to set a null reference. For example, suppose we execute the assignment statement `idNum = None`, after which `idNum` will be a null reference, as shown here:

Constants

Some languages support the creation of constant variables. A *constant variable*, or simply a constant, is a variable whose value cannot be changed after it has been assigned an initial value. Python does not support constant variables, but it is common practice to specify constant variables with all capital letters, as illustrated in the following example:

```
TAX_RATE = 0.06
MAX_SIZE = 100
```

It is important to note, however, that there is no way to enforce the concept of a constant variable and keep its value from being changed. But by following the standard convention, you provide information to yourself and others that you intend for a variable in all caps to be constant throughout the program.

A.2.4 Arithmetic Operators

Python supports the common mathematical operations for both integers and reals:

+	addition	*	multiplication	//	floor division
–	subtraction	/	real division	%	modulo operator
				**	power

The numeric type resulting from an arithmetic operation depends on the type of the two operands. If at least one operand is a floating-point, the result will be a floating-point and if both operands are integers, the result will be an integer. An exception is the real division operator (/), which always returns a floating-point. The floor division operator (//) mathematically computes $\lfloor a/b \rfloor$ but returns an integer if both operands are integers and a floating-point if at least one is a floating-point. The modulo operator (%) returns the remainder left after computing floor division.

The operators have the expected order of precedence as found in mathematics but can be overridden using parentheses. All of the operators, except the power operator (**), are evaluated from left to right. Special care must be taken when using the power operator with negative literal values. A negative literal on the left side of the power operator is treated differently than one on the right side. For example, the Python expression -2 ** 2 is evaluated as -(2 ** 2) while the expression 2 ** -2 is evaluated as 2 ** (-2).

Python also supports the compound assignment operators that combine an assignment with an arithmetic operator:

```
+=    -=    *=    /=    %=    **=    //=
```

These operators perform the arithmetic operation on both operands and store the result back in the variable on the lefthand side. For example, the expression x += 1 is equivalent to the arithmetic x = x + 1.

New in Python 3.x: The functionality of the division operator (/) has changed. It now performs real division and returns a floating-point value even if both operands are integers. The floor division operator (//) has to be used for integer division.

A.2.5   Logical Expressions

Decisions in a programming language are made based on the boolean result (true or false) of a logical expression. Logical expressions are constructed using logical operators, which can be divided into two groups: relational operators and boolean operators.

Relational Operators

The relational operators are used to determine if a given relationship exists between pairs of values. For example, we may want to determine if a student has a failing grade where failing is any average below 60. The logical expression for that evaluation would be written as,

```
avg >= 60
```

the result of which is either `True` or `False`. The relational operators can be used with any of the built-in types. The numeric values are compared by relative magnitude while strings are compared lexicographically, character by character from left to right. The Python relational operators are shown here:

`a > b`	Is a greater than b	`a >= b`	Is a greater than or equal to b
`a < b`	Is a less than b	`a <= b`	Is a less than or equal to b
`a == b`	Is a equal to b	`a != b`	Is a not equal to b

Boolean Operators

The boolean operators are applied to boolean values. They allow for the construction of not only boolean expressions but also more complex logical expressions by combining multiple relational and boolean expressions. For example, consider the following logical expression:

```
avg >= 80 and avg <= 90
```

which determines if the given value is in the range $[80\dots90]$. The Python boolean operators are described next:

`not a`	A unary operator that inverts the boolean value of its operand.
`a and b`	True if and only if both `a` and `b` are True.
`a or b`	True if `a` is True, `b` is True, or both `a` and `b` are True.

The logical operators are evaluated from left to right based on their order of precedence which can be overridden using parentheses. The relational operators have the highest precedence followed by the boolean operators in the order listed.

New in Python 3.x: The <> operator, which in earlier versions could be used in place of !=, is no longer available.

Object References

Python provides the `is` and `is not` operators for comparing references, or the addresses stored in variables. For example, in the code segment:

```
name1 = "Smith"
name2 = "Jones"
result = name1 is name2
```

`result` is set to `False` since the two variables point to two different objects. If we modify the segment as follows:

```
name2 = name1
result = name1 is name2
```

`result` is now set to `True` since the two variables refer to the same object and are thus aliases. The `is not` operator returns the inverse of the `is` operator and is equivalent to applying the boolean `not` operator. For example, the following logical expressions are equivalent:

```
result = name1 is not name2
result = not (name1 is name2)
```

We test for a null reference with the use of the special value `None`.

```
result = name1 is None
result = name2 is not None
```

A.2.6 Using Functions and Methods

While Python is an object-oriented language, it provides both a class structure for object-oriented programming and a function structure for procedural programming. A *function* is a stand-alone group of statements, sometimes called a subprogram, that performs a specific task. A function is used by invoking it via a *function call*. For example:

```
y = abs( x )
```

computes the absolute value of variable x and stores the result in y. When a function is called during execution, the flow of execution jumps to the function, executes its instructions, and then returns to the point where the function was called. A function call consists of the function name and an argument list enclosed within parentheses:

```
func( arg1, arg2, ..., argN )
```

Arguments are simply values that are passed to the function for use by that function. The number of arguments passed to a function depends on the specific function. When multiple arguments are passed to a function, they are separated with commas and passed in the order specified by the function header. If a function requires no arguments, the parentheses are still required.

Some functions may return a value. This value can be used or ignored depending on the purpose of the function. If a function returns a value, the function call can be used anywhere a value of the given type can be used. For example, since the `abs()` function returns a numeric value, it can be used as part of an arithmetic expression:

```
y = x * z + abs( x )
```

As indicated earlier, all values in Python are stored in objects that are created or instantiated from classes. Once an object has been created, it can then be used. Objects are automatically instantiated or created for all literal values within a program. But we can also explicitly create objects by calling the constructor of the corresponding class for the given type of object. For example, we can create a string object by calling the constructor of the `str` class:

```
name = str( "Jane Green" )
```

As you are probably guessing, there is no need to use the `str()` constructor explicitly to create a string object since we can just specify a literal string in our code and have the interpreter automatically create an object for us. But the `str()` constructor can also be used to create string representations of other data types, both literal values and those referenced by variables:

```
x = 45
intStr = str( x )          # '45'
floatStr = str( 56.89 )    # '56.89'
boolStr = str( False )     # 'False'
```

Since Python's built-in types are represented as classes, they each have a constructor that can be used for creating objects of the given type. The following is a list of the constructors for the simple types:

`int( x )`	integer	`bool( x )`	boolean
`float( x )`	floating-point	`str( x )`	string

These constructors can also be used to convert between the various types. For example, we can convert the string representation of a numeric value to the given numeric type using the appropriate constructor:

```
i = int( "85" )      # 85
f = float( '3.14' )  # 3.14
```

Operations can be performed on objects by invoking a method defined for the class of the given type. We have already seen the arithmetic operators used with the numeric types. But methods can also be defined for use with objects. The dot operator is used to apply a method to a given object. For example, we can create a new string that is the lowercase version of an existing string using the `lower()` method defined by the `str` class:

```
name = "Jane Green"
newStr = name.lower()
```

A method is very similar to a function with one major difference. A function is a stand-alone subroutine that can be used independent of an object, whereas a method is defined by a class and must be applied to an object of that class.

A.2.7 Standard Library

Python is a relatively small language but provides the necessary components for creating powerful programs. The built-in types, which are part of the language itself, have class definitions defined directly by the language. In addition, there are a number of built-in functions such as `print()`, `input()`, and `abs()`, that are also provided directly by the language. Additional functionality is available from various components in the Python Standard Library.

The Standard Library contains a number of functions and class definitions in which related components are organized into individual files called *modules*. While built-in functions and methods can be used directly within your program, those

defined within a module must be explicitly included in your program. To use a
function or class from the standard library, you include an `import` statement at
the top of your program. For example, to use a function defined in the standard
`math` module, you would include the statement:

```
from math import *
```

at the top of your program file. The import statement loads the contents of the
named module and makes all definitions within a single module available for use
in your Python program. For example, after importing the `math` module, we can
use the `sqrt()` function, which is defined in the module:

```
y = sqrt( x )
```

You can import individual components of a module and make them available
within the current file using:

```
from math import sqrt
```

which includes the module, but only makes the `sqrt()` function available for use in
your program. Python has a second variation to the `import` statement that works
very much like the from/import version:

```
import math
```

but in this case, the components defined in the module are loaded into their own
namespace. Namespaces will be discussed in more detail later in this appendix. For
now, simply note that after using this form of the `import` statement, the included
components have to be referred to by both module name and component name
and separated by a dot:

```
y = math.sqrt( x )
```

A.3 User Interaction

User interaction is very common in computer programs. In GUI (graphical user
interface)-based programs, the interaction is managed through widgets or controls
displayed within a windowed environment. In text-based programs, user input
originates from the keyboard and output is written to the terminal.

A.3.1 Standard Input

In Python, there is a single function for extracting data from the user via the
keyboard. The `input()` function waits for the user to type a sequence of characters
followed by the Enter key.

```
name = input( "What is your name? " )
```

The string argument passed to the `input()` function is a ***user prompt***, which tells the user what information we are looking for. When the previous statement is executed, the Python interpreter will display the string on a new line in the terminal followed by the cursor:

```
What is your name?
```

and then it waits for the user to enter data. After the user enters a sequence of characters and presses Enter , the data is returned as a string and assigned to the variable `name`, which can then be used within the program.

The `input()` function can only extract strings. But what if we need to extract an integer or real value? In that case, the numeric value will be extracted as a string of digits that must be converted to a numeric value using the appropriate numeric type constructor. In the following example:

```
userInput = input( "What is your gpa? " )
gpa = float( userInput )
```

we extract a floating-point value from the user by passing the input string to the float constructor, which converts the numeric string representation to a real value. This code segment can be written by nesting the two function calls:

```
gpa = float( input("What is your gpa?") )
```

New in Python 3.x: In previous versions of Python, there were two functions for extracting data from the user: `input()` and `raw_input()`. The `input()` function has been changed to provide the functionality of `raw_input()` and `raw_input()` has been removed from the language.

A.3.2 Standard Output

In Python, as you have seen in a number of examples, the `print()` function is used to display information to the terminal. When the following is executed:

```
print( "Hello World!!" )
```

the string is displayed in the terminal followed by a line feed, which moves the cursor to the next line. The `print()` function can only output strings but Python will implicitly convert any of the built-in types to strings using the `str()` constructor. For example, when the following code segment is executed:

```
avg = (exam1 + exam2 + exam3) / 3.0
print( "Your average is" )
print( avg )
```

the floating-point value stored in `avg` will be converted to a string and displayed to the terminal. The result is:

```
Your average is
85.732
```

New in Python 3.x: The `print` statement has been changed to a function and now requires parentheses. In addition, keyword arguments have been added to the function for changing the default behavior.

Multiple arguments can be supplied to the `print()` function. In that case, each argument is printed one after the other separated by a single blank space:

```
print( "Your average is", avg )
```

which produces as output:

```
Your average is 85.732
```

The default behavior of the `print()` function produces a line feed after the last argument is printed. This can be suppressed by including the keyword argument `end` to the argument list. For example, the following code segment:

```
print( "Your average is", end = ' ' )
print( avg )
```

produces as output:

```
Your average is 85.732
```

because the first call to the `print()` function does not produce a line feed after the string is printed since it was suppressed by including the keyword argument `end = '\n'`. The default value for the argument is `end = '\n'`, which produces a line feed after the last argument.

Escape Sequences

Escape sequences are used in Python to represent or encode special characters such as newlines, tabs, and even the quote characters. An escape sequence is a two-character sequence consisting of a backslash (\) followed by a letter or symbol. Consider the following example:

```
print( "Start a newline here.\nusing the \\n character." )
```

which produces:

```
Start a newline here.
using the \n character.
```

The common escape sequences are shown here:

\\	Backslash (\)	\n	Newline	\"	Double quote (")
\'	Single quote (')	\t	Horizontal tab		

Formatted Output

Python overloads the modulus operator (%) for use with strings to produce formatted output. Consider the following example:

```
output = "Your average is %5.2f" % avgGrade
print( output )
```

which creates a new string using the format string from the left side of the % operator and replacing the field format specifier (%5.2f) with the value of the avgGrade variable. The resulting string is then printed to standard output:

```
Your average is 85.73
```

It is common to nest the formatted string operation within the print() function when used to produce standard output:

```
print( "Your average is %5.2f" % avgGrade )
```

More than one field format specifier can be used in the format definition. In this case, the replacement values must be provided as a tuple:

```
print( "Origin: (%d, %d)\n" % (pointX, pointY) )
```

The replacement values are associated with the field format specifiers in the order listed and must be of the appropriate type. The following code segment shows the use of the formatted output to produce a report containing dollar amounts aligned on the decimal point:

```
print( "Wages:        %8.2f" % wages )
print( "State Taxes: %8.2f" % stateTaxes )
print( "Fed Taxes:   %8.2f" % fedTaxes )
print( "Pay:          %8.2f" % takeHome )
```

There are different field format specifiers for the various primitive data types and several optional arguments that can be used to tweak the output. A field format specifier has the general structure:

$$\%\,[\text{flags}]\,[\text{width}]\,[.\text{precision}]\,\text{code}$$

- **flags** — Indicates zero fills or optional justification and is one of the following:

    0   Fill preceding blank spaces within the field with zeroes.
    +   Right-justify the value within the field.
    -   Left-justify the value within the field.

- **width** — Is an integer value indicating the number of spaces in the field used when formatting the replacement value.

- **precision** — Is the number of digits to be printed after the decimal place when printing a floating-point value.

- **code** — Indicates the type of data that is to replace the field specifier. It can be one of the following:

%s	String	%x	Hexadecimal integer
%d	Decimal or integer	%X	Same as %x but uppercase
%i	Same as %d	%e	Scientific notation
%f	Floating-point	%E	Uppercase version of %e
%c	Character	%g	Same as %e
%u	Unsigned integer	%G	Uppercase version of %g
%o	Octal integer	%%	Prints a literal %

A.4 Control Structures

To this point, we have reviewed statements that are executed in sequence, one after the other. Sometimes, however, it may be necessary to change the flow of control and only execute a statement or block of statements if some condition is met or to execute the same statement or block of statements multiple times.

A.4.1 Selection Constructs

Selection statements allow you to choose whether to execute a statement or block of statements based on the result of a logical expression. Python provides several forms of the **if** construct for making decisions and selecting certain statements for execution. The **if** construct can take several forms. The if-then form is used to select a statement or block of statements if and only if some condition is met. Consider the following example:

```
if value < 0 :
    print( "The value is negative." )
```

in which the **print()** function is executed if **value** is negative; otherwise, the statement is skipped.

The If-Else Statement

The if-else form of the **if** construct is used to execute a block of statements if a condition is true and a different block of statements if the condition is false. This form is identified by the inclusion of an **else** clause. In the following example:

```
if value < 0 :
    print( "The value is negative." )
else:
    print( "The value is positive." )
```

a value is tested to determine if it is negative or positive and an appropriate message is displayed.

Nested If Statements

There is no restriction on the type of statements that can be included within the blocks executed by the if statement. Sometimes, it may be necessary to nest an if statement within another if statement:

```python
if num1 < num2 :
   if num1 < num3 :
     smallest = num1
   else:
     smallest = num3
else:
   if num2 < num3 :
     smallest = num2
   else:
     smallest = num3
```

The if statement and its corresponding else clause must be aligned properly to produce the correct result. In the following example, the else clause must be aligned with the second if statement to produce the message "Passing but marginal" when the average grade is in the range $[60 \dots 70]$.

```python
if avg < 70.0 :
   if avg < 60.0 :
     print( "Failing" )
   else :
     print( "Passing but marginal." )
```

If the else were aligned with the first if statement, as shown below, the message would be incorrectly printed for averages greater than or equal to 70.

```python
if avg < 70.0 :
   if avg < 60.0 :
     print( "Failing" )
else :
   print( "Passing but marginal." )
```

Multiway Branching

A special form of the if construct can be used with selections that tests a series of conditions and performs an action for the one which results in true. For example, suppose we need to determine the letter grade to be assigned for a given average using the common ten-point scale. This can be accomplished using a series of nested if statements as shown below on the left:

```
if avgGrade >= 90.0 :            if avgGrade >= 90.0 :
  letterGrade = "A"                letterGrade = "A"
else :                           elif avgGrade >= 80.0 :
  if avgGrade >= 80.0 :            letterGrade = "B"
    letterGrade = "B"            elif avgGrade >= 70.0 :
  else :                           letterGrade = "C"
    if avgGrade >= 70.0 :        elif avgGrade >= 60.0 :
      letterGrade = "C"            letterGrade = "D"
    else :                       else:
      if avgGrade >= 60.0 :        letterGrade = "F"
        letterGrade = "D"
      else:
        letterGrade = "F"
```

But as more and more conditions are nested, the structure becomes more complex and the blocks continue to be indented further and further, which can make it difficult to read the code. Python provides a third form of the `if` construct that can be used to implement a series of conditions or multiway branches, as shown above on the right. The else part can be omitted if there is no default part to the multiway branch. The `if`, `elif`, and `else` clauses must be aligned to the same indentation level.

A.4.2   Repetition Constructs

There are many occasions when we need to execute one or more statements multiple times until some condition is met. For example, suppose we want to compute the wages for a number of employees given the number of hours each worked. While the wage computation is the same for each employee, it is has to be performed for multiple employees. Thus, we can have the computer repeat the data extraction and computation for each employee until the data has been processed for all employees. Python has two repetition constructs: `while` and `for`.

The While Loop

Loops can generally be categorized as either *count-controlled* or *event-controlled*. In a count-controlled loop the body of the loop is executed a given number of times based on values known before the loop is executed the first time. With event-controlled loops, the body is executed until some event occurs. The number of iterations cannot be determined until the program is executed.

The `while` loop is a general looping construct that can be used for many types of loops. Consider the following count-controlled loop, which sums the first 100 integers by repeatedly executing the body of the loop 100 times:

```
theSum = 0
i = 1                  # initialization
while i <= 100 :       # condition
  theSum += i
  i += 1               # modification
print( "The sum =", theSum )
```

The `while` loop, which is a compound statement, consists of two parts: a condition and a loop body. The body of the loop contains one or more statements that are executed for each iteration of the loop. The number of iterations is determined by the condition, which is constructed using a logical expression. The body of the `while` loop is executed while the condition is true.

Since logical expressions are constructed by comparing and examining the values of one or more variables, the variables must be altered in order to change the condition. Thus, every loop must contain an *initialization* and *modification* component. The initialization is performed before the condition is examined and the body is executed. It is used to initialize the *loop variable* upon which the loop condition is based. At some point within the loop body, the loop variable must be modified so the loop condition can change.

As an example of an event-controlled loop, consider the problem of entering multiple exam grades from the user and then computing the average grade. We need to enter multiple grades but we don't know how many will be entered. To accommodate this unknown, we can repeatedly execute the body of the loop until the user enters a special value, known as the *sentinel value*. In the following solution for this problem, the sentinel value is any negative number. The event of entering the special value terminates the loop, thus leading to the name event-controlled loop.

```python
total = 0
count = 0
value = int( input("Enter the first grade: ") )
while value >= 0 :
   total += value
   count += 1
   value = int( input("Enter the next grade (or < 0 to quit): ") )

avg = total / count
print( "The average grade is %4.2f" % avg )
```

Python also provides the `break` and `continue` jump statements for use in loops. The `break` statement is used to break out of or terminate the innermost loop in which it is used. The `continue` statement immediately jumps back to the top of the loop and starts the next iteration from the point of the condition evaluation.

When using real values (floats) with logical expressions, you may get results you do not expect due to the imprecision of real number arithmetic on computers. Consider the following code segment:

```python
total = 0.0
i = 0
while i < 10 :
   total += 0.1
   i += 1

if total == 1.0 :
   print( "Correct" )
else :
   print( "Not correct" )
```

which adds the fractional value $\frac{1}{10}$ ten times to variable total. Since total has an initial value of 0, mathematically, it should equal 1 after the loop terminates and the program should print the string "Correct". But due to the imprecision of floating-point numbers, total contains a value close to 1 but not equal to 1 and thus the program will print the string "Not Correct".

The For Loop

The for statement in Python is part of the built-in iterator mechanism used to traverse the individual items stored in a sequence or collection. The individual items in the given collection are assigned, one at a time, to the loop variable. After each assignment, the body of the loop is executed in which the loop variable is commonly used to perform some action on each item. The loop body will be executed once for each item in the collection. Consider the following code segment:

```
count = 0
for letter in theString :
  if letter >= "A" and letter <= "Z" :
    count += 1
print( "The string contained %d uppercase characters." % count )
```

which traverses over the individual characters of the string "John Smith", one at a time, to count the number of uppercase letters contained in the string. Python's for statement is equivalent to the foreach constructs found in other languages. Thus, when reading code containing a for loop, it's best to read the "for" clause as "for each". Consider the loop in the previous code segment, which we would read as "for each letter in theString do the following" where "do the following" represents the statements in the loop body.

Python also provides the range() function, which can be used with the for statement to construct count-controlled loops. Consider the following code segment, which prints the range of integers from 1 to 10, one per line:

```
for i in range( 1, 11 ) :
  print( i )
```

The range() function specifies a sequence of integer values over which the for loop can traverse. There are several forms of the range() function depending on the number of arguments supplied. Consider the following examples:

```
# Third argument indicates the increment amount; default is 1.
for i in range( 0, 31, 5 ) :      # 0, 5, 10, 15, 20, 25, 30
  print( i )

# We can decrement through the range of values.
for i in range( 30, 0, -5 ) :     # 30, 25, 20, 15, 10, 5
  print( i )

# A single argument will iterate through the range, starting at 0.
for i in range( 5 ) :             # 0, 1, 2, 3, 4
  print( i )
```

A.5   Collections

Python provides several data types that can be used to store and manage data collections: the string, tuple, list and dictionary.

A.5.1   Strings

Python also provides several built-in collection classes. Strings are very common and fundamental in most programming languages. In Python, strings are immutable objects of the built-in `str` class, which store the sequence of characters comprising the string. A number of basic operations can be performed on strings, some of which are described in this section. Two strings can be concatenated using the plus operator. For example:

```
strvar = 'This is '
fullstr = strvar + "a string"
```

results in the string "*This is a string*" being assigned to variable `fullstr`. To concatenate a string with a non-string value, you must first create a string representation of the non-string using the `str()` constructor:

```
result = "The value of x is " + str( x )
```

Python provides the built-in `len()` function that can be applied to any of the built-in collections. When used with a string, it returns the number of characters contained in the string.

```
print( "Length of the string = ", len(name) )
```

In an earlier section, we saw that the individual characters of a string can be accessed by traversing the sequence using an iterator. An individual character of a string can also be accessed by specifying an integer subscript or index representing its position within the string. Consider the following example, which prints the first and last character of a string:

```
msg = "This is a string!"
print( "The first character is", msg[0] )
print( "The last character is", msg[-1] )
```

Both positive and negative subscripts can be used. A positive subscript represents the offset of the character from the front of the string while a negative subscript indicates the offset from the end of the string, as illustrated here:

The subscript must be within the valid range for the given string; otherwise, an exception will be raised, resulting in an error.

Printing a dashed line is a common operation in text-based applications. One way to do it is as a string literal:

```
print( "---------------------------------------------" )
```

But Python provides a string repeat operator for duplicating or repeating a string that produces the same results:

```
print( "-" * 45 )
```

A.5.2 Lists

A Python list is a built-in collection type that stores an ordered sequence of object references in which the individual items can be accessed by subscript. A list can be created and filled using a comma-separated sequence within square brackets. For example, the first statement in the code segment:

```
gradeList = [ 85, 90, 87, 65, 91 ]
listA = []          # two empty lists
listB = list()
```

creates a five-element list containing the specified integers and stores a reference to the list in the **gradeList** variable. The resulting **gradeList** is illustrated here:

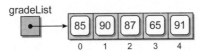

Element Access

List elements are referenced using the same square bracket subscript notation, used with strings. As with strings, the elements are numbered in sequential order, with the first element having index zero. Negative subscripts can also be used to reference the elements starting from the end.

```
print( 'First item = ', gradeList[0] )
print( 'Last item = ', gradeList[-1] )
```

A list can be printed using the **print()** function, as can most Python data types, or it can be converted to a string. Consider the following code segment:

```
aString = str( gradeList )
print( gradeList )
```

which produces the following output [95, 90, 87, 65, 91]. The elements of a list can also be accessed by traversing the list using the iterator mechanism:

```
for element in gradeList :
  print( element )
```

List Modification

The contents of a specific element of the list can be modified using the subscript notation with the variable name on the left side of an assignment statement. For example, the following code segment replaces grade 65 with 71:

```
gradeList[3] = 71
print( gradeList )    # prints [95, 90, 87, 65, 91]
```

New items can be appended to the end of the list using the **append()** method. The following code segment creates a list of 1,000 random values by appending each value to the end of an initially empty list:

```
import random

valueList = list()
for i in range( 1000 ) :
    valueList.append( random.random() )
```

The **extend()** method, which takes a list as its argument, can be used to append multiple items to the end of a list. For example, the following code segment:

```
listA = [ 0, 1, 2, 3 ]
listB = listA.extend( [ 4, 5, 6 ] )
print( listB )
```

produces as output [0, 1, 2, 3, 4, 5, 6]. The entire contents of the argument are appended to the end of the list for which the method was invoked. The **insert()** list method can be used to insert items anywhere within a list. Consider the code:

```
values = [ 0, 1, 2, 3, 4 ]
values.insert( 1, 8 )
print( values )
```

which produces the output [0, 8, 1, 2, 3, 4]. The **insert()** method inserted value 8 before the current item at position 1. The remaining items were shifted down to make room for the new item. Python provides several methods for deleting items from a list. The first approach uses the **remove()** method, which allows you to delete an item by value:

```
theList = [ 10, 11, 12, 13 ]
theList.remove( 11 )
print( theList )        # prints [10, 12, 13]
print( len(theList) )   # prints 3
```

To remove an item by index, you can use the **pop()** method, which retrieves and then removes the item at the given index. In the following code segment, we use the **pop(1)** method to retrieve and remove the item at index position 1:

```
x = theList.pop( 1 )
print( "list =", theList )    # prints list = [10, 13]
print( "x =", x )             # prints x = 12
```

The items following the removed item are shifted down and the size of the list shrinks by one. You can omit the index position for `pop()` and the item in the last element will be retrieved and removed.

```
theList.pop()
print( theList )    # prints [10]
```

Searching the List

Several methods and operators are provided that can be used to search the list. The `index()` method can be used to search for an item within the list. It returns the element index of the first occurrence within the list. If the list does not contain the given value, an exception is raised.

```
theList = [ 10, 11, 12, 13 ]
pos = theList.index( 13 )
print( pos )        # prints 3
```

A.5.3 Tuples

Another built-in collection type for creating an ordered sequence of objects is the tuple. Tuples are exactly like lists, except they are immutable. A tuple is created using a pair of parentheses instead of square brackets.

```
t = ( 0, 2, 4 )          # 3 element tuple
a = ( 2, )               # 1 element tuple
b = ( 'abc', 1, 4.5, 5 ) # 4 element mixed tuple
```

You have already seen the use of tuples when multiple values were passed as data fields in a formatted string that were listed within parentheses, as shown below. That was actually a tuple. Many of the operators used with lists can also be used with tuples, but there are no additional methods defined for tuples.

```
print( "(%d, %d)" % (x, y) )
```

A.5.4 Dictionaries

The Python dictionary is a built-in class that stores a collection of entries in which each entry contains a key and a corresponding value, sometimes called a payload. A dictionary can be created and filled using a sequence of comma-separated key:value pairs listed within curly braces or empty dictionaries can be created using empty braces, or the `dict()` constructor:

```
states = { 'MS' : 'Mississippi', 'VA' : 'Virginia',
           'AL' : 'Alabama', 'DC' : 'Washington' }
classLevel = { 0 : 'Freshman', 1 : 'Sophomore',
               2 : 'Junior', 3: 'Senior' }
emptyA = { }
emptyB = dict()
```

Element Access

The items stored in a dictionary are accessed based on the key part of the key/value pair. Accessing an entry in the dictionary also uses the subscript notation, but unlike a list or tuple, the subscript value is one of the keys in the dictionary.

```
print( 'The state name is', states['MS'] )
```

When using the subscript notation to access an entry in the dictionary, the given key must exist or an exception is raised. As an alternative, the `get()` method can be used, which returns the value associated with the given key if it exists or returns `None` if the key does not exist:

```
print( states.get( 'MS' ) )    # prints Mississippi
print( states.get( 'MD' ) )    # prints None
```

The collection can be traversed using Python's iterator mechanism provided through the `for` statement. The traversal is made over the keys in the dictionary. To access the corresponding value, simply use the subscript notation.

```
for key in classLevel :
  print( key, '=', classLevel[key] )
```

You can obtain a list of the keys or values stored in the dictionary using the appropriate method:

```
keyList = states.keys()
valueList = states.values()
```

Dictionary Modification

The value associated with a key in the dictionary can be changed using the dictionary subscript notation with the variable name on the right side of an assignment statement. For example, the following code segment corrects the entry for DC in the `states` dictionary and then prints the contents of the dictionary:

```
states['DC'] = 'District of Columbia'
print( states )
```

which results in:

```
{'VA': 'Virginia', 'AL': 'Alabama', 'MS': 'Mississippi',
 'DC': 'District of Columbia'}
```

New entries can also be added to a dictionary using the dictionary subscript notation. Thus, if the key exists, its corresponding value is modified; if the key does not exist, a new key/value pair is added to the dictionary:

```
states['OR'] = 'Oregon'
states['VT'] = 'Vermont'
print( len(states) )           # prints 6
```

An existing entry can be removed from a dictionary using the `pop()` method or the `del` operator. The given key must exist in the dictionary:

```python
states.pop( 'AL' )
del states['VT']
```

The `in` and `not in` operators can be used to determine if a dictionary contains a given key. These can also be used with strings, tuples, and lists.

```python
if abbv not in states :
  print( abbv, "is not a valid state abbreviation" )
if 100 in gradeList :
  print( "Student received at least one perfect score." )
```

A.6   Text Files

Data files stored on a secondary device such as a hard drive or USB stick can be used for the input of data into a program and the output of data from a program. For example, if we want to produce and print a report, we need we need to write the information to a file and then print the file. The data needed to produce that report may itself be stored in a file on disk. We would have to extract the data from the file, process it, and then produce the report.

In most languages, files are treated as I/O streams (input/output streams) in which data flows into or out of a program. Internally, standard input, in which data is extracted from the keyboard, is treated as an input stream and standard output, in which data is written to the terminal, is treated as an output stream.

There are two main types of data files that can be used with Python: text files and binary files. A **_text file_** contains a sequence of characters from the printable range of the ASCII code. This typically includes the ASCII values in the range $[32 \ldots 126]$ and ASCII values 13 and 9, which are used for newlines and tabs. Examples of text files include those created by any text editor such as the source files containing your Python programs. A **_binary file_** contains a sequence of binary numbers representing data values as they would be stored in memory. Examples of binary files include those created by word processors, spreadsheet applications, and databases. Binary files cannot be read and displayed by text editors since they contain byte values outside the printable range. In this section, we limit our discussion to text files since they are very common and easy to work with.

A.6.1   File Access

Files are a built-in type in Python that are represented by objects. This means no additional modules are required in order to access a file from within your program. Before a file can be used, it must first be opened and an object created to represent the file. A text file is opened using the `open()` function:

```python
infile = open( "records.txt", "r" )
outfile = open( "report.txt", "w" )
```

The function takes two string arguments. The first is the name of the file and the second indicates the mode in which the file is to be opened. The modes are:

'r' — Open the file for reading
'w' — Open the file for writing

New in Python 3.x: Python now includes multiple classes for working with files. The `file()` constructor no longer exists and cannot be used to open a file. Instead, you must use the `open()` function, which creates and returns an appropriate file object based on the supplied arguments.

If the file can be opened, the function creates a file object and returns a reference to that newly created object. This object is then used to access the file. A file opened for reading must exist and be accessible to the user running the program. If a file is opened for writing and it does not exist, a new file is created; but if the file exists, it will be erased and a new file created. If the file cannot be opened, an error is generated.

When you are finished using the file, it should be closed. By closing the file, the system will flush the buffers and unlink the external file from the internal Python object. A file cannot be used after it has been closed. To reuse the file, you must first reopen it. Python files are closed by calling the `close()` method defined for file objects:

```
infile.close()
outfile.close()
```

A.6.2 Writing to Files

Python provides several methods for outputting data to a text file. The easiest way to write text to a text file is with the `write()` method defined for file objects:

```
outfile.write( "Student Report\n" )
outfile.write( "-" * 40 + "\n" )
```

The `write()` method writes the given string to the output file represented by the given file object. To output other value types, you must first convert them to strings. Formatted output can also be written to a file using the string format operator:

```
outfile.write( "%4d  %6.2f\n" % (idNum, avgGrade) )
```

Note that the `write()` method does not add a linefeed or newline character after the string is written to the file. This must be done explicitly by including a newline character (\n) as part of the output string.

A.6.3 Reading from Files

Python provides two methods for extracting data from a text file, both of which extract data as strings. To extract other types of data from a text file, you must explicitly convert the extracted string(s) as was done with the `input()` function. The `readline()` method is used to extract an entire line from a text file. The end of a line is indicated by a newline character (`\n`). The extracted text is returned as a string:

```
line = infile.readline()
```

If the file is empty or the end of file has been reached, the `readline()` method returns an empty string (`""`) to flag this result:

```
infile = open( "data.txt", "r" )
line = infile.readline()
while line != "" :
   print( line )
   line = infile.readline()
infile.close()
```

The `readline()` method leaves the newline character at the end of the string when the line is extracted from the file. The `rstrip()` string method can be used to strip the white space from the end:

```
line = infile.readline()
stripped = line.rstrip()
```

To read individual characters from a text file, simply pass an integer value to the `readline()` method indicating the number of characters to be extracted:

```
ch = infile.readline( 1 )  # read a single character
```

Python provides the `readlines()` method that can be used to extract the entire contents of an open file and store it into a string list:

```
lines = infile.readlines()
```

An alternate approach to processing the entire contents of a text file is with the use of the file iterator. Consider the following example, which extracts the input file, one line at a time, and then writes it to the output file:

```
infile.open( "myreport.txt", "r" )
for line in infile:
   print( line )
infile.close()
```

The previous examples dealt with the extraction of strings from a text file. But what if we need to extract numeric values? Since Python only provides methods for extracting strings, we must handle the conversions explicitly. Consider the following sample text file containing three pieces of information for a student:

```
100
Smith, John
92.4
```

The first line is an integer identification number, the second is the name of the student stored as a text string, and the last line is the student's average computed as a floating-point value. To extract the information, each line must be read as a string and the two numeric values must be explicitly converted to the appropriate numeric type.

```python
idNum = int( infile.readline() )
name = (infile.readline()).rstrip()
avg = float( infile.readline() )
```

Typically, the newline character should be removed from strings that are part of data records. Otherwise, problems can occur when processing the strings, as would be the case when performing a string comparison. The removal of the newline character can be combined with the extraction as shown in the above code segment, or performed as two separate operations.

A.7   User-Defined Functions

Python allows users to define their own functions that can be used like any other built-in or library function. Functions allow for the subdivision of larger problems into smaller parts and for the reuse of code. In this section, we review the creation and use of user-defined functions.

A.7.1   The Function Definition

A Python function contains a header and body. The *function header* is specified using the def keyword while the *function body* is given as a statement block. The header consists of a name by which the function can be called and a parenthesized comma-separated list of formal parameters. Consider the following code segment:

```python
def sumRange( first, last ):
  total = 0
  i = first
  while i <= last :
    total = total + i
    i = i + 1
  return total
```

that defines the function sumRange(), which requires two arguments. The function sums the range of values specified by the first and last numeric arguments and returns the result. A user-defined function is called like any other function in Python, as illustrated in the following code segment:

```python
theSum = sumRange( 1, 100 )
print( "The sum of the first 100 integers is", theSum )
```

Function Arguments

When a function is called, the flow of execution jumps to the function. The arguments specified in the function call are copied to the function parameters in the order specified. The function is then executed beginning with the first statement in the function body. When a **return** statement is executed or the end of the function body is reached, execution returns to the point where the function was called.

In Python, arguments are passed by value. Since every value is an object, it is the object reference that is copied to a function parameter and not the object itself. For example, suppose we call `sumRange()` with two variables:

```
start = 5
end = 25
theSum = sumRange( start, end )
```

Inside the function, variables `first` and `last` are local variables that contain aliases to variables `start` and `end`, respectively.

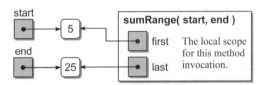

Python is a dynamically typed language and every operator in Python is a polymorphic operation. So, what keeps us from passing floating-point values into the `sumRange()` function? For example, the function call `sumRange(1.37, 15.78)` would be valid. So long as all operations within the function can be applied to the given values, the program will execute correctly. If an operation cannot be applied to a given argument type, an exception will be raised to indicate the invalid type. This flexibility is a powerful feature of Python. It allows a single function to be applied to different object types without having to define multiple versions.

Returning Values

As indicated earlier, the **return** statement can be used to terminate a function, but it's also used to return a value, or more specifically an object reference, back to the program where the function was called. For example, the `sumRange()` function returns the total that results from summing the range of values using the statement **return** total.

Most value-returning functions return a single value. But Python does not limit you to only returning a single value. Multiple values can be returned by specifying a comma-separated list as part of the **return** statement. For example, the following function prompts the user for their first and last names and then returns both strings:

```
def promptForName():
    first = input( "What is your first name? " )
```

```
    last = input( "What is your last name? " )
    return first, last
```

A function that returns multiple values can only be called as part of a multi-variable assignment statement:

```
firstName, lastName = promptForRange()
```

The multiple values returned by a function are assigned to the variables in the order they are listed in the **return** statement. Thus, if we execute the above function call and enter data as follows:

```
What is your first name? John
What is your last name? Smith
```

the string `'John'` will be assigned to `firstName` and `'Smith'` will be assigned to `lastName`. Note that when multiple values are returned by a function, Python actually returns a tuple with the values stored as elements. Thus, some books will show the assignment of the returned values using the following equivalent notation:

```
(firstName, lastName) = promptForRange()
```

Default and Keyword Arguments

Python allows functions to be defined with *default argument* values. For example, we can add a third parameter to the `sumRange()` function to be used as the step value and assign a default value to the argument:

```
def sumRange( first, last, step = 1 ):
    total = 0
    i = first
    while i <= last :
        total = total + i
        i = i + step
    return total
```

If the value of the third argument is omitted when calling the function:

```
theSum = sumRange( 1, 100 )
```

the default value is assigned to the parameter before the function is executed. If a value is specified in the function call for the third argument:

```
theSum = sumRange( 1, 100, 2 )
```

then that value is used instead of the default value. When defining functions with default arguments, all arguments following the first one with a default value, must be assigned default values. Otherwise, Python would have no way of knowing which argument is supposed to receive the default value.

The arguments specified in a function call are passed to the parameters of a function in the order they were specified. Python also allows you to specify the argument order by using *keyword arguments*. Consider the following function call:

```
theSum = sumRange( last = 100, step = 3, first = 1 )
```

in which we directly specify which argument is supposed to receive which value. As we've seen earlier, keyword arguments can be used with the `print()` function to change the separation string that gets inserted when printing multiple arguments and to change the string printed at the end of the function call.

A.7.2 Variable Scope

Variables are classified by their scope, which indicates where the variable was created and where it can be used. Python has four scope classifications. The ***built-in scope*** includes the variables and literal values defined as part of the language, which can be used anywhere within a program. The *global scope* includes the variables created at the top level of a source file or module (outside of all functions and classes). Unlike other languages in which a global variable can be used anywhere within a program, each module in Python creates its own global scope. The ***local scope*** includes the variables created within a function or method and are local to the given subroutine. Function and method arguments are local variables. And finally, the ***instance scope*** includes the variables defined as data attributes of a class. These will be discussed more in Appendix D.

Variables only exist within the scope in which they were created. The built-in and global scopes exist during the entire life of the program. Variables in the instance scope exist during the lifetime of the object for which they were defined. A local variable, however, only exists during the time in which the function is being executed. Each execution of a function creates a new local scope, which is then destroyed when the function terminates.

A.7.3 Main Routine

Every program must have a unique starting point: a first statement to be executed. In Python, the first statement to be executed is the first statement at file level (outside of all functions and class definitions). The statements within a function are not executed until the function is called, even though the statements are interpreted and converted to byte code as they are read. Thus, you can refer to one function from within another before the former has been defined. For example, consider the following code segment:

```python
def run():
    value = int( input("Enter a value: ") )
    print( "The double of your value is ", doubleIt( value ) )

def doubleIt( num ):
    return num * 2

run()
```

But this is not the case when calling a function from a statement at file level. When a Python source file or module is loaded by the interpreter, all statements at

> **NOTE**
>
> ⓘ **Use of a Main Routine.** In the text, we only use a `main()` function when the driver module contains multiple functions as illustrated by the `diceroll.py` program below. If the driver module does not contain multiple functions, as illustrated by the `driver.py` module, we omit the `main()` function and list all executable statements at the file level.

file level are executed during the loading process. If a function is called at file level before the function has been defined, as illustrated in the following code segment, the interpreter does not know about the function and has no way of executing it:

```
callIt( 5 )

def callIt( num ):
    return pow( num, 2 )
```

The order in which functions are listed within a file is not important, but the order of executable statements at file level is. When subdividing a program into various functions using a top-down design, it is good programming practice to place all executable statements within functions and to specify one function as the driver, as illustrated in the following code segment. With this approach, the driver function, which is commonly named `main()` due to that name being used in other languages, can be defined first with the remaining definitions following it. At the bottom of the file, a single file-level statement (not including constant variables) is used to call the driver function.

```
# diceroll.py - simulate the rolling of two dice.
from random import *

# Minimum number of sides on a die.
MIN_SIDES = 4

# Our very own main routine for a top-down design.
def main():
    print( "Dice roll simulation." )
    numSides = int( input("How many sides should the die have? ") )
    if numSides < MIN_SIDES :
        numSides = MIN_SIDES
    value = rollDice( numSides )
    print( "You rolled a", value )

# Simulate the rollowing of two nSided dice.
def rollDice( nSides ):
    die1 = randint( 1, nSides + 1 )
    die2 = randint( 1, nSides + 1 )
    return die1 + die2

# Call the main routine which we defined first.
main()
```

User-Defined Modules

As you learned earlier, Python includes a standard library containing modules of functions and class definitions that can be used in our programs. By using modules, the language itself can remain relatively small while still providing extended functionality.

B.1 Structured Programs

Python programs can quickly become very large and unmanageable, especially if the entire user code is placed within a single source file. To help structure and manage large programs, Python allows the user to create their own modules. A module, which is a text file that contains Python source code and has a `.py` extension, can be used to group class definitions and related functions.

Typically, a large program consists of a top-level source file and one or more supplemental modules. The top-level file acts as the ***driver***, which contains the statements for the main flow of execution, and the modules contain related components, which act as tools that are imported and used as needed.

The code segment below illustrates the use of modules in organizing a structured program. It consists of three Python source files: a top-level driver (`grades.py`), and two supplemental modules (`iomod.py`, and `compmod.py`). (Note, this is a small simple program used for illustration purposes. In practice, a short program like this would more likely be placed in a single module.)

```
# grades.py --------------------------------------------------------
# The driver module which contains the statements creating the main
# flow of execution.
import iomod
import compmod

gradeList = iomod.extractGrades()
avgGrade = compmod.computeAverage( gradeList )
iomod.printReport( gradeList, avgGrade )
```

```
# iomod.py ----------------------------------------------------------
# A module containing the routines used to extract and print grades.
def extractGrades():
  gradeList = list()
  grade = int( input("Enter the first grade: ") )
  while grade >= 0 :
    gradeList.append( grade )
    grade = int( input("Enter the next grade (or < 0 to quit): ") )
  return gradeList

def printReport( theList, avgGrade ):
  print( "The average grade for the ", len(theList),
         "grades entered is", avgGrade )

# compmod.py --------------------------------------------------------
# A module which defines a function for computing the average grade.
def computeAverage( theList ):
  total = 0
  for grade in theList :
    total += grade
  return total / len(theList)
```

To execute the program, you would enter the command:

```
python grades.py
```

at the command-line prompt since the driver program is the main file containing the starting point of execution. The Python interpreter will include each module specified within an `import` statement. In this example, that includes both `iomod.py` and `compmod.py` as indicated at the top of `grades.py`. The interpreter will only import a module once, even if it is encountered multiple times. Thus, you should always import a module within a source file if any component of that module is needed. Let the interpreter worry about omitting the module if it has already been included.

B.2   Namespaces

All identifiers in Python live within a ***namespace***, the context in which identifiers are defined. You can think of a namespace as a container or index in which various identifiers are stored. When an identifier is referenced in a Python program, a search is performed in a particular namespace to determine if that identifier is valid. The namespace concept allows programmers to create duplicate names, each existing in a different namespace.

In Python, each module constitutes its own namespace. Any identifier defined within a module may be freely used within that same module. But what about identifiers defined within other modules? It depends how they are imported. When the plain `import` statement is used:

```
import math
y = math.sqrt( x )
```

the contents of the module are made available for use in the current module, but they are not made part of the current module's namespace. That's why the identifiers have to be referenced using the dot/module name notation. When the `from`/`import` version of the `import` statement is used:

```
from math import *
z = pow( x, 3 )
```

the contents of the module are made available to the current module just like with the plain version. But the identifiers from the imported module are included in the namespace of the current module, which can then be used as if they were defined within the current module.

The `from`/`import` version of the `import` statement has two forms. When the asterisk is used as in the previous example, everything in the module is included and made available. Instead of including everything, you can specify individual components to be included:

```
from math import sqrt, pow
x = sqrt( x )
z = pow( x, 3 )
```

You may be asking, why are there two ways to import modules. Why not just use the `from`/`import` version and make all identifiers available within the current module? The short answer is, there are times when different module authors may use the same name for a function or class, yet provide different functionality. Identifiers are unique within a given namespace; there can be only one instance of each identifier. In Python, unlike other languages, an identifier can be redefined at any time with the new definition replacing the original. Consider the code segment below which illustrates a simple program consisting of a top-level driver (`main.py`) and two supplemental modules (`modA.py` and `modB.py`).

```
# main.py ---------------------------------------------------------
import modA
import modB

x = int( raw_input( "Enter value one: " ) )
y = int( raw_input( "Enter value two: " ) )
v = modA.userFnct( x, y )
w = modB.userFnct( x, y )

# modA.py --------------------------------------------------------
from math import *

def userFnct( x, y ):
    d = sqrt( x * x + y * y )
    return d

# modB.py --------------------------------------------------------

def userFnct( x, y ):
    return x + y
```

The driver needs to reference both instances of `userFnct()` from within its namespace. By using the plain `import` statement, both versions of `userFnct()` will be imported and made available within the `main.py` driver. We can then include the module name as part of the reference:

```
v = modA.userFnct( x, y )
w = modB.userFnct( x, y )
```

to direct the interpreter to a specific version of the function. Had we imported the two versions of `userFnct()` into the current namespace using the `from/import` statement, then only the version defined within `modB.py` would be available since the second definition of the function would have redefined the original from `modA.py`.

Exceptions

Unforeseen errors can occur in a program during run time due to faulty code or invalid input. Consider the following sample code segment, which attempts to access a non-existent element of a list:

```
myList = [ 12, 50, 5, 17 ]
print myList[ 4 ]
```

When this code is executed, the program aborts and the following message is displayed:

```
Traceback (most recent call last):
  File "<stdin>", line 1, in <module>
IndexError: list index out of range
```

The last line in the message provides information as to the type of run-time error that caused the program to abort. In this case, there are only four elements in the list numbered $0, 1, 2, 3$ and thus subscript 4 is out of range.

Python, like many other high-level programming languages, raises an exception when an error occurs. An *exception* is an event that can be triggered and optionally handled during program execution. When an exception is raised indicating an error, the program can contain code to catch the exception and gracefully handle it. When an exception is not handled, the program will abort as was the case in our example above.

C.1 Catching Exceptions

Consider the following example in which we want to extract an integer value from the user with the **input()** function:

```
value = int( input("Enter an integer value: ") )
```

What happens if the user entered 4x at the prompt instead of an actual numeric value? Python *raises* an exception which causes the program to abort with the following message printed to the terminal.

```
Traceback (most recent call last):
  File "<stdin>", line 1, in <module>
ValueError: invalid literal for int() with base 10: '4x'
```

Since Python cannot convert the string "4x" to an integer value, it raises an exception. Instead of having the program abort due to the exception, we can provide code to detect and *catch* the exception and request that the user try again.

```
while True:
  try:
    value = int( input("Enter an integer value: ") )
    break

  except ValueError :
    print( "You must enter an integer value. Try again." )
```

The try block flags the code in which we want to catch any exceptions that may be raised during execution. The except block indicates the action to take when the given type of exception is raised within the corresponding try block. If no exception is raised, execution flows normally and the except block is skipped. When an exception is raised, the normal flow of execution is interrupted. If an except block is provided for the type of exception raised, execution jumps to the first statement within that except block. On the other hand, if there is no corresponding except block, the program terminates.

C.2   Raising Exceptions

Python automatically raises exceptions when an error occurs during program execution for various language constructs and library modules. But you can also raise an exception when you detect an error in your code. Consider the following function, which accepts two arguments and returns the minimum of the two:

```
def min( arg1, arg2 ):
  if arg1 is None or arg2 is None :
    raise TypeError( "arguments to min() cannot be None" )
  if arg1 < arg2 :
    return arg1
  else :
    return arg2
```

If we define this function as accepting two comparable values other than None and return the minimum of the two, we need to make sure the arguments are valid. That is, neither argument is null. If one or both of the arguments is null, then we raise a TypeError exception to flag an error using the raise statement. Consider the function call:

```
y = min( x, None )
```

which results in an error and the exception being raised. The program aborts with the following message:

```
Traceback (most recent call last):
  File "temp.py", line 10, in <module>
    y = min( x, None )
  File "temp.py", line 3, in min
    raise TypeError( "arguments to min() cannot be None" )
TypeError: arguments to min() can not be None
```

Note the error message displayed in the last line of the output. This message comes from the second argument to the **raise** statement. When raising an exception, an optional string can be given to provide a descriptive error message to aide the programmer in debugging the code.

New in Python 3.x: The `raise` statement now requires the optional string message be included as an argument to the constructor of the exception class. In prior versions, the class name and the message could be separated by a comma.

C.3   Standard Exceptions

Python provides a number of built-in exceptions that can be raised by the language and its library modules. In Python, exceptions are defined as classes from which an object is created. The name of the class is given as an argument to the **raise** statement. Some of the more common exceptions are described next:

`IndexError`	Used when a list or tuple index is out of range.
`KeyError`	Raised when a dictionary key is not found in a dictionary.
`NotImplementedError`	Used in user-defined methods (especially in abstract classes) to indicate the method is being used but has not yet been implemented.
`RuntimeError`	Raised to flag an error when no other exception type is appropriate.
`TypeError`	Raised when an incorrect data type is supplied to an operator or method.
`ValueError`	Raised when the correct data type is supplied, but it is not an appropriate value.

C.4   Assertions

Python also provides the `assert` statement, which can be used to raise the special `AssertionError` exception. The `assert` statement is used to state what we assume to be true at a given point in the program. If the assertion fails, Python raises an AssertionError and aborts the program, unless the exception is caught.

The assert statement combines the testing of a condition with raising an exception. The difference between making an assertion and raising an exception is that the assert statements can be deactivated at run time. Consider the min() function defined earlier rewritten to use the assert statement:

```
def min( arg1, arg2 ):
    assert arg1 is not None and arg2 is not None, \
           "arguments to min() cannot be None"
    if arg1 < arg2 :
      return arg1
    else :
      return arg2
```

There are two forms of the assert statement, though both test the given condition and raise the AssertionError exception when the condition fails. The difference is the inclusion of the optional description, which provides information to the programmer as to the cause of the error.

```
assert value > 0
assert value > 0, "A positive value is required."
```

Exceptions should be raised in those instances where you expect errors may occur during execution that can be properly handled without aborting the program. For example, when checking for valid user input or verifying a successful network connection to a server, the program does not have to be aborted when the operation fails. Instead, you can catch the exception, inform the user, and provide an alternate course of action. This may not be the case, however, when a precondition fails due to a logical error in the program. For example, if the programmer incorrectly attempts to access a list element by supplying an out-of-range index, it may be impossible to recover from such an error. In this case, the program should abort as the proper course of action. Thus, assertions are best used for debugging a program and testing preconditions while exceptions are best used to catch recoverable errors.

As we stated earlier, assert statements can be deactivated at run time in the final product to prevent them from being executed. Since assertions are made to help debug and catch programming errors, once you have fully tested the program, we would not expect these errors to occur. By turning them off, the execution speed of the program can be improved in the final production environment. In addition, the end user of the program will have little use for the debug information.

When implementing abstract data types, it's important that we ensure the proper execution of the various operations by verifying any stated preconditions. The appropriate mechanism is to state assertions for the preconditions and allow the user of the ADT to decide how they wish to handle the error. In most cases, the appropriate step is to allow the program to abort. Thus, in the text, we focus on stating assertions and omit further discussion of catching those exceptions.

Classes

Python supports both the procedural and object-oriented programming paradigms. Whereas the procedural paradigm is focused on the creation of functions, the object-oriented paradigm is centered around the use of objects and classes. An *object* is a software entity that stores data. A *class* is the blueprint that describes the data stored in an object and defines the operations that can be performed on the object. Objects are created or *instantiated* from classes, and each object is known as an *instance* of the class from which it was created.

D.1 The Class Definition

Python, like all object-oriented programming languages, allow programmers to define their own classes. A class definition is a compound statement consisting of a header and a body. The class header contains the keyword `class` followed by an identifier used to name the class. The body of the class definition contains one or more method definitions, all of which must be indented to same indentation level.

Suppose we want to define a class to represent a point or coordinate in the two-dimensional Cartesian coordinate system. The objects will need to store two values, one for the x-coordinate and one for the y-coordinate. We will also have to decide what operations we want to be able to perform on the objects created from the new class. We can begin with a framework for the new class:

```
class Point :
    # The methods are defined in the body one after the other.
```

Notice that our class is named `Point`, which starts with an uppercase letter. While this is not a requirement of the syntax, it is common programming practice in order to distinguish a class name from variables and functions.

A *method* is a service or operation that can be performed on an object created from the given class. A method is very similar to a function with several exceptions:

(1) a method is defined as part of a class definition; (2) a method can only be used with an instance of the class in which it is defined; and (3) each method header must include a parameter named `self`, which must be listed first.

New in Python 3.x: All classes are automatically derived from the `object` base class even if it's not explicitly stated in the header definition.

D.1.1   Constructors

All classes should define a special method known as the *constructor*, which defines and initializes the data to be contained in the object. The constructor is automatically called when an instance of the class is created. In Python, the constructor is named `__init__` and is usually listed first in the class definition:

```python
class Point:
   def __init__( self, x, y ):
      self.xCoord = x
      self.yCoord = y
```

Data Attributes

The data contained in an object is known as the object's data fields or *data attributes*. The attributes are simply variables, like any other variable in Python, but are stored in the object itself. An object's attributes are accessed using the dot notation and appending the attribute name to the `self` reference. Any variables not prepended by the `self` reference are local to the method in which they are defined.

Since variables in Python are created when they are first assigned a value, the constructor is responsible for creating and initializing the data attributes. The constructor of our `Point` class needs to create two attributes, one for each of the coordinate components. This is done by the two assignment statements, which create and initialize the attributes named `xCoord` and `yCoord`. They are initialized respectively to the values of the two parameters, `x` and `y`. (Note that Python also allows default arguments to be defined for methods just as it does for functions.)

Object Instantiation

An instance of a user-defined class is created by invoking the constructor. This is done by specifying the name of the class along with any required arguments as if it were a function call. For example, the following statements create two objects from our `Point` class and assigns them to the variables `pointA` and `pointB`:

```python
pointA = Point(5, 7)
pointB = Point(0, 0)
```

The results are illustrated in Figure D.1. Note that we never call the __init__ method directly. Instead, Python allocates memory for the object, then automatically calls the __init__ method for the given class to initialize the new object. The attributes of an object are also known as *instance variables* since new attributes are created for each instance of the class. In our example, we created two objects and each object has its own variables named xCoord and yCoord.

Figure D.1: Sample Point objects.

The self Reference

You may have noticed that the constructor was defined with three parameters, but we supplied only two arguments when creating the objects. When a method is executed, Python must know on which object the method was invoked in order to know which attributes to reference. As indicated earlier, self is a special parameter that must be included in each method definition and it must be listed first. When a method is called, this parameter is automatically filled with a reference to the object on which the method was invoked. If the method defines additional parameters, explicit arguments must be passed to the method as part of the method call.

D.1.2   Operations

So far, we can create a new object, but we can't do anything with it. Next, we need to define additional operations that can be performed on our Point objects. Let's start by adding two methods that can be used to extract the individual x- and y-components of the point contained in the object. (Note that we only show the two new methods, but assume the constructor defined earlier is still part of the class as indicated by the # ... comment line.)

```
class Point :
# ...
  def getX( self ):
    return self.xCoord

  def getY( self ):
    return self.yCoord
```

We can use the new methods to extract and print the coordinates of one of the objects we just created:

```
    x = pointA.getX()
    y = pointA.getY()
    print( "(" + str(x) + ", " + str(y) + ")" )
```

When the getX() method is called, Python creates a local variable for the self parameter and assigns it a copy of the reference stored in pointA, as illustrated by Figure D.2. The body of the method is then executed. Since the instance variable is prepended with the self reference and self is an alias for pointA, the value in the xCoord attribute of pointA will be returned.

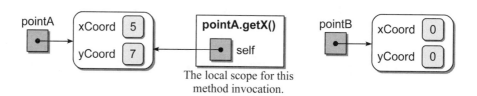

The local scope for this
method invocation.

Figure D.2: Use of the self reference.

Any object that stores data is said to have a state. The object's state is the current set of values that it contains. Objects are divided into two distinct categories: mutable and immutable. An ***immutable object*** is one in which the state cannot be changed once it has been created. If the data fields of the object can be changed after the object has been created, the object is said to be ***mutable***.

So far, the objects created from our Point class are immutable because we have no way of changing the coordinates stored in the objects. We can add a method to adjust or shift a point along both the x- and y-axes, which now makes our objects mutable since we have a way to modify the data attributes:

```
class Point :
  # ...
    def shift( self, xInc, yInc ):
        self.xCoord += xInc
        self.yCoord += yInc
```

If we apply this new method to our pointA object with the method call pointA.shift(4, 12), local variables are created for all three parameters and assigned the corresponding values, as illustrated in the top of Figure D.3. After the method is executed, the data attributes of the pointA object are modified, as illustrated in the bottom of Figure D.3.

Finally, we add a method to our class that can be used to compute the Euclidean distance between two instances of the Point class:

```
class Point :
  # ...
    def distance( self, otherPoint ):
        xDiff = self.xCoord - otherPoint.xCoord
        yDiff = self.yCoord - otherPoint.yCoord
        return math.sqrt( xDiff ** 2 + yDiff ** 2 )
```

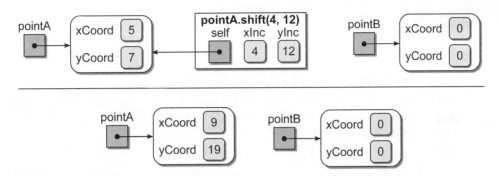

Figure D.3: The local scope (top) when calling `pointA.shift(4,12)` and the result after the call (bottom).

The distance is computed between the `self` point and the `otherPoint`, which is passed as an argument. Figure D.4 illustrates the local variables that are created when applying the method with the call `d = pointA.distance( pointB )`.

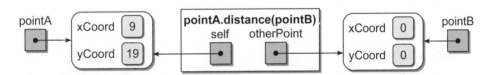

Figure D.4: The local scope when calling `pointA.distance(pointB)`.

D.1.3   Using Modules

A class definition is typically placed within its own module or combined with other common classes in a single module. This helps to organize and manage programs that consist of multiple classes. When a class is needed, it can be imported from the module just like we would do with any of the standard modules. For example, suppose the `Point` class is defined in the `point.py` module, as shown in Listing D.1. To use the `Point` class as illustrated by the earlier examples, we must first import it from the `point.py` module:

```python
from point import Point

# Create two point objects.
pointA = Point(5,7)
pointB = Point(0,0)

# Get and print the coordinates of pointA.
x = pointA.getX()
y = pointA.getY()
print( "(" + str(x) + ", " + str(y) + ")" )

# Shift pointA and compute the distance between the two points.
pointA.shift(4, 12)
d = pointA.distance( pointB )
```

> **Listing D.1**   The `point.py` module.

```
1   # Implements the Point class for representing points in the
2   # 2-D Cartesian coordinate system.
3
4   import math
5
6   class Point :
7     # Creates a point object.
8     def __init__( self, x, y ):
9       self.xCoord = x
10      self.yCoord = y
11
12    # Returns the x coordinate of the point.
13    def getX( self ):
14      return self.xCoord
15
16    # Returns the y coordinate of the point.
17    def getY( self ):
18      return self.yCoord
19
20    # Shifts the point by xInc and yInc.
21    def shift( self, xInc, yInc ):
22      self._xCoord += xInc
23      self._yCoord += yInc
24
25    # Computes the distance between this point and the otherPoint.
26    def distance( self, otherPoint ):
27      xDiff = self.xCoord - otherPoint.xCoord
28      yDiff = self.yCoord - otherPoint.yCoord
29      return math.sqrt( xDiff ** 2 + yDiff ** 2 )
```

While any form of the `import` statement can be used, in this text we will always use the `from/import` version and explicitly indicate the class to be imported from the given module.

D.1.4   Hiding Attributes

Object-oriented programming allows for the *encapsulation* of data and the operations that can be performed on that data. In other words, the data attributes of an object and the methods that are defined for use with the object are combined in a single definition and implementation. The class definition in turn provides an interface to a user-defined type.

The data attributes contained in an object are usually hidden from the client or user code that is outside the class. Only the methods defined by the class for use with the object should directly access the data attributes. This prevents the accidental corruption of the data that can occur when directly accessed by code outside the class. Sometimes we may also need to protect methods from outside use such as with a *helper method*. Helper methods are like any other method, but they are commonly used in the implementation of a class to allow for the subdivision of a larger method into smaller parts or to reduce code repetition by defining a single method that can be called from within other methods as needed.

While most object-oriented languages provide a mechanism to hide or protect the data attributes from outside access, Python does not. Instead, the designer of a class in Python is supposed to indicate what data attributes and methods are suppose to be protected. It's then the responsibility of the user of the class not to violate this protection. In this text, we use identifier names that begin with a single underscore to flag those attributes and methods that should be protected and trust the user of the class to not attempt a direct access to those members.

The class definition in Listing D.2 illustrates the use of the single underscore to indicate protected attributes. It defines a line segment, which is specified by Point objects that represent the endpoints. Several operations are also defined for use with a line segment.

Listing D.2   The `line.py` module.

```python
1   # Implements a LineSegment class constructed from Point objects.
2
3   from point import Point
4
5   class LineSegment :
6     # Creates a line segment object.
7     def __init__( self, fromPoint, toPoint ):
8       self._pointA = fromPoint
9       self._pointB = toPoint
10
11    # Gets the starting point of the line segment.
12    def endPointA( self ):
13      return self._pointA
14
15    # Gets the ending point of the line segment.
16    def endPointB( self ):
17      return self._pointB
18
19    # Gets the length of the line segment.
20    def length( self ):
21      return self._pointA.distance( self._pointB )
22
23    # Determines if the line is parallel to the y-axis.
24    def isVertical( self ):
25      return self._startPoint.getX() == self._endPoint.getX()
26
27    # Gets the slope of the line.
28    def slope( self ):
29      if self.isVertical() :   # not defined for a vertical line.
30        return None
31      else :
32        run = self._pointA.getX() - self._pointB.getX()
33        rise = self._pointA.getY() - self._pointB.getY()
34        return rise / run
```

You will note that we directly accessed the attributes of the `otherPoint` object from within the `distance()` method implemented earlier but we used the `getX()` and `getY()` methods to access the same values within the `Line` class. The reason for this is that `otherPoint` is an instance of the same class as the method we were implementing. In that case, it's acceptable to directly access its attributes without violating the protection. In the case of the `Line` class, however, `isVertical()` and `slope()` are not part of the `Point` class. Thus, we must access the values stored in the attributes of the two points by using the `getX()` and `getY()` access methods or we would violate the protection in this case.

D.2   Overloading Operators

In Python, we can define and implement many of the standard Python operators such as `+`, `*`, and `==` as part of our user-defined classes. This allows for a more natural use of the objects instead of having to call specific methods by name. For example, suppose we want to include an operation for comparing two `Point` objects to determine if they are the equal. Instead of including a named method such as `isEqual()`, we can implement the special method `__eq__`:

```
class Point :
  # ...
    def __eq__( self, rhsPoint ):
      return self.xCoord == rhsPoint.xCoord and \
             self.yCoord == rhsPoint.yCoord
```

which Python automatically calls when a `Point` object is used on the lefthand side of the equality operator (`==`):

```
if pointA == pointB :
  print( "The points are equal." )
```

If we need to determine if a point is at the origin, we can also use the equality operator by first creating an unnamed `Point` object whose coordinates are both set to zero:

```
if pointA == Point(0, 0) :
  print( "The point is at the origin." )
```

We can overload any of the operators by including a special method in our class definition. Table D.1 provides a list of the operators and the corresponding special methods that must be defined. Some of the special methods are actually called when an instance of the class is passed to a built-in function. Suppose we define the `__str__` method as part of our `Point` class:

```
class Point :
  # ...
    def __str__( self ):
      return "(" + str(x) + ", " + str(y) + ")"
```

Operation	Class Method
str(obj)	__str__(self)
len(obj)	__len__(self)
item **in** obj	__contains__(self, item)
y = obj[ndx]	__getitem__(self, ndx)
obj[ndx] = value	__setitem__(self, ndx, value)
obj == rhs	__eq__(self, rhs)
obj < rhs	__lt__(self, rhs)
obj <= rhs	__le__(self, rhs)
obj != rhs	__ne__(self, rhs)
obj > rhs	__gt__(self, rhs)
obj >= rhs	__ge__(self, rhs)
obj + rhs	__add__(self, rhs)
obj - rhs	__sub__(self, rhs)
obj * rhs	__mul__(self, rhs)
obj / rhs	__truediv__(self, rhs)
obj // rhs	__floordiv__(self, rhs)
obj % rhs	__mod__(self, rhs)
obj ** rhs	__pow__(self, rhs)
obj += rhs	__iadd__(self, rhs)
obj -= rhs	__isub__(self, rhs)
obj *= rhs	__imul__(self, rhs)
obj /= rhs	__itruediv__(self, rhs)
obj //= rhs	__ifloordiv__(self, rhs)
obj %= rhs	__imod__(self, rhs)
obj **= rhs	__ipow__(self, rhs)

Table D.1: Methods for overloading the common Python operators.

Now we can convert a Point object to a string or use the object directly within the print() function just as we would with an int or float object:

```
msg = "The initial point is " + str(pointA)
print( "Point B = ", pointB )
```

The __str__ method is automatically called when you attempt to print an object or convert the object to a string. If the __str__ method is not overloaded by a user-defined class, the default action is to print the object type and its reference address.

Finally, suppose we also want to allow the subtraction operator to be used in computing the distance between two points. We can define the __sub__ special method and have it call the `distance()` method:

```
class Point :
  # ...
    def __sub__( self, rhsPoint ):
      return self.distance( rhsPoint )
```

We could choose to only overload the subtraction operator for use in computing the distance instead of providing both a named method and an operator. In that case, we would provide the code for computing the distance directly within the `__sub__` method definition:

```
class Point :
  # ...
    def __sub__( self, rhsPoint ):
      xDiff = self.xCoord - rhsPoint.xCoord
      yDiff = self.yCoord - rhsPoint.yCoord
      return math.sqrt( xDiff ** 2 + yDiff ** 2 )
```

D.3 Inheritance

Python, like all object-oriented languages, supports ***class inheritance***. Instead of creating a new class from scratch, we can derive a new class from an existing one. The new class automatically inherits all data attributes and methods of the existing class without having to explicitly redefine the code. This leads to a hierarchical structure in which the newly ***derived class*** becomes the ***child*** of the original or ***parent class***. Figure D.5 illustrates a hierarchical diagram of derived classes representing the relationship between different types of bibliography entries. The parent-child relationship produced from the derivation of a new class is known as an ***is-a relationship*** in which the derived class is a more specific version of the original. In the hierarchical class diagram shown in Figure D.5, a book is-a publication and a chapter is-a more specific component of a book.

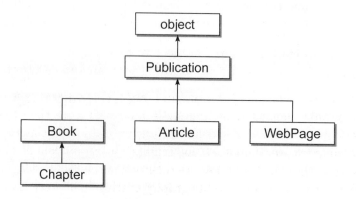

Figure D.5: Hierarchical class diagram representing types of bibliography entries.

Note the inclusion of the `object` class at the top of the hierarchy. This is a Python built-in class from which every class is derived, whether explicitly stated or not. Thus, all of the classes defined earlier in the appendix were derived from the `object` class even though it was not indicated in the class definition.

Inheritance allows us to reuse existing code without having to duplicate similar code. After inheriting the properties of the parent class, the new child class can be tailored to a specific purpose by adding new functionality or modifying the existing functionality of the parent class. To add new functionality, the child class can define new data attributes and methods while the functionality of existing methods can be overridden to provide new functionality as needed by the child.

D.3.1 Deriving Child Classes

To illustrate inheritance, we are going to define and implement the classes shown in Figure D.5, which can be used to build a bibliography. The idea behind this example is that publication references can be created for each source cited in a document and stored in a list structure. The collection of sources can then be printed at the end of the document to create the bibliography. Each class in our example will be used to store information related to a specific type of bibliography entry. Every entry will contain at least three pieces of information: a unique user-defined string code for identifying a specific entry, and the title and author of the corresponding publication. Additional information will be maintained for each entry, but it varies depending on the type of entry.

We start with the `Publication` base class used to store the minimum amount of information for each bibliography entry:

```
class Publication :
  def __init__( self, code, title, author ):
    self._code = code
    self._title = title
    self._author = author

    # Gets the unique identification code for this entry.
  def getCode( self ):
    return self._code

    # Returns a string containing a formatted bibliography entry.
  def getBibEntry( self ):
    return '[' + self.getCode() + '] "' \
              + self._title + '" by ' + self._author
```

Note the inclusion of the syntax (`object`) following the class name. This tells Python that the `Publication` class is derived from the `object` class. We could have omitted this explicit derivation as we did in the classes defined earlier in the appendix, but we included it for illustration of the default parent class.

In the `Publication` class, we only define the three data fields that are common to the different types of bibliography entries. The only information that we will need to obtain from each entry is the unique code value, which can be accessed using `getCode()`, and a string containing a correctly formatted bibliography entry.

The latter is obtained using the `getBibEntry()` method. Note that we have this method returning a string that contains the code, title, and author, which can be used as part of each entry. But this operation will have to be overridden by each entry type in order to produce a correctly formatted representation for the given type.

Next, we define the `Book` class, which will be used to represent book sources within our bibliography. It is derived from the `Publication` class since it is a more specific type of publication. A book entry will contain two additional pieces of information in addition to that contained in the `Publication` class: the name of the publisher and the year of publication.

```
class Book( Publication ):
    def __init__( self, code, title, author, publisher, year ):

        super().__init__( code, title, author )

        self._publisher = publisher
        self._year = year

    def getBibEntry( self ) :
        return super().getBibEntry() \
                + ', ' + self._publisher + ', ' + self._year
```

A constructor is also defined for this class that includes parameters for all of the data to be contained in a book entry. Each class is responsible for initializing its own data attributes. Thus, note the first line in the body of the constructor that is used to call the constructor of the parent class. That constructor requires three arguments: `code`, `title`, and `author`. After the parent class creates and initializes its own attributes, we can then create and initialize two new attributes needed by the child class.

The child class also overrides the `getBibEntry()` method from the parent class in order to build and return a string containing the bibliography entry for a book source. Our implementation calls the parent's version of the `getBibEntry()` method in order to format the code, title, and author part of the bibliography entry for a book.

D.3.2 Creating Class Instances

So what happens when we create an instance of the `Book` class? Consider the following code segment:

```
pub = Publication( "Test80", "Just a test", "Rob Green" )
book = Book( "Smith90", "The Year that Was", "John Smith",
                        "Bookends Publishing", 1990 )
```

which creates an instance of the `Publication` class and an instance of the `Book` class. The `pub` object only contains the three data fields defined by the `Publication` class, while the `book` object contains all five fields, the three from the parent class and the two defined in the `Book` class. Figure D.6 illustrates the contents of the two objects. In addition, the `book` object also inherits all of the parent's methods. But since we have provided new definitions for the constructor and the `getBibEntry()` method, the only method actually inherited from the parent is the `getCode()` method.

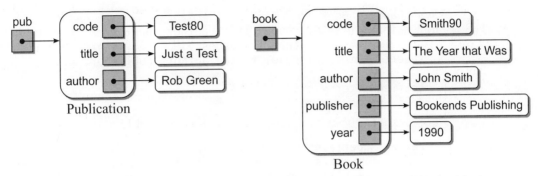

Figure D.6: The data attributes of the `Publication` and `Book` objects.

D.3.3 Invoking Methods

The methods available to objects of each class are shown in Figure D.7. Note that the `getBibEntry()` method of the `Publication` class is inherited and made available to the `Book` class.

Publication
Publication.__init__
Publication.getCode()
Publication.getBibEntry()

Book
Book.__init__
Publication.getCode()
Book.getBibEntry()

Figure D.7: The methods available for use with `Publication` and `Book` objects.

What happens if we use the `getBibEntry()` method on the `book` object as an argument to the `print()` function?

```
print( book.getBibEntry() )
```

It will print the bibliography entry shown here:

```
[Smith90] "The Year that Was" by John Smith, Bookends Publishing, 1990.
```

which it does by calling the `getBibEntry()` method defined by the `Book` class. That method first calls the parent's `getBibEntry()` method and then concatenates the result of that call with the publisher and year data needed to form a book entry. The methods of a child class can access the data attributes of the parent class. It's up to the designer of the class to ensure they do not modify the attributes incorrectly.

Next, we extend the `Book` class by defining the `Chapter` class, which is used to represent a single chapter within a book. It adds two additional attributes to the three already defined by the `Book` class and the two defined by the `Publication` class.

```
class Chapter( Book ):
  def __init__( self, code, title, author, publisher, year
                      chapter, pages ):
    super().__init__( code, title, author, publisher, year )

    self._chapter = chapter
    self._pages = pages

  def getBibEntry( self ) :
    return super().getBibEntry() + ', Chapter ' \
          + str(self._chapter) + ' pp. ' + pages + '. ' \
          + self._publisher + ', ' + self._year
```

Again, the constructor of the child class must call the parent's constructor with the use of the `super()` function. This time, the five fields needed by the `Book` class are passed as arguments to the constructor. The two new fields defined by the child class are then created and initialized with the values from the appropriate arguments. A partial implementation of the remaining bibliography entry classes are defined below in a similar fashion to those defined earlier.

```
class Article( Publication ):
  def __init__( self, code, title, author, journal, volume,
                     number, year ):

    super().__init__( code, title, author )

    self._journal = journal
    self._volume = volume
    self._number = number
    self._year = year

  def getBibEntry( self ) :
    ......

class WebPage( Publication ):
  def __init__( self, code, title, author, url, modified ):

    super().__init__( code, title, author )

    self._url = url
    self._modified = modified

  def getBibEntry( self ):
    ......
```

D.4 Polymorphism

The third concept related to object-oriented programming is that of ***polymorphism***. It is a very powerful feature in which the decision as to the specific method to be called is made at run time. Suppose we add the __str__ method to our Publication class and simply have it call and return the result of the getBibEntry() method as shown here:

```
# New version with a __str__ method added.
class Publication( object ) :
  def __init__( self, code, title, author ):
    self._code = code
    self._title = title
    self._author = author

  # Gets the unique identification code for this entry.
  def getCode( self ):
    return self._code

  # Returns a string containing a formatted bibliography entry.
  def getBibEntry( self ):
    return '[' + self.getCode() + '] "' \
               + self._title + '" by ' + self._author

  def __str__( self ):
    return self.getBibEntry()
```

Remember, when an object is used within the print() function, the __str__ operator method is automatically called for that object. So what happens if we print the pub and book objects created earlier?

```
print( pub )
print( book )
```

This results in the following output:

```
[Test80'] "Just a Test" by Rob Green
[Smith90] "The Year that Was" by John Smith, Bookends Publishing, 1990
```

But how is that possible since we did not define a __str__ method for the Book class? It has to do with polymorphism. Since the __str__ method is defined by the parent class, it will be inherited by the child class. Thus, when the __str__ method is executed via the print function:

```
print( book )
```

Python looks at the list of methods available to instances of the Book class and finds the getBibEntry() method defined for that class and executes it. Thus, the __str__ method correctly calls the getBibEntry() method of the child class, even though the __str__ method was defined in the parent class.

Bibliography

[1] Python v3.1.2 Documentation. http://docs.python.org/py3k, 2010.

[2] Alfred V. Aho, John E. Hopcroft, and Jeffrey D. Ullman. *Data Structures and Algorithms*. Addison-Wesley, Reading, MA, 1983.

[3] John L. Bentley. Programming pearls: How to sort. *Communications of the ACM*, 27(3):287–291, March 1984.

[4] John L. Bentley. Programming pearls: The back of the envelope. *Communications of the ACM*, 27(3):180–184, March 1984.

[5] John L. Bentley. Programming pearls: Thanks, heaps. *Communications of the ACM*, 28(3):245–250, March 1985.

[6] John L. Bentley. *Programming Pearls*. Addison-Wesley, Reading, MA, 1986.

[7] John L. Bentley. Programming pearls: The envelope is back. *Communications of the ACM*, 29(3):176–182, March 1986.

[8] Timothy Budd. *Classic Data Structures*. Addison-Wesley, Reading, MA, 2001.

[9] Thomas H. Cormen, Charles E. Leiserson, and Ronald L. Rivest. *Introduction to Algorithms*. MIT Press, Cambridge, MA, 1990.

[10] Nell B. Dale. *C++ Plus Data Strucutres*. Jones and Bartlett, Sudbury, MA, 1999.

[11] Nell B. Dale and Susan C. Lilly. *Pascal Plus Data Structures, Algorithms and Advanced ProgrammingSua*. Houghton Mifflin Co., Boston, MA, 1995.

[12] Charles L. Hamblin. Translation to and from polish notation. *Computer Journal*, 5:210–213, 1962.

[13] C.A.R. Hoare. Quicksort. *The Computer Journal*, 5:10–15, 1962.

[14] John E. Hopcroft, Alfred V. Aho, and Jeffrey D. Ullman. *The Design and Analysis of Computer Algorithms*. Addison-Wesley, Reading, MA, 1974.

[15] Bing-Chao Huang and Michael A. Langston. Practical in-place merging. *Communications of the ACM*, 31(3):348–352, 1988.

[16] Donald E. Knuth. *Fundamental Algorithms*, volume 1 of *The Art of Computer Programming*. Addison-Wesley, Reading, MA, 2nd edition, 1973.

[17] Donald E. Knuth. *Sorting and Searching*, volume 3 of *The Art of Computer Programming*. Addison-Wesley, Reading, MA, 2nd edition, 1981.

[18] B. J. McKenzie, R. Harries, and T. C. Bell. Selecting a hashing algorithm. *Software Practice and Experience*, 20:209–224, 1990.

[19] Bernard M. E. Moret. Decision trees and algorithms. *Computing Surveys*, 14:593–623, 1982.

[20] Rance D. Necaise. Transitioning from java to python in cs2. *Journal of Computing Sciences in Colleges*, 24(2):92–97, 2008.

[21] Rance D. Necaise. Python for Java Programmers. `http://python.necaiseweb.org`, 2009.

[22] Edward M. Reingold. A comment on the evaluation of postfix expressions. *Computer Journal*, 24:288, 1981.

[23] Igor Rivin, Ilan Vardi, and Paul Zimmermann. The n-queens problem. *The American Mathematical Monthly*, 101(7):629–639, 1994.

[24] Hanan Samet. *Applications of Spatial Data Structures*. Addison-Wesley, Reading, MA, 1990.

[25] Hanan Samet. *The Design and Analysis of Spatial Data Structures*. Addison-Wesley, Reading, MA, 1990.

[26] John W. J. Williams. Algorithm 232: Heapsort. *Communications of the ACM*, 7(6):347–348, 1964.

[27] Nicklaus Wirth. *Algorithms + Data Structures = Programs*. Prentice Hall, Upper Saddle River, NJ, 1976.

Index